Surrealism in Exile

Martica Sawin

Surrealism in Exile
and the Beginning of the New York School

The MIT Press Cambridge, Massachusetts London, England

This book was set in Sabon by Graphic Composition, Inc., and was printed and bound in the United States of America.

Library of Congress Cataloging-in-Publication Data
Sawin, Martica.
    Surrealism in exile and the Beginning of the New York School / Martica Sawin.
        p. cm.
    Includes bibliographical references and index.
    ISBN 0-262-19360-4 (alk. paper)
    1. Surrealism—France.   2. Art, Modern—20th century—France.
3. Artists—France.   4. Surrealism—United States.   5. Expatriate
artists—United States.   6. Surrealism—Influence.   7. New York
school of art.   8. Abstract expressionism—United States.
I. Title.
N6848.5.S96S28   1995
709'.04'063—dc20   95-10961
                                                                CIP

André Masson, *Adolescent in the American Woodlands (Portrait of Diego)*, 1943, oil on canvas, 21⅛ x 18⅛ inches; collection M. and Mme. Diego Masson.

Contents

We are living in an extremely disturbed moment of history, and it is not
necessary either that the painter should conceal the disquietude of his epoch.

André Masson, 1942

Introduction

Surrealism was born out of the traumas of the First World War and suffered its death throes during the Second. During the intervening years the Surrealists attempted to explore those areas of the human psyche where the propensity to violence lurked. They sought to demonstrate through paintings, poems, films, and games that man is essentially an irrational being; and they kept up sustained attacks on their dual anathemas, nationalism and rationalism. Their stated aim was to effect a revolution in consciousness that they saw as a prerequisite to social revolution. When ten artist members of this group, Salvador Dalí, Max Ernst, Leonora Carrington, Stanley William Hayter, André Masson, Roberto Matta, Gordon Onslow Ford, Wolfgang Paalen, Kurt Seligmann, and Yves Tanguy, along with its poet-spokesman, André Breton, took refuge in the United States during the war against fascism, two significant artistic developments ensued.

The first of these developments involves the displaced. Uprooted from their nurturing Parisian milieu, having experienced the ignominy and confusion of defeat, betrayals in high places, and, for some, harsh conditions, they found themselves in a country whose politics were suspect, to whose culture they were indifferent, a country that had scarcely appeared on the Surrealist map of the world. Yet during their years of exile many of these artists produced some of the strongest work of their careers, and at an extraordinary rate of output, work that stands out in comparison with that of the artists who remained in France and continued to exhibit under the auspices of the Vichy government. Indeed, their work of the early forties was possibly the most telling artistic witness to the experience of living on the *planète affolée,* the title of a 1942 painting by Max Ernst. The momentum of the survival effort may have fueled this efflorescence, but impetus also came from the particular set of circumstances of the milieu into which they were displaced and the urgent need to respond to what Masson called in 1942 "an extremely disturbed moment of history."

The second development arises from the impact of the displaced on the milieu into which they were injected. American art at the outset of the 1940s was stranded between the social realism that had dominated the thirties and formalist derivations of European abstraction. A number of young artists not content with either option were exploring various combinations of modernist styles and experimenting with materials and processes, including automatism. Much has been claimed and disclaimed regarding the extent of the effect that the presence of the Surrealist refugees had on the genesis of abstract expressionism. However, it is incontrovertible that not only was there a new mode of painting developing in New York by the mid-1940s,

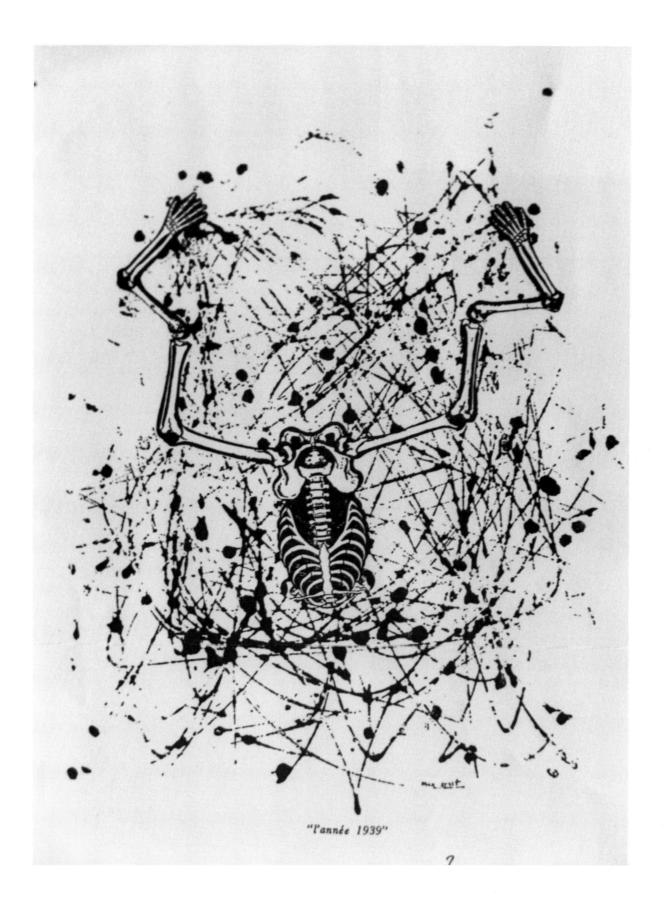

"l'année 1939"

Émigrés in Peggy Guggenheim's New York apartment, 1942; front row: S. W.
Hayter, Leonora Carrington, Frederick Kiesler, Kurt Seligmann; second row: Max
Ernst, Amédée Ozenfant, André Breton, Fernand Léger, Berenice Abbott; back row:
Jimmy Ernst, Peggy Guggenheim, John Ferren, Marcel Duchamp, Piet Mondrian.
Photography courtesy the Philadelphia Museum of Art.

Surrealist Map of the World, 1929.

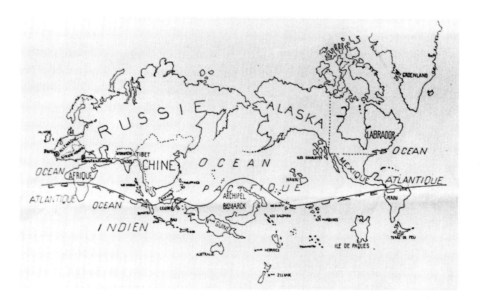

sometimes referred to as abstract surrealism, but also that it was emerging among those artists who had the greatest amount of contact with the Surrealist émigrés, painters such as Arshile Gorky, William Baziotes, Robert Motherwell, Gerome Kamrowski, and Jackson Pollock. The simplified version of this encounter has depicted a collective Surrealist arm extending the automatist brush to an outstretched American hand. In actuality the Americans were more or less familiar with automatist practices and had even invented some of their own. What they learned from the refugees was far more complex and has to do not only with ideas but also with the whole system of interconnecting factors that involves the perception and promotion of the artwork as well as its production. One might consider what took place during those years as a form of empowerment. Or as Meyer Schapiro put it: "It wasn't automatism that the Americans learned from the Surrealists, but how to be heroic." [1]

Surrealism differed from most art movements in that it was not only visual but literary and political. Its stated goals were extra-aesthetic, primarily directed toward the liberation of consciousness. During the 1920s and '30s it was highly organized; its members maintained a headquarters, the *centrale,* held daily meetings at an appointed café, and collaborated on the publishing of periodicals, books, and broadsides. Although the Surrealists attempted to hold the movement together in exile through collectively staged exhibitions and publications, inevitably it fell apart and it was never the same in its postwar incarnation. Again, quoting Masson who quoted Dante: "There are no quarrels worse than the quarrels among refugees."[2]

The chapters that follow offer a narrative account of the lives and work of the core figures of the Surrealist movement from January 1938, when their largest exhibition was held in Paris, to the summer of 1947 when a major postwar exhibition, including new American recruits, marked the return of the exiles to a less-than-welcoming France. Because of the historical circumstances and the movement's intellectual and political nature, I have tried to interweave the narrative of the art and artists with some account of the political history of the period. The story has been pieced together out of a combination of interviews with firsthand witnesses and participants, archives of letters and documents hitherto unavailable, relevant critical and historical writing, and, above all, the evidence of the artworks themselves.

The problem remains, however, that this is a history of a group of individuals. The dynamics of group interaction and the importance of the support system resulting from their common bond are intangibles that can only be approximated by assembling as much data as possible on the group activities while keeping track of the independent development of each individual. The difficulty posed by relying on interviews and memoirs was summed up for me by Jacqueline Lamba (Breton): "How are you going to make one truth out of all the lies people will tell you?"[3]

I cannot claim to have made "one truth." I have simply tried to place side by side fragments extracted from many sources that seemed to have some concordance, in the hope that the totality will dispel some misconceptions, correct some errors that have been written into art history, and shed some light on the genesis of America's postwar artistic "triumph." Most of all this book is intended as a chapter in the history of cultural change—not that all cultural change conforms to this model—because the cluster of artworks and events it chronicles offer such a clear-cut example of the role that displacement can play in stimulating significant artistic change. An amazing watershed in the history of art was in the making in the 1940s, mirroring, of course, larger global transformations. That it took the form it did may be ascribed at least partially to the stimulus provided by the refugees and the breakthroughs that the Surrealists themselves were making during the period of exile.

The story told here is only a fragment of a much larger cultural incursion. The years immediately preceding Hitler's invasion of Poland on the first of September 1939 saw the most momentous intellectual emigration in history, as scientists, psy-

André Masson, *Manhattan,* c. 1941, ink and wash on paper, 19 x 24¾ inches; private collection.

chologists, scholars in all fields, musicians, writers, artists, and architects fled Germany for the Western Hemisphere. Their flight not only assured that the atom bomb would be in Allied rather than fascist hands, but it deeply affected American culture from Hollywood films to urban architecture, from the symphony orchestra to the Broadway stage, from advertising to prestige publishing. A second wave of emigration began as France and England entered the war and it swelled following the fall of France in June 1940, as refugees availed themselves of the southern escape route still open through the unoccupied zone, either via Marseilles or through Spain to Lisbon. The second wave included Germans, Austrians, and anti-Franco Spaniards who had previously taken refuge in France, as well as French citizens who were in danger of being deported because they were Jewish or had a record unsavory to the Third Reich or were opponents of the Vichy government.

As the Manhattan Project took shape in Chicago, as former members of the Bauhaus faculty joined art departments or became heads of schools of architecture at universities in the United States, as increasing numbers of musicians and college

Kurt Seligmann and Yves Tanguy at Sugar Loaf, New York.

professors spoke with European accents, the isolationist America of the 1930s began to be drawn into an international culture even before it was drawn into combat against the would-be destroyers of that culture. Even when all-out war on the global scale absorbed much of the national energy and attention, the war years were a time of exciting intellectual and cultural growth, due in large part to the stimulus provided by the refugees. When the United States emerged at the end of the war as the world's leading military and economic power, the groundwork had already been laid for an appropriate cultural, particularly artistic, stance. The purpose of the chapters that follow is to explore the complex cluster of personalities, ideas, and artworks that constituted the Surrealist incursion and the extent to which this incursion determined the form the new American movement in the visual arts, i.e., abstract expressionism, would take.

Acknowledgments

My involvement with this story began at the grave of Kurt Seligmann on a farm in Sugar Loaf, New York. Seligmann was the first of the Surrealists to arrive in the United States, two weeks after the start of World War II in September 1939. He did not return to Paris after the war, but died in 1962 by a bullet from his own gun a few hundred feet from the knoll where he lies buried. It was in the boxes of mildewed and mouse-eaten papers found under his barn that the story of the exodus and the years of exile began to unfold. For this privileged access I thank posthumously his widow Arlette who is now also buried at the farm. Following the thread of the story led me to the many people named in the following paragraph, but most significantly to Gordon Onslow Ford who shared with me his archives, his illuminating comments on Surrealist paintings, including his own, and the story of his life, and offered the hospitality of his unique home within the nature preserve he has taken under his protection.

Among those who have shed light on this subject for me on both sides of the Atlantic are: Lionel Abel, Anne Alpert, Ethel Baziotes, Rosemarie Beck, Helena Benitez, Aube Breton, Elisa Breton, Peter Busa, Christopher Busa, Nick Carone, Leonora Carrington, Susanna Coggeshall, Pierre Courthion, Elaine de Kooning, Enrico Donati, Jimmy Ernst, Dallas Ernst, Ruth Francken, André Gomes, David Hare, Bill Hayter, Jean Hélion, Muguette Hérold, Edouard Jaguer, Martin James, Sidney Janis, Marcel Jean, Buffie Johnson, José Pierre, Ruben Kadish, Jacob Kainen, Gerome Kamrowski, Jacques Kober, Katharine Kuh, Jacqueline Lamba, Evelyn LaRoche,

Robert Lebel, Francis Lee, Michel Leiris, Angèle Levesque, Claude Lévi-Strauss, André and Rose Masson, Guite and Diego Masson, Malitte Matta, John Meyers, Robert Motherwell, Lee and Luchita Mullican, Helen Phillips, John Phillips, V. V. Rankin, Edward Renouf, John Rewald, Meyer Schapiro, Jean Schuster, Charles Seliger, Hedda Sterne, Dorothea Tanning, Germain Viatte, Patrick Waldberg, and Marie Wilson. I thank them all for their time and generosity and remember with gratitude those who are no longer alive.

I have also benefited from the input of a number of colleagues and friends, including Lourdes Andrade, Timothy Baum, Elizabeth Berman, Whitney Chadwick, Jacqueline Chenieux-Gendron, Michèle Cone, Nancy Grove, Stephan Hauser, Janet Kaplan, Stephen Miller, Francis Naumann, Susan Nessen, Cynthia Philip, and Thomas Windholz. Gratitude for a special form of support is due to Francis Naumann, Stephen Polcari, and Irving Sandler. My pursuit of this story was sustained by the willingness of Richard Martin to publish the articles that emerged from research for this book during his dedicated tenure as editor of *Arts*. A year of uninterrupted research and writing was made possible by a generous fellowship from the National Endowment for the Humanities.

Thanks are due for special help in the matter of reproductions to Joan Banach, Elizabeth Berman, Christopher Busa, Mikki Carpenter, Courtney di Angelis, Emily Edwards, Vera Hoar, Lillian Kiesler, Guite Masson, Zea Morvitch, Samar Qandil, Michael Rosenfeld, Elizabeth Roth, Adele Seronde, Dorothea Tanning, Mme. Vellay, and Christine Wachter. I am particularly grateful for the help provided by the staffs of the Archives of American Art in New York and Washington and by Janis Ekdahl and John Trause of the Museum of Modern Art Library and Rona Roob of the Museum archives, as well as by M. Chapon of the Fonds Doucet in Paris.

At the MIT Press my manuscript underwent the all-encompassing scrutiny of editor Matthew Abbate, whose eye for detail and constructive suggestions turned my work into a finished product. Designer Jean Wilcox managed to convert a sprawling text and 250 photographs into a coherent entity with a design that holds together the written and the visual material in just the kind of dynamic interplay I had hoped for. My deepest appreciation goes to Roger Conover for his faith in this project and his ongoing interest and support.

I have been fortunate in the sustaining combination of friendship and expertise offered by Virginia Zabriskie who has brought little-known aspects of Surrealism to the public eye in Paris and New York, and by Malitte Matta who shared with me

Diego, André, Rose, and Luis Masson in New Preston, Connecticut; photograph
courtesy Comité André Masson.

her astute perceptions in matters of cultural history. And Gina Sawin's encouragement and occasional prodding kept this undertaking on its halting course.

The methodology I have used is loosely based on the example of the French historian Pierre Renouvin, whose lectures on the origins of the First World War I attended at the Sorbonne in the winter of 1949. Renouvin examined history through the analysis of documents. As he stood in front of the class with one sleeve empty holding a piece of chalk between the two remaining fingers of his remaining hand he himself was a primary document. Using works of art, photographs, letters, material from the press, and personal interviews, I have tried to put together a documentary narrative that follows year by year for a decade the work and the intersecting lives of a small number of European and American artists, rather than arranging the material in support of a theory. Toward the end of the period under consideration Max Ernst said, "Art is not made by one artist, but by several. It is to a great degree the product of their exchange of ideas with one another." [4] Both the text and the artworks on the pages that follow provide an opportunity to test the validity of Ernst's statement, keeping in mind as well the singularity of the period covered and the inevitable artistic registering of the tensions and traumas of that "extremely disturbed moment of history."

I didn't seek this project. In Surrealist fashion, it found me, quite by chance, when I looked into the boxes of Kurt Seligmann's papers. Because my own formative years were those covered by this book, a time when I assumed all learning came with a European accent, the story found a willing instrument for its telling. To my surprise it turned out to be a different story than I intended. Originally I had thought simply to reconstruct what took place as the émigrés impacted on American art, but gradually I found what was happening to the displaced to be of equal or greater interest. And although these years marked the end of prewar Europe's last avant-garde, I learned in talking with so many people that Surrealism left no one that came in contact with it unaffected, myself included. In many ways it was an advance guard for a revolution in consciousness that has been ongoing for the last half-century.

Surrealism in Exile

[1] France, 1938: *The Railroad Station of the Imagination and the Dream*

On the evening of January 17, 1938, a row of elegant black automobiles lined the curb of the rue du Faubourg St.-Honoré near number 140, which housed the august Galerie des Beaux-Arts. Men and women in evening dress edged into the courtyard, jostling each other in order to peer into an antique taxi parked before the gallery entrance. Although the skies were clear, inside the taxi rain poured over a blonde-wigged mannequin on the back seat. Snails left trails of slime across her breasts and leafy vines obscured her feet. A crocodile chauffeur was seated at the wheel, his gleaming teeth bared.

Having gained the doorway, visitors found themselves in a corridor lined with mannequins poised beneath street signs, provocatively decked out like prostitutes beside their doorways along the rue St.-Denis. The head of one was encased in a bird cage, another was draped in widow's weeds; one body was covered with tiny spoons, another with scorpions; one cried crystal tears, another held a lobster as a telephone receiver.

"But there should be labels, explanations," a news reporter heard a heavy-set woman exclaim. "Ridiculous, lamentable," responded her escort.[1]

The crowd pushed on toward a large round gallery at the end of the corridor where guests were provided with flashlights so they could find their way in its cavernous darkness. The gallery's eighteenth-century décor was obscured by a dense array of dusty coal sacks hanging limply from the ceiling. An odor of roasting coffee prickled the nostrils, mingling with the *sous bois* fragrance of the dead leaves that carpeted the floor. Flashlights played over bizarre objects: a seat supported by four human legs in high-heeled pumps, a soup tureen covered with the feathers of a dove, and a tabernacle, mounted on female legs, with an arm raised in the papal benediction. On a white gramophone the shadow of a hand caressed two plaster breasts and another hand projected from a door in place of a knob. More hands floated on fluorescent liquids contained in a glass-topped table. Four beds in Louis XV style with rumpled linen stood near a pond, on which floated water lilies, surrounded by reeds and moss. In opposition to the cool water, red-hot coals gleamed through the perforations of a nearby iron brazier.

As the flashlight beams crisscrossed the "grotto" they flickered over paintings hanging on revolving doors that led nowhere. Like apparitions in the shifting light there hovered before the eyes landscapes that appeared to have been painted on another planet by Yves Tanguy, Salvador Dalí's *Great Masturbator,* Magritte's *Je ne vois pas la . . . cachée dans la forêt,* Paalen's *Fata Alaska,* Man Ray's *At the Hour of*

Top: Invitation to the International Exhibition of Surrealism, January 1938.

Bottom: A visitor greeting Masson's mannequin at the opening of the 1938 Surrealist exhibition, news photo from *Paris Soir.*

EXPOSITION INTERNATIONALE
DU
SURRÉALISME

INVITATION
pour le
17 Janvier 1938
TENUE DE SOIRÉE

A 22 heures
signal d'ouverture
par André BRETON

APPARITIONS
D'ÊTRES-OBJETS

L'HYSTÉRIE

LE TRÈFLE
INCARNAT

L'ACTE MANQUÉ

PAR

Hélène
VANEL

COQS ATTACHÉS

CLIPS
FLUORESCENTS

DESCENTE
DE LIT
EN FLANCS D'
HYDROPHILES

LES
PLUS BELLES
RUES DE PARIS

TAXI PLUVIEUX

CIEL DE
ROUSSETTES

Le descendant authentique de Frankenstein, l'automate " Enigmarelle ", construit
en 1900 par l'ingénieur américain Ireland, traversera, à minuit et demi, en fausse
chair et en faux os, la salle de l'Exposition Surréaliste.

GALERIE BEAUX-ARTS, 140, RUE DU FAUBOURG SAINT-HONORÉ — PARIS

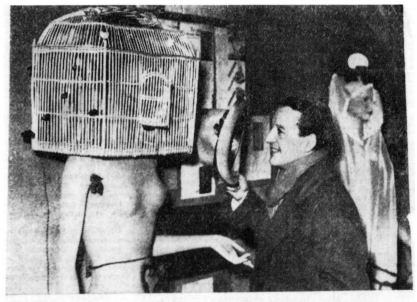

UNE VISITE AU SALON DES « SURRÉALISTES »

C'est dans une salle du faubourg Saint-Honoré que les « Surréalistes » présentent leurs œuvres. Toutes sont des mannequins vêtus de façon plus que baroque. L'imagination et la plus haute fantaisie y remplacent l'Art. Voici une élégante et son chapeau-cage.

the Observatory, Masson's anthropomorphic *Armchair,* two versions of Max Ernst's *Garden Airplane Trap,* and his 1927 *Au rendezvous des amis,* a group portrait of the early Surrealists and their chosen progenitors. Sculptures by Arp, Henry Moore, and Giacometti, early paintings by De Chirico, decalcomanias by Domínguez and others, one of Miró's *Dutch Interiors,* and Kurt Seligmann's recent *danse macabre* paintings were among the several hundred bewildering works caught in the crossfire of the flashlights.

The reactions of the guests ranged from nervous laughter to blatant scoffing. Disconcerted, they begged for explanations or offered each other their own interpretations. There was a large crowd on hand by ten p.m. when the poet Paul Eluard officially opened the exhibition and read a blessing on the occasion composed by the spokesman for the Surrealist movement, André Breton. The event's stage manager, the "technician of shock," Marcel Duchamp, did not stay around to see the impact of his handiwork, but was already en route to London. He later disclaimed any responsibility for the evening's climactic surprise, which occurred sometime after midnight when "a hairy sorceress, a specter in rags, aging and brittle" bounded onto one of the beds brandishing a live rooster, performed a wild dance, and jumped into the pond, splashing water over the assembled evening clothes. This was the dancer Hélène Vanel, an acquaintance of Dalí, performing "The Unconsummated Act." Although the invitation had promised his appearance, Frankenstein's offspring, Enigmerell, did not materialize.

"It was," read an account in the next day's newspaper, "moist, painful, and sad, as a return from the Bois de Meudon on a Sunday at the end of the world." The occasion was, of course, the first and last major manifestation staged in Paris by the pre–World War II Surrealist group, marking its fourteen-year occupation of the avant-garde territory. Since 1924 when André Breton had drawn up the first Surrealist manifesto, summoning writers to explore the unconscious by using "pure psychic automatism," there had been a barrage of publications, position papers, films, smaller exhibitions, and public wrangles that had given the movement visibility. The art produced under the Surrealist rubric or by artists Breton had annexed had been deemed important enough to have been the subject of two major museum exhibitions in the United States and one in London. Since 1934 the elegant, glossy publication *Minotaure,* financed by Albert Skira, had devoted its pages to articles and artworks by and about the Surrealists or to the gleanings from other periods and cultures that they designated as surreal.

Images and devices from the visual portion of Surrealism had been appropriated for use in advertising and packaging, most notably by Schiaparelli, for whom Dalí had designed a perfume bottle shaped like a torso. The biomorphic fantasies of Surrealist painters such as Miró had begun to influence furnishings and interiors on both sides of the Atlantic. One of the movement's most inventive individuals, the U.S.-born Man Ray, had revolutionized fashion photography through the same unorthodox techniques that he used in his surreal photographs. Their most famous patron was Marie Laure, Comtesse de Noailles, whose lavish balls they attended and whose husband had been threatened with excommunication for financing the Dalí-Buñuel film, *L'Âge d'or.*

The exhibition at the prestigious Galerie des Beaux-Arts, whose walls were usually devoted to the work of old masters (El Greco had immediately preceded the Surrealists), was not, then, the announcement of a revolution, but rather the grand finale of a movement about to pass from radical chic into history. World events, however, decreed that the artists involved would be given one last arena in which to continue their attempts to derail the senses. In October of 1942, when the art life of Paris was constrained under the Nazi occupation, nine of the artists from the Beaux-Arts exhibition (Carrington, Ernst, Duchamp, Hayter, Masson, Matta, Paalen, Seligmann, and Tanguy), along with their spokesman, André Breton, succeeded in causing a stir in New York with their "First Papers of Surrealism" exhibition, an event that officially signaled the transfer of Europe's last avant-garde to the Western Hemisphere. Few would have guessed that evening at the Galerie des Beaux-Arts that such a large contingent of the participants would within four years have fled the Nazis and reconstituted the Surrealist group across the Atlantic.

Thousands of people visited the exhibition in the Faubourg St.-Honoré and a dozen newspapers ran articles on it. Probably Maurice Morel and Jean Bazaine, writing in *Les Temps Présents,* came closest to an accurate assessment of what the "Exposition Internationale du Surréalisme" actually signified. Reviewing with respect the movement's origin in Dada, in the revulsion born of experiences during World War I, and in the Freud-inspired effort to bring about a revolution in consciousness, the writers questioned what had become of the avant-garde heroes of the 1920s among so many works of "derivative formulas, calculated cynicism, and banal perversities." They accused the Surrealists of seeming to take risks while actually being disengaged and lamented "one more revolution that fades into that which it wished to overturn." They found the artworks "terribly aged, in a vulgar salesroom, liquidat-

Top: Newspaper photograph of the 1938 Surrealist exhibition; at left is a painting by Kurt Seligmann.

Bottom: Newspaper caricature, January 28, 1938.

EXPOSITION SURREALISTE

— Coucou ! C'est moi le ministre-objet...
— Enchantée... je suis la majorité adéquatoïde...

ing all that remained of the postwar disgust. . . . This art, no longer dangerous, will wind up at the decorator, the advertising agency, the hairdresser, and the couturier. Seeing what had become of all their ideals, their need for purity, their rage, one wants to cry out 'à d'autres.' "[2] Morel and Bazaine's stand coincided with that of Georges Bataille, Breton's sometime collaborator and frequent antagonist, who found the event merely frivolous.

Eric Sevareid, who was to become famous as a war correspondent, reported in the following morning's *Herald Tribune* that a crowd of special police had been on hand to keep order outside the gallery and that overcrowding had forced them to close the doors a half-hour after they had officially opened, with the result that "the clash of colors in the corridors was accompanied by systematic crashes at the iron grill doors." He described the visitors stumbling in the dark through thick and dank autumn leaves under a ceiling hung with lumpy gunny sacks and moving into a second room that was well lighted by a chandelier artfully fashioned from an oversize pair of beribboned panties.

How had it come about that the rebels of the 1920s were being showcased in the Faubourg St.-Honoré, rubbing elbows with the haute monde? Apparently Raymond Cogniat, artistic director of the gallery, had approached Paul Eluard with the offer of a Surrealist exhibition, an initiative probably prompted by a suggestion from Kurt Seligmann, Swiss-born member of the group and nephew by marriage of Georges Wildenstein, owner of the gallery and publisher of the *Gazette des Beaux-Arts.* Summit meetings were held with Breton and Eluard at which the details were worked out: the Surrealists wanted carte blanche as far as the installation was concerned, but Wildenstein refused, on the grounds of bad luck, to have the ceiling hung with open umbrellas as Duchamp proposed. He finally agreed to the alternate scheme of using coal sacks to camouflage the décor after special insurance was arranged.

At a plenary session informing other members of the group an alert was sounded. The one principle they agreed upon was that nothing of the gallery décor should be visible, and Marcel Duchamp was charged with effecting the transformation. The empty sacks impregnated with coal dust dripping from the ceiling were intended to be, recalled Georges Hugnet, "like a steam engine that broke a breach in the ramparts of our senses large enough for the heroic charge of our dreams, desires, and needs."[3] The power of certain places to trigger associations and tap into the unconscious had long been exploited by the Surrealists. Breton made obsessive use of the Boulevard Bonne-Nouvelle and the Place Dauphine in *Nadja,* his seminal work of the 1920s; Louis Aragon revealed the hallucinatory power of the shop windows of the Passage de l'Opéra in *Paysan de Paris;* they and others of the group found themselves transported in the artificial rusticity of the Buttes-Chaumont. An exhibition was thus an opportunity to create a potent environment that would serve as a point of departure, a "railroad station for the imagination and the dream."[4]

A convoy of nudes was ordered. The first mannequins that arrived were pronounced too cute, and replacements were found that came closer to the "cardboard dream of the eternal feminine," stirring in each of the sixteen appointed male artists, according to Hugnet, the spirit of a Pygmalion. All sorts of mysterious packets were trotted in as each of the "couturiers of eroticism" decked out their fantasy females. Breton became furious with Leo Malet, author of *Ne pas voir plus loin que le bout de son sexe,* who hung a bowl with a goldfish in the crotch of his model, and confiscated his mannequin, which then fell to the elegant Austrian convert to Surrealism Wolfgang Paalen, who decked the rejected mannequin more decorously in moss and mushrooms. Breton also brought pressure to bear on Max Ernst to turn out the light bulb that glowed under the widow's skirts of his black-veiled mannequin. "Rrose Sélavy" inscribed across the pubes of Duchamp's mannequin, clad only in a man's jacket and hat, passed without comment. A favorite among these surrogate women was that of Masson, head encased in a cage, gagged with a black velvet band, the mouth replaced with a pansy, and clad in a G string inset with glass eyes.

As the pace of frenzied activity accelerated, there were increasing financial demands on the part of the exhibitors and Breton's tantrums multiplied. The artists protested, as usual, the placement of their works, but calm was eventually restored thanks to Eluard's patient diplomacy or Duchamp's smiling disdain. By the evening of January 17, all was in ordered disorder, with rain pouring inside the taxi thanks to a garden hose, the 1,200 coal sacks in place, the aroma of roasting coffee ready for release, flashlights stacked up for distribution, and the mannequins ready to solicit bewildered attention. Missing only was the man whom Gabrielle Buffet Picabia described as our "benevolent technician," he whom Breton called "surely the most intelligent and, for many, the most exasperating man of the first portion of the 20th century"—Marcel Duchamp.

Since Surrealism had been at its inception a literary movement, although arguably it made its greatest impact through visual art, Breton was particularly concerned with documentation. Books had been for a decade a major part of Surrealist activity, extraordinary books born of the collaboration of artists and poets, books whose very covers and formats were warnings of the time bombs concealed within. Exhibition catalogues, similarly, were regarded as creations as much as the works on display, intended to subvert the notion of a traditional catalogue with its listing of factual data, as well as to survive the ephemeral gathering of artworks. When a publication was in the offing the daily meetings at the café would be extended into evening work sessions at Breton's studio in the rue Fontaine, and the collaborative activity heightened the intensity with which the work proceeded. For the 1938 show, Breton and Eluard, with contributions from thirty-one of the group's members, put together a seventy-eight-page *Dictionnaire abrégé du surréalisme.* Its emphasis on the written word and on word-image juxtapositions, and the verbal participation of the artists, already had a precedent not only in *La Révolution Surréaliste* (1924–1929) and *Surréalisme au Service de la Révolution,* but also in the catalogue for an exhibition of Surrealist drawings held in December 1935 at the Galerie de Quatre Chemins to which each exhibitor contributed one sentence: for example Marcel Jean's "Wait no longer, the curtain has risen on a forest fire." In New York in 1942 Breton and Duchamp would produce the bullet-riddled *First Papers of Surrealism* catalogue, and a spongy breast with an invitation to touch would adorn the cover of the catalogue for the first postwar Surrealist exhibition at the Galerie Maeght in 1947.

The *Dictionnaire abrégé* includes a compendium of quotations from favorite Surrealist authors from Heraclitus to Novalis, including recent members of their literary pantheon such as Baudelaire, Lautréamont, Jarry, Raymond Roussel, and Tristan Tzara. Current and former Surrealists are listed and characterized: Magritte: "the cuckoo's egg"; Eluard: "the nurturer of stars"; Max Ernst: "Loplop, bird superior, painter, poet, theoretician of Surrealism from the movement's beginning until today." The names of the movement's heroes appear, accompanied by brief identifications. "Marx, Karl (1818–1883)—Transform the world, said Marx; change life itself, said Rimbaud; for us these orders are one and the same," wrote Breton, who also contributed the following comment on Hegel: "Hegel addressed himself to all the questions that could be raised in the areas of poetry and art; even the most difficult he has for the most part resolved with an unparalleled clarity . . . still today it is to Hegel that one must turn to inquire regarding the good or bad bases of Surrealist activity."[5]

The *Dictionnaire abrégé*'s selection of words and their definitions shed light on the history, theory, and practice of Surrealism. For example:

Cover of the catalogue for the 1938 exhibition, *Dictionnaire abrégé du surréalisme,* 1938, with drawing by Yves Tanguy. José Corti reprint.

OBJECT—the ready-mades and assisted ready-mades chosen or assembled since 1914 by Marcel Duchamp constitute the first Surrealist objects. In 1924 André Breton suggested making and circulating certain objects that one perceives only in dreams (oneiric objects). In 1930 Salvador Dalí fabricated and defined objects with a symbolic function (an object that lends itself to a minimum of mechanical functioning and which is based on phantoms and representations that might be provoked by unconscious acts). . . . Currently Surrealism has drawn attention to the various categories of objects existing independently: the natural object, the agitated object, the found object, the mathematical object, the involuntary object, etc.[6]

Illustrating the text are many of the items produced by the artists for the 1936 exhibition of Surrealist objects at the Charles Ratton galleries, as well as new ones fabricated for the 1938 show, such as Dalí's *Object Being,* Seligmann's *Ultra Meuble,* and Paalen's ivy-covered chair and sponge umbrella. Found objects of a provocative nature such as a dagger sheath in the form of a crucifix also appeared in the *Dictionnaire's* pages. Old steel engravings of bizarre initial letters from a printer's stock book were used to head each section of the alphabet, demonstrating that the printed word itself had an existence as an object.

While Surrealism during the 1920s had been the rubric adopted by a small group of writers—soon expanded to include visual artists—who met every day and worked closely together, by the mid-1930s it had taken on an international character and "Surrealist" groups had been founded in several countries, including England, Belgium, and Czechoslovakia, while individual practitioners were at work in far-flung places. The fact that the exhibition at the Galerie des Beaux-Arts included sixty artists from fourteen countries (Man Ray, Joseph Cornell, and Matta's wife, Anne Clark, were the only representatives of the United States) did indeed make it appear that Surrealism was a growing international movement and that it had entered on an expansionist phase. At the same time, Breton was eager to emphasize that it was by 1938 a movement with a history. Accordingly the major artists each showed a selection of works that covered their development within Surrealism, while the presence of a number of recent recruits such as Matta and Leonora Carrington contributed to the sense of the movement's ongoing momentum.

It was, however, an uneasy, tottering Europe that this international gathering of artists represented, and the works on view might well be seen as symptoms of the malaise. On the very eve of the exhibition's opening, Camille Chautemps, who had succeeded Léon Blum as premier during the Popular Front, that fragile coalition of leftist parties, had failed in his attempt to form the 104th government of the Third Republic. Described as adept at compromise, nonideological, and devoid of long-range goals, Chautemps repudiated Communist support of his policies, and the Socialist ministers, still loyal to the concept of the Popular Front, resigned and brought down the government. Neither Bonnet nor Blum succeeded in their attempts to form a new government and Chautemps was eventually recalled to leadership, but with a precariously narrow margin.

The policies toward fascism that France was to pursue were necessarily linked to those of England. On the day before the Surrealist opening, Anthony Eden, the British Foreign Secretary who was opposed to appeasement of fascist regimes, visited Prime Minister Neville Chamberlain at Chequers. The meeting turned into a serious altercation over Chamberlain's lack of interest in strengthening Anglo-American ties and the influence his pro-Mussolini sister-in-law was having on his conduct of foreign policy. By February 22, Eden, unable to shake Chamberlain's conviction that England had more to gain from doing business with Germany and Italy than from closer ties with the United States and France, resigned. With Eden went the last hope that there would be any opposition to the Anschluss, the annexation of Austria that Hitler was at that moment preparing. On March 3, when British ambassador Neville Henderson offered Hitler tacit British acknowledgment of Germany's right to her former colonies and asked for some contribution to European peace and security, Hitler ranted that "the most important contribution to European peace and security would be the suppression of the inflammatory international press, particularly offensive in England." [7]

On March 11, while Chamberlain was giving Ambassador Ribbentrop a farewell lunch at No. 10 Downing Street, messages arrived disclosing the massing of German troops on the Austrian border and the ultimatum to Kurt von Schuschnigg to cancel the scheduled plebiscite and resign in favor of the Nazi, Artur von Seyss-Inquart. A few days after Austria's capitulation, Mussolini in Rome ordered heavy bombing attacks on Barcelona. According to his son-in-law Ciano's diary, "he said he was delighted that the Italians should be horrifying the world by their aggressiveness for a change, instead of charming it by their skill at playing the guitar. In his opinion this will send up our stock in Germany too, where they love ruthless and total war." [8] On May 12 in Geneva the League of Nations Council accepted the proposal of Lord Halifax that the League take no action regarding Italian sovereignty in Ethiopia, despite Haile Selassie's eloquent pleas for his country in the face of Italian

Kurt Seligmann, *La Ronde,* 1940, oil and tempera on glass, 61 x 73 inches; The
Museum of Contemporary Art, Chicago.

aggression. In such fashion, step by step, the heads of the European governments performed the complicated appeasement dance, rather like the grotesques in the *danses macabres* that Kurt Seligmann had begun to paint, a rehearsal for the Munich quadrille that was to come in the fall.

How did the participants in the 1938 Surrealist exhibition see themselves in relation to the fateful game that was being played on the European chessboard? The political position of Surrealism had long been an important policy matter for the group, and it had split more than once on the question of allegiances and priorities. The very origins of Surrealism lay in the ludicrous tragedy of the First World War with its death toll of a million and half young men in France alone, the reasons for their deaths still unfathomed. That the international socialist movement might have prevented the war if nationalist patriotism had not been used to break up socialism's solidarity was a lesson not ignored by André Breton, as he called for resistance to the emotional ties of nationalism.

As a former medical student, Breton's World War I military assignment was in the hospital of St.-Dizier, but for a time he was sent to the front as an inexperienced orderly. Working behind the lines at Verdun where the battle raged for nine months and left hundreds of thousands of casualties, Breton had "the spectacle of wholesale death imprinted on his mental horizon." There he not only moved among the dead and horrendously wounded, but for the first time he confronted, among the shell-shocked, the derailments of the human mind.

Breton's early idol, the poet Apollinaire, died after an extended illness due to head injuries received in the war. André Masson was severely wounded at the front when a bullet ripped through his chest. "I am dead, the greatest of human adventures," he remembered thinking. He learned at first hand, he said, the capacity of man to be a sadist. He was confined in a psychiatric hospital, and the breakdown resulting from his trauma had long-lasting effects on his mental and physical health. Marcel Duchamp's brother Raymond Duchamp-Villon had died from war wounds. Onslow Ford's father, who as an army doctor had witnessed the senseless slaughter at Gallipoli, suffered a severe depression and early death that left an indelible mark on his eight-year-old son.

On the German side, Max Ernst spent four years at the front as an artillery engineer, was twice wounded and invalided out in 1917. He and Paul Eluard, who was gassed, were appalled to learn that they had been on opposite sides of the same front in February of 1917 and could have been firing at each other. It was against this background that members of the group took an antinationalist, antiwar stance, vowing not to be seduced by the nationalism stirred up by the arms industry or the idea that war was anything but a cruel delusion.

Antinationalist as they may have been, the Surrealists did not abstain from political commitment. In the movement's first official publication, *La Révolution Surréaliste,* founded in 1924, Breton envisioned Surrealism as leading the way to social revolution by breaking through the walls of psychological repression. As the international communist movement gathered momentum during the 1920s, the word revolution came to be synonymous with worldwide communist revolution. Hence in 1929 Breton changed the periodical's title to *Le Surréalisme au Service de la Révolution.* For the next five years the Surrealists, some more in name than in action, were aligned with the Third International Communist Party. When he broke with the Party at the time of the Congress for the Defense of Culture in 1935, Breton reasserted his conviction that "the future of culture is in the transformation of society by the proletarian revolution," and he cited a record of Surrealist participation that included a call to join the demonstrations of February 10, 1934, the immediate adherence to the Intellectuals' Committee of Vigilance (which had temporarily reunited him with Georges Bataille), and their presence in the streets in the very "bosom" of all the major workers' demonstrations. In resigning from the Third International, Breton described the Soviet Union as the negation of what it should have been and criticized it for favoring the French arms build-up:

If we assert ourselves against all attempts to resurrect the ideal of *la patrie* above all else, of national sentiment, in a capitalist regime, it is not only because from our profoundest selves we are totally incapable of subscribing, not only because we see in it the fanning of a sordid illusion which has all too often inflamed the world, but above all because even with the best will, we cannot help seeing it as a symptom of a widespread illness. . . . Nor have we ceased to be uneasy over the idolatrous cult through which certain zealots seek to bind the working masses, not only to the USSR, but to the person of its leader.[9]

Breton, Dalí, Eluard, Ernst, Dora Maar, Magritte, Messens, Oppenheim, Péret, Man Ray, and Tanguy signed this document in August 1935. While they thus protested against the Soviet Union and the imprisonment of writers such as Victor Serge, these artists by no means abjured political involvement. The cause of the Spanish Republic drew responses that ranged from actual participation (Péret, Remedios

Varo, Masson, and Marcel Jean were in Barcelona in 1937) to contributing to an edition of etchings, printed by Stanley William Hayter at Atelier 17, in order to raise money for Spanish children who were victims of the civil war. The English Surrealist Roland Penrose was also in Barcelona in 1936 and later arranged to bring Picasso's *Guernica* to England in 1938 to help arouse public opinion there. Pierre Mabille, medical doctor and Surrealist writer specializing in anthropological subjects, attributed major significance to the Spanish Civil War, "not only because the destiny of Europe was decided there, but because of the subsequent hold this tragedy has had." He saw in it "elements of a powerful myth which would rest in the collective consciousness of future centuries." [10]

In the spring of 1938 the opportunity arose for Breton to meet his political idol Leon Trotsky, who had been granted political asylum in Mexico after his expulsion from the Soviet Union in 1936. The trip came about because Breton decided, following the birth of his daughter Aube, that he should have a source of income and asked Alexis Léger (the poet St.-John Perse), then a foreign service officer in charge of cultural affairs, to send him somewhere as a cultural ambassador. (Breton had long made a point of living frugally. Since the 1920s he had occupied a small top-floor studio in a back building off the rue Fontaine near Montmartre's Place Blanche. The occasional sale of an artwork kept him going and he maintained that "poverty would be the ransom to be paid for non-slavery.") Offered the choice of giving lectures on French poetry and painting in either Czechoslovakia or Mexico, he chose the latter because it would provide an opportunity to visit Trotsky. Although Breton had broken with the Third International, he remained fervently antinationalist and dedicated to the cause of world revolution. He had not met Trotsky when the latter was in Paris, but had long admired him and had been profoundly influenced by his book on Lenin.

Also Mexico loomed large on the Surrealist map of significant places. During the presidency of Lázaro Cárdenas (1934–1940), Mexico's willingness to accept political refugees of all stripes had made it an international haven for European intellectuals fleeing Hitler and Stalin. For the Surrealists Mexico offered the added romance of the Indian culture. There was even a fascination with the ritual slaughter of the Aztecs in which Georges Bataille claimed to see human nature unmasked. The creator of the theater of the absurd, Antonin Artaud, an early adherent of Surrealism, later an apostate, had made a trip of several months to Mexico in 1934 during which he had come probably as close to participation in vestigial Indian rituals as is possible for a European. His accounts must also have fired the Surrealist imagination. "Red earth, virgin earth, impregnated with blood," Breton was to write of Mexico.[11] Pierre Mabille had even prophesied in *Égrégores:* "The dominant role of the European nations nears its end in favor of a transfer of civilization toward America. A special place will be reserved for Mexico."[12]

Breton and his wife, Jacqueline Lamba, arrived in Mexico in February without funds, only to find, according to the latter, that no arrangements had been made either for paid lectures or accommodations. (Public announcements of the lectures exist, but there are conflicting accounts as to how many were actually given.) Breton's first impulse, Lamba recalled, was to get back on the ship for its return voyage to France, but Diego Rivera stepped into the breach and invited them to be his guests in the linked studio buildings that he and Frida Kahlo shared in San Angel.

Other problems arose for Breton due to advance warnings that arrived from members of the French Communist Party, including a scurrilous letter from René Blech accusing him of perfidious action against the Spanish Republic. However, Pierre Naville had written a most positive response to a letter of inquiry about Breton from Trotsky's secretary, Jean van Heijenoort, who sent for copies of Breton's books in preparation for Trotsky's meeting with him. Shortly after the Bretons' arrival in Mexico, they were escorted by the Riveras to the "blue house" in Coyoacán that Diego had loaned Trotsky (today the Frida Kahlo museum).

Writing about this meeting after his return to Paris, Breton described the quickened heartbeat with which he entered the gate and crossed the garden "with its pink and violet bougainvilleas glistening in the sunlight and its paths lined with solemn cactus and pre-Columbian stone carvings." As Trotsky rose when they entered his book-lined study, Breton's first reaction was surprise at finding him so youthful, "this veteran who had led the 1905 revolution and had been one of the principals in October 1917." He described a man with deep blue eyes, abundant silvery hair, and a freshness of complexion—a man who seemed to wear a mask that concealed all trace of the precariousness of his circumstances, "ousted by his comrades, threatened every moment by Stalin's henchmen who were determined to hunt him down, denied asylum by the capitalist and communist countries alike, haunted by the memory of his four murdered children."[13]

Trotsky started the conversation with a discussion of the word "surrealism," against which he preferred realism, "in the precise sense that Zola gave the word." He also asked for news from Paris and inquired in particular after Gide and Malraux.

André Breton, Diego Rivera, and Leon Trotsky, Mexico, 1938, photograph by Fritz Bach.

Following this initial visit they met frequently for lengthy discussions. Jacqueline Lamba recalled long walks in the country, during which the two men who "shared the will to change the world, were ecstatic in front of nature, marveling at butter- flies."[14] In the weeks they spent together, Breton's image of Trotsky as a legendary hero was gradually replaced by a more vivid and human actuality—Trotsky scowling over the Paris newspapers in a garden in Cuernavaca under a burning sun, fishing for axolotls in a rushing forest stream, climbing the pyramid of Xochicalo, picnicking on the edge of a frozen lake in the crater of Popocatepetl, or listening to schoolchildren sing in the ancient Tarascan tongue. Incongruously, one of the pleasures afforded by the trip that the Trotskys, Bretons, and Riveras took to Lake Pátzcuaro in the interior was the opportunity to see an American western at a village movie theater, something that was too dangerous for Trotsky to attempt closer to civilization. In his written account of this trip, Breton conveys an image of Trotsky as a man of boundless curi- osity, energy, and childlike enthusiasm, as well as a ferocious capacity for work.

The major question that Breton was anxious to resolve with Trotsky involved the issue of artistic freedom, the right of the artist to be free from political dictation, a question that had plagued him since his affiliation with the Communist Party in 1926. Breton objected particularly to the term "social realism" and sought to pre- serve the integrity of artistic research independent of political goals. Gradually, ac- cording to Breton's version of the meetings, Trotsky came to agree that the revolutionary and the artist share the common goal of human liberation. However, Trotsky's suspicions were aroused by the value that Breton attached to chance and

he suggested that perhaps he kept a window open on the "au-delà" (mystical). Reassured, finally, Trotsky agreed to work on a statement that the two could issue jointly that would define the position of art vis-à-vis politics.

"Van" Heijenoort, the secretary who translated daily what Trotsky had written in Russian, described the way the two men worked: each separately wrote a part of the statement and then discussed together what they had written, following which Trotsky would cut and collage the sections together. As he worked the problem through, Trotsky ended up calling for an anarchist regime in the matter of intellectual liberty, with no authority, no constraint—"here Marxists and anarchists can walk hand in hand." When Rivera and Breton agreed on the statement "All freedom in art is permitted except against the proletarian revolution," it was Trotsky who warned against the new abuses to which even that single restriction could give rise, and he struck it out.[15] The essential message of the four-page statement was the defense of artistic freedom. Yet it also concluded that "the supreme task of art in our time is to participate consciously and actively in the preparation of the revolution, but the artist must feel it within. However, the artist can only serve the struggle for emancipation when he is subjectively permeated with its social and individual import and when he freely seeks to give artistic form to his interior world."[16]

Although Rivera had not played a significant role in its formulation, Trotsky insisted that Diego's name rather than his own appear alongside Breton's as coauthor. The reason given was that he did not wish to appear to be identified with a single art movement. The original of the document he gave to Breton, departing from his usual practice of keeping all originals in his archives; perhaps he did not attach great significance to it. It was nonetheless soon published in the United States in a translation by Dwight McDonald in *Partisan Review,* in England in *The London Bulletin,* and in France in *Minotaure.*[17]

Breton returned to France at the end of July, and he and Rivera subsequently took the initiative in founding the International Federation of Independent Revolutionary Artists. In a letter to Breton of December 22, 1938, supporting the Federation, Trotsky forcefully reiterated the principles of their July manifesto:

The struggle for the ideas of the revolution in art must begin anew with the struggle for artistic truth, not in the sense of a specific school, but in the sense of the fidelity of the artist to his interior self. Without that there is no art—You will not lie—that must be the challenge. . . . The International Federation of Independent Revolutionary Artists can ozonize the atmosphere in which artists breathe and create. Truly independent creation in our time of convulsive reaction can't help but be revolutionary by its very nature; each artist must carry on the search in his own way without waiting for outside commands, even rejecting dictation and those who submit to it.[18]

More immediate political concerns seem to have prevented the Federation from gathering momentum. Rivera broke with Trotsky while Frida was in Paris for an exhibition of her work arranged by Breton, and Trotsky moved out of the Riveras' blue house to the house a few blocks away where, despite the heavy iron shutters on the windows and doors of his room, he finally met his assassin.

While the number of artists who actually read the Breton-Trotsky statement may have been small, the attitude it expressed was to make itself felt in the United States, particularly through critics of a Trotskyist persuasion, most significantly in the intellectually influential *Partisan Review* circle. In essence it liberated politically radical artists from enslavement to social realism by sanctioning as revolutionary in itself the unfettered creative process. It also freed left-wing art critics such as Clement Greenberg and Harold Rosenberg from the obligation to extol social realism and instead made creative freedom the standard by which art should be judged. By the late 1930s a justification had been established for an "independent revolutionary art," while the artworks that were to fill this void had yet to come into existence.

Breton was not the only Surrealist to travel to the Western Hemisphere that summer. Kurt and Arlette Seligmann spent the summer of 1938 in British Columbia in order to study *in situ* the art and life of the Northwest Coast Indians. For a decade the development of French ethnology had been interwoven with Surrealism. The Seligmanns went with a mandate from the American section of the recently opened Musée de l'Homme to bring back material from a region not yet represented in the museum's collection. The Seligmanns stayed for nearly four months in a trading post, observing, interviewing, taking notes, and photographing the ceremonial dress, carved wooden house facades, and towering totems of the Tsimshian Indians. Seligmann also recorded the stories of the totems as they were recounted to him by the older Indians. "Already," he later wrote in an article in *Minotaure,* "the younger Indians were no longer interested in these legends and no longer felt the magic force of the carvings."[19]

Seligmann determined to make good on his commitment to the Musée de l'Homme with a spectacular acquisition. He selected the 60-foot-high Mat Totem of

Tsimshian totems *in situ*, British Columbia, 1938, photograph by Kurt Seligmann.

Top: Kurt Seligmann observing Tsimshian painted carvings, 1938, photograph by Arlette Seligmann.

Bottom: Mat totem packed for shipment, 1938, photograph by Kurt Seligmann.

Gedem Skanish, one of four totems still standing in 1938 where they had been placed in front of a Tsimshian chief's hut sometime before 1859. In order to purchase the totem it was necessary to obtain the consent of all those who were considered descendants of Gedem Skanish, and a meeting with some seventy clan members was called. Before the deal could be completed the Seligmanns were required to become members of the clan and receive Tsimshian names. Parts of the huge cedarwood carving were restored, especially around the base where it had rotted in the ground, and worn portions of the features were replaced, using other totems as models. The totem then was carefully wrapped and shipped to Paris.

Too high for the museum's interior, the totem still stands half a century later under the entrance portico, the plaque acknowledging its source obscured by pigeon droppings. For the *Journal de la Société des Américanistes* in 1939 Seligmann wrote a precise description of the towering sculpture, the traces of color, the method of carving, the circumstances surrounding its purchase, and, most valuable, the story told by its images, as it had been handed down through the clan's oral tradition. A similar scholarly impulse prompted Seligmann to begin to amass rare books on magic and the occult, an interest that would lead to the publication in 1947 of a unique compendium of information on those subjects, *The History of Magic.*

For the other Surrealists the summer of 1938 passed rather uneventfully in various corners of France. Masson, his wife Rose, and their two sons had returned from Spain to live in Lyons-la-Forêt in Normandy. Masson was not especially comfortable in that conservative provincial atmosphere, where the Spanish refugees who appeared at their home from time to time were looked upon with suspicion. However, because of the aftereffects of his war injuries he usually avoided living in cities, and this Normandy village served as a quiet setting in which to paint the tumultuous works that were coming from his brush after he had witnessed the defeat of the Loyalists in Spain.

Max Ernst was living in St.-Martin-d'Ardèche in the south of France with his new love, Leonora Carrington. Carrington had grown up in the Irish country home of her affluent family, had attended art school in London, and was introduced to Ernst at an exhibition in 1937. During the two years they spent together Carrington, barely twenty, produced some extraordinary paintings tinged with elements of Celtic mythology, while Ernst, perhaps in sympathetic reaction, began to employ a fantastic fairy-tale imagery that recalls nineteenth-century German illustration. Together they worked on fanciful concrete sculptures for their garden.

Ernst and Carrington went up to Paris in June to see Max's eighteen-year-old son Jimmy, who was preparing to leave for the United States. In his memoirs, Jimmy recalls a farewell apertif with them at the Café de Flore where they were joined by Paul Eluard, Hans Arp, Alberto Giacometti, Man Ray, and, summoned by phone, his mother, Lou Straus Ernst.[20] Jimmy's employer, who headed a printing firm in Glückstadt, had helped arrange for his visa and passage on a New York-bound ship, realizing that Jimmy, with a Jewish mother and a father whose work was included in Hitler's 1937 exhibition of degenerate art, could no longer stay in Germany. Jimmy himself had seen the lines of people waiting to get into the trailers in which this show was being circulated. He had seen and heard enough in Germany to be angrily impatient with his mother and her friends who had come to Paris to wait "until the trouble blew over." His urging that she try to join him in the United States was countered by that optimism which had served her so well in coping with poverty and single parenthood, and which now could not admit that Germans could actually behave to fellow Germans in such a barbaric fashion.[21]

During the summer of 1938, Peggy Guggenheim swept the remarkable Yves Tanguy, with his polished dome of a head sprouting a few unruly tufts of hair, off to England for an exhibition of his work in her gallery. Separated from her husband, the painter Laurence Vail, Guggenheim, with the guidance of Herbert Read, had begun to put together a collection for a museum of twentieth-century art, and, as she detailed unreservedly in her memoirs, had also commenced her collection of artist-lovers, among whom she claimed Tanguy. Returning from England in an unaccustomed state of affluence, Tanguy reportedly threw wads of money at people in cafés.

Both Tanguy's life style, which was basically one of neglect of material needs—he was reputed to live on alcohol and insects—and his art earned him the admiration of the recent recruits to Surrealism, Gordon Onslow Ford, Matta, and Esteban Frances. As Onslow Ford describes it, Tanguy had found a way to "break the barriers of the world of sight" and evoke a limitless space and a sense of suspended time.[22] Tanguy would cover the whole surface of his canvas with paint thinned with turpentine to an almost liquid consistency, carefully grading the tones. Then he drew into the prepared ground his small precise structures (Onslow Ford calls them *personnages*), wiping the wet paint away and introducing notes of brilliant hallucinatory color. Although Tanguy grew up in Paris, he was of Breton origin and visited relatives in Brittany during the summers. Surely he knew the local tradition of giving names and even personalities to the menhirs that hauntingly preside over the coastal land-scape. The dolmen, made up of giant slabs of stone resting across upright slabs, offers mute testimony to prehistoric worship and burial practices. This form is echoed re-peatedly in the shapes that populate Tanguy's horizonless spaces.

His young admirers, Onslow Ford and Matta, spent a rainy summer holiday in 1938 in an abandoned stone customs house at Trevignon near the Finistère coast of Brittany, Tanguy's ancestral terrain. Photographs show them perched on top of those mysterious menhirs that rise out of the flat landscape in a manner strikingly reminis-cent of Tanguy's structures. Confined indoors by the wet weather, they read a great deal and had long discussions about psychic phenomena and the writings of P. D. Ouspensky. In his *Tertium Organum* Ouspensky held that the artist must be a clair-voyant and help others who are "confined to the prison house of sight [to] see what they do not see by themselves." He dwelt on the inadequacy of three-dimensional geometry, the incompleteness of visual perception, and the necessity for a spatial understanding of time. "Our eye," he wrote, "distorts the external world in a certain way to enable us in looking about to determine the position of objects in relation to ourselves. But we are never able to look at the world not from our point of view; we are never able to have a view not distorted by our eyesight." [23]

According to Onslow Ford, Matta's drawing *Star, Flower, Personage, Stone* of 1938 was directly influenced by Ouspensky. Onslow Ford interpreted it as two per-sonnages evolving from either side of the horizon, merging and giving birth to a flower that becomes a star; at the side is a philosopher's stone. The suggestion of an alchemical transformation is combined with a warping of planes that is intended to denote a time dimension. Both artists adapted the use of warped planes from the models made to demonstrate the theories of the most widely read mathematician of the day, Jules Henri Poincaré. Max Ernst had discovered these objects in the Palais de la Découvert. Photographed by Man Ray, they were featured in the special issue of *Cahiers d'Art* devoted to the object in 1936. The curving planes, transparent linear webs, and exploded solids of these objects helped both artists to overcome the con-ventions of one-point perspective, yet in no sense were their aims to be confused with those of analytical cubism. In fact, one Onslow Ford drawing of this period contains a section resembling analytical cubism that is crossed out and inscribed "No sir."

Marcel Duchamp's *Rotary Discs,* suggesting ways of introducing another di-mension through optical illusions created by revolving concentric circles, provided these young Surrealists with an additional aid to breaking the time barrier. "Matta

Roberto Matta, *Star, Flower, Personage, Stone,* 1938, colored pencil on paper, 16 x 25½ inches; private collection.

and I wanted to extend the fields of consciousness beyond sensory perception," Onslow Ford recalled. "The eye only perceives a section of reality and psychological morphology gives a fuller view."[24]

When Breton questioned Matta as to what he meant by "psychological morphology," Matta wrote out the following explanation for him:

Reality is the sequence of explosive convulsions which shape themselves in a rhythmically pulsating and rotating milieu. The eye, tool of memory, is a means of simplifying. The optical image is only a theoretical cut in the sequential morphology of the object . . . psychologically, a morphology of optical images only concerns the theoretical section made at a single instant in the morphological age of an object. I call psychological morphology the graphic mark of the transformations resulting from the emission of energies and their absorption in the object from its first appearance to its final form, in the geodesical, psychological milieu. . . . The object situated at one moment in this milieu intercepts pulsations which suggest transformations in an infinite number of directions.[25]

Man Ray, *Poincaré Mathematical Object,* photographed for the *Cahiers d'Art*
special issue on the object, 1936, gelatin silver print, 11 x 8 inches; copyright the
estate of Man Ray, courtesy Robert Miller Gallery.

Roberto Matta, *Psychological Architecture,* 1938, colored pencil on paper;
courtesy Maxwell Davidson Gallery.

Clearly what Matta was proposing has very little connection with the earlier concerns of Surrealism while it drew heavily on Ouspensky's visionary writings. Although trained in academic figure drawing in his native Chile, Matta had specialized in interior design, with the thought that it might be useful in the family furniture business. When he arrived in Paris in 1935, he went to work as a draftsman in the studio of Le Corbusier, where he was occupied chiefly on visionary projects since there wasn't much actual work at the time. It wasn't until 1936, when he saw reproductions of Marcel Duchamp's work and read an article about him by Gabrielle Buffet Picabia, that he realized that visual art could depict time and change. Using his facility for spatial rendering, he began to experiment with ways of drawing objects in physical transformation in spaces that exploded the confines of the conventional three dimensions. Matta was grappling with ideas of growth, process, extended time, and simultaneity; neither veristic Surrealism nor "pure psychic automatism" were suitable models for what he was trying to visualize.

Through relatives in Spain Matta met García Lorca, who gave him a letter of introduction to Dalí in Paris. Only when he heard about Lorca's murder by the Falangists—news that deeply affected him and prompted him to write a long scenario for a play, "The Earth Is a Man"—did Matta actually call on Dalí. Following Dalí's suggestion he showed some drawings to Breton who, ever eager to prevent hardening of the Surrealist arteries by annexing young artists, welcomed him and also Onslow Ford into the Surrealist group. Breton included them because he perceived that they could make a new and original contribution rather than because they conformed to existing Surrealist practices. Thus it was by no means a monolithic Surrealism that was to be shortly transported to the United States, but a cluster of activities and individuals who provided each other with a support system and were united in their dedication to exposing the fallacies of rationalism and attempting to change human consciousness.

Onslow Ford had met Matta in 1937 at dinner in the pension where the latter was staying. After dinner Matta showed him some of his drawings, and the young Englishman found them to be "like nothing I had ever seen." Onslow Ford was the grandson of Edward Onslow Ford, who was regarded as having sculpted the best likeness of Queen Victoria and is particularly remembered for his sculpture of the drowned poet for the Shelley Memorial at Oxford. When Gordon reached his teens his guardian determined on a career for him as a naval officer and he was sent to prepare at Dartmouth. He served in the Royal Navy until the age of 25, in his spare time painting watercolors of his ship's ports of call around the Mediterranean. Over considerable opposition he resigned his commission in 1937 and arrived in Paris determined to be a painter. The years at sea, standing the night watch under the stars and seeing the dawn break on the horizon, had left their mark and set him in pursuit of the visionary, which he was struggling to find a way of realizing in his painting. The meeting with Matta brought him a friendship with an artist of facile draftsmanship and improvisatory train of thought who shared his intuition of a world beyond the visually perceptible. Together they made tentative forays in its pursuit, attempting to find ways to give form to the unseen. Tanguy's work provided them with inspiration and a direction that they did not find in the more Freudian-inspired Surrealists.

The summer of 1938 with its voyages and visits, its leisurely discussions and indulgence in the spirit of play, came to an end and the group gathered in Paris once more to issue a proclamation. The annual Nazi party rally with Hitler's inflammatory speech was held in Nuremberg on September 12. On September 27, the day on which

Hitler agreed to play host to a four-party conference in Munich on the Czechoslovakian question, an orange broadside appeared in Paris with the heading: "Ni de votre guerre, ni de votre paix" (Neither your war nor your peace). It accused the democracies of having allowed Italy to annihilate Ethiopia, of refusing Spain since July 1936 the arms that would have spelled a quick end to fascism, and of delivering China to Japanese imperialism. It ended with the statement "Capitalism survives only with the complicity of the second and third internationals," and it was signed "The Surrealist Group."

Two days later the French premier Daladier took off for Munich in the early morning fog from Le Bourget in a silver twin-engine plane. At the same time Chamberlain, saying good-bye to his assembled cabinet at Heston airport, quoted from Hotspur in *Henry IV:* "Out of this nettle, danger, we pluck this flower, safety." Meanwhile Mussolini sped toward Munich on a special train. En route—eyewitnesses differ as to where and how—he was joined by Hitler and his Chief of the High Command, General Keitel. Acknowledging that the western front was completely exposed, Hitler reassured Mussolini that Czechoslovakia would be overrun before its allies could mobilize.

By the small hours of the next morning the Czech emissaries in Munich, Jan Masaryk and Dr. Vojtech Mastny, were allowed to see the document sealing their country's fate that had been signed by the four heads of state. Without a shot having been fired Hitler had obtained from Chamberlain and Daladier exactly what he wanted, the Sudetenland. On their return to their respective capitals each head of state was greeted by enthusiastic throngs chanting "Peace, peace." Huge crowds lined Daladier's route from the airport and chanted outside the Quai d'Orsay. Daladier, standing at the window looking down at the crowds, is reported to have said, "Imbeciles. They don't know what it is that they are cheering." [26] Meanwhile an emotionally and physically exhausted Chamberlain uttered the words that would come back to haunt him: "Peace with honor, peace in our time," words he very soon asked the House of Commons not to take too literally.

Toward the end of his life Masson stated flatly "I detest politics," but there is no doubt that in 1938–1939 he was fully attuned to a "world convulsed," and knew where to lay the blame for the causes of that convulsion. Violence had been no stranger to his paintings of the earlier 1930s as he painted his series of massacres and rapes, but the lyricism of his calligraphy and the cubist-derived division of space tended to dissipate the impact of specific acts of aggression. By 1938, however, reconciled with Breton and entering his second Surrealist phase, Masson introduced harsh form and lurid color into violent, action-packed paintings. Jagged, angular bodies composed of discordant elements thrust forward from flaming or lightning-struck settings. Perhaps his most brutal assault on the viewer is the 1938 *Dans la tour du sommeil* (*In the Tower of Sleep*), in which a gigantic muscular figure, like Samson destroying the temple, seems to be bringing a collapsing world down around him as fluid gushes from his penis and a gaping head wound spills forth seeds. Masson considered it one of his richest paintings, revealing an oneiric, sadistic world. The large flayed figure, he said, "came from a memory of the war, a figure lying in the mud of a trench with its head split open." [27] A castration is taking place; a fire is burning fed by bundles of straw; blood runs everywhere; at the upper right a piano-minotaur has intercourse with a woman whose nipples are like swordpoints. It all takes place in a tower, "from which there is no way out except into the abyss."

Calm by comparison but nonetheless ominous is *Labyrinth,* in which a hulking skeletal minotaur stalks the land like a Goya colossus, torso and limbs bursting open to reveal inner architectures and organs. Recalling the central figure/structure in Hieronymus Bosch's *Hell* from the *Garden of Earthly Delights* triptych, the mino-taur's legs are like hollow tree trunks growing out of water, rock, and earth; at the terminus of one leg projects the webbed foot of an aquatic bird. Beyond the chasm of the earth is a stormy sea and a sky dark with thunderclouds. Masson had been living in Spain when the civil war broke out. Still war-wary, he was not a combatant, but there was no question where his sympathies lay. He must have known when he returned to live in a small town in Normandy that what he had witnessed was only a prelude to the horrors to come. "I was haunted by the idea that Europe was going to be overwhelmed with blood and fire." [28] While he may have drawn on timeless mythological subjects for his paintings, there is no mistaking the premonitory terror in the compositonal maelstroms and garish forms and colors.

Masson was not alone in registering the mounting anxiety of the late thirties. Kurt Seligmann had, earlier in the decade, put together a scrapbook of clippings gleaned from the September 1932 issue of the glossy newsmagazine *Le Journal.* Call-ing it "Bourrage de Crâne" (mendacious propaganda), he pasted into the book pho-tographs of the hedonistic life on the Riviera and society figures in elegant restaurants alternately with military photographs showing officers reviewing drilling soldiers or meetings of high-level uniformed officials. Handwritten on an inserted sheet of paper were the words "systematic distribution of poison. Worse than before the war. And

André Masson, *Dans la tour du sommeil*, 1938, oil on canvas, 32 x 39½ inches;
The Baltimore Museum of Art, gift of Saidie A. May.

André Masson, *Labyrinth,* 1938, oil on canvas, 47½ x 24 inches; Centre Georges Pompidou, Musée National d'Art Moderne.

the same things exist. How soon will the next war come, for it certainly will?" He lists topics suggested by the photographs: "War has never ceased to exist"; "The taste for heroism is cultivated by movies and theater"; "The Communists are financed by the capitalists." He concludes "Long live the *bourrage de crâne* and the *petit bourgeois* with a stomach strong enough to digest all this while eating his brioche and drinking his coffee."

Clearly Seligmann understood as early as 1932 Europe's collision course and detected the symptoms of incipient war that most Europeans, still trying to recover from the earlier war, preferred to ignore. His own painting was gradually changing from the hard-edged and austere abstractions that he had exhibited with the Abstraction-Creation group (although these also appear to have contained encoded images; witness the Guggenheim Museum's *Portrait* of 1928, which clearly refers to his academy classmate Giacometti)[29] to paintings and graphic works that were inspired by the late Renaissance artists of his native Basel. A specific catalyst in this change was the 1934 retrospective and catalogue raisonné of Urs Graf, a sixteenth-century artist whose graphic works abound in bizarre fantasies.

Another source on which Seligmann drew was the traditional Basel carnival, a three-day event during which the quiet, generally reserved citizenry goes berserk and the streets are filled with masked figures day and night. It is probably more than coincidence that he wrote an article on this revived tradition for the magazine *Sud* in 1935, the year in which his canvasses became populated with cavorting grotesques. His fascination with the carnival dated from early childhood, but it was only in the mid-1930s that he began to adapt the carnival imagery to his own artistic ends as well as to use the images of the earlier Bâlois graphic tradition exemplified by Urs Graf to give form to the specters he saw on the European horizon. In his new paintings, hollow-faced figures assembled of both mechanical and organic parts appear to gyrate in a clumsy *danse macabre,* which Seligmann with his fatalistic irony may have intended as a parody of European statesmen and generals. Or perhaps he had a foreboding of the living skeletons of Hitler's grisly work force which within a decade would confront the world like skeletons rising from the grave in a fifteenth-century Last Judgment.

Next door to the Seligmanns' studio-house in a short impasse called the Villa Seurat lived Salvador Dalí and his wife Gala, the former wife of Paul Eluard. Dalí had marched directly into the Surrealist limelight when he arrived in Paris from Spain in 1929 with paintings that for many soon came to personify the visual side of Surre-

Kurt Seligmann, *The Beautiful Disturbers of the Night,* 1940, oil and tempera on glass, 32 x 36 inches; Dallas Museum of Art, gift of Mr. and Mrs. Bernard Reis.

Urs Graf, *Knight in the Grasp of the Devil,* 1516, ink on paper, 29.5 x 21 cm;
Basel Museum of Art.

Salvador Dalí, *Still Life with Boiled Beans, Premonition of Civil War,* 1936, oil on canvas, 29⁵⁄₁₆ x 39⅜ inches; Philadelphia Museum of Art, the Louise and Walter Arensberg Collection.

alism. Although he became persona non grata in the late 1930s because of his self-promoting antics and suspected tolerance of fascism, he led the way in giving visual form to the specter of war in 1936 with his *Still Life with Boiled Beans, Premonition of Civil War*. A year later his *Enigma of Hitler* suggested a sinister force at work. A giant telephone receiver hangs from the dead branch of a partially severed tree which also supports an almost transparent umbrella, the latter a favorite Surrealist fetish (later a symbol of Chamberlain and appeasement). From the phone is suspended a large drop of viscous liquid, like spittle, above a soup dish containing a few beans and a photograph of Hitler; a bat is poised on the edge. The phone takes on the character of a menacing object through which a disembodied voice transmits declarations of war, military commands, and decisions affecting millions of lives. While the two neighbors, the quiet Bâlois and the flamboyant Catalan, may have had little in common, it is conceivable that they shared a certain clairvoyance about the future of Europe. And Seligmann may have chosen his motif of the late Renaissance dance of death after seeing the hideous bony specter bestriding a dry, desolate landscape in Dalí's *Still Life with Boiled Beans*. Even Masson may not have been immune to its influence, although he regarded the arrival of Dalí on the scene as a downturn for the movement.

Another prescient Dalí painting was the 1937 *Inventions of the Monsters*. In a letter to the Chicago Art Institute which bought the painting in 1943, Dalí commented: "According to Nostradamus the apparition of monsters presages the outbreak of war. This canvas was painted in the Semmering mountains near Vienna a few months before the *Anschluss* and has a prophetic character. The horsewomen equal maternal river monsters. The flaming giraffe equals a cosmic masculine apocalyptic monster . . ."[30]

In the Seligmanns' farmhouse in upstate New York there hung for half a century the first and smallest version of Max Ernst's *Garden Airplane Trap*. Death from the skies was the theme of Picasso's *Guernica* in 1937; is it possible that this is also the subject of these works by Ernst, the conjoining of the earthly and airborne in a death grip? Like Masson, forever seared by war wounds, Ernst's work is frequently tinged with violence. The French title for this painting is *Gobe-avion* or airplane swallowing; in northern Renaissance art the enclosed garden is a symbol of Mary; does it suggest here a female symbol that traps with its elaborate décor the phallic plane? The union of earth and sky, at the root of many mythologies, becomes also an image where eroticism and aggression meet and a foreshadowing of the first war

Salvador Dalí, *Inventions of the Monsters,* 1937, oil on canvas, 51.2 x 78.4 cm;
Art Institute of Chicago, Joseph Winterbotham Collection.

to be waged from the skies. Another way of seeing the plane is as a stand-in for Ernst's favorite subject, a bird; he owned an early nineteenth-century book on trapping birds.

Even Miró, although he avoided alignments and the confining implications of political labels, was capable of producing work tinged with foreboding. His 1937 *Still Life with Old Shoe* is distinctly an anomaly in his oeuvre. When painting this work, Miró departed from his customary procedures and set up a still life composed of ordinary objects that typified for him his Catalan homeland. The objects were painted in a realist manner that asserted their substantiality, a style that lent a convincing intentionality and had implications of revolutionary solidarity. The auras that surround the shoe, bottle, fork, and bread appear to charge them with radioactivity as if the painting were emitting danger signals.

Whether the apprehension was consciously conceived or infiltrated the paintings from a preconscious level, it is undeniable that by 1938 Surrealist art was registering, like a seismograph, signs of an approaching upheaval. This could not have been said of the School of Paris paintings that had dominated the International Exposition held in Paris in 1938, an event that, with the exception of *Guernica* and Miró's

Max Ernst, *Garden Airplane Trap*, 1935, gouache and watercolor on canvas, 15¾ x 19¾ inches; private collection.

destroyed mural *The Reaper* in the Spanish pavilion, managed to avoid discordant works and troubling signals from the avant-garde. Breton was one of the few to write openly on this time lag between art and life:

Art in France seems above all anxious to throw a carpet of flowers over a mined world. Although a wind of destruction was blowing at all the gates, to judge by what many painters exhibited one would think that life was going on sweetly and even with ostentation. At the time when Barcelona was suffering privations under a hellish sky or elsewhere the days of freedom seemed numbered, their work reflected nothing of the tragic apprehension of the time. . . . The problem is no longer, as formerly, to know if a painting "holds up" in a field of wheat, but whether it holds up beside the daily newspaper.[31]

Joan Miró, *Still Life with Old Shoe,* January 24 to May 28, 1937, oil on canvas, 32
x 46 inches; The Museum of Modern Art, New York, gift of James Thrall Soby.

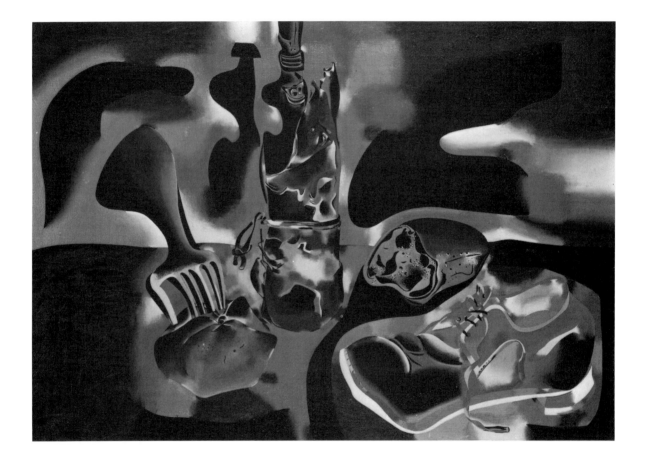

Wolfgang Paalen, *Untitled* (illustration for Lautréamont), 1937, ink on paper, 24¾
x 18¾ inches; Solomon R. Guggenheim Museum, New York, gift of Katharine Kuh,
1979.

² France, 1939: *"The Curtain Has Risen on a Forest Fire"*

Munich purchased for western Europeans a scant year in which to avert their heads from the grim facts of fascism's ends and means under the illusion that confrontation could be indefinitely postponed. Although armaments budgets were increased in England and France, it was scarcely in the spirit of preparation for all-out war. The French continued to pour concrete to strengthen their Maginot Line without giving much thought to the possibility that the German tanks might outflank it. The definitive collapse of the Spanish Republic caused few ripples, since that collapse had been ordained when the democracies denied assistance three years earlier.

The pages of *Le Plaisir de France* continued to justify the title with descriptions of opulent festivities, such as a lavish banquet at Monte Carlo accompanied by photographs of the dancing girls who served it. It featured the fashions of Molyneux and Maggy Rouf, drawn by René Bouché or photographed on models whose faces were like masks with highly stylized painted eyebrows and lips, framed by upswept hair topped by hats perched forward and slanted over one eye, with flirtatious little veils dangling as far as the tip of the nose. Along with ads for ermine coats and that armored encasing for the female body, the girdle, there were photographs of exotic places whose inhabitants are mere picturesque adjuncts to the landscape, a faceless Third World throng not yet prepared to throw off the yoke of the industrialized powers.

Paris was described as having a fit of prosperity and gaiety, with money and music in the air. Employment and exports were both up; the hotels were full; lavish costume balls and parties followed one after the other; the most talked-about was Lady Mendl's international garden party for 750 guests and three elephants. As a member of the international press corps put it, "It has taken the threat of a war to make the French loosen up and have a really swell and civilized good time."[1]

Art in general mirrored the ostrichlike behavior of the French population, with the glaring exception of the Surrealists. Among the Surrealist works of 1939 that might be seen as "holding up beside the daily newspaper" is the last painting Kurt Seligmann painted in Europe, *Sabbath Phantoms,* which strongly suggests flight before an oncoming storm. The skeletal figures gesticulate and beckon as they move in a ghostly flight from what appears to be a stone jetty on the left where one figure still stands firmly, a bony arm raised to a head whose shape is derived from one of Seligmann's own sculptures, as if surveying the situation. In view of his practice of encoding personal meanings even in his abstract paintings, it seems quite possible that the apprehensive figure on the jetty is the artist himself, hesitating at the prospect of emigration.

Kurt Seligmann, *Sabbath Phantoms,* 1939, oil and tempera on glass, 21½ x 28 inches; collection of Stephen Robeson-Miller (formerly collection of the Museum of Modern Art).

Max Ernst, *A Moment of Calm,* 1939, oil on canvas, 66⅞ x 128 inches; National
Gallery of Art, Washington, Gift of Dorothea Tanning Ernst.

Max Ernst's last prewar painting, *A Moment of Calm,* also probably reflected
the headlines of the daily newspaper. This large canvas, painted almost entirely in
multicolored wedges made with deft pulls of the palette knife, has as its subject a
dense shadowy garden in which three birds huddle on a branch and a fourth bird
flies. As one's eye adjusts to the dark blackish greens with flecks of bright color, a
stalking black cat becomes visible at the lower left, a rather pedestrian theme for the
ever-improvising Ernst unless read as a metaphor. Did he sense as he worked on it
that France and Germany would soon be at war and that he would be arrested and
interned before the painting was complete?

Matta also presents the viewer with an apprehensive vision in his dark, vaporous oil of 1939, *The Eve of Death.* According to Onslow Ford, Matta said to him at
the time of making this work, "the object of painting is to prepare yourself so that
you are at peace with the world an hour before you die." The remark may have
been a reflection of the Jesuit teachings with which he had been raised rather than a
meditation on the threat of war, but the cataclysmic nature of the painting suggests
that it is more directly foreboding of world events.

Perhaps the most interesting innovation among those artists who adhered to
Surrealism in 1939 was to be seen in a group of canvases produced by Gordon On-

Roberto Matta, *The Eve of Death,* 1939, oil on canvas, 30 x 36 inches; private collection.

Opposite: Wolfgang Paalen, *Combat of the Saturnian Princes II,* 1938, fumage
and oil on canvas, 57 x 45 inches; private collection.

slow Ford through a process he called *coulage.* The Surrealists had long exploited
change effects to trigger a process of free association. Such devices included *frottage*
(or rubbing) introduced by Max Ernst; the tracing of lines made by loops of string
dropped on paper; Arp's torn papers; Domínguez's decalcomania; and most recently
Paalen's *fumage* which involved passing a canvas coated with wet, thinned paint over
a lighted candle. *Coulage,* literally pouring or flowing, came about when Victor
Brauner was working one day in the same room with Onslow Ford and the little
figures Brauner was painting began to disrupt the Englishman's concentration. Exas-
perated, he picked up some cans of fast-drying Ripolin enamel and began to pour
the paint onto a canvas lying flat on the floor. He tried several different colors,
allowing them to flow together as the paint quickly hardened into a lavalike surface.
Onslow Ford thus became the first artist to make poured paintings, and he brought
several of these with him when he arrived in New York the following year.

As the enamel dried Onslow Ford found that he could peel off layers of the
enamel skin, revealing other colors beneath. He then imposed a white rectilinear grid
over the chaotic color of the hardened enamel surface. The grid appears to have been
for him and Matta a means of indicating a plane and at the same time introducing
depth; it also played a role in their system for denoting time and space. The kind
of shorthand system these two artists developed was useful for working in a rapid,
spontaneous manner, something on which they both put a premium. "We had discovered," said Onslow Ford, "that when you work spontaneously, you express reality.
Our aim was to work faster than the speed of thought." Onslow Ford also aimed to
circumvent conscious thought by keeping paper and pencil at his bedside in order to
draw his dreams while still in a half-waking state.

As the underlying sense of crisis mounted, Georges Duthuit posed the question
of how individual artists felt about the relation of art to surrounding events. "Can
the work," he inquired of Miró, Masson, Braque, and Laurens in *Cahiers d'Art,* "exist outside of the historical periods, valid for all time and ways of life? Does creation
thus impose on its author the requirement to ignore what is going on and the fate of
common humanity?"[2] Miró responded:

There are no more ivory towers. Withdrawal and escape are no longer permitted. But what
counts in a work is not what too many intellectuals want to see in it, but what it carries along,
in its ascending movement, of actual experience, of human truth. One mustn't confuse the
alliances proposed to the artist by professional politicians and other specialists in agitation

Gordon Onslow Ford, *Without Bounds,* 1939, coulage, Ripolin enamel on canvas,
28¾ x 36½ inches; private collection.

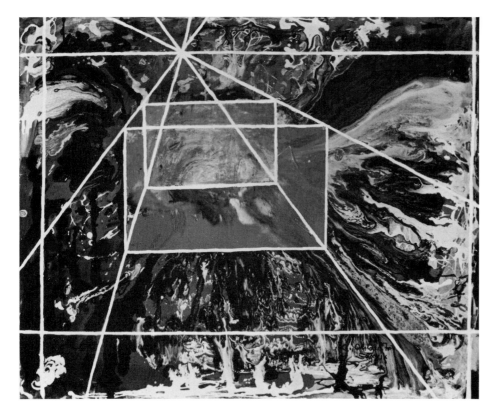

with the deep necessity which makes him take part in social upheavals, binds him and his
work to the flesh and the heart of the future and makes the necessity of the liberation of all
his own cause.

Masson was more outspoken:

To wish not to recognize the concern of being in the world and of being part of the collective
tragedy, to avow one's ignorance of the totality of existence, to take refuge in the practice of
an art for art's sake, indifferent to the woes of the time, to exclude all representation of fear,
of violence, and of death—that might have been possible in a period of euphoria such as that
which preceded the capitalist war that began in 1914. But this prudent coldness is nothing
more than a derisive stance toward a world convulsed, prey to anguish and to war. The only
justification of a work of art is to contribute to human development, to the transmission of
values, to the denunciation of the dominant class, responsible for the imperialist war and
fascist regression.

Despite the appearance in print of such outspoken statements of commitment to social purpose, the Surrealists were criticized in certain quarters for dilettantism and lack of engagement, and such criticisms were to proliferate in the accusatory aftermath of World War II. The principal challenge to those who had held the avant-garde literary and artistic territory for nearly two decades came from a former *lycée* teacher, Jean Paul Sartre. It was launched in 1939 in *Le Mur,* a collection of five of his short stories, at least three of which may be seen as attempts to discredit Surrealism.[3]

In the story, "L'Enfance d'un chef," Sartre tells of a young student who is introduced by a friend to the circle of Achile Bergère (is the correspondence of initials only a coincidence?). To establish a hold on the youth by playing up the slightest neurotic symptom as a source of genius, Bergère continually asks, "Êtes-vous inquiet?" The story contains authentic Surrealist details such as the description of the contents of Bergère's apartment, which includes a piece of human-legged furniture similar to Seligmann's *Ultra Meuble.* However, Sartre's account of Bergère's seduction of the young man runs directly counter to Breton's well-known homophobia. Several years earlier the Surrealist leader had actually struck the head of the French Communist Party, Ilya Ehrenburg, for referring to Surrealist activity as "péderastique."

In the story "Erostrate," the hero tries to commit Breton's ideal Surrealist act, to shoot at random in the street, and fails. In another story a young woman romanticizes the degenerative illness of her husband as he progresses from madness to imbecility, finding in it a poetic truth that sets them apart from the hypocrisy of society. Here Sartre touches on one of the core problems of Surrealism, how to exploit hallucination and psychosis while keeping them under control. The distinction between madness as a key to hidden truths and as a disease that incapacitates and kills is difficult to maintain. However, the fascination with madness that Sartre debunks is essentially more a legacy of romanticism—as in Blake passing Bedlam: "The madmen have locked up all the sane people"—than a uniquely Surrealist fallacy.

Patrick Waldberg, a long-standing ally of Breton and also a friend of Sartre, dismissed the idea that *Le Mur* was directed against the Surrealists, pointing out the collaborations between Sartre and artists such as Masson. However, the correspondence of names and the holding up to ridicule of practices that might be associated with Surrealism strongly suggest an intention to discredit Surrealism as "petulant, cowardly, and, above all, ineffective, producing useless works for a bourgeois audience and turning the mind away from serious preoccupations."[4]

From his fourth-floor apartment at 42 rue Bonaparte Sartre could almost see the daily meetings of the Surrealists at the café Deux Magots on the Boulevard St.-Germain. Perhaps he was already formulating the philosophy of engagement and commitment to action that would move him to center stage among the French intelligentsia at the end of the war and garner him an overnight international reputation. His turf would by then be the adjacent Café de Flore, where during the heatless mid-1940s he wrote some of his major works.

In what turned out to be the last issue of *Minotaure,* André Breton introduced the newest recruits to Surrealism in an article, "Des Tendances les plus récentes de la peinture surréaliste." Commenting briefly on Paalen, Domínguez, Frances, Matta, and Onslow Ford, he described their having opted for automatism, their innovations in this area, and their profound yearning to transcend the three-dimensional universe. He went on to praise the "psychic fourth dimension" of Brauner, the objects of Seligmann, and the photographs achieved through the "pale hyphen of [Raoul] Ubac's eye."

During the lull of the summer of 1939, Gordon Onslow Ford rented a château in a wooded park overlooking the Rhône at Chemillieu, in the Ain near the Swiss border, that had been occupied by Balthus the previous summer. Accompanying him were Matta and his American wife Anne (known among the Surrealists as Pajarito, the name meaning little bird that Matta had given her), Esteban Frances, a young Spanish painter who had left Spain after Franco's victory, and Tanguy. André Breton arrived and was greeted ceremoniously at the gate with the keys to the château. Jacqueline Breton and their daughter Aube, who had been visiting the Surrealist photographer Claude Cahun on a Channel island, also decided to join them, and requests for an invitation came from two American women in pursuit of Tanguy, Peggy Guggenheim and Kay Sage. The latter, still officially the Princess di Faustino, arrived and stayed in a nearby pension.

Sage had been introduced to Surrealism as a result of a chance meeting with Kurt Seligmann in a hotel where both were staying in 1936. His paintings—at that time in transition from his Abstraction/Creation period toward Surrealism—which she saw through the open door of the room, made a strong impact on her. The next year she moved from Italy to Paris, fell under the spell of the work of De Chirico and then Tanguy, and began to follow Surrealist exhibitions closely. In the fall of 1938 she met Breton and became part of the Surrealist circle, which often gathered at her Île St.-Louis apartment. Thus it came about that a Chilean, a Spaniard, an En-

Top: Château at Chemillieu; photograph courtesy Gordon Onslow Ford.

Bottom: Surrealists in the garden at Chemillieu, 1939; left to right: Anne Matta, Ithiel Colquohoun, Matta, Onslow Ford, Frances; photograph courtesy Anne Alpert.

Onslow Ford, Matta, and Esteban Frances at Chemillieu, 1939;
photograph courtesy Gordon Onslow Ford.

glishman, two Americans, two Frenchmen and a Frenchwoman, and also briefly an Englishwoman, Surrealist artist Ithiel Colquohoun, spent the final months before the war in a French château, passing the time in what appears in retrospect to have been an almost trancelike state. Sage's enthusiasm for Surrealism in general and Tanguy in particular did not prevent her from writing a witty spoof of a dinner table dialogue among this polyglot group.[5]

As Onslow Ford described that summer there were long walks in the Rhône valley and afternoon gatherings around the table in the garden, and in the evenings Breton read aloud from Baudelaire, Rimbaud, Lautréamont, Apollinaire, Jarry, and others from the Surrealist pantheon, as well as from the German romantics. They played poker using drawings and small found objects for stakes. Breton also recounted for the group's new young members stories of Surrealist activities of the twenties, which Onslow Ford saw as a tradition to draw upon, "a family tree" of which he and his cohorts were now part. For festive occasions they produced elaborate decorations made of colored paper, among them a large bird of paradise. And to reinforce the rumor that the château was haunted, a ghost appeared one night at the foot of Onslow Ford's bed.

They made an excursion to the fantastic structure known as the Palais Idéal du Facteur Cheval. Built largely of concrete by a reclusive postman in a slow process of accretion over many years, this fairy-tale palace was made up of elaborate columns, caryatids, twisting passageways, relief sculptures inside and out, and a wealth of fabulous details, the outpourings of an untutored imagination. Its flowing sculpted surfaces projected a look of instant decay, giving it the air of an exotic ruin that might have been there for centuries. Here was an actualized version of the deserted château that played a mythic role in the European imagination, the château of Alain-Fournier's *Le Grand Meaulnes* or Julien Gracq's *Château d'Argol* or the locale of the orgies described by the Surrealist cult hero, the Marquis de Sade. In the bizarre concretion concocted by Cheval there was another and absolutely authentic form of the "railroad station of the imagination and the dream," where fantasy assumed tangible form, an enchanter's domain that the artists could literally walk into or clamber about.

On another outing they visited the nearby home of Gertrude Stein. Onslow Ford was acquainted with Stein and arranged for a meeting between her and Breton at which the American writer Thornton Wilder was also present. One partisan observer was struck by the difference between Breton's gracious and courtly manner

Below: Matta at the Palais Idéal du Facteur Cheval, 1939; photograph courtesy Anne Alpert.

Opposite: Papier-mâché bird of paradise, made collectively at Chemillieu, 1939; photograph courtesy Gordon Onslow Ford.

and Stein's brusque, confrontational style. Perhaps she was put on the defensive by Breton's avowed homophobia and his chauvinistic attitude toward women. Breton, in turn, possibly found it difficult to deal with a woman, American at that, on a basis of professional equality.

From Paris Kurt Seligmann wrote Breton that since there was no more *tablée* at the Deux Magots, there was more work and more sleep. Breton responded that he hoped the Seligmanns would pass through Chemillieu on their way to Switzerland and sit with them under the magnificent trees. He reported that Surrealist painting was proceeding full steam ahead, the poetry more slowly. He mentioned that he had heard from Wolfgang Paalen in New York and hoped Paalen wasn't so completely seduced that he wouldn't return.[6] A few days later, on July 23, he wrote to Paalen voicing his fear of what was to come and reiterating his dislike of newspapers. Gordon, Matta, and Esteban, he reported, had worked a great deal and were in better form than ever.[7]

Although they regarded the visionary works of Tanguy as part of their ancestry and also looked beyond him to his source of inspiration, De Chirico, these three

Gordon Onslow Ford, *Man on a Green Island,* 1939, oil on canvas, 28¾ x 36⅜
inches; private collection.

artists, then in their mid-twenties, were creating paintings that were radically different from those of the preceding generation of Surrealists. Matta had brought from
architecture a great facility in the depicting of multidimensional space. To this he
added drawings made from a book of botanical photographs. The enlarged details
he used as a point of departure for fantastically elaborated and meticulously drawn
"abstract dramas." At the urging of Onslow Ford, he then began to supplement
his line drawings with amorphous sweeps of color, applied to the canvas with
large brushes in such a way that they had the effect of dematerializing the drawn
spaces and linear constructions. Like Frances and Onslow Ford, Matta veered away
from specific references to figures and objects, opting instead for expanding, non-
Euclidean spaces.

    Onslow Ford had been working on a series of "transparent mountains" in
which he tried to deal simultaneously with solidity and transparency. As the paintings testify, he was less concerned with the aesthetics of the results than he was with

Gordon Onslow Ford, *Mountain Heart,* 1939, oil on canvas, 28¾ x 36 inches; private collection.

the new ground he was attempting to break in giving visual form to his visionary ideas. Another work of this period is seminal for what he was to take up later; *Man on a Green Island* includes a small configuration of the kind he was later to call "live line beings." This *personnage* (his term for spirit presences) is isolated in a limitless space over which the artist imposed a grid of lines, almost like navigational coordinates plotted on a chart.

From the little that can be retrieved of the work of Esteban Frances, it appears that he was working in a direction similar to that of Matta and Onslow Ford. At this juncture he was the most sophisticated of the three in terms of artistic background and experience. His technical polish gives his work a drier, less experimental look, but his interest in non-Euclidean structures with conflicting perspectives and multiple vanishing points coincides with theirs. Shortly the war was to disrupt their work and scatter these three young men; had it been otherwise, they would very likely have been perceived as the nucleus of a new mode of painting, rather than simply latter-day Surrealists.

Yves Tanguy, *Chemillieu,* 1939, inscribed "pour Gordon Onslow Ford, mon ami;
Chemillieu, 1939"; private collection.

The Surrealists at Chemillieu planned a new issue of *Minotaure,* no. 13. Its
contents were to include works produced there at the château: paintings by Matta,
Onslow Ford, Tanguy, and Frances, as well as a poem, "The House of Yves Tanguy,"
by Breton. Although there was never to be a *Minotaure* no. 13, Onslow Ford took
the material to England where it was subsequently published in the British Surrealist
review *The London Bulletin* (1940). Among the paintings reproduced was Tanguy's
Arrières pensées which, according to Onslow Ford, has an extra "personnage" that
was added when a cleaning woman at Chemillieu knocked a broom against Tanguy's
easel, leaving a mark in the wet paint. Onslow Ford's description of Matta's intentions, in the painting of his that was reproduced in the same journal, also aptly characterizes his own aims in painting: "Matta's horizonless space in which solids melt
and turn to vapor conveys not so much cataclysm, but the sense of a universe in
which everything is interchangeable and spirits disembodied float free of time."[8]

While the Surrealists were making papier-mâché fantasies for their fêtes at
Chemillieu, the news arrived of Stalin's nonaggression pact with Hitler. Once again
the French left was split. Die-hards followed the line that Stalin had simply outma-
neuvered the capitalist countries who were counting on Hitler to polish off the Bol-
sheviks. Others heeded the words of escaped revolutionaries such as Boris Souvarin
who told of Stalin's admiration for Hitler and his role in the Nazi leader's rise to
power. Breton, who had broken with the Third International in 1935, was able to
say "I told you so."

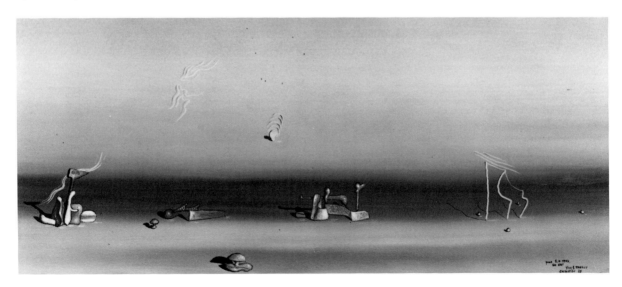

Miguel Covarrubias, painting of the Tlingit hut façade purchased by Wolfgang
Paalen in British Columbia, summer 1939.

During that summer Masson was staying at La Baule with his wife Rose and two young sons. Pierre Mabille was living nearby, and Masson recalled their long political discussions, which culminated in their agreement on the necessity to "disengage oneself from all politics."[9] In St.-Martin-d'Ardèche Max Ernst and Leonora Carrington were enjoying their garden and the bizarre concrete sculptures they had created for it. British Surrealist Roland Penrose and American photographer Lee Miller visited them only a few weeks before the French police led Ernst off to an internment camp for enemy aliens. From British Columbia Wolfgang Paalen, who was following the route the Seligmanns had taken the previous summer, wrote of his excitement over discovering the art of the Pacific Northwest.[10] Like Kurt Seligmann, Paalen made a stupendous purchase, the carved and painted facade of a Tlingit hut. During this trip he developed a passion for Native American and pre-Columbian art, an obsession that was ultimately to lead him into a self-destructive course.

Meanwhile Hitler was preparing once more to test the French and English will to stand by their eastern European alliances. Would they abandon Poland as easily as Czechoslovakia? Toward the end of August an incident was arranged that would justify the German invasion of Poland: prisoners were taken from German concentration camps, drugged, dressed in the uniforms of the Polish army, shot, and strewn around a German signal station near the Polish border. In retaliation for this "attack" German divisions marched across the border and swept through Poland, quickly reclaiming the territory lost in the Versailles Treaty.

Although England was clearly unprepared to fight on the continent, Parliament declared war within twenty-four hours and France had no choice but to follow suit. A phony raid, costumes for dead men, and the Western world was plunged into the most massive war of all time, a new kind of war in which death came blindly and without warning from the air. A small effort called Surrealism had tried to dramatize the pitfalls of rationalism, the ludicrousness of politics, and the violent enemy lurking within the human psyche.

"L'Européen—c'est presque fini." On September 16, 1939, Breton penned a letter of introduction on behalf of Paalen to Trotsky's secretary, Van. He wrote on stationery headed "Café l'Européen" and in small letters after the printed heading he added in his habitual green ink, "It's almost done for."[11] At the same time he wrote to Paalen in Mexico that a "reformed" Tanguy was considering leaving for the United States and Matta as well, that Esteban Frances had obtained a passport for Chile, that Eluard was a lieutenant at Montargis, and that he had no news of Ernst,

Miró, or Dalí. "A new spirit will form here," he wrote, "but it's too soon and these are days of such total eclipse that it is difficult to live."[12] Soon he himself would be in uniform, part of a medical staff attached to a pilot training school near Poitiers.

Following the declaration of war, Sage began making plans with Yvon Delbos, the French minister of education, for a series of exhibitions in New York, the proceeds of which would be used to help artists involved in the crisis in France. According to Sage's biographer, Stephen Miller, it was decided that the artists chosen for the series would travel to America.[13] Tanguy was to inaugurate the series and would join her in the United States later in the fall. Sage's efforts back in New York resulted in the founding of the Society for the Preservation of European Culture, which helped bring not only Tanguy and the Mattas but eventually Gordon Onslow Ford to the United States.

Nine days after the German invasion of Poland, Kurt and Arlette Seligmann sailed for New York where he was to have an exhibition at the gallery that Karl Nierendorf had transplanted from Berlin. Apparently the Seligmanns simply left their house in the Villa Seurat and locked the door, not intending to make a prolonged sojourn in the United States. Arlette had no idea they were leaving as refugees and her husband may not have thought of their departure in that way, but certainly the ex-Berliner Nierendorf knew the danger they were in and may have arranged the exhibition to expedite their departure. Once in New York they were urged not to return to their home in Paris, and by the first of November they had moved from temporary quarters in the Plaza annex to a studio apartment in the Beaux Arts Building at 40th Street and Fifth Avenue, which would be their New York City home until 1959.

The works Seligmann had shipped for the exhibition that opened at Nierendorf on September 27 were perceived as ominous by at least some of the New York audience. The reviewer for *Art News* described the paintings as "presenting the horrors of war," despite the fact that they had been painted before the outbreak of hostilities. Oddly the reviewer felt that these were not Surrealist paintings because "this man is painting with deadly seriousness of themes which haunt the conscious mind of anyone alive today."[14] Such a perception of Surrealism, relegating it to fantasy and failing to comprehend the relationship it sought to establish between human behavior and the unconscious mind, underscores the difficulty it faced among viewers in the United States, including critics. Accustomed to the simplistic polarities of formalist abstraction and pictorial realism, such an audience saw Surrealist art as little more

Kurt Seligmann, *Unwelcome Guests,* 1940, oil on glass; present whereabouts
unknown.

Letter to Seligmann from Paalen, November 1939, Seligmann papers (MS).

than the illustration of nightmares. At least the reviewer grasped the premonitory
nature of the Seligmann *danses macabres* and the present relevance of his archaic
style and imagery.

Misapprehension of a different sort is apparent in James W. Lane's review of
the exhibition that Pierre Matisse mounted in December of paintings by his old
friend Tanguy. "It is beauty of form and color alone that interest this imaginative
painter," Lane wrote, describing the smaller works as "comforting and endearing." [15]
Here is the seed of an oft-repeated mistake that critics in the United States were to
make, that of seeing in purely formalist terms works in which there was a strong
latent content. Indeed American viewers who relied on critics to tell them what they
were seeing were bound to end up confused. Lane's comment on Matta's work at
Julien Levy in the spring of 1940 was that he painted "shards and roots of teeth,
spars and mangled bodies. What does it matta that Matter is mad as a hatta?" [16]

From Mexico in November Wolfgang Paalen wrote to the Seligmanns that he
and César Moro, the Mexican artist and poet, were arranging a Surrealist exhibition,
and he asked for the loan of several of his paintings as well as for help in locating
Matta and Tanguy. [17] This was the first word that the Seligmanns had received that
other members of the Surrealist group were also in New York. Tanguy had sailed
early in October to join Kay Sage and was installed in an apartment in Greenwich
Village. Sage had some independent means, if not a lavish income, and Tanguy had
a guaranteed sum of money each month from his former schoolmate, New York art
dealer Pierre Matisse, in exchange for paintings. Matta, however, who had also arrived in New York in October with his American wife, Anne, was in desperate straits.
Tanguy wrote in December to the Seligmanns, asking them to help by purchasing a
Matta drawing: "The Mattas are in a bad situation, no money and little hope of
selling in this terrible country. We have tried to help, but our means in this accursed
country are too limited." [18]

Seligmann, because of his Swiss nationality, was able to get funds transferred
to U.S. banks during the war years. Thus, while most of his fellow refugees had no
means of support other than through the sale of art, he was in a position to afford
both a New York apartment and a farmhouse in the country, to buy an etching press
and paper of the finest quality, amass a collection of rare books on magic, and help
his stranded friends in a variety of ways. Although their style was not lavish, the
Seligmanns were at least free of the gnawing financial anxieties that were a fact of
life for many of the refugees. In addition, the fact that he spoke English made it

possible for him to secure teaching positions, first at Briarcliff College, then at the New School, and eventually at Brooklyn College where he was a member of the art faculty for ten years.

Seligmann's teaching career in the United States actually started with private lessons, and these had a curious beginning as well as a momentous consequence. One day during the early months of his New York sojourn he was visiting the nearly empty galleries of the Museum of Modern Art and fell into conversation with a visitor of a scholarly mein similar to his own. Thus began a long friendship with the art historian Meyer Schapiro, a friendship that included visits to the Shapiro summer home in Vermont and an erudite correspondence on arcane sources of information on magic and the occult. Realizing that additional income would be a help to the Seligmanns while their European finances were still in limbo, Professor Schapiro proposed that one of his graduate students in art history who was also interested in painting take lessons with Seligmann.

The student in question was Robert Motherwell, who had left his graduate studies in philosophy at Harvard to come to New York to study with Schapiro. He had already spent a year in France in 1938 in order to do research on Delacroix's journals and had become interested in trying his hand at painting. When he brought some of his early attempts to show Schapiro, the latter suggested that he might benefit from the discipline of regular work with a professional artist. On the other hand Schapiro said, "You're an intellectual and should make contact with the Surrealists." To Motherwell's response that he hated Surrealism Schapiro replied that "they were the last generation inheriting the tradition of symbolist poetry." Convinced, Motherwell began going once or twice a week to Seligmann's studio, where he remembered learning something about the profession of the artist and did indeed soon meet the other members of the Surrealist group. The slips of paper with the dates of *les leçons Motherwell* indicate that these sessions took place during the spring of 1940 and the winter and spring of 1941.[19] According to Motherwell, Seligmann's art, based as it was on draftsmanship, meant little to him, but what he acknowledged as being of value was the entré into Surrealist circles as they gradually re-formed in and near New York.[20] While such was Motherwell's view in later years, he did write at the time to the Seligmanns saying, "All the time I am very conscious of how much I have learned from Kurt. I am sure I would never have gotten out of my original muddle by myself."[21]

Two other private pupils during the same period were Monica Flaherty, daughter of the great documentary filmmaker Robert Flaherty, and Barbara Reis, daughter of Bernard and Becky Reis. Bernard Reis was the accountant for Julien Levy and therefore familiar with the Surrealists by reputation. He had become a collector by offering his services as a financial advisor to artists as well as to Levy in exchange for paintings instead of fees. Becky Reis had worked in a Paris gallery and later became manager of Louis Carré's New York gallery. The couple liked to entertain and their apartment became a congenial meeting place for the refugee artists. They took the Seligmanns on a tour of the New England countryside and Kurt wrote of the particular pleasure he took in the shapes of American barns. Typically it was the American vernacular to which the Europeans were drawn, rather than the country's attempts to emulate Europe in the creation of a high culture.

France, in the meantime, was passing through that oddly quiescent period known as *la drôle de guerre* (the phony war), during which the Germans consolidated their gains in eastern Europe without interference from the USSR and with little effective opposition from the western powers. France and England, relying on the invincibility of the Maginot Line, waited for Hitler to turn toward the French frontier. Conscription began. Breton, who had said he would refuse to put on a uniform, capitulated when the time came because, he said, he did not want his child to have a father in jail. His long-time cohort Benjamin Péret, however, chose prison over the draft. Max Ernst had no choice; as an enemy alien he was interned in a camp in Les Milles. When the police arrived he was working on the mural-sized painting described above, *A Moment of Calm*. Hans Bellmer, another German-born Surrealist, was also in Les Milles. The camp was a former brick factory; everything lay under a heavy coating of brick dust. Bellmer made a portrait of his cellmate, Ernst, as if he were constructed of bricks.

Called back to his post in the Royal Navy, Onslow Ford sailed for England, taking with him the fruits of the summer's collective work at Chemillieu which were published in the *London Bulletin* that winter. Back in London he arranged a window for a Surrealist show at the Zwemmer Gallery which featured a bed with rumpled linen and a dagger thrust into its center.

The atmosphere in Paris during the phony war is conveyed by Arthur Conte as he describes the eve of the New Year of 1940. An unaccustomedly heavy snow was falling all over Europe, as far south as Rome. The streets of Paris were darkened for air defense, but the nightclubs were packed. At the Ritz, Noel Coward and Jean Cocteau drank the new year in with officers of the Royal Air Force. At midnight the president's official message was broadcast: "1940 will be a happier year for all humanity." People still spoke of the phony war and lackadaisical soldiers refused to dig trenches. Among the communists confusion reigned over the fact that fighting fascism also meant opposition to Hitler's ally, the Soviet Union. Some of the party members who opposed the war, such as Maurice Thorez, went underground, to emerge later as leaders in the Resistance. At Nancy the thirty-five-year-old Sartre, mobilized as a private second class, was making notes for *Being and Nothingness* in a notebook that was lost during his subsequent imprisonment. "The howls of the Surrealists," wrote Conte, "were heard no more." [22]

3 New York, 1939: *The Prepared Ground*

One of the most improbable and inappropriately timed events of the decade was the New York World's Fair that opened on a landfill in the Flushing Meadows in June 1939. Its mated symbols, the trylon and perisphere, presided over an international playground whose theme was "the world of the future." Although many of the participating countries would be at war by the time its gates closed in the fall, no reminder of the looming threat of fascism clouded the confident displays of the wondrous life technological advance would bring, was indeed bringing. The horns on the little blue trains and motorized carriages that carried visitors around the vast fairgrounds sounded cheerful tunes to warn pedestrians. Moving belts conveyed astonished crowds around the inner circumference of the perisphere or through the General Motors building. In both spaces huge scale models were laid out showing a "world of the future" in which metropolis, suburb, and newly electrified rural checkerboard were linked by a system of gleaming highways, crisscrossing at cloverleaf intersections. Elsewhere one could ask questions of a robot who uttered monosyllabic answers, see the newest thing in farming, a cow hooked up to a milking machine, or glimpse a far-out vision of an automated workerless factory. The Italian building was a target of ridicule and was regarded as looking as vulgar as Il Duce himself, but too cardboard in appearance to be taken seriously. Topped by a sculpture of a regally enthroned woman, behind whom water cascaded down the terraced stories of the tall building, it was compared by some to a flushing toilet. There was no German pavilion, but it is unlikely that visitors to the fair were giving much thought to what else might be preoccupying the Germans after they had made their annexation of Czechoslovakia complete that spring.

Over in the Amusement Park, along with the parachute jump, Billy Rose's Aquacade, and Frank Buck's "Bring 'em back alive" wild animal show, was a pavilion whose molded plaster facade was inscribed "Dream of Venus." A giant head of a fish and a plaster leg obstructed the entrance; a fifteen-foot cutout of Botticelli's Venus was framed in a kidney-shaped opening above the door; through another door appeared another cutout, this one of Leonardo's coyly beckoning John the Baptist, while through a third opening there emerged a hybrid with a human body ending in a forked fishtail. The dream of Venus, born from the sea, was of her prenatal home: a room under water. To represent this room, the pavilion's impresario, Salvador Dalí, had devised a large aquarium, within which ten pretty young women were to swim or float, play a soft piano, or warm themselves at an underwater hearth.

The idea that there should be a Surrealist pavilion at the World's Fair had been concocted by the New York art dealer Julien Levy, who had already held three exhibi-

Façade of Salvador Dalí's "Dream of Venus" under construction, New York World's
Fair, 1939; gelatin silver print, 7 x 7⁷⁄₁₆ inches, attributed to George Platt Lynes;
The Museum of Modern Art, New York, gift of Julien Levy.

tions of Dalí's work and had introduced that of other Surrealists as well. His financial backers, however, well aware of Dalí's flair for publicity, insisted that Levy turn the conception and execution entirely over to the artist. Whether Dalí's *Dream of Venus* would have become a popular peep show at the fair remains purely in the realm of conjecture. One of the backers of this venture was a manufacturer of molded rubber objects who was determined to turn the girls in the tank into mermaids by providing them with molded rubber tails, a gimmick strenuously opposed by Dalí. When another backer, the British art collector Edward James, gave a champagne party the night after the opening that ended with an after-hours swim in the aquarium, the "rubber man" seized on this breach of rules to force Levy to sell out so that he could remake the pavilion to his own taste, rubber tails and all.

This was the rude awakening, after one day's public viewing, of Dalí's *Dream of Venus.* The Spaniard, however, managed a parting shot before returning to Europe. He composed a rather lengthy manifesto, a takeoff on the Declaration of Independence, in which he proclaimed the right of man to his own madness, and had hundreds of copies dropped from a plane over New York City. "Man is entitled," Dalí declared in his broadside, "to the enigma and simulacrums that are founded on these great vital constants: the sexual instinct, the consciousness of death, the physical melancholy caused by time-space." The "middlemen of culture" were condemned by Dalí because they come between the creator and the public, and he called on artists and poets to "loose the avenging thunder of your paranoiac inspiration." He hailed New York as being "mad as the moon, won by the Surrealist Paranoia Kinesis." In retrospect it seems almost like an advance announcement·of the Surrealist incursion that would start within a few months.

It is small wonder that for the American public the term Surrealism was synonymous with the name Dalí. As early as 1928 he had exhibited in the important Carnegie International, and by 1939 he had had four one-man shows in New York, had lectured at the Museum of Modern Art, and had attracted attention in the tabloid press through his parties and escapades. In March of 1939 he shoved a bathtub (fur-lined) through the Fifth Avenue window of the Bonwit Teller department store during a fracas that ensued when he found that the window display he had been hired to do had been tampered with. Although reportedly Dalí himself was nearly decapitated by a piece of falling glass, the attendant publicity did no harm to his exhibition that had just opened around the corner on 57th Street.

Ironically, the man who was most identified with Surrealism's visual image was no longer an official member of the group. Expelled over his publicity-seeking tactics, his increasingly fascistic pronouncements, and what Breton deplored as his rank commercialism, his name had been turned by the latter into a mocking anagram, Avida Dollars. Because of his excommunication and the banal conservatism of much of his later work, the power of what Dalí created between 1929 and 1939 in writing as well as in painting and film has been underplayed, and his paranoiac-critical method insufficiently credited with a power to touch the nerve centers of human experience during the decade darkened by advancing totalitarianism.

Dalí's dealer, Julien Levy, had made his gallery into a veritable beachhead of Surrealism in the United States. Levy was a product of the same Fine Arts Department at Harvard that, under the guidance of Paul Sachs, had produced Alfred Barr, Chick Austin, and Henry-Russell Hitchcock, all of whom were there as tutors or postgraduates when Levy was an undergraduate. He put together much of the work for the first U.S. exhibition of Surrealism, which Austin mounted at the Wadsworth Atheneum in Hartford under the title "The New Super Realism." Levy, Barr, and Austin were all three involved in expanding the parameters of visual art by showing photography and film and sponsoring avant-garde performances, such as Virgil Thomson's opera based on Gertrude Stein's *Four Saints in Three Acts* which had its premier at the Wadsworth Atheneum in 1930. Levy lived Surrealism as much as he merchandised it. In 1927 he had met Marcel Duchamp when the latter was installing a Brancusi exhibition at the Brummer Gallery and the two of them soon embarked for France, intending to join forces with Man Ray to produce an experimental film from a scenario by Levy. Since they passed Man Ray at sea the project came to naught, but through Duchamp Levy met various members of the Paris Surrealist circle, as well as Joella Loy who became his first wife. Joella was the daughter of Mina Loy, the prototypical bohemian whose great love had been Arthur Cravan, boxer and poet, whose disappearance in the waters off Mexico in 1918 remains as much an enigma as the life he led.

On his return to New York a small legacy from his mother made possible the opening of the Julien Levy Gallery at 602 Madison Avenue with an exhibition of American and European photographs. During the 1930s the gallery served as a trans-Atlantic bridgehead for the work of Max Ernst, Eugene Berman, Dalí, Alberto Giacometti, Pavel Tchelitchew, Leonid, Jean Cocteau, René Magritte, Yves Tanguy, Giorgio De Chirico, and Leonor Fini, as well as introducing the Americans Joseph Cornell, Alexander Calder, Walter Quirt, Peter Blume, Abraham Rattner, and a number of major photographers who were strangers to the gallery world at that time. Mina Loy served as his agent in Paris, keeping him informed of what was going on among the Surrealists and selecting works from the artists for showing at Levy's gallery. His correspondence indicates that he depended on her discriminating eye as well as counting on her to negotiate with the artists and to send him entire exhibitions. One of her missions was to secure the Dalí/Buñuel film *L'Âge d'or,* which he presented at the Film Society with great success. He staged an exhibition of her work in 1933, arranged for its inclusion in an exhibition at the Wadsworth Atheneum the same year, and was able to send her some money from sales.

Levy was a friend to his artists as much as a dealer, and he enjoyed the escapades that resulted from these friendships. Although he did once show the work of Ben Shahn, there is no mention in his memoirs of his two decades as a dealer of anything that touches on the Depression years or of the social realist and regionalist art that dominated the thirties in New York. In his book on Surrealism Levy staked out its position between the Scylla of social realism and the Charybdis of abstraction: "In the history of art, surrealism is a revolution, first against the bondage of realism, secondly, against the snob monopoly of abstract painting."[1] The American artists whose work he exhibited were, in various ways, exploring independent options that had affinities with Surrealism, ranging from the Miró-inspired sculptures of Calder to the surreal social commentaries of Peter Blume.

One American painter in particular haunted the Julien Levy Gallery, the Armenian-born Arshile Gorky. This tall man with drooping mustache and sad eyes lingered in the gallery until he had read the whole of Levy's book on Surrealism. Once he left a portfolio of his drawings, as if by accident, in the back office. Although Levy visited his Union Square studio, it was not until ten years later, in March 1945, that he was to give Gorky his first one-man show. While Gorky wanted to learn all he could about Surrealism, in 1936 he was still doing work that was heavily indebted to Picasso. However, the murals for the Newark Airport, which he was working on at the time, show a definite inclination toward flattened biomorphic shapes and a mode of constructing a painting not dissimilar to that of Miró of the early 1930s. Gerome Kamrowski visited Gorky's studio while he was working on the studies for the Newark murals and recalled that he had a reproduction of Duchamp's *Bride* tacked on the wall. (Julien Levy owned *The Bride* at the time and recollected that Gorky had seen it in his apartment.) Gorky's passionate attachment to a sequence of different artists has been documented in a number of ways; there is much that he

Arshile Gorky working on the Newark Airport murals, 1936.

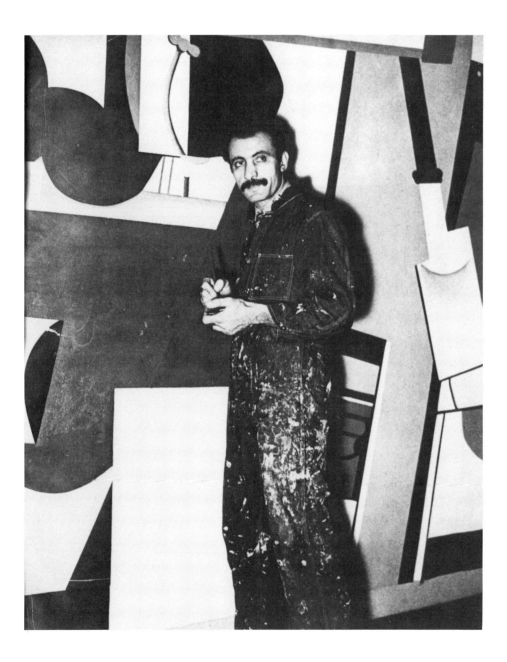

Opposite: Marcel Duchamp, *The Bride,* 1912, oil on canvas, 35¼ x 21¾ inches; The Philadelphia Museum of Art, The Louise and Walter Arensberg Collection.

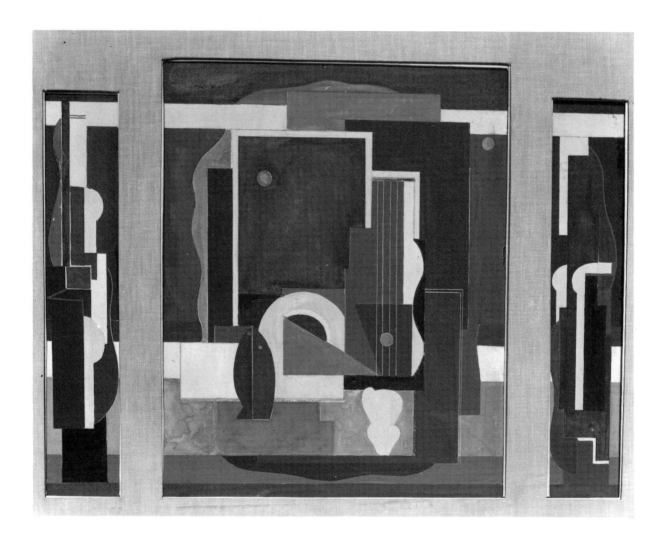

Gerome Kamrowski, *Mural Design for Northrup Auditorium at the University of Minnesota,* Federal Art Project, 1936, gouache on paper, 14¼ x 11¾ inches center panel; 13 x 2½ inches side panels.

gleaned from other artworks, much that he took possession of and transformed and concealed within his own mysterious paintings, and Surrealism was a not inconsiderable source for him.

At the time he visited Gorky's Union Square studio Gerome Kamrowski was working for the WPA in the Midwest, but made frequent trips to New York on a poultry train in order to be able to see good examples of abstract art unavailable in his hometown. He had been introduced to abstract art while a student in his native Minnesota by Cameron Booth, who had studied with Hans Hofmann in Munich and had exhibited with the Paris-based Abstraction/Creation group. The murals Kamrowski did for the WPA, such as the one for the Northrup Auditorium at the University of Minnesota in 1936, were painted in a severe geometric style, but Kamrowski also became interested in Surrealism after seeing the Museum of Modern Art exhibition "Fantastic Art, Dada, Surrealism," which traveled to Minneapolis. He started perusing the pages of *Minotaure* and learned something of automatist ideas and techniques. During a semester at the newly opened Chicago Bauhaus of Moholy-Nagy in 1937, Kamrowski heard firsthand stories about Dada days and reminiscences of Kurt Schwitters and saw the Duchamp *Rotoreliefs,* which Moholy owned. A stipend from the Baroness Rebay, director of the Museum of Non-Objective Art and beneficiary of Solomon Guggenheim's largess, enabled him to move to New York, where he soon met William Baziotes and where he signed up in the same unit of the WPA as Jackson Pollock. Even before he met any of the Surrealist émigrés, Kamrowski was experimenting with the automatist use of a variety of new and unorthodox procedures. Leafing through boxes of old works on paper in his studio he described some of them:

This is what you could get with blind chance with the carbon; it was carbon from holding the paper over a candle, like Paalen's fumage technique, then you would spray it with a diffuser. Jimmy Ernst used to get diffusion patterns by blowing on the wet paint through a straw. Here are effects produced with decalcomania—this could be a transfer or you applied the paint and then blotted it with another piece of paper—and these are flottages, made by floating your oil paint on top of water and dipping the canvas or paper into it, the same principle as marbelized paper. There was a high risk factor in working this way; you would lose things and then everything wouldn't be marvelous. Sometimes things would get overly labored and sometimes you'd just be reinventing the wheel. It was a period of adventure and you were not particularly interested in turning out a commodity unless it was something to please the Baroness.[2]

Gerome Kamrowski, *Alienated Emissaries,* 1939, gouache and casein on board,
17¾ x 14¾ inches; courtesy Washburn Gallery.

Automatism as defined by Breton in the first Surrealist Manifesto in 1924 was conceived of as a way to pry raw material from the unconscious, not as a way to produce an artwork. Breton had specified "no moral or aesthetic considerations," but inevitably this was not strictly adhered to by all of the painters whom Breton claimed as Surrealist. In the United States, as artists began to experiment with automatist processes, there was an interest not only in the chance images produced, but also in the new effects obtainable just for their own sake. As part of their WPA work David Smith and Francis Criss conducted an experimental materials workshop. In his mural-painting workshop in the heart of the artists' territory on Union Square, David Siqueiros urged his assistants not only to drip paint freely but to try applying commercial techniques such as airbrush and to incorporate extraneous materials including photographs.

In the basement of the Museum of Non-Objective Art, according to Kamrowski, several of the artists who were recipients of stipends from Baroness Rebay and worked at various jobs at the Museum tried some automatist dripping with a lacquer made by melting worn-out phonograph records. The Baroness liked to have classical music played in the museum as an accompaniment to the paintings. As the worn-out records accumulated, one of the resourceful artists working in the storeroom began melting them down to make a fine dark lacquer for marking crates. The same substance if dripped and swirled on paper dried instantly, much to the fascination of the other artists on the staff who soon began dripping melted Bach on whatever surfaces were available. Even before the arrival of the Surrealist émigrés, then, American artists were familiar with a variety of automatist practices, including some that they had invented. For the American painters, however, automatism was not necessarily an open sesame to the unconscious; using these techniques was often simply a way of getting into a painting, just as later some of the abstract expressionists would write a name or numbers on the bare canvas just to get a painting going.

When Kamrowski met William Baziotes in 1938 the two found they shared an interest in automatist practices, and they would leaf through the pages of *Minotaure* together. Baziotes, despite his early training at the conservative National Academy of Design, had Surrealism on his mind. His early receptivity to Surrealism was indicated in a letter to his wife written in April 1940, during a visit to his family in Pittsburgh. He described his brother as "painting Surrealist pictures—straight from the unconscious. I believe he puts down what everyone feels. My brother doesn't know what they mean."[3] It is likely that he was reading his own ideas about painting

William Baziotes, *Untitled,* c. 1936, watercolor and graphite on paper, 11⅞ x 9 inches; estate of William Baziotes, courtesy Blum Helman Gallery.

into his brother's work, for he maintained that he often didn't know until after completion, sometimes long after, what the subjects of his paintings were.

Peter Busa, another artist from the WPA, worked collaboratively with Baziotes at the beginning of the 1940s.

He told me [Busa recounted] that my painting *Seven* was too fragmented. So, picking up the brush, as if in a trance, he worked on the left side of the painting, simplifying areas toward the notion of larger sweeps or movements. He didn't like overlapping and his comments were that the large painting was not flat enough. The right parts are in my hand, but on the left you can see Baziotes' love for paint and surface. Later Jackson said that he liked the title but not the painting; having heard that Baziotes worked on it he gave a scornful grin and I had to protest his gesture when he grabbed the brush and said "You need a big 7." [4]

Among the New York artists who were working in the 1930s in a way that paralleled European Surrealism was Boris Margo, who had arrived from Russia at the start of the decade. As a student he had already cultivated a predilection for fantasy and had attended the school started by the independent-spirited Pavel Filonov, who encouraged spontaneity of method and untrammeled expression. [5] By 1935 Margo was working in the decalcomania process, that is, laying paper over a freshly painted surface and then pulling it off, a process that often results in eerie effects of decay and putrefaction. It was about the same time that Oscar Domínguez started working with decalcomania in Europe, and by the late 1930s it had become a favorite technique for Max Ernst. For Margo it was a step toward lurid Boschian scenes and vistas into a macabre underworld; staring at the hallucinatory effects of his surface, he would elaborate on certain shapes with the brush, wipe off areas of paint, or draw into it with a sharp point. At some point he encountered the work of Tanguy and developed a great admiration for this kindred dreamer. He was not eligible for the WPA until after he became a citizen in 1938, but his close friend Gorky arranged to hire him as an assistant on the Newark murals. Gorky and Margo shared a studio, and it has been suggested that the period of free and spontaneous flowing on of paint and the cultivation of the visionary at which Gorky finally arrived may have been triggered by their close association, as well as from proximity to the Surrealists. [6]

Although the use of "blind chance," experiment with materials and techniques, and an interest in psychic automatism were already known among American artists by 1939, the major dilemma for most was still, as Julien Levy pointed out, between

Peter Busa and William Baziotes, collaborative work, c. 1941, ink, watercolor,
and collage; courtesy Christopher Busa.

Arshile Gorky and Peter Busa on Fourteenth Street; courtesy Christopher Busa.

representational art and abstraction, and more particularly between the social realism endorsed by the Communist Party and the appeal of new aesthetic formulations. Jacob Kainen's introduction in the little catalogue for the 1936 Walter Quirt exhibition at the Julien Levy Gallery summed up the conflict confronting the American artist when the Federal Art Project was in full sway: "The painter finds himself expected to pictorialize political scenes for the masses on the one hand, and to develop fresh new plastic methods on the other. He is caught between a culturally untrained working class and the tradition of modern painting." The dilemma grew more complex as both artistic and political ideologies splintered and proliferated. One thing was clear: avant-garde art and old left politics did not march shoulder to shoulder, suspicious U.S. senators to the contrary. Peter Busa remembered that he and Gorky were constantly being attacked as bourgeois because they showed an interest in abstraction. "Gorky," he recollected, "would be shouted down at Artists Union meetings when he tried to discuss aesthetic questions."[7] However, someone noted down and preserved his statement that "proletarian art is poor pictures for poor people." Abstract painters like Ilya Bolotowsky soon came under attack by the Union as being Trotskyist.

A perusal of the pages of *Art Front,* the monthly journal published by the Artists Union between November 1934 and the fall of 1937, indicates that the seeds of a future mistrust of Surrealism had already been sown. Samuel Putnam, in an essay on "Marxism and Surrealism," wrote:

The real, then, is Marx' starting point. Nothing in Marx justifies the assumption that there is any reality above the real. . . . Marxist art is a dialectical deepening of reality in its human essence . . . the essence of the human is the sum total of social relationships. . . . The Surrealist proposes not to change the world, but the reflection of the world in consciousness. He is being utterly false to Marxist principle by asserting that consciousness conditions being, not being consciousness.[8]

He cites Lenin's objections to philosophical idealism and falls back on Schiller's intent "to build a meaning in truth itself."

This Marxist emphasis on the actual as voiced by Putnam and others in the 1930s was upheld by most artists of the old left and is echoed as well in Trotsky's apprehensiveness over Breton's interest in the "au-delà." It sheds some light on the rise of formalist criticism as practiced by critics who had been conditioned by Marx-

Boris Margo, *Untitled,* 1939, oil on masonite, 18 x 24 inches; courtesy Michael
Rosenfeld Gallery.

ism, such as Clement Greenberg and Harold Rosenberg. They generally emphasized form as nonreferential, as having its own inherent actuality. Thus a discussion of content, veiled or otherwise, was missing from the contemporary writing on abstract expressionist art.

In an earlier issue of *Art Front,* Jerome Kline had condemned the artists of Dada and Surrealism, saying that they were "neurotically incapable of giving their efforts a point of leverage in the real world, having dodged the vital issues of revolutionary art."[9] And in January 1936 Joe Solomon described Dalí's paintings as "looking like old color charts from some treatise on venereal disease." However, there were some contributors to *Art Front* who saw with less political prejudice. Charmion Von Wiegand, in her review of the "Fantastic Art, Dada, Surrealism" show at the Museum of Modern Art in the January 1937 issue, wrote that the Surrealists were "not all corrupt with the festering sores of dying individualism . . . [Surrealism] contributes new discoveries of the inner life of fantasy by pictorializing the destructive process of the subconscious mind."[10]

Since the Federal Art Project favored social realism, the major portion of the work done under its auspices fell into that category. However, as one artist put it, "we had a mole on the Project [Burgoyne Diller]," so that some abstract murals by artists such as Peter Busa, Stuart Davis, and Gorky were approved. There were even a few murals that were tinged with Surrealist fantasy, such as those Walter Quirt did for Bellevue Hospital. In fact traces of Surrealist influence flickered across a number of American canvases of the 1930s, including those of Quirt, Federico Castelon, Boris Margo, Lorser Feitelson, and several others, but the subversive purposes of European Surrealism and the highly organized "research" conducted by the group were not part of the agenda of those who tried to duplicate the style in the United States.

After the revelations of the Moscow trials, which split the American left, a new group was formed, largely Trotskyist in orientation, the American Artists' Congress, which later became the Federation of Modern Painters and Sculptors. Tolerating a diversity of styles and subjects, this group provided an alternative for those artists who still wanted to transform the world but believed that the transformation could be better effected by an art of aesthetic merit than by pictorial propaganda. So by the end of the 1930s, in addition to the old left which decreed that art must have legible social content, there was a new left which upheld the principle of freedom in both style and content, particularly after the publication in the summer of 1938 of

Dwight Macdonald's translation of the Breton-Trotsky joint statement in *Partisan Review.*

Partisan Review had moved, or its editors had, from the Stalinist to the Trotskyist camp. The fact that it provided a platform for Clement Greenberg during the 1940s is critical to understanding the verbal web that was woven around the New York School, and indeed for the whole formalist interpretation given to both European and American modernist painting in the following decades. The prejudice against social realism that resulted from the enmity of these factions of the left tinged art criticism for half a century. Since geometric abstraction could hardly be made to stand alone on the side of artistic freedom, something new was needed, something free, emphasizing the individual, yet grand enough to be the successor to European modernism. Greenberg was not the only anti-Stalinist critic in search of an art that would suit his political position.

The most visible avant-garde group in the later 1930s was the American Abstract Artists, whose members largely veered in the direction of Mondrian and neo-plasticism or toward an amalgam of geometric abstract styles of the type often lampooned in *New Yorker* cartoons. For most, the mystical content that underlay the work of Mondrian or the Kandinskys hanging in the Baroness Rebay's Museum of Non-Objective Art posed no problem since they were unaware of it, and the appreciation of these works became a matter of analyzing the formal relationships. The presence in the United States of influential teachers from the Bauhaus—Moholy-Nagy in Chicago, Josef Albers at Black Mountain College, Walter Gropius at Harvard—lent authority to geometric abstraction.

One witness who had a more than parochial understanding of the 1930s was Fritz Bultman, who had studied in Munich, spoke French and German, and had a good grasp of the various nuances of European modernism. He saw the artists who arrived from Germany soon after the Nazis closed the Bauhaus in 1932 as "the first wave." These émigrés spread the theories that had been hatched at the Bauhaus or, in the case of Hofmann, an expressionist version of cubism, and they had already made their influence felt in art departments and schools of architecture by the time the "second wave" began to arrive from France after Hitler invaded Poland in September 1939. In contrast to the usual description of the Depression years, Bultman felt that the late thirties in New York were tremendously exciting and that there was the sense of a new potential in the air.

Certainly there were artists there who were thinking about new possibilities and were not satisfied with any existing answers to the questions of what and how to paint. The lack of a strong marketplace left artists feeling free to work experimentally, since their work was not going to sell anyway. Nor were they inhibited by the consideration that a museum curator might be looking over their shoulder. The Museum of Modern Art's director, Alfred Barr, was more preoccupied with importing European modernism—and in the process beating museums abroad in the recognition of this work—than with showcasing American art of *any* persuasion. The Federation of Modern Painters and Sculptors delivered attacks on MoMA in 1942, 1943, and 1944, protesting the museum's callous attitude toward American artists and overemphasis on Europe. In response, James Thrall Soby, who became assistant director of MoMA in 1943, pointed out that what was going on in Europe in the arts was a great deal more interesting than what was going on in America. "You cannot possibly present twentieth century American painting," he argued, "as we have presented School of Paris painting."[11] It was a challenge, rather than approval, that MoMA was offering American artists.

If one were to survey what those artists who were to become the major figures of the New York School by midcentury were doing in 1939, one might be inclined to agree with Soby. Tentative is a word that could be applied to most of them, meaning that they were seeking but had not yet found a way of working both appropriate to the time and fulfilling the need for individual expression. They were in no sense a group; while some were acquainted from the Federal Art Project, others would not meet until as late as 1946. Yet they had in common the sense of being propelled beyond existing solutions, an interest in conveying a mythic content, a curiosity about Surrealism and the escape route it offered from both the mundane and the rigidly formalistic; and most of them also knew John Graham. No history of those years is complete without mention of Graham, the eccentric White Russian who served for a time as secretary of the Museum of Non-Objective Art. Striking in appearance, cosmopolitan in background, Graham exerted a significant influence over the more intellectually adventurous among the New York artists through his connoisseurship of primitive art, his up-to-date awareness of modern developments abroad, his knowledge of the occult, and his wide-ranging discourses on aesthetics. Graham remains an elusive yet distinctive presence in the New York art scene of the 1930s and early 1940s, a background figure who never quite emerges into the foreground. His interest in Jung and his belief in the unconscious as the driving force in creativity

Jackson Pollock, *Composition with Woman*, 1938–1941, oil on masonite, 17¾ x
10⅜ inches; private collection, Japan.

had a profound impact on many New York artists during the interwar years. The
exhibition he arranged at the McMillen Gallery in 1942 brought together well-
known Europeans and unknown Americans and was the occasion as well for the
first showing of key members of the future New York School, including Pollock and
de Kooning.

In 1939 Jackson Pollock had started his work with a Jungian analyst, attempting to bare his psyche in a visual rather than a verbal stream of consciousness
by producing images that he and his analyst interpreted together. His paintings were
an amalgam of qualities from many different sources, the primary one being a personal turbulence, which seemed to register on the canvas in the viscous flow of the
paint. A circular mode of organizing a composition may have been acquired from his
teacher, Thomas Hart Benton, while at the Siqueiros workshop near Union Square
he would have been encouraged to drip and spray paint in an explosive manner and
to use unorthodox materials. For the totemic images in a 1939 painting such as
Composition with Woman, a number of sources seem likely, including Native American art and Jungian archetypes. There was an undeniable power in the rhythms of
the paint, a paint that appeared to have been applied with such an outflow of physical
and psychic energy that it often appeared to obliterate more than it defined.

William Baziotes had hitchhiked as a youth from his native Pittsburgh to Philadelphia to see the work of Paul Klee and Max Ernst's *Hundred Headless Woman.*
From 1936 on, while studying at the conservative National Academy of Design, he
had made a practice of doing automatist drawings. In 1939 Mark Rothko was still
painting his incongruously vaporous subway stations with weightless human apparitions or flattened figures in grid-structured interior spaces. All during the thirties
Rothko seemed to avoid dealing with the figure in a volumetric fashion, minimizing
its lifelikeness and preferring contracted or distended proportions and simplified
forms. He tended to organize his compositions along vertical and horizontal axes
and to paint thinly, often apparently even wiping excess pigment from the canvas.
The awkwardness and lack of a firm stylistic direction left Rothko open to the possibilities of experiment in a way that some of his contemporaries with a more clearly
formulated direction were not. What is impressive is his persistence in working his
way through these awkward stages in hundreds of canvases and works on paper
during the later 1930s and early 1940s as he struggled to suppress the external motif
in favor of an ambiguous symbolism.

Mark Rothko, *Untitled (Figures around a Piano)*, 1935–1940, oil on canvas, 23⅝ x 31¾ inches; National Gallery of Art, gift of the Mark Rothko Foundation.

Between 1938 and 1941 Rothko met often with his long-time friend, Adolph Gottlieb, to discuss the need for a new artistic direction in America and to try to work out what that direction might be. The two artists had exhibited in a group known as "the Ten," nine artists who exhibited together in a variety of places between 1935 and 1939 and who were perceived by critics as trying to straddle the space between figurative and abstract art. Both were also friends with Milton Avery, an artist whom Rothko greatly admired and whose influence can be seen in paintings such as *Untitled (Figures around a Piano)*, 1935–1940; perhaps it was from Avery that he learned how to soften edges to achieve his characteristic effect of floating, hovering forms.

Gottlieb also showed the influence of Avery in works such as *Untitled (Self-Portrait in Mirror)*, c. 1938. He and his wife had been living in Brooklyn Heights, but from September 1937 to June 1938, because of Esta Gottlieb's health, they lived in Arizona. There he painted forms suggested by bones and cacti and some strong, stark landscapes, and he also discovered Indian rock paintings. In 1939 he painted a mural for the post office in Yerrington, Nevada. A passing interest in veristic Surrealism is evident in a 1939–1940 painting that includes the World's Fair symbols, the trylon and perisphere. His 1940 show at the Artists Gallery included the Arizona still lifes and the more recent *Souvenirs of the Sea,* in which shells are isolated in the frame of a crate, also found on the beach, a device that prefigures the grid of his later "pictographs."

As for de Kooning, who would later be regarded as the unofficial leader of the New York School, he appears to have been an enigmatic presence on the downtown scene. Rarely completing a painting, never showing his work, he nonetheless commanded a certain amount of respect among painters. What he did produce ran a gamut from professionally accomplished commissioned work, such as the 16-foot four-part *Legend and Fact* of 1940, to exploratory, somewhat disjointed figure paintings. For him Surrealism was not a particularly important issue or a mode of painting to be worked through, although at times, such as in *The Wave* of 1943, a certain kind of Miróesque biomorphism is present.

Others who would contribute to the momentum of the New York School and who were already at work in the late thirties were occupied roughly as follows: Franz Kline was exhibiting heavily painted cityscapes or industrial landscapes such as *Palmerton, Pa.* and modest-size figure paintings, hung on fences in the semiannual Greenwich Village outdoor art exhibitions. Gorky was applying paint up to a half-

inch thick to cover his canvases with compositions often referred to as Picassoid, but which actually are more freely improvisatory than most of his earlier work—a sign of his move into a more confident individual mode. Richard Pousette Dart at the age of twenty-one was preparing for his first New York exhibition at the Artists Gallery, painting heraldic or totemic bird and fish images embedded in flattened compositions bordering on the abstract. At the Marine Air Terminal James Brooks was starting on one of the largest murals ever undertaken in the United States, the 240-foot *History of Flight* for the main rotunda. Barnett Newman had studied painting but was also drawn to writing and in the meantime ran for mayor of New York on an anarchist platform. Ad Reinhardt had graduated from Columbia University where he had done an abstract cover for the literary magazine and had joined the American Abstract Artists. Robert Motherwell had left his pursuit of a graduate degree in philosophy at Harvard and had come to New York to study art history with Meyer Schapiro.

There was little to suggest that these same artists would, ten years later, be sitting around a long table with Alfred Barr in earnest discussion of, among other things, the appropriate designation for the new art they had launched. Some knew each other from the Federal Art Project or from the Artists Union and there were close friendships among several of them, but in no sense was there either artistic or social cohesion at the outset of the 1940s. What there was was an open-ended experimental approach to art on the part of artists who were not ready to settle for the existing alternatives.

Franz Kline, *Palmerton, Pa.*, 1941, oil on canvas, 21 x 27⅛ inches; National
Museum of American Art, Smithsonian Institution.

As far as the museums were concerned, there was little support for an innovative American art, despite the fact that advanced European art found more favor with the Museum of Modern Art's curators than it did among European museums. The Museum of Modern Art was the first purchaser of a painting by Masson and the first museum to acquire works by many of the Surrealists, including a whole curiosity cabinet of Surrealist objects that came almost directly from the object exhibition at the Charles Ratton gallery in Paris in 1936. Perhaps it was Barr's distance from the politics and polemics of European art centers that allowed him to take an overview of contemporary art and to stage major exhibitions, in the same year, of such stylistic opposites as International Style architecture and "Fantastic Art, Dada, Surrealism."

The latter exhibition served something of the same function as the pages of *Minotaure,* gleaning bizarre images from the fantastic art of the past and placing them alongside contemporary celebrations of the irrational. It was shown in Minneapolis and San Francisco as well as New York and offered American artists and the

museum-going public a view of Surrealism as a part of the established canon of twentieth-century art, along with cubism, futurism, neoplasticism, and the rest, and not simply the result of the collective activities of an outrageous, scrappy avant-garde. Americans knew little of its poetry (nothing by Breton was translated into English until the mid-1940s with the exception of a brief excerpt from *L'Amour fou,* published in *transition* in 1938) and less of its politics. Surrealism at MoMA was presented as part of the menu of artistic styles that the artist who wished to be modern could pick from, smorgasbord fashion, rather than as a way of life and a dedication to revolution.

When it came to American artists, however, the perceptive director of MoMA was less broad-minded. He was slow to acquire even the early American moderns such as Hartley, Dove, Storrs, and Schamberg and hesitant to admit that there was a valid modern movement in the United States. Despite picketing by American artists protesting this neglect, it wasn't until the large "Abstract Painting in America" show in the winter of 1950–1951 that MoMA gave them the official nod.

The prepared ground for the exodus of European Surrealists was one where Surrealism was partially known and incompletely understood. It was a territory split between Depression-era realism, including regionalism, and partially digested modernism, a division that mirrored the broader division between isolationism and a more European-oriented outlook. The bitter feuding between the Stalinist and Trotskyist factions of the left and their underlying political agendas persisted for many years, affecting the critical reception of art if not the artists themselves. There was also bound to be a chauvinistic residue on the part of some of the artists irritated by MoMA's persistent showcasing of European modernism, although others, unable to travel abroad in the Depression, welcomed the opportunity to broaden their artistic horizons. Among these others might have been those mentioned above, the independent experimentalists working not out of a theoretical program or proclaimed manifesto but in the hope that what they were doing might turn out to be what was needed to fill the void in American art.

It was into this situation that the catalyst of the Surrealist displacement was injected. Here and there, individually and collectively an artistic interchange was to take place that would affect both the displaced artist-refugees and the milieu into which they were displaced. A cluster of "events"—exhibitions, publications, friendships, patronage—developed between 1941 and 1945 that changed Surrealism and pushed American art into uncharted waters.

James Brooks working on *History of Flight,* Marine Air Terminal, La Guardia
Airport, New York, 1939–1940, photograph courtesy Charlotte Brooks.

It would be vain to argue that it was the introduction of an external element
alone that brought about this change, but even more so to contend that the new art
would have emerged in the form it did without such a catalyst. The years during
which these encounters took place were among the most momentous in human history, as global awareness was forced on the inhabitants of what Max Ernst called *La
Planète affolée* by the war that encircled it. From the crucible of the war years, forged
out of strange encounters, a hitherto unseen form of visual art was to emerge.

Installation view of the exhibition "Fantastic Art, Dada, Surrealism," The Museum
of Modern Art, New York, December 7, 1936–January 17, 1937; photograph
courtesy The Museum of Modern Art New York.

I have always been drawn to what is not a sure bet.
A tree marked out by the storm
The glimmering boat brought in by the ship's boy.
André Breton, *Pleine marge,* 1940

In the bitter cold of January 1940 Breton wrote to Paalen in Mexico, giving him what news he had of the scattered Surrealists. Max Ernst had been released from the detention camp where he had been interned since the mobilization. "Matta, Tanguy and Seligmann write from New York without enthusiasm," he reported. "Picasso and Dora are at Royan. He continues to paint, but lives in a more and more fierce isolation." [1]

In March Kurt Seligmann heard from the poet Benjamin Péret, who wrote from Nantes asking him to try to find a buyer for a De Chirico painting he wished to sell in order to supplement his allotted fifty centimes a day. He also alluded to "les Matta et Cie." as "des vielles vaches qui ne donnent plus signe de vie." [2] (Throughout his correspondence Péret reveals himself as a hardline Surrealist with little tolerance for anyone who in his view deviated in the slightest from true Surrealism; few besides Breton met that test.)

Seligmann also received a collective letter written on May 23, signed by Victor Brauner, Oscar Domínguez, Jacques Hérold, René Magritte, Robert Rius, Raoul Ubac, and Remedios Varo. The letter explained that it was essential for them to leave Paris and that they could only do so if their living expenses were guaranteed. Hence they were asking for the pledge of a monthly sum to assure their support in the Midi "until the cessation of hostilities," to be repaid in paintings. This appeal, they wrote, was being made "only as a last resort." [3]

There is no record of Seligmann's reply to this plea. Perhaps he received it only after the French surrender in June, when financial transfers became too problematic for him to send help. The signers of this letter did get out of Paris, as did roughly two-thirds of the city's 6,000,000 inhabitants whose makeshift caravans clogged the roads to the south for weeks. The above artists found shelter in or near Carcassonne thanks to Joe Bosquet, a paraplegic writer confined to a wheelchair with enough means to contribute to the support of the refugees. From there most of them joined the ranks of anxious would-be émigrés in Marseilles during the winter of 1940–1941.

Undaunted by the war, Peggy Guggenheim was making the rounds of Paris studios on a buying spree. Under the guidance of a former Los Angeles gallery owner, Howard Putzel, she rounded our her collection of twentieth-century art with such acquisitions as Giacometti's *Woman with Her Throat Cut* and Brancusi's *Bird in Space,* the latter acquired while the Germans were bombing factories on the outskirts of Paris. When the panzers were less than forty miles from the city, she sat at the

Dome drinking champagne with a new lover, by no means the only expatriate to view the war as nothing more than a temporary inconvenience.

By June of 1940 it was all over. The British troops had been evacuated from Dunkerque in an amazing fleet made up overnight of any kind of vessel that would float; the German army had occupied Paris and France had been partitioned, with the collaborationist Pétain government established at Vichy. It was an outcome that few had anticipated and one that will be long debated, particularly the alacrity with which the Third Republic voted its own demise, agreeing to all Hitler's conditions for what was euphemistically called an armistice. A few cabinet members balked at the provision calling for the "surrender on demand" of all Germans in France who had fled the Nazis, as violating the historic right of asylum, but it was a point on which the Germans insisted. The Pétain government was to prove assiduous in tracking down these "enemies of the Reich." The eighty-four-year-old Marshal Pétain, now virtual dictator of France, soon showed his fascist colors in proclaiming the infamous Statut des Juifs.

The Abstraction/Creation painter Jean Hélion, who had left his home in Rockford Springs, Virginia, to return to France for the mobilization in 1939, has left a stirring account of a soldier's bewilderment during the rout, the general confusion, the lack of information, and the lack of leadership during the invasion and the weeks following the surrender. The French army rank and file had allowed themselves to be rounded up by the Germans in the belief that they would be mustered out and permitted to return to their homes. In accepting the armistice terms, however, the French government had agreed that the million and a half prisoners of war would remain in German hands until the conclusion of peace, and they were shipped off in freight cars to labor camps in Germany. Hélion made an astounding escape from his camp in eastern Germany, crossed the borders into Belgium, France, and the unoccupied zone and arrived back in New York in 1942, where he published the details of his story in *They Shall Not Have Me* in the following year.

In England Onslow Ford had received an assignment to a naval convoy, but illness prevented his sailing with his ship. It was the first ship sunk in the war; hit by a torpedo from a German U-boat, it went down with its whole crew. Meanwhile, through efforts made on his behalf across the Atlantic by Kay Sage he received an invitation to come to the United States as a kind of cultural emissary. Kay Sage's young cousin, David Hare, was married at the time to Susanna Wilson, daughter of Frances Perkins, Secretary of Labor. In 1940 immigration was still under the Department of Labor (in 1941 it was transferred to the Justice Department with visas handled at the State Department), and apparently Mrs. Perkins was able to expedite visas for some of Tanguy's Surrealist confrères. Onslow Ford persuaded the British Admiralty to grant him a leave to fulfill this obligation to represent the European

Kay Sage, *Danger Construction Ahead,* 1940, oil on canvas, 44 x 62 inches; Yale
University Art Gallery, gift of Mrs. Hugh Chisholm Jr.

culture that the West hoped to save. In June 1940 he crossed the Atlantic on a crowded Cunard liner and disembarked in New York with a few pound notes and a gold cigarette case in his pocket.

In New York he was reunited with Matta, who had already made his presence felt. Julien Levy had published an attention-getting broadside on the occasion of Matta's first exhibition in April 1940. According to Levy, he had appeared in the gallery "confident, exuberant and mercurial and produced a portfolio of explosive crayon drawings, vowing he would complete enough canvases for an exhibition in the next two months if I were interested." Matta, he wrote in retrospect, "burst on the New York scene as if he considered this country a sort of dark continent, his Africa where he could trade dubious wares, charm the natives and entertain scintillating disillusions. He was chock full of premature optimism and impatient disappointment; believing ardently in almost everything and in absolutely nothing, as he believed ardently and painfully in himself. For me he was easily the most fertile and the most untrustworthy of the younger Surrealists."[4]

Through Tanguy and Kay Sage, who were living on Waverly Place in Greenwich Village, the Mattas met David Hare and his wife Susanna and were invited to spend part of the summer of 1940 at Frances Perkins's home on the Maine coast. When Onslow Ford arrived he was asked to join them, continuing the tradition of shared summer holidays that they had formed in Europe. Newcastle, Maine, lies along a tidal estuary with a sparsely settled wooded shore. There were visiting dignitaries and a certain amount of protocol in the Perkins household, so the young Surrealists moved out into a nearby cabin on the shore which became the base for a summer of boating and picnicking with the Hares.

It was also a summer of work. While there Onslow Ford painted his most substantial canvas to date, *Propaganda for Love,* a provocative work recapitulating the themes that had occupied the painter during the previous two years: transparent mountains, shadows cast by unseen presences, undulating planes, grids, and the lines and dotted circles that he used to denote different sections of time. At the center a monster hatches the "world egg," from which protrudes an intestine excreting a sinister dark chain. According to the artist it was "a rather horrible painting, reflecting my feeling about the war and the state the world was in." His use of such a specific but personal iconography followed from his belief in Jung's concept of a collective unconscious, through which his images would have resonance for others.

From the Maine coast Seligmann received a postcard from Onslow Ford and a letter from Matta, who informed him that Mrs. Perkins had authorized him to use her name if it would be useful in getting the affidavits for the would-be émigrés. Susanna recalled writing affidavits for the Bretons and for Duchamp and urging her

Below: Matta, *Rocks,* 1940, oil on canvas, 96.9 x 152.7 cm; The Baltimore Museum of Art, Bequest of Saidie A. May.

Opposite: Gordon Onslow Ford, *Propaganda for Love,* 1940, oil on canvas, 40½ x 66 inches; private collection.

mother to be sure they got visas. She also bought some small works from Matta. "He never had any money and was selling his drawings for $15 or $20. In Newcastle he met Henry Clifford, who took to him right away and later bought *La Terre est un homme* right off the walls at Pierre Matisse." [5]

Back in New York in the fall, Onslow Ford took up residence in a cold-water flat on Eighth Street, not far from the Mattas. The American painter William Baziotes helped him to construct an improvised partition to separate studio and living areas, and it may be at that time that Baziotes saw the two coulage paintings that the British artist had managed to bring with him; the others which he had left in his Île St.-Louis studio disappeared after the war's end. He had met Baziotes through a young photographer and filmmaker, Francis Lee, who had attended the National Academy of Design at the same time as Baziotes. Lee was the son of an Italian aristocrat who had died of tuberculosis while in the army and a mother from a family of Boston Brahmins. He spoke French and Italian and had a large loft in an industrial

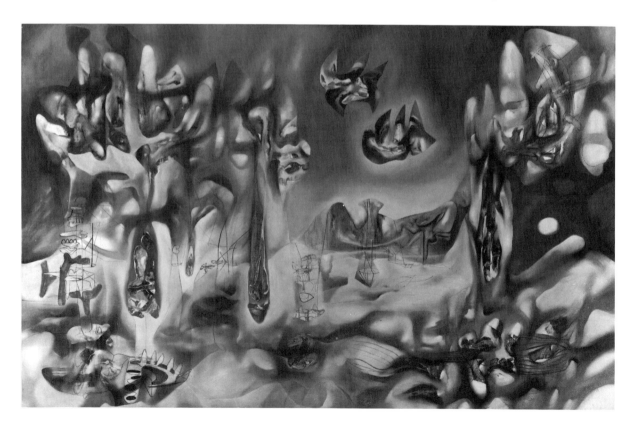

building on Tenth Street, which because of its size became a gathering place for a mixture of European émigrés and young American bohemians. "We lived in cramped, cold apartments and had no cafés to meet in so we went to Francis' loft several times a week," according to Matta.[6] Lee made experimental films and provided the slides that were projected onto a mannequin in the corner of Seligmann's studio during one of the latter's evenings of magic. Through Lee Baziotes met Matta and was captivated by the latter's rapid flow of ideas. Although Baziotes was the more silent and Matta invariably took the conversational lead, a close understanding developed between them. According to Baziotes' widow Ethel, Matta really felt that Baziotes understood what he was saying, and the originality of his thought left a deep imprint on her husband.

Another English artist who had been associated with the Surrealists in Paris and who crossed the Atlantic in June of 1940 was Stanley William Hayter, at whose Atelier 17 prints by Masson, Miró, Ernst, and others had been produced. Hayter's training was in science and he had worked as a geologist for the Anglo-Iranian Oil Company before settling in Paris in the mid-1920s, where he learned printmaking from a master engraver. He opened a print workshop where he printed his own work and that of others, including several portfolios to which artists contributed to raise money to feed and clothe children who were victims of the Spanish Civil War. His scientific background made him particularly interested in technical experiment, which combined with his interest in automatism to generate an approach that was to profoundly influence printmaking the world over. Invited to teach during the summer of 1940 at the California School of Fine Arts in San Francisco, he crossed the North Atlantic to Halifax on a freighter that had been mounted with heavy guns as

Yves Tanguy, *Palace with Rock Windows,* 1942, oil on canvas, 64 x 72 inches;
Centre Georges Pompidou, Musée National d'Art Moderne.

a protection against German U-boats, but which Hayter claimed would have sunk their own boat had they been fired.

In July Hayter wrote to Seligmann, praising the California climate and the enthusiasm of his students and giving him the news that he had married a San Francisco sculptor, Helen Phillips. He said he was looking forward to seeing Seligmann in the fall, as he had arranged with the New School for Social Research to reopen his Atelier 17 on its premises in October, and he mentioned that Ozenfant would be teaching there, along with others of his "copains d'autrefois." An exhibition of his work was scheduled to follow that of Picasso at the San Francisco Museum at the end of July and he was also doing radio broadcasts.[7]

In Reno with Kay Sage who was awaiting a divorce during the summer of 1940, Tanguy wrote to the Seligmanns bemoaning the lack of news from abroad and voicing his anxiety about the war, the news from France, and the fate of his confrères. He knew only that Miró had returned to Spain, which shocked him, given the latter's hatred of the Falangists. Tanguy found it strange to have a studio in that "funny little country out of a comic opera, where everyone goes about disguised as cowboys, without thought of the terrible things that are happening," but he found the "paysage magnifique" and urged the Seligmanns to make the trip.[8] Indeed, within a day's drive of Reno is a landscape of fantastic rock formations that may well have fueled some of the changes that appeared in Tanguy's paintings of the early 1940s. His *Palace of Windowed Rocks,* 1942, shows a solidity and complexity of structure and clarity of light that differ markedly from the smaller, more widely dispersed shapes and the nuanced atmosphere of his prewar works.

In August Tanguy passed on the news that Jacqueline Breton had written from Royan where she was staying with Picasso and Dora Maar, saying that André was well and still in the army medical corps, Magritte and Scutenaire were at Carcassonne, Mabille in Provence, and Péret in prison at Rennes. The latter, who had gone to jail as a war resister, was soon released from jail by the occupation troops who thought he had been there as a German sympathizer. (Some accounts say that he paid a bribe for his release, but since his letters indicate that he was wholly without funds this seems unlikely.) Péret returned to Paris where he stayed well into the fall, and then, hidden in a wagonload of straw, he made a slow journey to the unoccupied zone and eventually to Marseilles where he rejoined Remedios Varo.

André Masson with his wife Rose and their two young sons were living in the north in Lyons-la-Forêt in the first half of 1940. There he painted two large canvases

for Pierre David Weil, one of which, *The Birth of the Minotaur,* he learned after the war had been used as a tarp to cover canons when the Germans ransacked the David Weil house. The Massons became more nervous as the Germans advanced, partly because they sensed hostility on the part of the local residents. They had been living in Spain when the civil war started, and although Masson had been a noncombatant he had made drawings against Franco, and they also had friends among the refugees from Spain who came to see them and were dubbed "les rouges" in that conservative community. Since Rose was Jewish there was no knowing what might be in store for them, so in June they decided to move south to Fréluc in the Auvergne. There they were joined by Rose's sister, the actress Sylvia Makles, wife of Georges Bataille, and by the psychologist Jacques Lacan whom Sylvia would later marry. The complex intellectual relationship of those three men, compounded by the marriages with the Makles sisters, was of far greater significance for Masson than his ties to the Surrealist poets. After the 1920s the connection with the organized Surrealist group made little difference in the way Masson carried on his work. "Je suis né surréaliste," he liked to say, implying that it was in no one else's power to declare him in or out of the movement.

During the months at Fréluc, Masson did the drawings for *Anatomy of My Universe* that would later be engraved at Hayter's Atelier 17 and published by Curt Valentin with a dedication to Lacan in memory of their discussions at Fréluc. The introduction was also written there in October: "At the beginning of all things is the underground world of unsatisfied instinct." Masson proceeded to explore in words and lines the question of the unifying forces underlying all phenomena. For the second plate, *The Unity of the Cosmos,* he wrote: "There is nothing inanimate in the world, a correspondence exists between the virtues of minerals, plants, stars and animal bodies." Other drawings treat the "Theme of Desire" and a "Morphology of the Passions." Now that the war that he had foreseen so apprehensively was under way and the specter of fascism had materialized into battalions of steel-helmeted men, Masson's concerns seemed to turn away from the premonitory violence characteristic of so much of his 1930s work and to stress rather a morphology of nature and the theme of regeneration, subjects that would be expanded on in the exuberant and colorful paintings of his American years.

Demobilized in the Gironde, André Breton wrote to the Seligmanns on August 10 from Salon where he had joined Pierre Mabille. After long conferring, they had decided, he wrote, "that our work can best be carried out where you are, since the period of reconstruction in France will certainly not be auspicious for an artistic revolution."[9] He proposed that he give a series of lectures in New York on subjects that Seligmann might find appropriate and asked him to help secure an invitation from an important cultural organization so he might be given an exit visa from Vichy France. He also mentioned that, due to their financial circumstances, a sum of money would have to be sent in advance. Seligmann contacted Alfred Barr and others to set in motion the necessary process to bring Breton, Masson, and Pierre Mabille to the United States. It was Margaret Scolari Barr who took charge of the efforts to bring artists out of Europe and acted as liaison with the Emergency Rescue Committee that had been set up three days after the fall of France to help artists, scholars, and political figures who might be in danger of deportation get to the United States. Seligmann gathered the necessary information and wrote résumés which he delivered to Mrs. Barr, and he also wrote a plea on behalf of Péret to Inez Warburg, who was running the Emergency Rescue Committee office in New York, and set about procuring the necessary affidavits of support from reliable U.S. residents. By October he was able to write to Breton that Barr would be delighted to help arrange a lecture series and that there remained few obstacles to his coming to New York.

Pierre Mabille was a medical doctor with a strong interest in anthropology, aligned with the Surrealists through his interest in magic and the occult. The publication of his *Mirroir du merveilleux* in 1939 along with articles written for *Minotaure* had gained him respect and recognition in Surrealist circles. However, he was not well enough known in the United States to have easy access to a visa, and he arrived in Martinique from Casablanca in November 1940, where he stayed while Seligmann tried to find the means to get him to New York. Eventually he secured a position in Port au Prince, Haiti, and he and Seligmann continued to correspond on the subject that obsessed them both, early writings on magic. Indeed Seligmann was continuing in New York to seek out rare tomes to add to his collection on the subject, accumulating a library that would eventually include more than 250 titles on magic and the occult and preparing his compendium, which would appear as *The Mirror of Magic* in 1947.

In May 1940, the last month before the capitulation of France, 406 boats carrying 135,000 passengers had sailed from Marseilles. Then the "armistice" in June put shipping under German control and the number of departing ships dwindled, so there was little for the refugees who had poured into Marseilles to do but sit in the cafés and wait, among them actor Louis Jouvet, playwright Henri de Montherlant, and many other recognizable figures from the world of arts and letters. In order to leave one needed not only a ticket on a steamship but a visa from the country of destination and an exit visa from Vichy, the second not available without the first. Little was done in Washington to expedite the visa process and many applicants were

André Masson, *Unity of the Cosmos,* from *Anatomy of My Universe,* 1940;
published by Curt Valentin, Buchholz Gallery New York, 1943.

turned down, particularly on grounds of past political affiliation but also for lack of someone in the United States ready to sign affidavits testifying to probity of character and a willingness to provide support. Roosevelt did get around the visa quota for each country by establishing a number of what were known as Roosevelt visas, which were of limited duration and did not count toward the period needed to become a naturalized citizen. Occasionally there was a bonanza, as when the Czech consulate closed down and turned over all its visas to the American consulate. The German-born art historian John Rewald who had been making regular trips to the consulate in Marseilles happened to come in on the day these Czech visas became available and was able to get one with little difficulty.

During the summer of 1940 a young American Quaker, Varian Fry, arrived in Marseilles to begin a year of intensive work for the Emergency Rescue Committee. The Committee had been established with private contributions on the initiative of a few individuals concerned mainly with the fate of members of the European intelligentsia. The New York office under the direction of Inez Warburg carried on an active fund-raising campaign and worked on assembling the biographical material, affidavits from individuals and cultural institutions, and invitations to teach or lecture that were a prerequisite to getting a visa from Washington as well as an exit permit from the Vichy government. Funds were needed not only for their passage, but also to keep the refugees going in Marseilles during the months of waiting.

Fry and his French counterpart, Daniel Bénédite, at first worked out of Fry's room in the Hôtel Splendide where they began receiving long lines of refugees who needed funds for survival, help with U.S. visas, and a place on a waiting list for passage. Ships leaving Marseilles for Casablanca or Martinique were few, usually Portuguese as that country's neutrality would hopefully give its ships immunity from German U-boat attack. Many had to try an alternate route through Spain and Portugal and thence by plane or ship from Lisbon, and this meant entry and exit visas for both of those countries. For some these were not obtainable or they didn't dare wait. Among the latter was Alma Mahler Werfel who has left a dramatic account of the slippery ascent of the Pyrénées made by herself and Franz Werfel, together with Heinrich and Golo Mann, while Fry took their luggage across the border on a train.[10] The process of even attempting to leave was long, tortuous, and constantly threatened with strangulation by bureaucratic impediments, dilatory action at the U.S. consulate, and the obstructionism of the Vichy government.

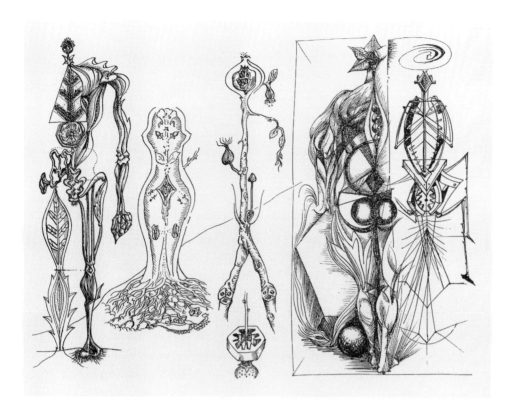

Armed with hastily compiled lists, made up with the help of Thomas Mann and Alfred Barr, Fry attempted to locate the various individuals he had been sent to rescue. Among the difficulties he encountered was the task of persuading some of those on the list of the necessity of departure. He had been in Germany and had observed at first hand Nazi anti-Semitism in action during Hitler's first pogrom on July 15, 1935; unlike some of his clients he was under no illusion about the danger of their situation. Jacques Lipchitz, in a letter of condolence on Fry's death in 1967, wrote: "I owe Varian Fry my life. I did not want to go away from France. It was his severe and clairvoyant letters which helped me finally to do so." [11]

The original plan of the Emergency Rescue Committee had been to locate leading intellectuals and political refugees, to solve the problem of visas, and to care for those whose resources were exhausted. Word quickly spread of the activities of Fry and Bénédite on behalf of the refugees and soon they were handling 120 interviews a day. An office was set up in the rue Grignon and procedures were established to determine priorities among those who applied for help. Bénédite described the meetings that Fry held at the end of each day, during which each interviewer would outline the "cases" seen during the day and propose appropriate financial assistance in the form of an allowance or a loan, visa application, and, if necessary, a hiding place.

The Emergency Rescue Committee office in Marseilles, 1941; left to right, Max
Ernst, Jacqueline Breton, André Masson, André Breton, and Varian Fry;
photograph courtesy the Musée Cantini, Marseilles.

Among those whose failure to recognize the danger of their situation had tragic consequences were former German government officials Rudolf Hilferding and Rudolph Breitsheid. These two, concerned for their wives' traveling comfort, turned down transport in steerage class on an outbound ship, despite Fry's urging, and returned to Nice to await other accommodations, only to have their exit permits withdrawn and almost immediately to be placed under house arrest. Shortly after they were picked up by the Gestapo and heard of no more. The dramatic narrative of his year in Marseilles, including hideaways behind concealed doors in the city's seamiest districts and ever-risky underworld cooperation, was recounted by Fry after his expulsion from France in *Surrender on Demand* and years later by Bénédite in *La Fillière marseillaise,* as well as in fragments here and there by many of the participants, including a memoir by Mary Jayne Gold, *Crossroads Marseilles.*

This last author was a wealthy American expatriate who joined Fry's staff and participated in the strangely assorted ménage that occupied a vacant villa in the suburb known as La Pomme. Housing was virtually unobtainable and the hotels packed to overflowing. Bénédite's wife Théo, accompanied by Mary Jayne Gold, set out to canvas the suburbs, walking from house to house, knocking on doors in search of lodging. On their first sortie they stumbled on the Villa Air Bel, a stately house, elegantly furnished and set in an ample park. They located the owner, Dr. Thumin, an eccentric amateur ornithologist, who, after some hesitation, agreed to let them have it for 1,300 francs a month, scarcely more than the going rate for a hotel room yet it would accommodate ten persons comfortably. Bénédite and his wife had already agreed to share a home with the Belgian-born veteran of the Russian Revolution Victor Serge, his companion Laurette Séjourny, and son Vlady; Mary Jayne Gold and Varian Fry were asked to join them and Serge proposed that they take in André, Jacqueline, and Aube Breton who were in precarious financial circumstances. At the end of the summer the Bretons and the Mabilles had moved south to Montargis. Living in a cabin near the shore, Breton wrote *Plein marge* whose publication he entrusted to Jean Ballard, editor of *Cahiers du Sud.*[12] Mabille left for Martinique in the fall and Breton, feeling hopeful about his chances of getting across the Atlantic, came to join the anxious would-be émigrés in Marseilles. In proposing to add the Bretons to their ménage, Serge told the others: "He has the reputation of being difficult, but I assure you that he is a charming and truly stimulating companion."[13]

Thus it came about that Serge, a founder of the Third International later exiled by Stalin to Siberia, the provocative Surrealist *chef d'école* Breton, his wife Jacqueline Lamba, who had been an aquatic dancer in a fishtank in a Paris bar when they met, and the quiet, Harvard-educated Fry, together with the Bénédites and assorted children, became housemates during one of the coldest winters the region had known. The Battle of Britain was being waged in the northern skies, but ships of neutral nations could still cross the Atlantic with their cargoes of refugees who slept on hastily constructed scaffoldings in the hold. The odds of getting onto one of those crowded ships were poor and the Villa Air Bel was nicknamed by its inhabitants "Villa Esper-visa," which could have been applied to the entire city of Marseilles. When the U.S. State Department took over the visa process, the granting of visas slowed down and the criteria became more stringent.

For Serge it was the fourth exile and seventh flight in twenty years. He described their existence as "hanging by slender threads. . . . the long-awaited visas are not here, still not here. . . . Our wretchedness contains as much talent and expertise as Paris could summon in the days of her prime; and nothing of it is visible, only hunted, terribly tired men at the limit of their nervous resources. . . . If it had not been for Varian Fry's American Relief Committee, a goodly number of the refugees would have had no reasonable course open to them but to jump into the sea from the height of the transporter-bridge, a certain enough method." [14]

It was a long mild fall, what the French call a St. Martin's summer. On Sundays the inhabitants of the Villa Air Bel lunched at a table set outdoors under the *platanes*. On those days they might be joined by Victor Brauner and Jacques Hérold, Surrealist painters who had come together to Paris from the same town in Romania, by René Char and Hans Bellmer, by Oscar Domínguez from the Canary Islands, by a new recruit, Cuban-born Wifredo Lam, and his German-born wife Helena, by the writers Jean Malaquais and Pierre Herbert who lived in an adjoining suburb, and by Sylvain Itkine who brought along members of his far-left theatrical group, performers of satirical comedy. They drank wine ordered in cartons and under Breton's directon made collages or "exquisite corpses." The latter were composite drawings made by three or four people drawing in turn on a piece of folded paper without seeing what the others had done, the best being greeted with applause and whistles. Sometimes there were auctions of artworks with Itkine acting as auctioneer and the paintings hung from the branches of the trees. Sometimes even the residents were in the trees—a photograph shows the decorous Fry and Consuelo de St.-Exupéry perched in the spreading branches of a venerable *platane*.

On September 19 Masson received a letter from Breton who wrote cryptically: "Isn't it time you went to America to prepare an exposition. It is a long way from our former homes that we will find each other again—what do you think?" [15] The idea of using the pretext of an exhibition to get the Masson family out of France had already been proposed. His dealer, Daniel Henry Kahnweiler, had arranged for Curt Valentin, who had worked in the Flechtheim Gallery in Berlin until 1933 and had become the director of the Buchholz Gallery in New York, to handle all Masson's work in the United States. From his correspondence it is evident that Kahnweiler thought it would be a good idea to get not only Masson's paintings but also his family to New York.

Plans for a Masson exhibition were being set in motion from another quarter as well. Kay Sage was in touch with an influential collector of Masson's work, Mrs. Saidie May of Baltimore, about plans for a show at the Baltimore Museum. Mrs. May had visited Masson's studio in 1938 and bought the still unfinished *In the Tower of Sleep* and she had acquired several more canvases since then. She and her assistant and traveling companion, Alfred Jensen, had both studied painting in Paris and kept up a correspondence with Masson.

Late in the fall Masson kept the rendezvous Breton had proposed in Marseilles. He was given a hunting lodge to live in on the estate of the Countess Pastré in the suburb of Montredon. Lily Pastré, heiress to the Noilly Pratt fortune, was a celebrated patroness of the arts in a city that was not lacking in cultural enterprise. At her home some forty refugees found shelter, including Darius and Madeleine Milhaud, Georges Auric, Francis Poulenc, Pablo Casals, Josephine Baker, Christian Bérard, Madeleine Grey, and Rudolph Kundera. Her great interest was in music; dinners in her formal dining room were often followed by concerts. She called her rescue operation "so the mind may live" and she spent generously to shelter as comfortably as possible the extraordinary artists who came her way. Theatrical performances were held on her estate under the directorship of Sylvain Itkine. The high point of the period for her came in the summer of 1942 with an outdoor performance by moonlight of *A Midsummer Night's Dream,* with costumes and décor by Christian Bérard and an orchestra composed of Jewish musicians who could no longer perform in public under Vichy law.

Marseilles in 1941 has been described as having a festive air despite the prevalent anxiety. There was even an air of optimism as members of its refugee arts community continued to create and perform to fill the void of the uncertain waiting period. Under the wary eye of Vichy, the city became an artistic and intellectual cen-

Would-be émigrés at the Villa Air Bel, 1940, photograph by André Gomes.

Below: André Masson, *Ghost in My Room at Montredon (the Room of Napoleon),* 1941, lead pencil on paper, 32 x 43.3 cm; collection Diego and Guite Masson.

Opposite: André Masson, *Marseille,* 1941, wax crayon with penciled color notations, 24.5 x 31.5 cm (inspired by allegorical figure sculptures outside the Musée des Beaux Arts); collection Diego and Guite Masson.

ter, building on its tradition as a cosmopolitan cultural capital for the south of France, with a mixed population that included many Italians, Spaniards, and North Africans. In 1914 Marcel Pagnol had founded a literary magazine titled *Cahiers du Sud;* under the editorship of Jean Ballard it enjoyed a considerable reputation and had published a number of contributions by Surrealist authors. Its offices became a center for refugee writers, with sometimes as many as twenty people sleeping on the floor. The staff also found food for some of the German writers, such as Ernst Erich Noth whose novel *Die Mietskaserne* had been burned in Berlin, since as aliens they could not get food tickets. Given the "surrender on demand" clause of the armistice, the circumstances under which refugees like the Noths lived were fraught with danger. Noth and his family were helped by the Dominicans, who provided them with false papers, and they made it across the Spanish border and thence to Lisbon and New York.

Although it was an hour's tram ride from Montredon to Air Bel, Masson participated in some of the Surrealist activities there. During the winter of 1941 he made three drawings of Breton, remarkable in the lucidity with which he traced the profile of that powerful head, to which he then added the interior components to produce a psychological portrait. He also drew the room in which he worked in the hunting lodge at Montredon, including his own hands in the drawing as a variant on the animated metamorphic furniture that he had been developing in in some of his later 1930s paintings and graphic work.

Settled in for a waiting period of unknown length, the residents of Air Bel found varying distractions to relieve their anxiety. Bénédite was fascinated by the flora the garden offered and counted forty-five varieties of trees and shrubs, while Breton observed its fauna, commenting on the corpses of frogs who died in the act of procreation and on the profusion of praying mantises near the conservatory where he worked. These he liked to capture and set forth on the dining table, an allusion perhaps to the meal that the female mantis made of her mate after copulation. Varian Fry, who had made bird-watching a hobby, was particularly struck by Dr. Thumin's collection of drab and dusty stuffed birds. The old ornithologist escorted them through the collection one evening, exclaiming: "It is the most important in all of Provence; look how alive they are. . . . I found a true artist who made the glass eyes." [16]

While Fry and his cohorts were at the office in the rue Grignan, Victor Serge foraged for reading material in the villa's library where he was delighted to find a first edition of Saint-Simon and where he worked on a new novel, *L'Affaire Toulaev*.

Gathered in the salon in the evenings, they sang old French songs, discussed politics, or listened to Serge and Breton read aloud. The latter also discoursed on Surrealist painting or read from the Surrealist publications he carried in his suitcase or from the witty letters of Duchamp or Péret. Frequently conversations would be cut short by Breton's half-question, half-command: "Alors, on joue?" (Well then, shall we play?) To play, to really play, according to Breton, was a special way of galvanizing the mind to make sorties into the unfamiliar and the adventurous in spirit would usually fall in with his challenge. *Vérité*, a brutally frank form of truth or consequences, was a favorite, but there was also a game of grading famous individuals, started by the Dadas, and one involving moral judgments in answering questions such as "would you open the door if . . . ?" Charades by analogy, Murder, and a game in which a person takes on the identity of an object, as well as exquisite corpses—these were some of the forms of serious play to which Breton invited his friends. Later in New York when anthropologist Claude Lévi-Strauss was asked to participate in these games he said he regarded it as a kind of initiation ritual, a form of group rite.

During the mornings Breton paced the floor of the conservatory, pausing every so often to write a line in his fine delicate hand and customary green ink. It was here that he produced *Fata Morgana,* a long poem in which the force of love undergoes hermetic transmutation and ends as a sun, signifier of hope. To illustrate this new work he enlisted Wifredo Lam, who had joined the swelling ranks of refugees in the early fall. As an enemy alien Helena Lam had been interned in a camp near the Pyrénées. She had managed to get to that camp rather than Drancy near Paris through the help of Picasso, who advised her to see Frau Perls, mother of the New York gallery owner Klaus Perls. Frau Perls agreed to "adopt" her and used her influence to have them both interned near the Spanish border, much more favorably placed than Paris for possible escape if the situation worsened. After the partition of France Helena was released from the camp and was able to meet Wifredo in Marseilles.

Lam knew the Surrealists, but he had been working in a semicubist style much more closely resembling Picasso, who seemed to regard him almost as a protégé. In fact he left his paintings in Picasso's care when he joined the exodus from Paris. The months in close proximity to Air Bel marked a turning point in his work; Helena describes the collaboration with Breton as the opening through which Lam moved to a new realm of conceptualized archetypal images.[17] The day that Breton invited him to be his collaborator, Lam said to her: "Well, I guess I've been baptized now as a Surrealist." The working procedure was for Helena to translate the text into Spanish for her husband as Breton completed each section. He would then select a passage that evoked an image for him and proceed to make a drawing; of the perhaps three dozen drawings that he made, eight were selected for use in the book. The Editions de Sagittaire, whose director Léon Pierre Quint was Jewish, had retreated to Marseilles. They agreed to publish a limited edition, but only five copies were actually printed and the edition was deferred to a "time of peace." *Fata Morgana* appeared first in an English translation by Clark Mills published by New Directions in 1941, and the first French edition was put out by Roger Caillois in Buenos Aires in 1942.

André Gomes and his wife Henriette, formerly the assistant to art dealer Pierre Loeb who had shown Surrealist art since the 1920s, had come to Marseilles after the fall of France without any definite intention of emigrating. Perhaps because Henriette was Jewish they wanted to be in a better position to leave if necessary. In the end they stayed, leaving Marseilles and moving into the hinterland where they participated in Resistance activities. For nearly two years, however, Gomes chronicled with snapshots the residents of Air Bel and their friends as they gathered in the gardens of the villa or met in the old port at their designated café, the Brûleur au Loup. These often-reproduced photographs capture the spirit of solidarity that sustained the group and the humor with which they met the tribulations of cold, hunger, and uncertain fate.

Jacques Hérold with Wifredo and Helena Lam in Marseilles, 1940, photograph by André Gomes.

Wifredo Lam, drawing for *Fata Morgana* by André Breton, 1940–1941, published
in Helena Benitez, *Wifredo Lam Interlude Marseille* (Copenhagen: Edition Blondal,
1993).

"We laughed a lot," Gomes recollected a half-century later. But there was an irony in the clowning. The photograph of Wifredo Lam and Jacques Hérold wearing a single coat was a comment on the bitter cold of the winter of 1941 and the unpreparedness of the refugees for such conditions. And an eloquent although unintended testimony to the toll that life in Marseilles was taking on its throng of transient inhabitants can be seen in the four photographs taken of Helena and Wifredo Lam on the streets of Marseilles at intervals during their stay. The relaxed smiles and light clothing of the early fall were replaced by increasingly tense faces and huddled postures as the months wore on.

By December the shortage of food was making itself seriously felt. Diners at the Villa Air Bel sat in carved high-backed chairs in the formal dining room to partake of stewed carrots, rutabagas, turnip greens in lieu of spinach, sparse rations of bread, and "coffee" made from acorns with no sugar available for sweetening. The building lacked central heat and wood for the fireplace was scarce. Dr. Thumin forbade their collecting scraps of wood from the park around the house. Angèle Levesque, who was living in a shack on the edge of the city while waiting for passage, kept until her death a painting done by a friend that winter showing their street blanketed with snow, an unprecedented occurrence for Marseilles. She also remembers heating bricks in the fire and putting them under their feet in the bus for their frequent trips down to the American consulate and heating them again there for the return trip.[18]

The situation was exacerbated by the increasingly tight hold of the Vichy government. It had been decreed that only those refugees who could prove that they were leaving would be allowed to stay in Marseilles. Since this was nearly impossible to prove until one was on the boat, living there was more and more dangerous, more so than in the surrounding countryside. Antifascists from all over Europe had poured into the city and the police were nervous; there were more controls, search, arrests, and deportations, and the law decreed the surrender on demand of aliens and other suspects. The growing capacity of Vichy for paranoid reaction and breaches of human rights was brought home forcibly to the refugees during the preparation for Pétain's official visit to the city in December. Air Bel was searched, and a drawing with a caption that was viewed as a slur against Pétain was considered sufficient evidence to warrant rounding up the residents without warning and herding them on to a ship, the *Sinaia*, which was anchored in the harbor. There they were held incommunicado, along with hundreds of others, for three days, without knowing the reasons for this abrupt action or having any idea of the fate in store for them. People began to disappear. Julien Cain, former director of the Bibliothèque Nationale, was arrested on February 12, 1941, and sent to Buchenwald. Claude Lévi-Strauss haunted the offices of the steamship lines he knew from his previous trips to South America.

Lam and Hérold sharing a coat, winter 1940–1941, photograph by André Gomes.

Political considerations in Washington were making Fry's work at the Emergency Rescue Committee increasingly difficult. It was made clear in a variety of ways that known Communists were not to be helped by the Committee. Fry's sometimes loose interpretation of this stricture was perhaps responsible for the letter Eleanor Roosevelt wrote to Fry's wife in May 1941: "There is nothing I can do for your husband. The government cannot stand behind what he has done."[19] Or possibly this reproof was prompted by the illegal means to which Fry resorted to try to get people out of the clutches of Vichy when their papers were not in order or they could go nowhere on their German passports. Doubtless there were objections to his use of the Committee's resources to help people who couldn't get U.S. visas go to Mexico, which under the Cárdenas government had a liberal immigration policy. Among those he helped in this way was Victor Serge, whose revolutionary past, although he

Oscar Domínguez and André Breton at the Villa Air Bel, 1940, photograph
by André Gomes.

had become a vociferous anti-Stalinist, made his entry into the United States impossible.

Max Ernst had come to Marseilles in December in real fear that the Gestapo was after him. For a year he had been in and out of internment camps as an enemy alien, first at Largentière, then at Les Milles. Eluard had helped secure his release from Les Milles and at Christmas he returned to work at St.-Martin, but in May he was denounced again and for the next few months he was shifted about from one camp to another, with several escapes and recaptures until finally release papers arrived. After his first internment, Leonora Carrington had fled to Spain, suffered a breakdown, and been committed by her family to a sanatorium in Santander. Ernst continued to work, doing a number of decalcomania paintings that focused directly or obliquely on Leonora, a series in which *Europe after the Rain,* started in 1941 and finished later in New York, became the final episode. However, the "surrender on demand" law made it unsafe for him under the Vichy government, and he also joined the "espère visa" crowd in Marseilles. A historic photograph shows Varian Fry in his office surrounded by the senior Surrealists, Breton, Max Ernst, and Masson, along with Jacqueline Lamba. Thanks to Fry's efforts and to cooperation on the other side of the Atlantic, this cenacle would in a few months be operative far away from the old haunts in the Place Blanche and St.-Germain-des-Prés. The months in Marseilles also provided an opportunity for a reconciliation of sorts between Breton and Ernst, who had broken off because of Breton's proposed boycott of Eluard for his intransigent allegiance to the Third International.

One of Gomes's photographs shows paintings hung in the trees at Air Bel on the occasion of a Sunday sale and auction. They appear to be mostly paintings by Ernst, but curiously there are at least two paintings by Leonora Carrington, her well-known self-portrait of 1938 and her *Portrait of Max Ernst* in which the artist's delicate birdlike head protrudes from a red-feathered shaman's robe. Since Carrington had decamped in a terrible state of mind, it is possible that she left her paintings behind in St.-Martin, even though she had disposed of the house. Ernst must have packed them up along with his own.

Breton had been hoping to mount a Surrealist exhibition in Marseilles. When this plan fell through, he devised another group project, the collective designing of a new deck of Tarot cards. Researching the origin of playing cards in the Marseilles Library, he learned that the derivation was military, the trefoil representing the soldier's country, the diamond arms, etc. He decided to substitute for the traditional

Preparing for auction of artworks in the garden at Air Bel, 1941, Jacques Hérold
helping to hang paintings by Max Ernst and Leonora Carrington; photograph by
André Gomes.

suits four major preoccupations, each with its own symbols: the flame for love, a black star for the dream, a bloody wheel for revolution, and a key for knowledge. In order to eliminate the old hierarchies, he deprived the king and queen of their power, replacing them with genius and siren, while the jack was freed from his subordinate rank and became a wiseman. Each of these was given the identity of a historic or literary personage. The joker, naturally, was Ubu, as his creator Jarry had drawn him. The other cards were produced as follows: Hegel and Helene Smith by Brauner, Paracelsus by Breton, Pancho Villa by Ernst, Sade and Lamiel by Hérold, Novalis and Baudelaire by Masson, and the "dream figures" Freud, Alice, and Lautréamont divided between Domínguez and Lam. It was their intention that the deck, by retaining its old black and red colors, be used for all the existing card games, but that it also inspire new variations through associations provoked by the themes and characters. This talisman deck, known as the *Jeu de Marseille,* memorializes that tense and uncertain interval during which the Surrealist artists, poised in a void, redid the playing cards, symbols of the ultimate powers of fate.

A more spontaneous and unknown talisman testifying to the shared concerns of the group is a small book made for Helena Lam. On the day of her birthday she decided to stay alone and not join the group at Air Bel. There was nothing to send her as a present, so those assembled each drew or wrote on a page or two in a little notebook. First a poem to Helena by Breton, then drawings and paintings by Domínguez, Brauner, Hérold, Jacqueline Lamba and her sister, Huguette, and finally a drawing by the four-year-old Aube with her words written down by Breton. The booklet is scarcely larger than a file card and the paper is poor-quality wartime paper, but it looms large as a gesture of solidarity and concern toward this young woman, not a Surrealist but a chemist by training, a German alien and thus doubly endangered. Amid the fears, uncertainties, and privations of that awful winter, the refugees used their art—or their poetry or music—almost in the spirit of an incantation, as protective actions that could ward off disaster and despair.

Masson had not at first been certain that he wanted to leave France, but a combination of factors pushed him toward a decision. When he heard on the radio the announcement of the Vichy government's racial laws, he literally vomited, he later told an interviewer, and declared to Rose who was Jewish that they must leave as soon as possible. "I couldn't participate in the Resistance. I was already suspect. Anyway, I had no taste for war. It isn't lacking courage to preserve life and values."

André Masson, *Novalis,* maquette for the *Jeu de Marseille,* 1941, ink and
watercolor on paper, 26.8 x 21 cm; collection Diego Masson.

Jeu de Marseille, maquettes by Victor Brauner, Oscar Domíniguez, Max Ernst, Jacques Hérold, Wifredo Lam, Jacqueline Lamba, and André Masson, 1940, published in *VVV,* 1943; private collection, Paris.

Evidently he also spent a considerable amount of time drinking in cafés, since he lacked space in which to carry on his work. And as he drank he became vociferous in his antagonism to the Vichy government. Breton cautioned him that he would get them all in trouble and his family came to agree that it would be safer to get him out of the country, so they too became clients of the Emergency Rescue Committee. Mrs. Saidie May sent enough money to the Committee in New York to pay for the Masson family's passage, and on February 8, 1941, he wrote telling her that he had received his American visa and would shortly have his exit visa.[20]

Passage was finally secured for the Breton family, Victor Serge, and the Lams on the *Capitaine Paul-LeMerle,* a ship departing for Martinique on March 25. According to Claude Lévi-Strauss who was also on board, the departure resembled that of a convict ship. The quayside was cordoned off and "helmeted gardes-mobiles, with automatic pistols at the ready, severed all contact between the passengers and the relatives or friends who had come to see them off. Good-byes were cut short by blows or a curse." Three-hundred and fifty passengers were crammed onto a ship that had cabin space for seven. The dark, unventilated hold was turned into an improvised dormitory with straw pallets on a scaffolding constructed by the ship's carpenter. On the deck were communal sanitary facilities, again crudely improvised and soon nauseatingly rank. Lévi-Strauss, thanks to his previous crossings to Brazil which had made him known to officials of the shipping company, was one of the seven who shared the two cabins. His description of the thirty-day crossing in *Tristes Tropiques* includes observations on several of his noteworthy traveling companions: "Breton, by no means at ease in such a situation, would amble up and down the rare empty spaces on deck, looking like a blue bear in his velvety jacket. We were to become firm friends in the course of an exchange of letters which we kept up throughout the interminable journey; their subject was the relation between esthetic beauty and absolute originality."[21] It's a wonderful image even if only partly true, the founder of structural anthropology and the *chef d'école* of one of the century's most influential artistic and literary movements, amid the foul odors and horrendous overcrowding, fleeing horrors as yet unknown toward an uncertain destiny, engaged in a dialogue that wholly transcended their situation—a situation that perhaps neither was prepared to verbally evaluate.

The Massons left a week later on the *Carimare* for the same destination. John Rewald, who was also on that ship, remembered the family's problems: Rose sick, the two boys tearing all over the ship, and the father maintaining a detached, withdrawn attitude. When they arrived in Martinique, they found the Bretons in an internment camp near Fort-de-France. Regarding the refugees as riffraff, a despotic local police in steel helmets and shorts appeared to be treating them as scapegoats for the fall of France. Jacqueline Lamba recalled that although this treatment came as a shock after the arduous voyage, the experience was hardly traumatic. The camp or *lazaret* was by the sea in a beautiful setting, and the benign climate was a relief after the severities of the Marseilles winter. Breton's account of Martinique, published in *Pour la Victoire* in New York in February 1942, details the corruption and poverty and the murder of anyone who attempted reform in the place the ship's captain had called "the shame of France." The former leper colony where they were interned was worse than the ship in terms of adequate food, light, and sleeping quarters. The Jews among the refugees suffered particularly insulting treatment from the guards. As comfort, however, there were the fragrances of the trees and a small beach where they were allowed to bathe. Breton appealed to the civil governor, pointing out that he had served in the French army medical corps until the demobilization, but he and his family were under secret police surveillance for the duration of their stay.

Masson and Breton collaborated on a little book, *Martinique, charmeuse de serpents,* completed after their arrival in the United States but not published until 1947. They chose a title from a painting by Henri Rousseau because it suggests the mysteries of the tropics as envisioned in the European imagination and evokes a territory somewhere between memory and dream. Breton chose to write the text in two opposing voices, one lyrical, the other confined to descriptive information. In this way he hoped to convey their own divided perceptions, enraptured on the one hand, hurt and indignant on the other. Woven into the poetic portion of the text was the sensation that both Frenchmen experienced of having known the place before, and their awe before its savage nature—the trees surpassing cathedrals, the latent force of the volcano, the precipices and vegetal energy. Seeing the women of Martinique, Breton recalled Baudelaire's line "even when she walks she dances," and Masson drew the landscape as the body of a woman. The following year in Connecticut he embodied the spirit of the place in the rich colors and voluptuously undulating forms of *Antilles.* Being in the tropics inspired an unaccustomed lyricism in Masson, and his ink-dipped brush ran fluently over the paper seeking the all-over rhythms of the luxuriant foliage. For the book he drew metamorphoses in which the fingers on human hands appear to be transforming themselves into an entire jungle. One drawing is particularly specific about the locale, showing the volcano Pele and a rock crystal island described in Breton's text.

Their happiest moment in Martinique came when Breton discovered the writing of the poet Aimé Césaire and arranged for the first of many meetings with "le grand poète noir." Later in New York Breton was instrumental in bringing about the publication of his work and wrote an essay on him for the review *Tropiques.*[22]

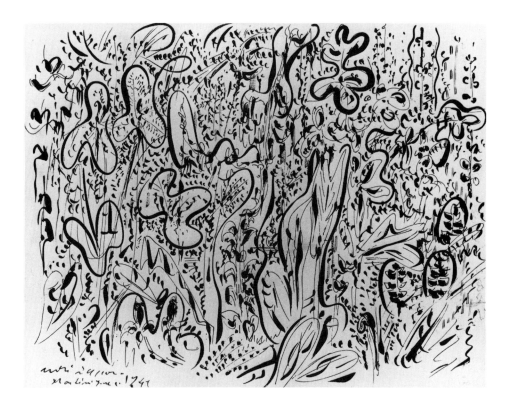

At the end of May passage became available on a ship bound for New York, and a telegram sent to the Seligmanns announced the Bretons' imminent arrival. There was one more delay, however, in the Dominican Republic, where the dictator Trujillo was attempting to detain doctors, dentists, and others whose services were needed. From there Breton wrote to Seligmann, thanking him for the efforts made on his behalf and expressing relief that the journey was accomplished. "There will be no backward glances," he promised, asserting that "all thought will be for our collective future task. I am strong in the knowledge," he wrote, "that historically the word is with us alone; circumstances have justified the positions of opposition which we took; I believe that ours asks only to be affirmed, made more precise and abundantly illustrated afresh." [23] He also explained that the authorities in Ciudad Trujillo had impounded his correspondence so he had no other addresses, and he asked Seligmann to let Calas, Onslow Ford, and the Mattas know of their prospective reunion.

Stanley William Hayter remembered meeting the ship carrying the Bretons and claimed that he took Breton for a pastis that very day at New York's only outdoor café, the sidewalk terrace of the Brevoort on lower Fifth Avenue. Tanguy and Kay

Opposite: André Masson, page from *Martinique, charmeuse de serpents,* 1941; text by André Breton, illustrations by Masson.

Above: André Masson, *Martinique,* 1941, ink on paper, 48 x 63 cm; collection Diego and Guite Masson.

Sage had found an apartment for them on Eleventh Street, a small top-floor walk-up. Onslow Ford had helped to find and hang on the walls paintings by Matta, Magritte, De Chirico, Tanguy, and his own *Propaganda for Love* so that Breton would feel himself in familiar surroundings. On June 24, Jacqueline Breton sent a letter to Varian Fry in Marseilles, thanking him for their deliverance. "America is truly the Christmas tree of the world," she wrote.[24] Forty-five years later she still described Fry as a "magnificent man—he thought only of others, never of the danger he himself was in."[25]

The arrival of the Masson family in New York was less auspicious. There was no one to meet them, their resources were meager, and they did not know in what direction to move. To make matters worse, a customs inspector took offense at one of his drawings in which a landscape with a cave was also clearly the body of a woman with a small figure entering the cavity of her vagina. A debate ensued as Masson tried in French to explain the mythological content. Finally the box of drawings was impounded. "You have no mythology," he told the customs officials, a lament that was to be a refrain for both the émigrés and American artists during the 1940s. Later he asked Archibald MacLeish to intercede on behalf of the drawings, but evidently several were missing when the carrying case was returned to him. The Massons stayed in the Hotel van Rensselaer on East Eleventh Street right after their arrival, and from there he wrote to his patron in Baltimore, Saidie May, saying: "New York pleases me, but it's devouring me. I hope to live in the country." In thanking her for her help he added, "I think I would be dead if I had stayed there."[26]

A few weeks later, on June 22, he wrote her again, this time from Washington, Connecticut, where they had rented a house for three months and where, he said, he was already getting back to work. And a fruitful summer of work it was. For a year he and his family had been on the move, from Normandy to the Auvergne to Marseilles, thence to Martinique and finally, with a stopover in Puerto Rico, to New York. He had never stopped drawing, but painting on the move was more problematic. When he started again it was as if a pent-up force had been released, and he entered on a richly productive period and a new stylistic and thematic phase of his art. This phase related closely to the visible nature around him and to regenerative processes within the earth. His escape, again, from death, as well as the knowledge that he had brought his family to safety, must have impelled him toward an art of affirmation that strongly contrasted with the violent images from the 1930s.

In August he wrote to Alfred Jensen, "For me the observation of nature remains essential," and to Mrs. May he said, "Painting for me remains dependent on nature, on universal forces."[27] And he described with delight the delicate, waxlike Indian peacepipe plant that grew in the shady recesses of the surrounding woodlands. As he was later to say, there in New England, in what seemed like wild country in its abundance of flora and fauna, he turned inward on himself and arrived at what he called telluric painting. Isolated by a language barrier he never broke, although his sons went to the local school and became fluent in English, he seems to have absorbed himself in contemplation of his natural surroundings. Instead of returning to New York in the fall as originally intended, the Massons stayed for a time with Eugene and Marie Jolas at Lake Waramaug and then rented a converted barn in nearby New Preston for the winter.

Meanwhile in Fry's Marseilles office a letter had been received from Alfred Barr stating that Max Ernst was "in danger because he is a German citizen who refused to return to Germany after the Nazi regime came to power. His active dislike of all totalitarian forms of government is well known and he has made no secret of it . . . his wife is Jewish." Although Max had been divorced from his first wife, Lou Straus, since the early 1920s and had since been married and divorced again, Jimmy Ernst, who had found a job as a mail clerk at the Museum of Modern Art, had developed this stratagem for getting his mother out of Europe. When Fry met with them in his office, he insisted, evidently on specific instructions from Eleanor Roosevelt, that she could not get by with posing as Ernst's wife, as it would jeopardize not only her departure but his entire operation. When the visa was denied by the American vice-consul, Ernst offered to remarry her on the spot, but Lou Straus was too proud and too bitter to accept her former husband's offer. Although Fry warned her that she would not easily get another visa and that she was in mounting danger, she insisted on waiting for her own papers.[28]

That same winter of 1941 Peggy Guggenheim was in Grenoble arranging for the exhibiting and storing of her collection. It began to dawn on her that the Guggenheim name was no protection against the exterminating arm of Hitler and she made plans for repatriation. Arriving in Marseilles, she was welcomed at Air Bel by Brauner and Max Ernst, Breton having already departed, and she purchased a number of Ernst's paintings. He invited her and Varian Fry to have dinner with him in the Old Port on the evening of his fiftieth birthday and an affair began, the immediate result of which was that Ernst replaced Brauner as the companion Guggenheim proposed to bring with her to the United States. They agreed to rendezvous in Lisbon where the Guggenheim family was to send a plane to collect Peggy.

Lisbon was also for Ernst the site of a devastating encounter with Leonora Carrington, who had escaped from the mental institution in which her family had placed her and taken refuge in the Mexican consulate. There she was taken under the protection of diplomat Renato Leduc who married her to help her leave Europe. The entourage that departed in July from Lisbon in a Pan Am Boeing B13 clipper included not only Peggy Guggenheim and Ernst but her children, Pegeen and Sinbad, her former husband, Laurence Vail, his former wife, novelist Kay Boyle, and Boyle's four children.

Gordon and Jacqueline Onslow Ford accompanied Jimmy Ernst to the Marine Air Terminal to meet the plane, but Max was swept off immediately to Ellis Island by the immigration authorities who failed to understand why he should have a German passport after living in France for twenty years. What was to be the last in Ernst's series of internments was of short duration. It is an often-told story, how Jimmy, armed with a letter from Nelson Rockefeller, went to Ellis Island to confront the authorities, only to be told that if he could support his father on his twenty-five-dollar weekly salary, they would let him take Max away with him. Ernst's was the only one of the Surrealist arrivals to be noted by the press.

In July Kurt Seligmann wrote to a former girlfriend in England, Ivy Langdon, telling her of the arrival in New York of Max Raphael, a Marxist writer on aesthetics. At Ivy's urging Seligmann had made great efforts to raise money from prominent Jewish leaders to pay for Raphael's passage and to secure his release from the detention camp where he was being held pending deportation. "His health is satisfactory," Seligmann wrote. "No traces of concentration camp life . . . so much for the good news; I think it is plenty. Now the medium news: one by one all our friends from Paris arrive here. To give you some of their names: there are Ivan Goll, André Breton, Max Ernst (actually on Ellis Island), Jacques Lipchitz, Marc Chagall, André Masson, Louis Buñuel, Yves Tanguy and many others whom you might not know as you had left Paris sometime ago. I call this news medium because I do not know how all these *chers collègues* will behave and if their attitude towards one another will be pleasanter than when they were in Paris. There is some hope that events may have taught them a lesson, but for my part I doubt it, and I think that the same atmosphere of intrigue and pushy-pushy will soon reign in the American capital. You see that I am as sceptical as I was before." [29]

Similar words of attraction/repulsion are a recurrent motif in the letters and reminiscences of the Surrealists. The notion of the group, with Breton at its center, was in part what allowed them to plunge as deeply as they did into unfamiliar waters, yet the party line was a source of frustration and irritation and they chafed against it, and in the end most argued with Breton and were expelled or simply drifted away, but indelibly marked. For the stronger artists, Breton's seal of approval was not what defined them artistically. Along with Masson they would for the most part have said, "I was born a surrealist." Surrealism ultimately was a state of mind—or a state of spirit—not something to be applied or withdrawn at the whim of one individual.

In August 1941, Varian Fry was arrested and expelled by the Vichy authorities for "being pro-Jewish and anti-Nazi and for having sent help to a known Communist in a camp in Morocco." [30] The year of work he had done in Marseilles not only saved the lives of well over a thousand refugees, but also brought to the United States many remarkable individuals whose presence changed American culture, sometimes in totally unforeseen ways. This catalytic force made itself felt particularly where the Europeans were present in number, as part of groups that provided a support structure and even generated an orbit into which Americans were drawn. Such was certainly the case in the instance of the Surrealist group, augmented as it was through Fry's efforts by the presence of its three most noted senior members, Breton, Ernst, and Masson. In no way can Fry be blamed for the other side of the story—for the many thousands who were not rescued, for the failure of the U.S. government to launch a massive campaign to save those awaiting deportation at Drancy and elsewhere, for the obstructionism of the State Department in the matter of granting visas. He acted as an individual to do the utmost he was capable of doing in the face of inertia, suspicion, and bureaucratic obfuscation. That fall in New York he received a letter from Victor Brauner which began: "It is raining at Air Bel and we are here mourning your departure." [31]

Victor Brauner at Villa Air Bel, 1941, photograph by André Gomes.

Marcel Duchamp and Jean Arp playing chess in Sanary, 1942, photographs by
André Gomes.

After most of the Air Bel group had departed, Henriette and André Gomes went to stay in nearby Sanary where Duchamp, having made the decision to try to emigrate, was waiting in the hope that his friends in the United States could provide travel funds and secure a visa for him. Arp was also there, his presence recorded by Gomes's camera as he played chess with Duchamp. Arp and his wife, Sophie Tauber, decided not to leave for the United States even though the way had been prepared for them, and they withdrew to Switzerland where they stayed during the war years.

Gomes was still there photographing when one of the last ships pulled out in March 1942, with Marcel Duchamp poised on its prow, arms extended in a farewell wave. Perhaps the most poignant of all his photographs is the one of the figures on the quay to whom Duchamp was waving, Victor Brauner and Jacques Hérold, standing in front of the iron bars of the closed gate to the free world. Some say that these two were unable to get visas because the small quota for Romanians had been used up, but still they might have qualified for non-quota Roosevelt visas if there had been someone with enough money and the right connections working for them across the Atlantic. Also thwarted in the matter of visas was Rose Masson, who was overcome with anxiety about the possible fate of her mother and her sister Sylvia as Jews in Vichy France. The Massons appealed for help in a variety of places, but the process was slow and it became extremely difficult to get anyone out of France after the American entry into the war at the end of 1941. Then it was too late altogether. When American troops landed in North Africa in November 1942, the Germans, fearing a strike from the south, moved troops into the *Zone Libre* and occupied Marseilles, setting fire to the Old Port. The refugees who were not rounded up filtered off into rural areas, finding places where they could live as inconspicuously as possible, some in hiding, some participating in Resistance activities, some protected by the villagers, some denounced, some, such as the painter Otto Freundlich or the theater director Itkine, turned over to the Nazis by the local French authorities and sent to their death.

Brauner and Hérold in front of closed gate, Marcel Duchamp on prow of ship,
1942, photograph by André Gomes.

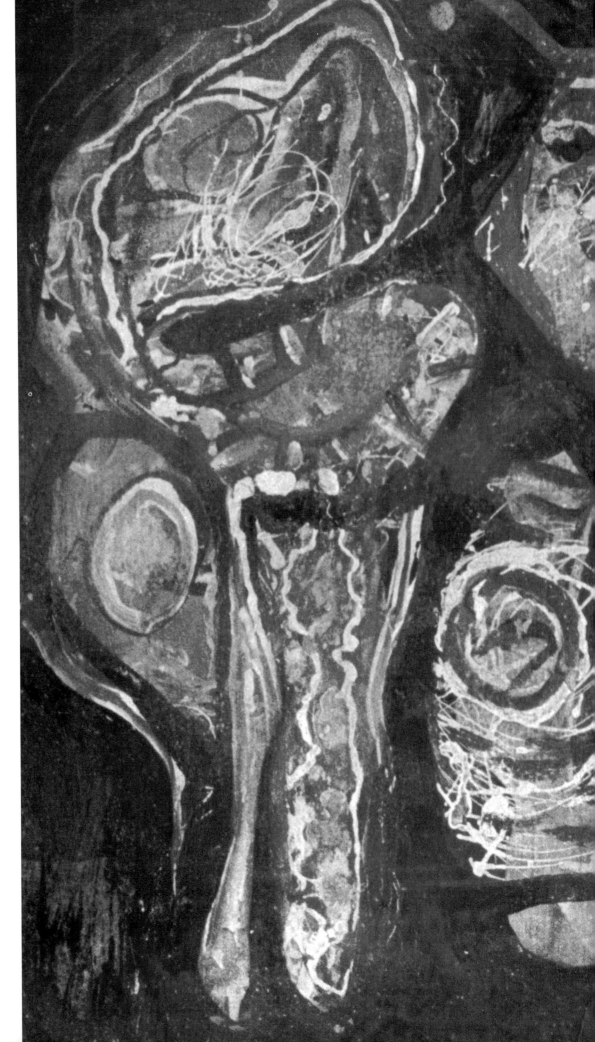

⁵ New York, 1941:

In a

Land

without

Myth

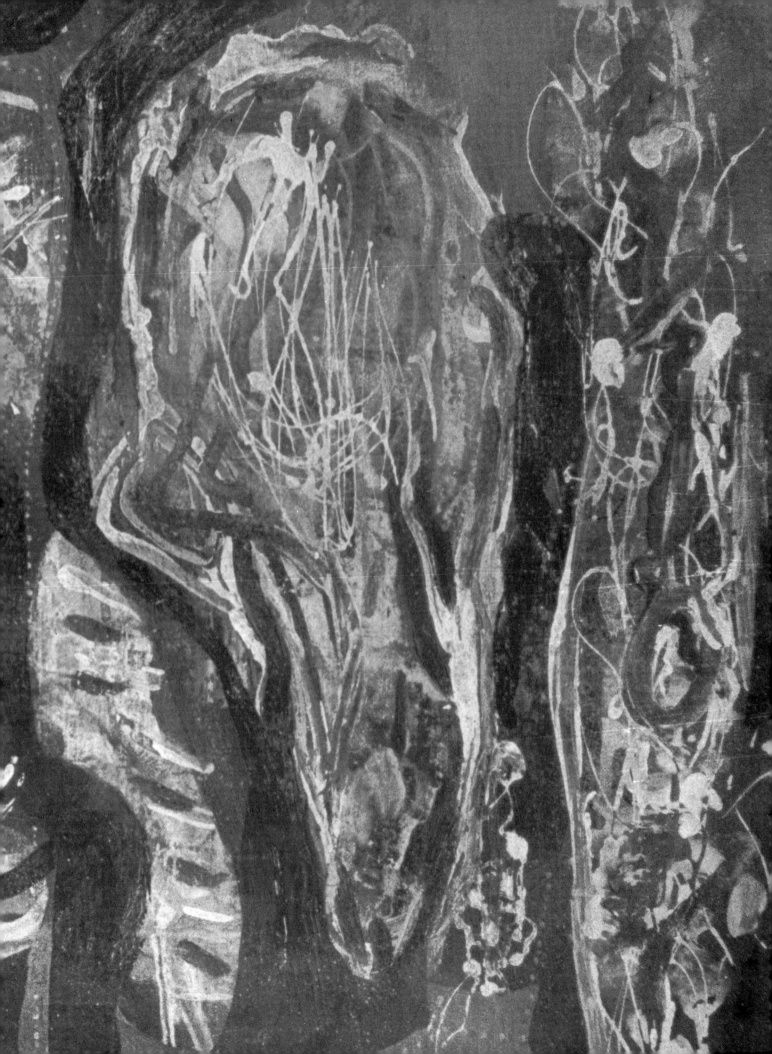

"I ask myself, where am I now? In a place that denies myths and sees the world in flat ordinary colors . . . without exaltation, ecstasy or any of the enlightened visionary elements."[1] So mused Paris-born Anaïs Nin in her diary in the summer of 1940 as she attempted to settle into a new life as a refugee in Greenwich Village. Her words evoke the sense of dislocation experienced by many of the artist-refugees deprived of the reminders of shared myths and symbols of historical continuity woven into the fabric of European cities. The environment into which they had been displaced lacked precisely that which gave resonance to the places from which they had come. Those sculptural and architectural icons that fulfilled the need for unifying symbols, the streets, buildings, and squares resonant with the ever-present past, had few counterparts in the urban environments of the new world. The desire for a new unifying myth accompanied by meaningful visual symbols was to be a leitmotif during the next few years for the deracinated Europeans, as well as for some of the younger American artists who had outgrown the styles and subjects of the 1930s. What legends or symbols held validity for the contemporary world at war? what bridged the gap between the old world and the new? between Mediterranean civilization and the pre-Columbian Western Hemisphere? The questions were asked by American artists of the generation that came of age in the 1930s, Rothko and Gottlieb, Baziotes and Newman, just as they were asked by veterans like André Breton who would himself propose a new myth in the first issue of the review he launched in New York in 1942, *VVV.*

The Americans made some attempt to recycle Greek myths and titled their works *Pasiphaë, Persephone,* or *Tiresias,* and some of the Surrealists dug into the writings of the nineteenth-century occultist Eliphas Lévy, or the sixteenth-century mystic Paracelsus. The Jungian concepts of the collective unconscious and the trans-cultural validity of symbols were beginning to gain currency. A French volume of Jung's collected writings had been published in 1939 and Jolande Jacobi's English translation of many of these writings appeared in the United States soon after. By the later 1940s, when the first volumes of the Bollingen edition of his complete works appeared, Jung was a familiar name in the downtown studios. Also germane to the rising concern with myth and the occult was the desire for an element of ambiguity, an avoidance of overt statement in favor of the hidden or latent symbol emerging through the automatist process or submerged beneath the surface of abstract form. U.S. critics of a Marxist orientation, however, preferred to deal with the visible epidermis and tended to ignore the question of symbolic content or the allusions to myth. Such a circumscribed view was to lead to considerable confusion for the next generation of artists and critics, who were raised on the formalist dicta of critics such as Clement Greenberg or who looked at abstract expressionism through the restrictive lens of Harold Rosenberg's notion of action painting.

The beachhead established by the émigrés of 1939 and 1940 had fanned outward and its numbers had been enlarged by 1941, so that even before the last arrivals from Marseilles Surrealism was enjoying an increasing visibility in Manhattan. Gallery exhibitions, magazine articles, reviews in the daily and art press, and the Museum of Modern Art's Dalí and Miró exhibitions cumulatively drew attention to Surrealism's presence. In the spring of 1940 a periodical was launched that was to involve the Surrealists' participation and publish their work. *View,* whose first two issues appeared as scarcely more than broadsides in 1940, was the brainchild of southern-born poet Charles Henri Ford. Ford lived with Pavel Tchelitchew, a painter whose work comes more under the heading of magic realism than surrealism but whom Ford sought to identify more closely with the Surrealist group.

In a letter to Kurt Seligmann dated May 27, 1940, Ford discussed the prospective launching of the new "poetry paper" and told him that his name was being printed among the sponsors on the announcement. According to Ford, Seligmann was one of his principal sources of help and encouragement in this undertaking; due to his participation the review came to include a number of short pieces on magic and the occult, which were a Seligmann specialty. Surrealists Matta, Tanguy, and Nicolas Calas are also listed on the *View* letterhead, along with such literary figures as Pablo Neruda, Thomas Merton, Wallace Stevens, and William Carlos Williams.

Calas was a poet of Greek origin who had lived in Paris since 1934 and had been welcomed as a bright young protégé by Breton. As a second-generation Surrealist he had been one of those, along with Mabille, Matta, Brauner, and Brunius, who tried to broaden its scope. Soon after his arrival in New York in early 1940 he received a visit from James Laughlin, publisher and general editor of New Directions books, with a proposal that he edit a Surrealist anthology for the 1940 New Directions annual. He invited Calas to stay at his home in Norfolk, Connecticut, during the summer while working on the anthology.

At least a portion of what Calas assembled, his "Surrealist Dictionary" and his introduction to Surrealism in the form of an interview, offered a helpful clarification of the movement's basic premises. He then launched into his own "Towards a Third Surrealist Manifesto," an unfortunately garbled polemic that can only have baffled the reader and that Breton later severely criticized. Calas's selections of poems and prose excerpts, all appearing in English translation for the first time, are from the work of pre-Surrealists such as Rimbaud and Apollinaire as well as from the full range of Surrealist writers and some painters as well. For some reason, perhaps as a form of disavowal, Laughlin decided to end the anthology with essays by two out-spoken critics of Surrealism, Herbert Muller and Kenneth Burke. Literary Surrealism was thus launched in the United States in a somewhat ambivalent fashion, but at least there was a source of information on the litany and the cast of characters for anyone who might want to be enlightened. Since Laughlin later told Calas it was the worst disaster of his publishing career, apparently not many readers took the opportunity to be introduced to the movement that was even then descending on New York.

Charles Henri Ford gave a welcoming party for Calas and invited him to con-tribute to *View.* His first appearance in that publication was in the form of a letter in which he threw down the gauntlet to *Partisan Review* and its art critic, Clement Greenberg.[2] He accused the latter of initiating a Jesuit form of attack against Surreal-ism and pointed out several examples of Greenberg's ignorance, although it is clear that Calas knew him well enough to have been in his home and to have heard conver-sations between him and Kurt Seligmann. Greenberg reportedly responded with fist-icuffs when they next met as well as publishing a scathing reply. Given Greenberg's later role in establishing abstract expressionism and discrediting Surrealism, this early publicly declared feud may have been a seminal event.

The New School for Social Research had established in 1936 a graduate faculty in the social sciences made up largely of German scholars fleeing the Nazis, and in 1940 it became host to the Ecole Libre des Hautes Etudes, a faculty made up of French university professors in exile. It provided a particularly hospitable center for refugees representing a broad spectrum of cultural endeavors; the theater of Erwin Piscator, the films of Maya Deren, the music of Edgar Varèse were all presented at the New School, along with lectures and courses offered by refugees in an amazing variety of subjects. In addition to an exhibition program that in 1940 had presented the graphic work of Kurt Seligmann and exhibitions of Matta and Esteban Frances, and introduced the future Surrealist Enrico Donati, the New School was responsible in 1941 for two catalytic activities that brought together the European Surrealists and some of the younger American artists.

One of these was the reopening in the fall of 1940 of the print workshop Atelier 17 that Stanley William Hayter had previously operated at 17 rue Campagne Pre-mière in Paris. Thanks to the cooperation of the Maltese maintenance staff it ran until the small hours of the morning in the New School premises, and artists began making a habit of dropping in to work or talk. Hayter had learned printmaking originally from a Polish master of the burin, Joseph Hecht, but by the early 1930s he had started to develop some of the medium's automatist possibilities, rubbing over engraved lines with coarse carborundum or using a burnisher to blur figure-ground distinctions. Even then he was alert to the possibilities inherent in combining various methods of working the plate in order to achieve the chance results and paradoxical effects sought by the Surrealists. He started exhibiting with the latter in the early 1930s and was one of the organizers of the London exhibition in 1936.

He described his operation at the New School as follows: "My notion of a workshop is like a far-out research department; we are not there to produce editions. The fundamental thing that is useful in a workshop is that the thinking is done in the medium itself. You find what you want during the operation, by means of the operation. If you don't finish with more than you had in the beginning, I consider it a waste of time."[3] The "operation" for Hayter meant a constant expansion of the boundaries of printmaking through technical experimentation. Engraving was combined with soft-ground etching and drypoint; allover textures were created by pressing loose-weave fabrics, silk stockings, or crumpled paper into the soft-ground; leaves, grasses, and other materials were incorporated in the same way; even varying the pressure used in wiping the ink from the plate became an automatist gambit.

Hayter remembered his association with the New School as particularly fruitful due to the presence on the faculty of Max Wertheimer, who was lecturing on the

Stanley William Hayter, untitled drawing, c. 1942, present whereabouts unknown.

psychology of perception, and Ernst Kris, who was teaching a course entitled "Problems in the Social Psychology of Art." Questions that arose from the conditions of printmaking, in which the artist had to deal with mirror images, made Hayter particularly responsive to Wertheimer's suggestions for experiments in visual perception. They exchanged ideas and even lectured to each other's classes, and the dialogue continued with Rudolf Arnheim, a student of Wertheimer, when he began teaching at the New School. It is possible that discussions of such subjects as reversals of positive and negative shapes and visual field scanning contributed to the changing notion of the canvas as an allover surface to be activated and to the breakdown of traditional concepts of positive/negative polarity that would become central to New York School painting.

Not only was the exchange with fellow faculty members stimulating, but Hayter began to attract a rather unique "gang," as he called it, of co-workers. (He avoided the term student during a lifetime of teaching.) Tanguy, Ernst, Chagall, Lipchitz, and Masson did prints there, while Baziotes, Jimmy Ernst, and Motherwell each spent time experimenting with burin lines and soft-ground etching and that combination of techniques known as intaglio. Calder made his *Big I* print in the latter medium, and Pollock worked on at least seven plates there in the winter of 1944–1945. Ruben Kadish worked there in 1944 and Adolph Gottlieb in 1945, as did Miró in 1947 when he was in New York to work on a commission. Matta added his lively presence from time to time and produced what he called his New School series—a suite of erotic etchings in a fine delicate line. Masson did eighteen prints at Atelier 17 during his years in the United States, starting late in 1941 with *Emblème,* an original print produced for inclusion in the deluxe copies of his *Mythology of Being* which Wittenborn published in early 1942. The central image—or the emblem—is a skull with additional emblems set within it, defined by the contrasting soft-ground tonalities. The ideas developed at Atelier 17 were to carry over into Masson's postwar graphic work and may even have played a role in the changing structure of Masson's painting, which in 1942 was to consist more and more of a dark ground over which color moved in a linear flow.

"Everyone at the studio was on his own," Jacob Kainen recollected. "Hayter would tell them to ruin the plate. He urged them to start without sketches, take proofs, re-etch, add drypoint, do everything. The idea was to make the artist lose his fear of the plate and also to make it an intuitive process. I think it had a lot to do with the development of the automatic point of view."[4] Anaïs Nin includes a description of this workshop in her journal:

The place was enticing to me, with piles of paper, inks, the presses, the vats with acid, the copper being worked upon. The miraculous lines appearing from the presses, the colored inks, the sharpened burins. The group working with him, absorbed, intent, bent over under strong naked bulbs. He always moved about between the students, cyclonic, making Joycean puns, a caricature, a joke. He was always in motion. I wondered how he had ever spent hours bent over copper plates, delicate, demanding, exacting work. His lines were like projectiles thrown in space, sometimes tangled like antennae caught in a windstorm . . . to me he was a wire sculpture, a man of nerves.[5]

Atelier 17 was to have far-reaching effects on American printmaking, both in expanding the number of practitioners and in strengthening its status as a medium for direct creative expression. For the next few decades there was scarcely an American printmaker who did not come from Atelier 17 or who hadn't at least studied with one of Hayter's alumni. Even when the artists who worked there did not produce much in the way of finished prints, as was the case with Motherwell, Baziotes, and Rothko, Hayter felt that out of the experiments

all kinds of things resulted that were applied in painting and sculpture. A lot evolved. We had an experimental approach and created an environment where things could happen. We were not teaching people to carry out the operations of printmaking. This is an example of what we did: a drip can hung on a compound pendulum. It was an ordinary can with the top and bottom cut out and a cone inserted that was filled with guck, a kind of bitumen. It swung in a discontinuous cyclical motion and the stuff dripped in some very odd patterns. It was a toy to play with, used and seen by many.[6]

Thinking back on that time in his Paris studio in 1985, Hayter said:

Possibly more important than the prints we did was the talk. The artists were living in very difficult circumstances and had no place to get together. There was a little room at the Jumble Shop tearoom [referred to by the émigrés as *le Jeumble*] on MacDougal Street where we used to meet to talk on Fridays. This was the forerunner of the Artists Club. Actually the New York School really came together at Atelier 17.[7]

The second of the catalytic events held under New School auspices was a series of four lectures given in January and February of 1941 by Gordon Onslow Ford. Since Onslow Ford's official invitation to visit the United States and his consequent leave from the Royal Navy had been based on the premise that he was a worthy representative of that culture the free world must fight to save, the time came when it was incumbent on him to fulfill this mission, and a series of lectures on Surrealism was duly scheduled. The flyer put out by the New School read: "Surrealist Painting: an adventure into Human Consciousness; 4 sessions, alternate Wednesdays. 8:20 to 10 p.m. $4. Far more than other modern artists, the Surrealists have adventured in tapping the unconscious psychic world. The aim of these lectures is to follow their work as a psychological barometer registering the desire and impulses of the community." [8]

Not yet thirty years old and lacking in lecturing experience, Onslow Ford decided to depend heavily on the visual material and simply give a personal interpretation of the paintings as he went along. To this end he spent most of the lecture fee on having Francis Lee make slides, and he enlisted the help of Howard Putzel to hang concurrent exhibitions of Surrealist works in an adjacent room at the New School. Putzel was a man of adventurous and discerning taste who had advised Peggy Guggenheim during her last art-buying spree in Paris. They were able to borrow works

from the Museum of Modern Art and the Rockefeller collection without difficulty since Surrealist works were little valued at the time. A few, such as Max Ernst's *Tottering Woman,* had been purchased from Onslow Ford by the Museum.

The first of these small exhibitions opened on January 22 and was devoted to Giorgio De Chirico, "child of dreams," as Onslow Ford described him, and paterfamilias of the Surrealist movement. It consisted of ten of his works, including *The Melancholy of Departure, Portrait of the Artist,* and *The Jewish Angel.* There followed on February 5 a display of ten paintings by Max Ernst and six by Miró. The exhibition for the February 19 lecture featured Magritte—"the poetry of the object"—and Tanguy—"the internal landscape"—with *The Lost Bells, Out of the Blue,* and *Second Thoughts* by the latter. The theme of the fourth exhibition, hung for the March 5 lecture, was "adventures in Surrealist painting during the last four years." This included works by Delvaux, Brauner, Paalen, Seligmann, Matta, Onslow Ford, Jimmy Ernst, and Esteban Frances. A garbage pail marked "Dalí" stood by the door to emphasize the rejection of the outrageous Spaniard by the movement with which he was so completely identified in the public eye. At the last show sheets of pink paper were hung on the wall and the public was invited to draw on them "in the split second after a few minutes of complete mental relaxation," following which they were folded over for the next person's contribution to produce an ad hoc "exquisite corpse."

Apprehensive about his lack of lecturing experience, Onslow Ford wrote out pages of longhand notes for the lectures in advance and even tried them out at Frederick Kiesler's nearby apartment beforehand. The following account is based on the surviving notes, although the artist says that he spoke spontaneously about each painting as it was shown rather than depending on his prepared text. One can only assume that this commentary was similar to that in the prepared notes.

As for the audience at the talks, estimates of attendance and reports of the identities of the attendees vary wildly depending on the eyewitness. There are a few

Above: Matta, *Red Hat Green Hat: Green Hat Lecturing at the New School, Red Hat in the Audience,* c. 1960, crayon and pencil on paper, 8 x 11½ inches; private collection.

Opposite: Jimmy Ernst, *Portrait* (said to be a portrait of Max Ernst), c. 1941, oil, 20 x 28 inches; estate of the artist.

persons one can place with certainty in the audience. One is Matta, who in the mid-1950s made a book of drawings illustrating the story of his friendship with Onslow Ford, depicting one of them as "red hat" and the other as "green hat." One drawing shows "green hat" lecturing with "red hat" in the audience. William Baziotes heard the lectures and reported on them enthusiastically to Gerome Kamrowski, who saw the exhibitions but did not hear the talks. Susanna Wilson and her husband David Hare went, as did Tanguy and Kay Sage. Robert Motherwell attended, very likely with or at the suggestion of Kurt Seligmann, and brought with him a graduate student from Stanford University, Jacqueline Johnson. Frederick Kiesler, Nicolas Calas, and Jimmy Ernst were also in the audience. Robert Lebel went to at least one of the lectures; according to his recollection neither Onslow Ford's lectures nor those given by Claude Lévi-Straus during the same period were heard by more than fifteen people. However, Hayter recalled that there were at least a hundred, and other accounts of the attendance fill the room to overflowing and add the names of Pollock, Rothko, and Gorky. (Gorky, according to Onslow Ford's recollection, came frequently to his Eighth Street apartment in the evenings to ask questions about Surrealism.)

In his introduction Onslow Ford urged his listeners to "tear down the veils one by one that hide the reality of our own incomprehensible universe,"[9] to explore their dreams, and to join the Surrealists in the pursuit of the marvelous. Some of the ideas to which he gave voice found their way into the thinking that underlay the development of the New York School, especially in the dependence on Jung and the notion of a collective unconscious to which the artist must gain access by "plunging into the depths of the unknown self." Those who attain this greater consciousness, according to his notes, "will be capable of creating a work of art that will speak to the unconscious of every sensitive person." He reminded his audience of the state of crisis of civilization and the "control by the military authorities of the people of most countries, forced to be cogs in war machines." However, he offered a hope for a future culture in which "the individual will have the courage to liberate the latent forces in his mind and to situate his actions in the functioning of the universe." The artists whose works he planned to show, he announced, were men who would "lead us to strange regions of the human mind. They have closed the circuit between dreams and waking state and established communications between the interior and exterior world."

Other subjects touched on in his introductory words included "the neurosis that impels the artist to paint," which involved the need to exorcise internal conflicts, and the idea of psychic communication that makes the work of art a "barometer registering the desires and impulses of the community," a notion that had been put forward by the British aesthetician Charles Collingwood. He also described the eye as an imperfect instrument that gives us a distorted image of the world in which we live. This last is a motif that runs through both his and Matta's statements from their early years and reflects Ouspensky's comments on the "prison house of sight." Onslow Ford referred to the "barriers that for our intelligence separate the different parts of space as they separate the different parts of time." Characterizing them as artificial, he said, "The barriers dividing time into past, present and future must be broken down to give man a greater consciousness." Here he introduced the ideas about time, space, and simultaneity to which he and Matta had been attracted. "The ordinary eye is a slave to the present moment, but in our imagination we are free to move along the time length. . . . To see Hayter's *Three Dancing Women* you have to switch your eye to a speed that is different from the normal, where the present moment can be expanded at will to embrace an action."

He urged his listeners to turn on the "cycloptic eye in the middle of the forehead to look inside yourselves at the internal landscape." The idea of the cycloptic third or inner eye was part of the Surrealist tradition, but it had particular significance for Onslow Ford in his effort to give form to the "inner worlds"; an important work finished just before he left England was entitled *Cycloptomania.* This notion of the cycloptic eye offered to American artists an opposing path to that of the social and regional realism with which they had grown up, as well as a way beyond the limbo of cubist-derived semiabstraction where many of the more adventurous were becalmed.

The first three talks were devoted to an interpretive analysis of the paintings of De Chirico, Miró, Max Ernst, Magritte, and Tanguy. Onslow Ford's analysis of De Chirico may well have been close to Breton's, as he had acquired several of his De Chiricos from or through Breton and was not likely to deviate from the authority of the man he still called "maître." Showing a slide of *Nostalgia for the Infinite,* he spoke of the vital relationship between the arcade and the tower—yet, rooted to the ground, they could not meet. He traced through other paintings the theme of lovers similarly thwarted. In *The Child's Brain,* he pointed out the symbolism of the column, the curtain, and the naked father and interpreted the book with a marker as symbolizing intercourse.

In the next lecture he showed Ernst's *Two Children Are Menaced by a Nightingale,* connecting the subject with Ernst's collage novel *The Dream of the Little Girl Who Wanted to Enter Carmel,* Marceline-Marie. "This picture is of the day she lost her virginity. It offers the first glimpse of the conflict which will run through the

future works of the artist, the eternal conflict of lion and bird." In effect, when he discussed the older Surrealists he kept close to the Freudian interpretations of Breton, but when it came to the recent members of the group, such as Matta, he turned to a more Jungian mode of interpretation or applied his own concept of psychological morphology.

In his last lecture he turned to those who had joined Surrealism during the 1930s, Hayter, Brauner, Seligmann, Paalen, Matta, and himself, differentiating between the aims of the older and younger generations. "The young generation today are expressing the desires of the collective unconscious in new ways of looking at the world. We all now have the discoveries of Freud in our blood; the young generation knows him by instinct, as we also have the psychological adventures of the first part of Surrealism in our blood." His words coincided with the growing appeal of Jungian ideas for American artists and intellectuals during the forties. Jackson Pollock had been in therapy with several Jungian analysts, and a number of artists including Tony Smith were beginning to pick up a smattering of Jungian thought from the volume of collected works that Jolande Jacobi had translated into English. Thus there was a shared interest in myth, symbol, and archetype, as well as in the idea of a collective unconscious from which and to which the artist might directly communicate. While not rejecting Freud, Onslow Ford here welcomed Jungian theory as leading away from a focus on the individual psyche and toward a commonality of psychic experience.

Whatever understanding the members of his audience may previously have had of Surrealism, they must have been impressed by the actual Surrealist giving them the insider's view of the associative processes through which the images were arrived at as well as of the mysterious links that pulled these artists into a common orbit. Instead of seeing the Surrealist works removed from context on the walls of the Museum of Modern Art or in one or two galleries, his American listeners were now able to pick up the underlying currents of ideas and emotions that had given Surrealism its collective presence. The excitement must have heightened when he came to the last lecture and discussed artists who were there in the room, Seligmann, Matta, Hayter, and himself, and welcomed to their ranks some of the young Americans who were in the audience.

His greatest eloquence in the last lecture was reserved for Matta, whose 1938 drawing *The Birth of a Flower* he described as follows:

The horror at the sight of wet bread and the joy at the sight of a red balloon have married and given birth to a green flower of brilliant conversation. Imagine depth dimension to represent time length, breadth to represent the space compartments and height to represent a measure of sexual power. In the distance two feelings were formed which finally unite and a flower is born.

As he showed Matta's *Invasion of the Night,* he said:

One of the reasons why I feel full of life is because I have had the privilege to watch and perhaps almost to take part with pick-axe and shovel in the development of the world of Matta. Imagine that we look inside ourselves at the psychic landscape and we see the nights all joined together to form a band of yellow ground . . . at first there are no objects on the scene; they all lie buried in the unconscious behind the surface of the blue and yellow bands. Suddenly there is an upheaval. These bands start to palpitate like water just before it boils. The blue sky of night starts to invade the yellow ground of day, pouring down in pulsation after pulsation to form an ever-growing mountain that lifts part of the ground into the sky. Some unseen subterranean pressure makes the mountain continue to grow until it can bear the strain no longer and its summit bursts open in a volcano to hurl upwards out of the picture a stream of fire and smoke and objects that have long been buried in the unconscious, to make unseen clouds and constellations that cast their shadows on the blue sky of night and yellow ground of day.

Opposite: Gordon Onslow Ford, *Cycloptomania,* 1940, oil on canvas, 35 x 50 inches; private collection.

Opposite: Matta, *Invasion of the Night,* 1941, oil on canvas, 96.5 x 152.7 cm;
San Francisco Museum of Art, bequest of Jacqueline Onslow Ford.

Some of the objects ejected by the volcano have already come back to sight and by the auras that they emit they appear to have a big influence on their immediate surroundings. In the blue sky of night there is a floating red stone that is perhaps a knife that has been for years spinning in a direction of murder. An object that resembles some heavy flying bird that is perhaps the thoughts of the moon as she gazes at the earth's biggest volcano. On the yellow ground of day there is a woman imprisoned in an iron corset of her dreams . . . fleshy vegetation, floating objects and that is not all. This is but a glimpse of that marvelous world that is perhaps buried in each of us; once we can become aware of it, it can lead to a fuller life.

Onslow Ford's interpretation of this Matta painting offers some insight into a mode of visualizing that combination of collective unconscious and time-space continuum with which both painters were concerned. The attuning of the unconscious to cosmic events, the sense of all time being present in each moment, the substitution of spatial flux for a world defined by conventional linear perspective, and the ascendancy of subjective over objective vision represent a mode of thinking that differed drastically not only from the dominant realism in American art, but also from the Picassoesque semiabstraction and geometric formalism that characterized the work of most of the members of American Abstract Artists. It differed also from the Surrealist program as it had been codified in the 1920s, in that it cut loose from a Freudian interpretation of the human psyche. These were liberating words to the American artists who heard them; as Onslow Ford himself says, "an incitement to revolution."

Matta, with his impatient energy, graphic facility, and darting mind, found it an easy matter to give visual form to "psychological" morphology. Onslow Ford, perhaps because of his rigorous educational background, followed a more cerebral and deliberative process in working out the complex compositions of his elaborately symbolic paintings. Where Matta's brush spun lines swiftly across the canvas and flowed on paint in colorful drifts, Onslow Ford worked out a literal symbolism and proceeded to draw and fill in with paint in a more traditional manner of execution. This conventional approach to unconventional imagery is well exemplified in his major work of the previous summer, *Propaganda for Love,* which was hung at the New School and which he interpreted for his audience as follows:

This painting shows part of the psychic landscape—its three different zones, pale grey, blue, and dark green, are perhaps indications of the states of consciousness that correspond to light,

shadow and gloom of space. At the nucleus there is a purple monster; her head is a column, her hair two whirlpools, her feet six projecting claws; her six eyes concentrate their gaze on two points on a triangular plane. In the purple mother's womb there's an egg that is at the same time a hole whose presence turns the latent atmospheric energy into fourteen lines of force. That joins the chance encounters of the other characters that go to make up the dialogue. From the egg hole has just been hatched a green reptile who is spitting out his venom in the form of black bubbles . . . the bottom left-hand corner suggests three roads which sexual desire can take, the normal wife of flesh, an abstract wife of earth and an abstract wife of metal. . . . Rising from the zone of darkness there is a sea of flesh which is forever breathing in different shapes. Its skin is clearly marked with life lines and there is a maggot forever eating its way in and out. The sea of flesh is married to a yellow scaly form and together they penetrate the first abstract wife; a green three-peaked mountain arises and astride the valley of this mountain there rises a creature I call the seducing machine. Its two heads are suction pipes; the feet are nature-destroying vermin . . . there is a black planet covered with hairs . . . a skeleton chess board, hypnotic trees dancing from move to move, a web round a deep sea and a luminous star as their goal. . . .

Below: Boris Margo, *Personages in Radiant Motion,* 1941, oil on canvas, 25 x 30 inches; courtesy Michael Rosenfeld Gallery.

Opposite: William Baziotes, *The Accordion of Flesh,* 1940, oil on canvas, 20 x 26 inches; estate of William Baziotes, courtesy Blum Helman Gallery.

More significant than this mélange of cosmic, folkloric, alchemical, and erotic imagery was the conclusion to this analysis, in which he maintained that the foregoing words were only labels and that each object should mean something to each viewer in terms of his or her own psyche. Thus the ground was prepared for a mode of painting intended to circumvent conscious symbolic interpretation in order to speak directly from the unconscious of the artist to the unconscious of the viewer.

The concluding remarks in Onslow Ford's prepared lecture notes offered the following challenge:

Tonight I have given you a brief glimpse of the works of the young painters who were members of the Surrealist group in Paris at the outbreak of the war. Perhaps it is not by chance that all of us except Brauner and Dominguez have managed to find our way to these shores. . . . Here in America we have by our side: Kay Sage whose bleak landscapes are slowly creating an atmosphere where some important drama is bound to be enacted. Boris Margo whose powerful collages are strong enough to burst the walls of any room. Helen Phillips whose face in negative is in my opinion one of the most important busts of recent years. Bill Baziotes whose whirlpools of water have not yet settled down into definite form, but may one day astound him as well as others. Jimmy Ernst whose personages are slowly fading into the land where they want to live. But in spite of this we are not yet a group. We are just a crowd of painters

Opposite: Arshile Gorky, *Garden in Sochi,* 1941, oil on canvas, 44¼ x 62¼ inches; The Museum of Modern Art, New York, purchase fund and gift of Mr. and Mrs. Wolfgang Schwabacher.

and as such only limited action is possible until we have contacted poets and writers moving in a direction similar to our own. But I am overjoyed to tell you that I hope soon André Breton will be with us and that Pierre Mabille has got as far as Martinique and will come here the moment it appears possible for him to make a living. I think I can speak for all my friends when I say that we are completely confident in our work and slowly but surely with the collaboration of the young Americans we hope to make a vital contribution to the transformation of the world.

Just as the audiences can't be reconstructed, so also it is impossible to gauge the reaction of these words envisioning a joining together of Americans and émigrés in a unified contribution to the Surrealist mission of transforming consciousness. Susanna Hare Coggeshall recalled that the "American artists' eyes were popping out of their heads." Gerome Kamrowski testified to Baziotes's excitement over the lectures; Tanguy had mentioned in an earlier letter to Seligmann that he had some misgivings about Gordon's interpretation of Surrealism, but he was very moved when Onslow Ford raised the projection screen to reveal hanging on the wall the last painting he had painted in Europe, *Si c'était.* On the other hand Robert Lebel minimized the lectures' impact and Elaine de Kooning recalled that although she and Willem saw all the Surrealist exhibitions, she had never heard of Onslow Ford or his lectures. At any rate his reputation as a spokesman for Surrealism spread sufficiently so that Alfred Barr wrote the following year asking for his interpretation of Max Ernst's *Two Children Are Threatened by a Nightingale.* Motherwell's ideas about continuity with European culture may have received an initial impetus from Onslow Ford's vision of Americans and Europeans working together toward a common artistic goal. Jimmy Ernst described the earnest group of listeners that gathered around him after these talks. "To some of us he seemed to say for the first time, 'Why not?' rather than 'It has to be.' We were not getting the last word from Europe, but rather the possibility for a further horizon that implied individualism." [10]

One consequence of Onslow Ford's lectures was that he unintentionally became something of a Surrealist guru, a position that made him uncomfortable. Julien Levy read the Tarot cards for him and foretold disaster if he stayed in New York. He had become involved with Jacqueline Johnson, who had attended his lectures with Motherwell, and they decided early in the summer to leave for Mexico where they settled in a Tarascan village that was to be their home until after the war. The impact of his words, however, remained.

In a 1941 letter to his sister Gorky wrote: "I am using divisions on a two dimensional surface—my canvas—so as to reflect the life pattern that exists in the universe, its tension, oppositions, actions and counteractions, and to explore the cosmic pattern by the way I move the planes back and forth in all directions to form the complete living unit."[11] These words, so different from Gorky's usual lyrical style of writing, are very likely a reflection of the ideas absorbed from Onslow Ford either at the lectures or during studio visits. They seem to have little relation to his own works of the time, and in writing them Gorky seems to be following his not infrequent custom of incorporating passages extracted from other sources into his letters.

Jimmy Ernst used to tell the following story:

One evening at the Jumble Shop after one of Gordon Onslow Ford's lectures we were all sitting around. Matta and Gorky were there. Gorky didn't have much use for Matta personally and they were always at each other's throat, particularly since Gorky then was seemingly heavily influenced by Matta in his approach. Matta, referring to a prior visit to Gorky's studio, said "There's something in the upper right-hand corner of the last painting—how did you do that?" . . . Gorky said "Well, first you take a glass or a palette and you squeeze paint on that, then you have brushes, then you have a little cup with turpentine and some oil. You dip the brush in the cup and in the paint and you transfer it to the canvas." Matta said, "Yes, but how did you do it?" "That's how I did it," said Gorky.[12]

One of the few press notices of this Surrealist event was in *Decision,* a publication put out by another émigré, Klaus Mann.

The fifth week of Surrealism (the title has the ring of a plague) is now in full possession of the galleries of the New School for Social Research. Contemporary mannerism has gone far enough. It has exploited the irrational through all stages of subjectivity, narcissism and incoherence. Self-imposed insanity is an open refusal to accept all forms of responsibility.[13]

This review signaled the beginning of an anti-Surrealist campaign that Mann was to carry on until he enlisted in the U.S. army in 1943. It is likely that left-wing political feuding caused him to adopt such an antagonistic attitude toward the Trotskyist Surrealists.

Almost all the artists mentioned above lived in or near Greenwich Village in the early forties. Dropping around to each other's studios was a commonplace practice, as was casually meeting at a coffee shop, stopping in at Atelier 17, or, for the Surrealists, gathering in a small outdoor enclave they discovered on Canal Street. Cold-water flats and walk-up tenement apartments were the rule and Francis Lee was the only loft-dweller, so his place became the locus for larger parties. It was there that Matta and other refugees met Baziotes, Pollock, and Kamrowski. Through Kurt Seligmann Motherwell came to know Matta and through Matta Baziotes, who became a close friend and colleague for a time. Gradually there developed an informal group, made up of younger Americans and the first wave of Surrealist émigrés. Jimmy Ernst's memoir convincingly conveys something of the loose-structured, nonideological nature of this group, linked principally by their search for a way beyond existing styles.

One evening in the winter of 1940–1941, Baziotes brought Jackson Pollock over to Kamrowski's studio, and the three artists began experimenting with quick-drying lacquer paint that Baziotes had bought at Arthur Brown's art supply store. They spread some cheap canvases out on the floor and began brushing and then dripping the paint onto them. In the process of "fooling around," as Kamrowski called it, they all worked on the same canvases and during the course of the evening produced a number of collaborative spontaneous works. All three artists already had some knowledge of Surrealism and were familiar with the concept of "pure psychic automatism," and they were trying to find ways in which the new quick-drying paint developed for commercial use could be put to this end. When Kamrowski moved out of that studio—the artists moved with regularity in order to avoid paying rent during the summer months when they wanted to be out of the city—he threw out most of these experimental canvases but kept one as a kind of souvenir, and this three-man canvas has surfaced in a number of recent exhibitions as a kind of proto–abstract expressionist work. Although each artist made use of dripped paint and a gestural approach in combination with other techniques during the next few years, it wasn't until 1946 that dripping lacquer began to be the basis for an entire painting and that Pollock reached what Kamrowski referred to as "his greater freedoms."

Of interest to both the European refugees and the American artists was the exhibition "Indian Art of the United States," held at the Museum of Modern Art in the winter of 1941. For this exhibition a pictograph from the sandstone walls of Barrier Canyon in Utah was reproduced full-size (12 by 60 feet) on a wall of the museum by the Utah Federal Art Project. By all accounts the show was masterfully installed under the aegis of the Austrian émigré René d'Harnoncourt. One came upon the mural on leaving the confines of "dark ceremonial chambers," which gave it an aura of revelation after a mysterious dark passage. There was also a replica of a kiva mural with feathers, spirals, and birds, painted by four Hopi artists whose ancestors had painted the original in a pueblo that had fallen into ruin. Navaho artists were on hand to demonstrate sand painting, an ephemeral art form that tradition required to be destroyed by sundown. There were masklike objects cut from

Navaho sand painting. Installation view of the exhibition "Indian Art of the United
States," The Museum of Modern Art New York, January 22–April 27, 1941;
photograph courtesy The Museum of Modern Art, New York.

the sides of large white shells, mica ornaments from Ohio's Hopewell mounds, and complex spiral designs on pottery jars from Louisiana that had contained skeletons. Thanks to d'Harnoncourt's installation the urban audience had an opportunity to grasp the ceremonial and magical significance attached to this work, rather than to see it as form isolated from context. (Another part of d'Harnoncourt's agenda was to promote the sale of Indian crafts, and to this end he emphasized their compatibility with modern interiors.) The fact that Pollock brought his Jungian analyst to see the show and that Lee Krasner was hired to take over the painting of the pictograph give some indication of the involvement of contemporary artists with the exhibition.

However, for those who had experienced Native American art *in situ*, the show was a pale reflection of the real thing. Kurt Seligmann described the exhibition in a letter to Wolfgang Paalen. "There is currently an exhibition of Indian art at the Museum of Modern Art. It is rather meager and it's a pity that your objects, especially the front of your Tlingit hut, are not in the show. At the entrance there is a modern totem painted in oil, carved two years ago. As for my totem, I fear that it must now adorn a museum in Germany."[14]

Two exhibitions that opened in November at the Museum of Modern Art also contributed to the general awareness of Surrealism, although one of the featured artists, Miró, was in Mallorca and did not come to New York until after the war. The other artist was the outcast Dalí, whose flirtation with fascism had made him anathema to his former cohorts but who nonetheless fascinated the public. The curator of the Miró exhibition was James Johnson Sweeney, a writer well acquainted in international avant-garde circles and increasingly influential as a critic and impresario. In the catalogue accompanying the exhibition Sweeney quoted Breton's description of Miró as "the most Surrealist of us all," as well as Miró's own statement on the importance of subject matter to replace the "deserted house of abstraction."

"To me," Miró had said, "it seems vital that a rich and robust theme should be present to give the spectator an immediate blow between the eyes before a second thought can interpose." Sweeney assigns Miró a pivotal role: "Tomorrow a new epoch in painting will have opened. Yesterday a period closed. Miró's work belongs to the youth of a period that is opening, rather than the old age of a closing one. He has brought western painting to new forms and new evocations."[15] Miró was to become not only an important inspiration for American painters such as Motherwell and Gorky, but the subject of a book in 1947 by abstract expressionism's principal advocate, Clement Greenberg.

Miró's painting was not new to New York. Pierre Matisse had presented it in half a dozen exhibitions since 1932 and a number of his works had entered American museum collections. The Museum of Modern Art show included a 10-foot mural done for the children of Pierre Matisse that may have helped to nudge Americans toward the idea that a large scale could be as appropriate for personal expression as it had been for the public-interest themes of WPA murals. The show's inclusion of paintings that incorporated writing, such as *Painting Poem,* 1938, may have been the inspiration for Motherwell's incorporation of the written word in his compositions, although it was several years before this began. More obvious is the use Gorky made of the central shape from Miró's 1937 *Still Life with Old Shoe* in his first, 1941, version of *Garden in Sochi.*

Both Sweeney and the author of the Dalí catalogue, James Thrall Soby, were taken to task in *Partisan Review* by George L. K. Morris.[16] Morris's own complex abstract canvases and his leading role in American Abstract Artists did not blind him to Miró's accomplishment, but he did take exception to Sweeney's sweeping generalizations and casual use of terms like "spiritual values." As for Dalí, he debunked the myth of his technical prowess en route to criticizing Soby for his ignorance of modern painting. Unfortunately Morris's criticism of the abuses of language in art writing fell on deaf ears, and the faults he pointed out proliferated as the American art world expanded, contributing to the confusion that has plagued attempts to give an objective account of the artistic developments of the 1940s. As Clement Greenberg stated in the opening sentence of the review that followed the one by Morris, "It is possible to get away with murder in writing about art."[17]

Quite apart from museum exhibitions, the émigré artists, far more than their American contemporaries, were fortunate in having in New York a ready-made

showcase among the transplanted European art dealers, both those who were long established in New York such as Pierre Matisse and those who had left Berlin in the 1930s, Karl Nierendorf, Curt Valentin, and J. B. Neumann, or Otto Kallir from Vienna, not to mention such major names from Paris as Paul Rosenberg and Georges Wildenstein. Added to these were the sympathetic American dealers who had spent some time in Europe before the war, such as Julien Levy, Marian Willard, and Betty Parsons, then at the Wakefield Gallery. Thus there was a network of dealers receptive to and supportive of the émigré Europeans well before November 1942, when Peggy Guggenheim opened the doors of Art of This Century, a gallery where the more adventurous Americans would soon be seen alongside the Surrealists. The New York art market was by no means dormant; *Art News* reported the best auction season in twelve years for 1940–1941, up 54 percent over the preceding year.

Actually Peggy Guggenheim found little in New York when she first arrived to convince her that the city deserved her art collection. Perhaps she was unnerved by the presence of Leonora Carrington who had arrived in New York that summer as the wife of a Mexican diplomat, bringing with her a body of Ernst's work. At any rate she decided to cross the continent to determine whether California would be more hospitable to the museum she wished to create. Accordingly she flew to Los Angeles, accompanied by her sixteen-year-old daughter, Pegeen, and by Max Ernst and his son Jimmy. They stayed in the Santa Monica home of her sister, Hazel Mc-Kinley, where Max set up a studio on the enclosed porch. It was there that he painted *Napoleon in the Wilderness,* a work that one is tempted to read as a self-image, the conqueror as exile, his world in ruins behind him, next to a column suggestive of a Northwest totem pole, on the right Leonora enfolded in exotic vegetation, with the blue Pacific in the background.

The transcontinental return trip was made in a Buick convertible and had a decisive impact on Ernst's future and that of his painting. It was on this trip that he first saw Hopi Indian dances and acquired the bulk of his collection of Hopi and Zuñi kachinas, and it was also at this point that he was first struck by the Arizona landscape around Flagstaff. In his memoirs Jimmy described his father's amazement as he recognized in those rock formations one of the invented landscapes from a painting done when he was still in the Ardèche. (This land of red rocks took such a hold on his imagination that he was later to return to build a homestead facing a breathtaking view where he and Dorothea Tanning lived for six years.) When the party reached New Orleans, Max Ernst, inspired by the Navahos, made sand paintings on the shores of Lake Pontchartrain.

During that same summer and fall Masson, in rural Connecticut, was also responding to his New York surroundings. *Iroquois Landscape,* considered to be his first American drawing, harks back to an image from the previous year, *Landscape*

Max Ernst, *Napoleon in the Wilderness,* 1941, oil on canvas, 18¼ x 15 inches; The Museum of Modern Art, New York, purchase and exchange.

André Masson, *Iroquois Landscape,* 1941, ink on (American) paper, 21 x 28.2 cm; collection Diego and Guite Masson.

in the Form of a Fish, whose theme was metamorphosis or the interrelatedness of all processes of growth and transformation. To that theme has been added desolation and flight before a menacing claw that can also be read as the Nazi double-headed eagle. Although the war was never far from the Massons' minds, anxious as they were about Rose's mother and sisters, Masson allowed himself to submit to what he saw as "l'Amérique sauvage de Chateaubriand," and to use it as the basis for a major new development in his work. He described for Kahnweiler a nature of abundance and extremes of climate, and a rustic house that was "très Fenimore Cooper." Even the vegetable garden was alarming in the size of the tomato plants it produced and its untamable weeds. Skunks, rattlesnakes, wildcats, oversize tortoises, northern lights, poison ivy, tiger lilies, the prisms of the ice-covered landscape refracting the light, the quartz and mica glinting from the rocks, and the "autumn trees looking as if the sky had poured pots of paint over them"—all acted on his imagination to give rise to a body of work markedly different from the prewar years.

His palette and mode of applying paint also changed. He used more fully saturated color, made almost iridescent by the underlying dark ground which seems to have been intended to suggest being within the earth. Cubist and volumetric think-

ing, still apparent in the late 1930s in paintings such as *Labyrinth,* have receded before a merging of form and space on a single plane. He mentioned that he used a brush instead of a pen in his ink drawings during the Connecticut years (already in evidence in some of the Martinique drawings), and this may have led him to wield the brush in a more calligraphic way in his oil paintings as well. In Marseilles he had written "Painting Is a Wager," which he later gave as a talk in America. "Lay the canvas flat on the floor," he wrote. "Seize your inspiration in that state of ecstasy and paroxysm in which mind and body coincide and regain their lost unity. Let execution be a lightning-swift and automatic act. . . . Think of creation as a risk to be taken and of the picture as a commitment and an adventure." [18] Whereas previously automatism had served as a prelude to a subsequent more conscious process, in Connecticut Masson put his new program of action painting into play.

At the end of October a Masson exhibition opened in the new Members Room at the Baltimore Museum, arranged, of course, by Saidie May. He lectured in French

Above: André Masson, *Millet Seed,* 1942, oil on canvas, 82.5 x 100 cm;
collection Diego and Guite Masson.

at the museum and found himself and his work the subject of more attention than either had ever attracted in France. This was the other side of the coin for the refugees. Uprooted, impoverished, anxiety-ridden as they may have been, they had in the United States more attention from museums, more patrons, and probably larger reputations than they had had in France. The Museum of Modern Art had acquired a Masson twenty years before any other museum, and Barr helped establish Surrealism's historical validity as part of a succession of significant twentieth-century art movements. The kind of encouragement he got from Curt Valentin and other dealers may also have nourished Masson's growth as a painter as he worked in his rural refuge.

The section of northwestern Connecticut beyond the commuter belt where the Masons had gravitated was quickly becoming an enclave of refugee artists and their American friends. Its nineteenth-century farmhouses with unused barns, surrounded by pastures and woodlands, were inexpensive and perhaps for the refugees offered a more secure haven than the city. Among these who settled in neighboring communities in the area were Marie and Eugene Jolas, Naum and Miriam Gabo, Hans Richter, and Robert Jay Wolf. The hilltop home of Alexander Calder with a studio barn that looked like a magician's lair was in nearby Roxbury, as was the home of David and Susanna Hare. Calder had known most of the Surrealists in Paris and had worked on his mercury fountain for the Spanish pavilion at the same time as Miró was doing his antifascist mural. His presence in that part of Connecticut acted as a magnet for the refugees. In 1941 Kay Sage and Yves Tanguy moved out from the city to Woodbury, and a few years later they bought a farmhouse there where they lived the rest of their lives. The Gorkys stayed in New Milford for three weeks in the early summer of 1942, and in 1945 returned to live in Roxbury in David Hare's house and then in Sherman. Julien and Muriel Levy followed the Gorkys and acquired a home in Bridgewater. Thus this corner of Connecticut became a virtual Surrealist outpost and was visited frequently by André Breton and his family, Marcel Duchamp, Enrico Donati, and others; Claude Lévi-Strauss visited the Massons and Chagall spent at least one vacation in New Preston. It was in the Connecticut woods that Breton was introduced to unknown flora and fauna: "the little Indian pipe, so timorous, so ambiguous, the scarlet tanager, the staghorn fern and the mysteries of American butterflies." [19]

Tanguy had lamented to Anaïs Nin that the streets of New York were no substitute for the streets of Paris. The latter he said had nourished him—every walk was

Page from *VVV* showing studio of Alexander Calder, Roxbury, Connecticut,
1943, photograph by Herbert Matter.

an adventure, every café a conversation. America he found to be a country of silence and impersonality. There is no doubt, however, that living in rural isolation with few diversions, he concentrated more intently on his painting, and as he did the work grew in scope and complexity. The serious attention he gave his painting may also have been a consequence of the arrangement Pierre Matisse had made with him to provide a monthly stipend in return for one painting a month. For the first time he had a serious business agreement with a dealer, albeit an old schoolmate, and as his paintings became commodities it may have been less possible to be the spontaneous, erratic Tanguy of old. His first two years in the United States saw an increase in size of the constructions that populated his horizonless spaces and a greater density to their deployment. The focus became sharper, the colors brighter, and the nuanced grays of Parisian skies gave way to a strong, clear light. It seems quite possible that some of the fantastic rock formations he had seen in the American West in the summer of 1940, the gigantic upright flat pierced rocks in Nevada, for example, may have reemerged as shapes on his canvases. Ten years earlier a trip to Morocco had left its imprint on Tanguy in the *Palais promontoire* and several other works of 1930–1931, and the western landscape seems to have had a similar impact.

Tanguy's way of working was highly improvisatory. His intricate conglomerate "personages" and biomorphic constructions emerged as he worked intently, one shape leading to another, without premeditation. This does not mean, however, that certain actual configurations had not imprinted themselves in his mind to come forth later as spontaneous images. Nor should one forget that during his last fifteen years his work was done in close proximity to Kay Sage and that the decisive shapes, sharp edges, and strong light of her paintings may have quietly infiltrated his work.

Kurt and Arlette Seligmann also bought a country place, but they chose the cheaper and more isolated Sugar Loaf, New York, a hamlet about sixty miles from New York City that they had heard about from Meyer Schapiro's brother-in-law, Dr. Joseph Milgrim. As long as Kurt taught in the city they also kept their apartment in the Beaux Arts Building on 40th Street, but for Arlette, who remembered her childhood on her grandparents' farm outside Paris, the gardens and barnyard of the Sugar Loaf farm constituted a paradise regained. The letters Seligmann sent back during the war years to his sister and brother-in-law in Geneva constantly reiterated the bucolic side of their lives.

In France artists' prints had normally been done by a master printer. Now Seligmann learned how to print his own graphic works and set up an etching press in his

Kurt Seligmann, *Les Environs du Château d'Argol*, 1941, restored by the artist,
1952, oil on glass; Art Institute of Chicago.

Kurt Seligmann, polarized photograph of cracked glass, used as a basis for his
"cyclonic" compositions.

studio. Meyer Schapiro recalled that a number of artists, including Tanguy and Calder, did etchings and engravings at the Seligmanns' farm, and he bemoaned the fact
that unknown treasures of etching plates were buried beneath the ruins when a cyclone leveled the studio barn in 1949.

Seligmann seemed to have little difficulty settling into a new life. He had a
modest income; he showed in 1939 and 1941 with Nierendorf and then from 1943
on at the Durlacher Gallery; he was in constant touch with Chicago collector Earl
Lugdin, a good friend and patron whom he had known already in Europe; he had
private students and college teaching positions; the close friendship he developed
with Meyer Schapiro gave him someone with whom he could share his obsession
with rare books on magic and the occult, which he continued to acquire even during
the war from booksellers abroad. He was supportive of Charles Henri Ford when the
latter was getting *View* under way and was the first to purchase shares when Ford
hit upon this method of financing his publication; his drawings and articles appeared
frequently in its pages. His technically impressive works had an old-masterish authority that impressed at least some of the critics, and his paintings began to enter
museum and private collections. The fact that he spoke and wrote English facilitated
the carrying on of his professional life, lecturing, serving on exhibition juries, and
arranging exhibitions, as well as the expansion of his circle of acquaintances.

He also made efforts, as we have seen, on behalf of his Surrealist cohorts in
Europe, helped financially where he could, and personally raised the money and secured the affidavits to bring the Marxist art historian and critic Max Raphael, al-

ready in a detention camp, out of Europe. Meyer Schapiro contributed to this effort, but warned Seligmann to keep Raphael away from the Stalinists when he arrived. However, once in New York, Raphael's intransigent Stalinism prevented a sympathetic interchange with Schapiro who, like so many other adherents of the old left, had broken with the Third International after the Moscow trials. In 1951 Raphael committed suicide, perhaps in part overcome by the guilt of the survivor. Did Kurt Seligmann, prophet of the horrors to come in the years before the war, also suffer from this guilt? What is encoded in his dark paintings of 1940 and 1941 that might give some hint of the hidden thoughts of this ironic and in some ways very private person, whose own death twenty years later was probably a suicide? "My mind is as black as the background in my paintings," he wrote on a scrap of paper.

In his second exhibition at Nierendorf in the spring of 1941, five of the twenty paintings shown are grouped under the heading "wrapped and cyclonic landscapes." Here he has introduced a new element, an ominous, agitated shape that appears to twist like a cyclone. These eccentric shapes were arrived at through a quasi-automatist process, described by Meyer Schapiro as projecting broken glass through a slide projector and tracing the outlines of the image thus obtained. In the *Environs of the Château d'Argol* he used this technique actually on glass. For some years he had made use of the Swiss folk art practice of painting on the reverse of glass and passing the glass over a candle flame to blacken the background, and in this work he compounds the mystery of the process. The title of the work comes from a novel by Julien Gracq, a young writer whose work the Surrealists had acclaimed.[20]

The presence of the refugee artists was noted in a variety of ways during 1941. An exhibition at the Addison Gallery of the Andover School in Massachusetts was devoted to works by European artists teaching in America that year, among them Albers, Bayer, Grosz, Hayter, Moholy-Nagy, Ozenfant, and Seligmann. Each was represented by a work done prior to and one done after their arrival. Excerpts from student essays on the show were published in the *Magazine of Art* in December. A senior named Hessey wrote: "American art in 1939 seemed toneless. Millions had seen in Thomas Craven's book and in *Life* magazine the picturization of their own land in essentially the same technique until they were tired of it. A new impetus was needed. It is my opinion that the source of that impetus is in the talented men and women driven here by the war. . . . Something fresh, pleasantly disturbing."[21] These words of a senior at an elite prep school forecast the mood of a new generation, one that would come into its own in the postwar years to fuel the enthusiasm for a new American art that had responded to the impetus provided by the refugees.

Another exhibition of work by refugees was held at the National Art Club on Gramercy Park, New York, to raise money for a fund to help refugee artists. *Fortune* magazine acknowledged their presence in its December 1941 issue with an article titled "The Flight of Culture," illustrated with glossy reproductions of works by Surrealists Masson, Seligmann, Tanguy, and Tchelitchew, as well as Chagall, Léger, and Ozenfant. "It's as if one transplanted a whole culture from one continent to another," wrote Thomas Craven in the accompanying commentary. And for the November-December issue of Klaus Mann's *Decision,* art collector Sidney Janis wrote an essay, "The School of Paris Comes to New York." He confined his interviews and comments to three representative artists, Ernst, Léger, and Mondrian, and one "young artist of talent and temperament—the irrepressible Matta."

Matta's aim, as reported by Janis, was "to be conscious of the web of relations which is the structure of life; to paint the colossal structure of life as science relates it, in a town-like geometry." He writes of a penetrating visual perception that "X-rays reality . . . by a fusion of techniques from painting, architecture, fumage and photography, his images are superimposed on the screen of his canvas where the composite becomes, in effect, an X-rayograph." Janis warns in conclusion, "It is not for our artists to follow the outward character of their [the Europeans'] work, but to gain insight by which to express their own ideas."

Since Janis still had his amateur standing as a collector of art, not yet a purveyor, it is surprising to find him ending his essay with these words: "New York is supplanting Paris as the art center of the world. This naturally means that the whole of America will play its part. . . . An extensive and imaginative merchandising plan aimed to encourage a vast American public to participate by purchasing the works of their time, will be a step in the right direction." Sidney and Harriet Janis had collected paintings by members of the School of Paris during the 1930s and had traveled abroad and knew some of the artists personally, so their apartment was a place to which the émigrés gravitated. Janis recalled arguments between the French and American artists heating up as they drank together at his parties. And as he observed this commingling, an idea for a book and an exhibition began to take shape, one that would present the cultural fusion or perhaps infusion that Janis discerned and was eager to describe. The result, which did not actually emerge until 1944, was the first book on American art to go beyond the realist styles of the 1930s and to take cognizance of the artistic transfer that was taking place: *Abstract and Surrealist Painting in America.*

Janis was not the only one to be dazzled by Matta. Rosamund Frost, a regular reviewer for *Art News,* singled him out in a "School of Paris" group show at Pierre Matisse: "Matta, the young man people are keeping an eye on, has done his best work to date, *Deep Stone,* a cosmic whirlwind of color with the glint and clink of unset jewels." [21] And she waxed poetic over his one-man show the following spring:

Imagine a white hot furnace. Imagine the breaking down and reconverting of the essential substances of the world. Imagine these substances rendered explosively, powerfully reacting on but not modifying each other. Imagine a painter of thirty who has invented an idiom so outside the run of experience that this seems the only line along which to approach his work.[22]

After André Breton arrived in late May 1941, the Surrealists in exile resumed their discussions on such subjects as the Tarot cards, true and false Surrealism, and magic and alchemy, as well as playing again *vérité* and *cadavres exquises*. They found a small "terrasse" downtown that, while not a café, afforded them an outdoor meeting place, and they often lunched together in a coffee shop on 57th Street. Among those attending the lunches was Robert Motherwell, who described himself as a young acolyte who was tolerated because he was a source of information on curious local customs. The Europeans wished to be enlightened, he recalled, on such subjects as what was the purpose of a hamburger, what could be used as a substitute for unobtainable olive oil, and was the imposition of censorship on overseas mail a forewarning of military dictatorship? According to Motherwell, "The Americans were filled with bitterness at the end of the Depression. They resented the Europeans for their prestige. I had come out of a golden university world; I didn't have that defeated quality. I floated in and out of the Surrealist milieu because I had no stake—I wasn't thought of as a painter."[23]

These lunches would often be followed by a postprandial stroll down Third Avenue past the windows of its secondhand stores as Breton directed them to discover and point out true Surrealist objects, much as they had in the Paris flea markets. In *L'Amour fou* Breton had written of his practice of "wandering in search of everything" and described a stroll near the flea market in the company of Alberto Giacometti during which they let their eyes roam "over the objects that, between the lassitude of some and the desire of others, go off to dream at the antique fair."[24] During that particular visit each was ultimately attracted to an object and acquired it, Giacometti a steel half-mask and Breton a wooden spoon with a small shoe carved as a support for the handle. For the former the mask helped him to overcome a contradiction in the sculpture he was working on, *The Gift,* while for the latter a meditation on his object led him to understand the significance of the glass slipper in the Cinderella story. Breton's own apartment in the rue Fontaine contained carefully culled flea market objects in provocative arrangements on every available horizontal surface, while the walls were covered with African and South Pacific masks and paintings by Picabia, Miró, and other colleagues. Similarly the parlor of Kurt Seligmann's upstate New York farmhouse, whose contents, like those of the Breton apartment, remain much as they were at the time of his death, contained a large wooden moon-shaped head that he and Breton had found in a prewar flea market,

Pages from Robert Motherwell's Mexican sketchbook, 1941, India ink and
watercolor on paper, 9 x 11½ inches; The Museum of Modern Art, New York.

along with china hands, a moose inkstand, a carved fish from a weather vane, and several small inlaid wooden masks from British Columbia, as well as his own paintings on reverse glass and works by Ernst, Onslow Ford, and others. In these settings each object seems to emanate a certain aura of provocation, sometimes in isolation, often in uneasy juxtaposition with other objects.

In the United States, however, it was not so much flea market castoffs that the Surrealists collected but Native American artifacts. They discovered a small shop where Julius Carlebach sold Indian ceremonial objects and pried out of him the secret of his source of supply. Shortly thereafter two taxis full of the artists and their friends set off for a warehouse in the Bronx that was filled with the surplus collections of the Heye Foundation, proprietor of the Museum of the American Indian. There they were able to buy for sums averaging $15 a variety of masks, kachinas, and carved objects from all regions of North America.

Anaïs Nin, living in a skylit studio five flights up on West Thirteenth Street, recorded in her diaries fleeting glimpses of the regrouping in New York of the circles she had known in Paris, her reunion with Caresse Crosby, who had run the Black Sun Press in Paris, at a party given by Kay de San Faustino [Sage] and Tanguy, visits with Edgar and Louise Varèse in a brick house on Sullivan Street, parties at which she danced with Pierre Matisse and Luis Buñuel, groups of refugees dancing until dawn at the Savoy Ballroom in Harlem, and André Breton "with all the dignity and royal bearing he genuinely possesses, with his long hair brushed away from his leonine face, his large eyes and bold features, leaning over my hand to kiss it on the top of a Fifth Avenue bus."[25]

With Breton and his family installed on Eleventh Street, near Meyer Schapiro whom he saw frequently, Matta on Ninth Street, Jackson Pollock and Onslow Ford on Eighth Street, Kiesler and Baziotes on Fourteenth, Gorky at 36 Union Square, Noguchi in Macdougal Alley, and Motherwell and Kamrowski also in Greenwich Village, it could be said that by the end of 1941 there was a network of downtown artists that included both the Surrealist émigrés, especially the younger ones who spoke some English, and a handful of disaffected young Americans. It has been claimed that Breton, who was paralyzed by the thought of speaking a language in which he could not express himself precisely, was aloof and did not fraternize. This is contradicted by the closeness he felt to the Gorky family, described in his 1945 book *Arcane 17*, by the fact that he gave titles to the paintings of Gorky and Enrico Donati and perhaps others, by the English-language publication he engineered which was an integrated Franco-American endeavor, and by causal comments in letters here and there such as that of an American woman artist: "Making love to André was like taking a bath in molten steel."

Early in their stay in the United States the Seligmanns apparently felt sufficiently ill at ease to consider taking steps to relocate in South America and made inquiries at several consulates. They also considered moving to Mexico and planned a trip to reconnoiter in the summer of 1941. They invited his pupils, Robert Motherwell and Barbara Reis, to join them and passage was booked on a ship traveling to Mexico. At the last moment a problem with the transfer of funds from Europe made them apprehensive about leaving New York and the Mattas went on the trip instead, traveling second class while their companions looked down from the upper deck.

The pages of Motherwell's Mexican sketchbook are a clear indication of the kind of apprenticeship to Matta that he served during that summer. Drawings such as those illustrated indicate that he was attempting to deal with a multidimensional space similar to that developed by Matta in his drawings of 1938–1940. However, his background in American pragmatic philosophy may have made him less susceptible to the mystical content that Matta read into his work, since his paintings of the following years tend to have quite specific references. Nonetheless he did state in 1950 that "Abstract art is a form of mysticism. . . . One's art is one's effort to wed oneself to the universe." [26] Recollecting this trip, Motherwell said, "I was as close to Matta then as anybody can be. He is a kind of intellectual Don Juan who seduces and then moves on." [27]

Writing to the Seligmanns from Taxco in June, Motherwell grumbled about living conditions in Mexico, although he admitted that Barbara Reis and the Mattas did not share his negativism and ill-humor. He gave a vivid description of the encounter one evening of a flower-bedecked procession carrying the tiny white pine coffin of a child. It is perhaps noteworthy that he picked this of all the sights in Mexico to describe, in the light of the recurrent theme of death in his work. He also wrote that "Taxco is so dull that there is nothing to do but work. I have rather radically changed the way I paint—much more flatly than I was—and I think perhaps I am on a track that will lead to some good things." [28]

Matta's recollections of the trip are of a different sort: "We spent the whole summer in Taxco, met everyday in a bar opposite the cathedral. It was by chance that my work began to take the form of volcanoes. I saw everything in flames, but from a metaphysical point of view. I was speaking from beyond the volcano. The light was not a surface, but interior fire . . . I painted that which burned in me and the best image of my body was the volcano." [29] Born in the geologically active region of Santiago, Chile, Matta must have felt the reverberation of something long familiar kindled by the Mexican experience. Volcanic imagery is felt with a new force as it permeates paintings such as *Listen to Living,* one of a series of works in which the

earth spews fire and glowing rocks. It is even possible that these glowing rocks are intended as the gems that to pre-Columbian societies were the transmigrated souls of important people. Breton had also identified his body with a volcano when he described in *L'Amour fou* the ascent of the volcano Tiede during the Surrealists' visit to the Canary Islands in 1935: "It is my heart beating in your depths."

While in Mexico City, Motherwell met Wolfgang Paalen, and despite his earlier discontent he stayed on in Mexico to learn what he could from Paalen, an association that was to have interesting future consequences. (He also met a Mexican actress, María Emilia Ferrcira y Moyers, who subsequently became his first wife.) Paalen, he said, gave him a year-long course in Surrealism in six weeks. He visited his home in San Angel daily and did some of his early paintings in Paalen's studio. Paalen's cultivated background, his erudition and cosmopolitan world view impressed the young

Above: Matta, *Listen to Living*, 1941, oil on canvas, 29½ x 37⅜ inches; The Museum of Modern Art, New York, Inter-American Fund.

Meyer Schapiro, *Surrealist Picnic under the Tree of Liberty. The Great Master of Modern Liberty Distributes Very Ancient Apples as Prizes for the Best Manifestations of Modern Liberty,* c. 1941–1942, ink and watercolor on paper. Courtesy of the artist; photograph by Jack Peters.

American, who became a translator for and contributor to Paalen's periodical *Dyn*. In 1945 when Motherwell worked with George Wittenborn on the Problems of Contemporary Art series, Paalen's *Form and Sense* was the first book to appear.

The Seligmanns, meanwhile, visited Meyer Schapiro and his family in South Londonderry, Vermont, and enjoyed it enough to return to stay at a nearby guest house in August. Their correspondence reveals not only the keen interest they shared in hermetic writings but also their enjoyment of the pastoral life, picnicking, berry gathering, and attempting to dam the small stream that flowed past the Schapiro farmhouse. Schapiro made a drawing for Seligmann of André Breton under a tree handing down apples to the gathered Surrealists. They also worked on etchings together, and Seligmann appears to have confided in Schapiro some of his difficulties with the Surrealist group and, on a more anguished level, his anxiety over events in Europe.

In October 1941 there appeared a special Surrealist issue of *View*, with Nicolas Calas as guest editor. This was in large part devoted to an interview Calas had done with Breton and served as an official notice of the latter's presence in New York. Asked what changes he foresaw taking place in art in view of world events, Breton predicted "the birth of a new spirit from the present war. It is certain that whatever persists in growing as if nothing were happening stands self-condemned." [30] His response to Calas's question about the present orientation of Surrealism is the first English translation of Breton's own words on the movement. In describing what is ending in Surrealism he settles a few grudges (with Dalí and Eluard); under the heading of what is continuing he lists those Surrealists who currently have his seal of approval, including the Americans Joseph Cornell and David Hare, and he stresses collective activity. Finally he summarizes his philosophy in the section on what is beginning:

Conquerors and conquered appear to me headed for the same abyss if they do not instruct themselves before it is too late in the process which set them one against the other. . . . It is rationalism, a closed rationalism which is killing the world. . . . The program of Surrealism is to render to man the concrete empire of his functions; the plunge in the diving bell of automatism, the conquest of the irrational. [31]

Breton concluded the interview by promising a Third Manifesto of Surrealism.

The Breton interview filled the front page of *View*, which was still in newspaper format, except that in the center was Leonora Carrington's *Self-Portrait* last seen hanging from a tree at Air Bel. It must have arrived with the work Ernst had shipped from Europe. Drawings by Ernst, Sage, Matta, Domínguez, Lam, and Tanguy are scattered through the issue, which also contains Seligmann's article "An Eye for a

Top: Matta, *Thanksgiving Turkey,* a version of the crayon drawing given to the Reises, Thanksgiving 1941. Courtesy Latin American Masters Gallery, Los Angeles.

Bottom: André Breton, *Surrealist Composition with Postcard and String,* collage for *VVV* portfolio, 1941, 18 x 14 inches; The Baltimore Museum of Art, Bequest of Saidie A. May.

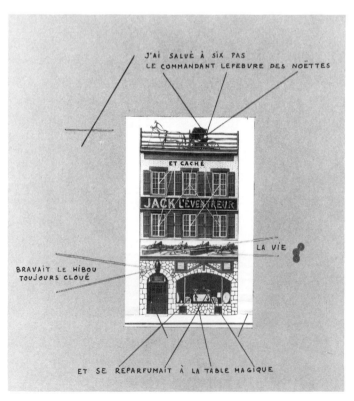

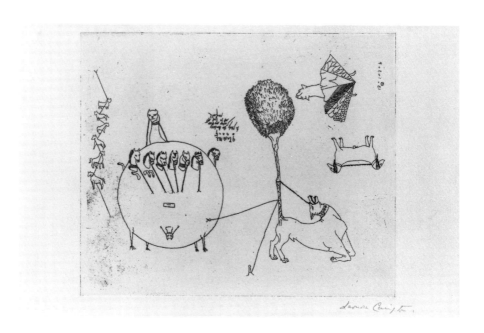

Tooth" and a Gotham Book Mart ad for "Surrealist specials." *View*, although it had begun as a literary review that Ford had originally called "The Poetry Paper," had moved by the end of a year of publication directly into the Surrealist camp and was focused particularly on material by and about the émigré artists. Thus in some ways it functioned as the continuation of the series of periodicals, *La Révolution Surréaliste, Surréalisme au Service de la Révolution,* and *Minotaure,* that had served as mouthpieces for the movement in Europe. This was something that no group of American artists had during the Depression and war years (with the exception of the politically oriented *Art Front*), and it certainly played a role in the regrouping of the émigrés and in establishing a sense of continuity between the two cultures. However, unlike the earlier publications it was not directly under Breton's control, and this led to a certain amount of friction between his coterie and the circle around Charles Henri Ford, exacerbated by the former's homophobia. It would not be long before he felt the need for an American journal of his own. In the meantime he was kept busy working on the text for a book about Peggy Guggenheim's collection, in return for which she supported the Breton family during their first year in New York.

At a Thanksgiving dinner held at the Reises plans were hatched for financing the new publication that Breton and his cohorts envisioned. Bernard Reis proposed that they each contribute a print for a portfolio to be published in a limited edition of fifty copies, each containing ten prints, to be sold for $100 each. Subsequently Calder, Carrington, Chagall, Masson, Seligmann, and Tanguy each prepared a plate and these were printed by Seligmann on his own etching press. Ernst did a handcolored frottage, David Hare a photograph, and Matta and Motherwell did individ-

Above: Leonora Carrington, *Animals,* c. 1941, etching for *VVV* portfolio, 8 x 10 inches; The Baltimore Museum of Art, Bequest of Saidie A. May.

ual works in ink and watercolor for each portfolio. André Breton made an original collage for each portfolio using a French postcard and adding handwritten phrases and stitching string and sequins to each page. The Reises and Pierre Matisse helped to market the portfolios, but evidently only twenty were produced and sold rather than the fifty that had been envisioned. In any event the impetus had been set in motion to launch a new journal the following spring.

Late in the day of December 7, 1941, Meyer Schapiro received a phone call from Breton. "What," he asked, "was the date of publication of Newton's *Opticks?*" When Schapiro replied 1699, he was disappointed. He had hoped that it was 1713, which when elided (and using a French 7) would have been his initials; he had wanted to use it as a signature in a box he was doing on Newton. Then, as an afterthought, Breton asked, "Do you think there will be war?" True to form, even as the U.S. Pacific fleet sank at anchor and a substantial air force lay in ruins, Breton maintained his stance of disengagement.

The entry of the United States into the war placed it now officially in the position of defending European culture and democratic freedoms against fascism. Just as the mechanisms of defense production, already in motion for Lend-Lease, accelerated and expanded, so did the propaganda machinery gear up to convince the American public of the necessity of making common cause with England and the Free French. Henceforth the intellectual and artistic refugees became allies, representatives of the cultural heritage of the Western democracies that Americans were now being called on to make an all-out effort to save. Extra-aesthetic value began to be ascribed to the artists in exile, and the United States began to be perceived not just as their refuge but as defender, avenger, and legitimate heir. This shift in position gradually came to be reflected in the growing confidence and independence of its artists vis-à-vis the Europeans. First, however, came the dark night of the war, the radio broadcasts from London with the sound of bombs falling in the background, ignominy and retreat in the Pacific, and the gnawing awareness that something sinister beyond belief was happening inside German borders.

Writing during those grim months in the magazine *Art in Australia,* André Masson said: "In this night of the spirit only the U.S. and the British Empire, by respecting individual expression, are maintaining the essential values of civilization. . . . What counts in the history of man is the free expression, constantly being renewed, of life and destiny." He went on: "We are living in an extremely disturbed moment in history, and it is not necessary either that the painter should conceal the

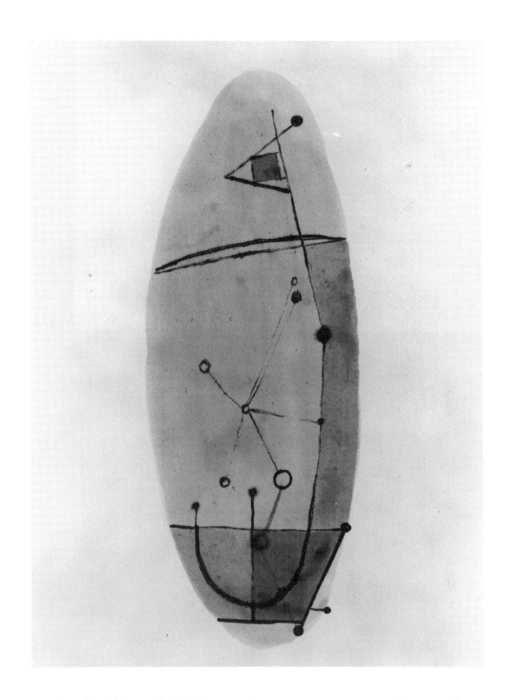

disquietude of his epoch."[32] These words, written in Connecticut by a Frenchman, published in English on the other side of the world, seem to be at the crux of this story of cultural change. That something convulsive, to borrow Breton's synonym for beauty, should happen in art is to be expected; that it should happen at the confluence of two groups, deracinated Europeans and Americans in a transition to global consciousness, almost takes on an aura of historical destiny.

Above: Robert Motherwell, *Yellow Abstract Composition, VVV* portfolio, c. 1941, gouache on paper, 8¾ x 4¾ inches; The Baltimore Museum of Art, Bequest of Saidie A. May.

6 New York, 1942: *Veils and Transparents*

In less than a decade, America has made room for the biggest intellectual and artistic migration since the fall of Constantinople. Outwardly the infiltration has been peaceful enough, yet the conflict is already on and, as there is no melting pot which fuses ideas, one side or the other must inevitably dominate. Another ten years will tell us which.

Rosamund Frost, *Art News,* March 15, 1942

While the U.S. war machine shifted gears from Lend-Lease to all-out production for global armed conflict, its propaganda apparatus speeded up its output of anti-Axis images. This endeavor enlisted the services of many artists who turned from social realism to grisly caricatures of fascist leaders or galvanizing images of fighting men at the front. Some artists entered the armed services as war reporters or staff artists for the service newspapers. Some who were not in the army designed camouflage or worked in defense plants. A very few risked a prison sentence as war resisters or did menial labor as conscientious objectors. The artists who were to be the nucleus of the future New York School were, for one reason or another, nonparticipants, as of course were the Surrealist émigrés. In fact artists returning from the service in the mid-1940s complained that they had "missed the beginning of abstract expressionism."[1]

Such extraordinary and anxiety-fraught times called for an extraordinary art, not one that could be plucked from the roster of existing styles but something that would express the urgency and the scope of the conflict that had erupted around the world. It was not enough to realistically depict human suffering, nor would the depersonalized relationships of geometric abstraction fill the bill; a new language, a new image had to be invented. With so many lives at risk the idea that art should also involve a risk must have seemed appropriate.

Although Surrealism had started as an attempt by several medical students turned poets to explore the human psyche largely through verbal experiments, twenty years later it was identified more widely with its visual manifestations, some of which had their origins in automatic processes. The presence of the émigrés in New York and the visibility of their work in its small art arena gave the American artists an opportunity to observe automatism at work and to examine at first hand the art that it generated, though they had little awareness of Surrealism's original objectives. What they saw, however, did in some instances function as a catalyst in releasing previously untapped forces in their approach to making art. Further, the milieu in which these two groups of artists connected with each other—that is, art dealers, curators, patrons, critics, and a diversified intellectual community—provided feedback and a support system that reinforced the experimental directions in which the young Americans were moving.

The first months of 1942 saw brilliant gallery exhibitions of the work of Masson, Ernst, Tanguy, and Matta in addition to Pierre Matisse's now famous gathering, "Artists in Exile." These were only a prelude to the newsworthy events of the late fall, the "First Papers of Surrealism" exhibition and the opening of Peggy Guggenheim's Art of This Century, a showcase for her own collection and a gallery featuring Surrealist artists and their friends. *View,* which devoted special issues to Max Ernst and Tanguy, was joined by two new reviews, *VVV* under the direction of Breton and Ernst, and *Dyn* published by former Surrealist Wolfgang Paalen. It was the period during which, as Robert Lebel said, "everybody met everybody. The influence was collective and this is how it spread. Each one met someone through another one. The Reises had a party at least once a month; everyone met at Peggy Guggenheim's parties—Pollock, Baziotes, and Rothko; the Janises invited all of us and there was an open house at the Askews every Sunday. Later the Americans hid their Surrealist paintings, but when we saw Pollock during the war he was like a little boy in front of Max Ernst."[2]

The émigrés, then, despite their poverty, had a visibility in print and a support network that the American painters on the whole lacked, especially after the Federal Art Project dwindled away at the outset of the 1940s. This network included literary spokesmen, connections to wealth and private collectors, even to influence in Washington through Frances Perkins and others, connections to the museum world through Sweeney and Soby, dedicated and established dealers, and, of course, reputations that had preceded them, thanks to Alfred Barr, Julien Levy, and others. By the end of 1942, they would also have several extraordinary showcases for the works they continued to produce, complete with a press response American painters had not even begun to dream of. Naturally all these supporters had a certain stake in these artists, whether one of aesthetic judgment or financial investment. This was not a calculated situation since it had arisen out of a series of unforeseeable circumstances and chance connections. The American support derived from a combination of sympathy for the plight of the refugees, excitement generated by their work and their presence, and a desire to graft onto this European stock some new developments in American culture.

Within Surrealism—if it is still possible at this point to say "within"—certain distinct tendencies could be perceived, the most important of which was a greater degree of occultization. This may be ascribed in part to the charismatic proseletizing of Matta, who had an intense interest in the occult and urged his American friends to read the nineteenth-century French occultist Eliphas Lévi. Also reinforcing this direction was Kurt Seligmann with his erudite articles on magic, the arcane symbolism of his intricate etchings that seemed only a few steps beyond Bosch, and the popular evenings of magic demonstrations he held in his studio. And then came Breton's surprising proposal for a new myth, one that was the very essence of mystification, the "Great Transparents." References to alchemy abound in the artworks and in the pages of *View,* an interest reinforced by Jung's writings, which found in alchemy parallels for psychological processes.

Morphology was another distinct preoccupation. This refers to the form and structure of an organism considered as a whole, that is, inner and outer, as it evolves and changes—one might say the intersection of form and process. Some of the Americans, notably Gerome Kamrowski, had been influenced by D'Arcy Thompson's *On Growth and Form* and were particularly receptive to this aspect of Surrealism.

Above: Kurt Seligmann, *Life Goes On,* 1942, ink on paper; present whereabouts unknown.

Opposite: Kurt Seligmann, *Announcement for Magic Evening,* c. 1942.

Masson was becoming more and more involved, as we have seen, in what he called the telluric, a sense for the regenerative forces within the earth and consequent vegetal growth. Matta had used microphotographs of botanical details as the basis for his drawings back in 1938. ("Je suis monté à cheval à travers la botanique" is the way he described his origins as a painter.)[3] Max Ernst applied his new technique of dripped and blotted paint to a subject matter of exotic vegetation and fantastic rock forms that seem to be in a simultaneous process of growth and decay. At the same time the earlier Surrealist predilection for uneasy juxtapositions of antithetical images appears to have been on the wane. It is almost axiomatic that when a painter is attempting to express process or transformation, edges will blur, leaving shapes ambiguous. Hence the more fixed, albeit hallucinatory, images of classic Surrealism gave way to effects of allover fluctuation. Even a veristic draftsman like Kurt Seligmann subsumed quirky detail in turbulent, whirlwind-like images that convey a twisting force, images that he referred to as cyclonic, "suggestive of a world in formation."

Transparency was also a frequent subject among the Surrealists in the New York years. Onslow Ford and Matta had been pursuing the idea of "transparent worlds" since reading Ouspensky on "the great transparent reality that surrounds us everyday." It was Matta, by most accounts, who introduced to Breton the notion of the Great Transparents that became the core of his new myth. That great transparent artwork, Duchamp's *Large Glass,* with its suspended images and tangible cracks,

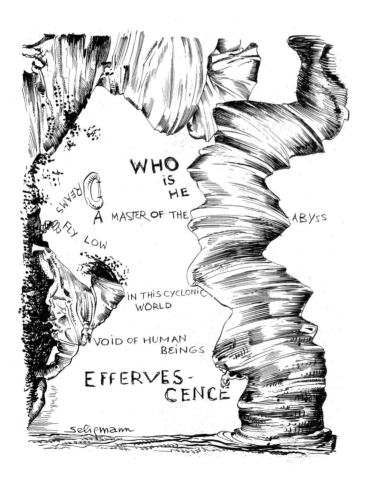

exercised a considerable fascination for the émigrés who could at last see it in Katherine Dreier's living room. As mentioned earlier, Kurt Seligmann used the mysterious technique of reverse glass painting in which the painting is seen through the glass on which it is painted, the painting support, as it were, rendered transparent. Breton had actually described in the pages of *Nadja* a transparent house of glass in which he dreamed of living. And Pierre Chareau, the architect in 1930 of the unique Paris house known as the "Maison de Verre," was also a refugee in New York, where he designed the façade and interior of the Free French canteen on Second Avenue and, in 1944, a house in East Hampton for Robert Motherwell. (The "Maison de Verre" more than any other building of the interwar period embodied Surrealist principles of contradiction and enigma, and in its façade of glass blocks Chareau certainly toyed with the idea of the transparent house.)

Thus automatism was merely one among a number of preoccupations current among the Surrealists during the early 1940s. It is important to keep in mind that Surrealism in its origins was à mode of experimentation. Its practitioners were not seeking a new style in art or a platform that could be slid into a historical niche. Although a gradual process of commodification took place during their U.S. sojourn as a result of their arrangements with New York galleries, in 1942 Surrealism's original experimental and clinical intentions still had momentum.

The year started with a Masson doubleheader: simultaneous exhibitions of paintings and pastels done since his arrival at Curt Valentine's Buchholz gallery and of ink drawings and etchings from 1938 to 1942 at the Marian Willard gallery. Some of his new work engaged themes he had already been working on in Europe, such as *Monument in a Desert,* which was based on the fourth drawing in his 1938 *Mythology of Nature,* or that perennial Surrealist favorite, the praying mantis, or the landscape as the body of a woman as in *Matriarchal Landscape.* In addition there were several paintings—notably *The Jungle, Woman of Martinique,* and the collage *The Street Singer,* inspired by his stay in the Antilles, and two oils of substantial size, *The Nasturtium* and *The Sleeper,* apparently completed in early 1942—that give clear evidence of his new preoccupation with observed nature and the interconnectedness of a variety of elements in the growth process. In contrast to the works on the theme of germination that he was to paint later in 1942 and in 1943, in *The Sleeper* he still used an anthropomorphic presiding genius or earth mother figure who shelters "a gestating plant-animal organism," as well as nurturing breasts and a pregnant woman implanted in the ground.[4] The Museum of Modern Art bought the *Street Singer* from this exhibition.

The works on paper in the Willard gallery exhibition offered the same diversity of themes and included the drawings for *Mythology of Being,* which Wittenborn had just published with a Masson poem, eight drawings, and an etching. Not only were the subjects drawn from a diversity of sources, but the styles ranged widely from Daliesque illusionism to allover abstraction, from combinations of supple linear brush drawings with amorphous drifts of color to a wholly painterly treatment such as that of *Landscape in the Shape of a Fish* with its dispersed shapes and shallow spatial fluctuation. In other words, the younger American painters seeing these exhibitions would have encountered a highly sophisticated artist yet one who could not be categorized, an artist of international reputation who was searching, experimenting in a free cursive mode, unencumbered by ideological considerations or by the exigencies of the marketplace.

The reviewer for *Art News* chose to cover the Masson shows together with exhibitions by Boris Margo (Artists Gallery) and Walter Quirt (Pinacotheca), calling them "Three Fantasists." She wrote, "Theirs may be the idiom most tellingly reflecting this convulsed epoch," and referred to the cruelty in Masson and the bluntness of Quirt, while Margo "belongs to the automatic school—smears paint around the canvas until it takes its own form.[5]

In March Pierre Matisse arranged an exhibition he called "Artists in Exile," and gathered the émigrés in the studio of George Platt Lynes for a now-famous photograph. Included were all the Surrealists plus Chagall, Léger, Lipchitz, Mondrian, Ozenfant, and Ossip Zadkine, as well as Eugene Berman, whose magic realism vaguely aligned him with the *View* circle. It was possibly the most impressive assemblage of artists in one room and in one photograph that the twentieth century has

Opposite: Pierre Chareau, façade of Free French canteen on Second Avenue, c. 1942; courtesy the Archives Maison de Verre.

George Platt Lynes, photograph for the announcement of the "Artists in Exile"
exhibition at the Pierre Matisse Gallery, March 1942. From left to right, first row:
Matta Echaurren, Ossip Zadkine, Yves Tanguy, Max Ernst, Marc Chagall, Fernand
Léger; second row: André Breton, Piet Mondrian, André Masson, Amédée
Ozenfant, Jacques Lipchitz, Pavel Tchelitchew, Kurt Seligmann, Eugene Berman.
Photograph courtesy the Museum of Modern Art, New York.

seen—as Jimmy Ernst commented, it would have been impossible in Europe to get
this same group together in one room. More than half of those present had arrived
thanks to the Emergency Rescue Committee. The photograph was published in a
small catalogue with a brief introduction by James Thrall Soby and a longer essay
by Nicolas Calas. Soby's text was both a welcome to the refugees and a plea for
internationalism in the arts as he warned against the forming of a xenophobic circle
by American artists and patrons. Calas's essay considered the historical significance
of the cultural displacement and described the current crisis as necessitating a "re-
shifting of the order of values in a kind of intellectual shake-up." He believed that it
was also necessary for the "pioneers of culture" from both continents to agree on
their outlook on the future and that this outlook would be affected by the fact that
it was formulated on a continent that lay between two vast oceans linking Europe
and Asia.

Pierre Matisse showed one work by each artist completed since their arrival,
including Masson's *Seeded Earth*, Seligmann's *Borealis Efflorescence*, and Tanguy's
Time and Again. Matta's *The Initiation* was hailed in *Art News* as "an arresting

piece of combustion in paint. . . . Matta brings something special to America and it reads like a new language . . . artists who must rack their brains for themes should get a load of this dynamo of things to come."[6] The most striking painting of this exhibition, however, must have been Max Ernst's *Europe after the Rain,* a long horizontal landscape begun in Europe and completed in the United States. Ernst used the decalcomania process for the earth and its strange excrescences while the blue sky and white clouds seem to have been lifted from the flawless calendar art of the day, an incongruity that added to the baffling unreality of the putrefying world that stretched across the canvas. Embedded in the crevices of the intricately textured bizarre formations, suggestive of rocks and ruins and fossilized growth, are a dozen or more figures, hovering, like hallucinations, on the edge of perception. Two larger figures, one a bird-headed man turned toward the viewer, the other a dark-haired woman turned away toward the distance, stand near what appears to be a fallen idol, a huge half-buried bull. Are Ernst and Leonora Carrington passing in the ruins of their world, as they passed from time to time in New York? Displaced, no matter how comfortably, in a strange country while his native Germany occupied his adopted France, subjected to harsh internment by that adopted homeland, suspect now as a German in the United States, shaken by the circumstances of the break with Leonora, Ernst had more than enough reason to paint a bizarre and desolate postcataclysmic world. The decalcomania technique with its veined effects and blurred edges was ideally suited to the conveying of a state of decay in which the various forms of matter seem to be eliding in a general state of putrefaction. Yet enough twisting shapes remain to remind one of the desolate rocky setting of the Dalí-Buñuel film *L'Âge d'or,* in which Ernst had appeared. *Europe after the Rain* was reproduced in the March 15 issue of *Art News,* and it was purchased from the exhibition by Chick Austin for the Wadsworth Atheneum.

A week before the "Artists in Exile" exhibition closed, the Valentine Gallery opened a show of Max Ernst paintings from 1937 to 1942. Ernst described his three

Max Ernst, *Europe after the Rain,* 1940–1942, oil on canvas, 54.8 x 147.8 cm;
The Wadsworth Atheneum, The Ella Gallup Sumner and Mary Catlin Sumner Fund.

Max Ernst, *The Robing of the Bride,* 1940, oil on canvas, 51 x 37⅞ inches; The
Solomon R. Guggenheim Foundation, New York, Peggy Guggenheim Collection,
Venice.

shows of that year, in New York, New Orleans, and Chicago, as "three absolute
flops. The press was either antagonistic or maintained a conspiracy of silence; the
public reaction negative." [7] Actually his New York show was given a long and not
altogether bad review in the *Times* by Edwin Alden Jewell; *What Is Going On in
Africa?* and *Antipope* were reproduced in *Art Digest;* and his show at the Arts Club
of Chicago got good coverage in the local press and a burst of enthusiasm in the
Chicago Sun. During the three previous turbulent years Ernst had not only been
productive on an unprecedented level, but had expanded both his means and his
imagery to give a new depth to his work. His earlier Dada-derived provocative juxtapositions of irreconcilable elements, the chancy frottages, collage novels, and wondrous transformations of medical illustrations, had played a major role in the
formulation of visual surrealism in the 1920s. By the later 1930, however, with his
pictorial imagination released by the adoption of the decalcomania process, his canvases took on an illusionistic appearance reminiscent of the German illustrative tradition. One had to look closely to discover how much of this effect had been arrived
at by the haphazard process of dripping and blotting the paint, especially since he
combined this technique with exquisitely precise Cranach-like painting to produce
enigmas like the *Robing of the Bride.* This painting and the similar *Antipope* were
described by Jewell in the *New York Times* as being beyond comprehension. Here
again human figures partially metamorphose into birds as feathery mantles enfold
heads and bodies. Perhaps we are seeing M.E. himself in the guise of the bird Loplop,
as well as hints of the conflicting feelings that beset him in his relationship with Peggy
Guggenheim. Certainly the face and body of Leonora haunt these paintings just as
she haunted his first year in New York.

The April issue of *View* was devoted to Ernst and, with a checklist inserted,
served as the catalogue for the exhibition. Among its contents were Breton's "The
Legendary Life of M.E., Preceded by a Brief Discussion on the Need for a New
Myth," "Max Ernst, Bird Superior," by Leonora Carrington, a photo of Ernst in a
feathery jacket seated cross-legged among his kachinas by James Thrall Soby, and
another photo of Ernst by Berenice Abbott. Joseph Cornell paid homage in a "Story
without a Name for M.E." told with collaged engravings. The collective image is of
a not quite human personage, one whose identity has merged with that of his alter
ego, the bird Loplop. There seems to have emanated from his slight frame and fine-
featured countenance, haloed by whitened hair and pierced by blue eyes, something
of the aura of one who has been miraculously saved. Twice wounded in combat in

Max Ernst with his collection of kachinas, 1941, photograph by James Thrall
Soby.

Dorothea Tanning, *Self-Portrait,* 1943, oil on canvas; private collection.

the First World War, interned and escaped three times in France at the outset of World War II, rescued from almost certain deportation by the Emergency Rescue Committee and the financial help of Peggy Guggenheim, he had brushed against death so many times that he must have seemed graced with invulnerability.

The inconveniences and humiliations of his status as an enemy alien after Pearl Harbor had finally brought about the marriage of Max Ernst to Peggy Guggenheim by a Maryland justice of the peace. She had rented a triplex apartment on Beekman Place where they lived in anything but domestic bliss, as described by Jimmy Ernst, whom Peggy had hired as her general assistant, and numerous other witnesses. The legendary parties, riotous gatherings where the émigrés and their American circle of friends and patrons drank cheap scotch and carried on polyglot debates, have been described often enough, not least by the hostess herself. There seems to have been no wartime damper on the social life of this group between the round of openings, cocktail parties, dinners in one studio or another or at Rocco's on Thompson Street, and weekends in Connecticut. "I went out every night," reminisced one woman painter who gravitated between European and American art circles in those years. At one of these social events, an opening at Julien Levy's gallery not many months after his marriage to Peggy Guggenheim, Ernst met Dorothea Tanning, a painter from the Midwest who was as fascinating as her unique surreal paintings. This encounter sealed the fate of the unstable marriage and prompted Peggy Guggenheim to look beyond the Surrealists in quest of new art and artists.

It is not hard to grasp why Ernst's extremely literary, often archaizing paintings did not attract followers among American painters. Much as they might have admired his ingenuity and fecund imagination, there was little in their artistic backgrounds, whether regionalism, social realism, or abstraction, that offered any resonance with Ernst's seemingly illustrational fairy-tale fantasies. There was, however, according to Ernst, one work, shown later that year by Betty Parsons at the Wakefield Gallery, that intrigued several of the American painters because of its unusual technique. With the benefit of hindsight, he recounts in his "Biographical notes—tissue of truth, tissue of lies" how he told them it was child's play. "Tie a piece of string, one or two meters long, to an empty tin can, punch a small hole in the bottom and fill the tin with thin paint. Then lay the canvas flat on the floor and swing the tin backwards and forwards over it, guiding it with movements of your hands, arms, shoulders and your whole body. In this way surprising lines will drip onto the canvas. Then you can start playing with free associations." [8] We have already read Masson's exhortation to lay the canvas flat on the floor and move the body above it as if in an inspired dance. Here is Max Ernst now also talking about canvases laid on the floor and painting by moving the entire body. Whether or not he actually said those words in 1942 is immaterial; the works themselves were evidence of the process and Ernst could also be seen that summer on Cape Cod swinging a paint can over a canvas spread out on the kitchen floor. Meanwhile we have Hayter's word that everyone was curious about the drip can on a compound pendulum that hung at Atelier 17. As we saw in chapter 3, experiments with dripping paint onto a horizontal surface were not lacking prior to the Surrealist arrival. In fact, with the exception of Onslow Ford's impulsive pouring of lacquers to produce his coulages, there

is little evidence for the émigrés having worked in this way before coming to the United States, and for none of them was the gestural drip an end in itself.

Pierre Matisse followed "Artists in Exile" with an exhibition of Matta's most recent work. It must have been a stunning show, including as it did his first major works, such as *Rain*, already owned by James Thrall Soby, *The Earth Is a Man*, purchased from the Matisse gallery by Henry Clifford, and *Locus Solus*, the title taken from a Surrealist favorite, the book of that name by Raymond Roussel. The words printed in Matta's catalogue were extracts from *Dr. Faustroll Pataphysicien* by another Surrealist demigod, Alfred Jarry, and include the totally contradictory and mock-pretentious definition of pataphysics, as if to give a clue to the contradictory nature of the worlds of his painting. He was working on a much larger scale than previously, and this gave the works an enveloping quality. One could experience without peripheral interference Matta's multidirectional, multidimensional spatial pulls, so different from conventionally constructed perspectival space.

Opposite: Max Ernst, *La Planète affolée,* 1942, oil on canvas, 110 x 140 cm; Tel
Aviv Museum of Art.

Above: Matta, *The Earth Is a Man,* 1942, oil on canvas, 182.9 x 238.8 cm; The
Art Institute of Chicago, gift of Mr. and Mrs. Joseph Randall Shapiro.

The Earth Is a Man was the culminating painting in the volcanic series partially
inspired by his trip to Mexico the previous summer. (Matta had used this title earlier
for the long poetic scenario he had written in 1936 on hearing of the murder of
García Lorca by the Falangists.) His particular technique of sponging on and wiping
off thinned pigment to produce translucent layers of color effectively conveyed the
convulsions that dissolve the boundaries between earth and sky, as the atmosphere
reddens with glowing volcanic matter and the earth becomes yellow-white with heat.
The space seems to engulf the viewer as the eye is pulled in multiple directions over
the canvas surface. In later years Matta commented that what he had been trying to
show at the time was "human energy as a system in expansion in the cosmos." [9]

James Thrall Soby saw this painting as the climax of Matta's early manner,
whereas *Locus Solus* was the beginning of a search for a "sterner architectonic order." At the suggestion of Breton Matta tried combining his diaphanous screens of
color with the complex linear perspectives of his drawings. As Soby, who was witness

to these years, put it: "In a number of canvases painted in 1941 and 1942, Matta pierced his thin sprays of color with triangular or rectangular corridors, white, solid, heavily lined, leading past walls of flame or cutting through banked mists of rose, yellow and blue."[10] *Locus Solus,* with its abrupt transitions from painterly to linear sections, becomes a powerful metaphor for the contradictory pulls between chaos and order. The sponged-on paint and the crisp brush-drawing of transparent structures offer a dialectic between two opposing modes of visual signifying.

This counterpoint of Matta's also became the key to the breakthrough that enabled Arshile Gorky to achieve the lyric brilliance of his final style. For Gorky this change appears to have begun during the summer of 1942 with the painting *The Pirate I,* a work that was done when he was staying at the home of Sol Schary in New Milford, Connecticut. Inspired by the intrusion of a neighbor's dog into their yard, this painting consists largely of pale washes of runny paint delicately touched with passages of the fluent line drawing that was to become the quintessential Gorky.

Masson later said that Gorky was the only American painter he knew, and it's likely that it was during this 1942 stay that they met since Gorky was to spend much of 1943 and 1944 in Virginia and Masson returned to Europe in 1945, although not until some months after the Gorkys moved into David Hare's house near New Preston. In any event Diego Masson remembers Gorky coming to their house, and the possibility of Masson's telluric painting inspiring Gorky to work more on themes from nature should not be discounted. The consummate draftsman in Gorky must have admired the same in Masson, as well as his willingness to take risks. For all their capacity for improvisation, both artists had a strong predilection for classical composition and retained throughout their careers a sense of themselves as part of the painting tradition. However, it was ultimately Matta, according to Meyer Schapiro, who showed Gorky how to flow on paint in thinned washes and to improvise with a thin, supple, brush-drawn line.

Soby mentioned Matta's fascination with something most people have forgotten, Thomas Wilfred's Clavilux, which must have both inspired him and confirmed his own visions.[11] Since 1913 Wilfred had pioneered in the creation of an art of color and light, touring the world giving performances on his color organ and building consoles containing screens across which colors wafted in an ever-changing interplay. The Clavilux was installed in its own space, known as the Art Institute of Light, in the Grand Central Palace, where public "lumia" recitals were given weekly from 1933 until 1943 when the building became an induction center. The seemingly va-

Opposite: Matta, *Locus Solus,* 1942, oil on canvas, 75 x 94.5 cm; private collection.

Below: Arshile Gorky, *The Pirate I,* 1942, oil on canvas, 29 x 40 inches; private collection.

View, cover of Tanguy/Tchelitchew issue, May 1942.

porous drifts of color were actually produced by revolving disks of painted glass, colored light bulbs, and polarizers, but watching the screen was like traveling through the layers of multidimensional space of a Matta painting of the early 1940s.

Following the Ernst issue of *View,* Charles Henri Ford implemented his plan to associate Tchelitchew with the Surrealists by producing a double issue in May that, opened from one side, was devoted to Tanguy, while reversed and opened from the other side it featured Tchelitchew. To this issue James Johnson Sweeney contributed an essay, "Tanguy, Iconographer of Melancholy," illustrated with a photograph of Tanguy by his cousin by marriage, David Hare; the continuity between reproductions was written by Hare's half-brother, John Goodwin, whose father Phillip was a trustee as well as architect of the Museum of Modern Art. Breton's contribution, "What Tanguy Veils and Reveals," was translated by Lionel Abel, a poet who was to be involved with the Surrealists for the next few years. Breton's longtime first lieutenant, Benjamin Péret, sent an essay on Tanguy from Mexico. Such was the extended family of Surrealism in exile.

Breton's use of the word "veils" in relation to Tanguy suggests that to conceal may actually be to reveal, a notion that Rothko was to make a cornerstone of his work a few years later. "With Tanguy," writes Breton, "we enter a world of latency for the first time . . . the inner landscape changes every minute . . . it consists of indistinct markings which melt one into the other. We are behind the scenes of life."

It must have galled Breton that a publication so focused on Surrealism as *View* was not only out of his control, but also under the editorship of someone of whom he did not wholly approve. That spring he faced a new challenge from an unexpected quarter. Wolfgang Paalen, to whom Breton had been addressing warmly cordial letters for several years, launched his own periodical, *Dyn,* and led off with the announcement of his resignation from Breton's group in his essay "Farewell to Surrealism." Although published in Mexico, *Dyn* was written in French and English, not Spanish. The tone of its articles, as well as the advertisements it ran for New York institutions like the Gotham Book Mart and *Partisan Review,* indicate that it was addressed primarily to a New York audience, in particular the émigré artists and their American colleagues. In effect *Dyn,* which ran until 1944, represented Paalen's bid to become the center of a new group that would go, as he put it, "beyond Surrealism." The contents of this publication, both its articles and the art reproduced in its pages, were of considerable importance for the direction American artists were to pursue for the next few years.

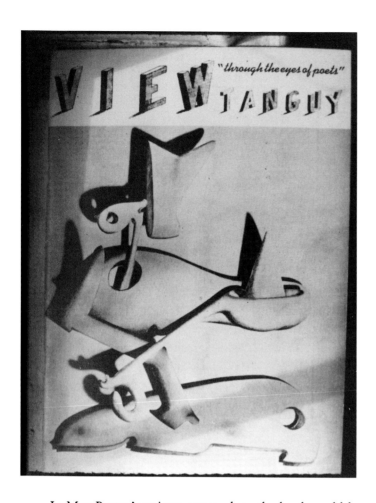

In May Breton's unique approach to the book could be seen in the catalogue Peggy Guggenheim published of her collection entitled *Art of This Century*. Most of the decisions, such as using photographs of the eyes of the artists next to their works, were his, as was the selection of artists' statements. Several important documents of twentieth-century art were included as appendixes. The book, of which 2,500 copies were issued, had a cover by Max Ernst and was printed partially in green ink, the color in which Breton habitually wrote. Breton's long essay, "Genesis and Perspectives of Surrealism," was essentially a survey of the modern movement, culminating in Surrealism. For the first time in English a definition of automatism was available:

Automatism is the only mode of expression which gives entire satisfaction to both eye and ear by achieving a rhythmic unity . . . there is a grave risk, however, that a work of art will move out of the Surrealist orbit unless, underground at least there flows a current of Automatism. The Surrealism in a work is in direct proportion to the efforts the artist has made to embrace the whole psycho-physical field, of which consciousness is only a small fraction.[12]

Breton knew from long experience the important role a publication could play in holding together a group and attracting new adherents, and having control of a publication was crucial to the carrying on of his work in the United States. Goaded by Matta and others of the more abstract-automatist members of the group, Breton spearheaded the founding of a new mouthpiece for New York Surrealism, *VVV.*

Dyn no. 1, April 1942, cover by Wolfgang Paalen.

Through his collective enterprise he must have hoped to give an impression of an expanded Surrealism with a new American following, hence the inclusion of Charles Henri Ford and his coterie and as many Americans as possible. One can sense the atmosphere from the lines Matta wrote to Gordon Onslow Ford in May: "This winter in New York was a very hot one—all energies were lost in personal quarrels. I was fighting most of the winter for the publication of *VVV;* now it is at the printer's. André at full strength—sabotage of all the click around *View* (Calas, Seligmann, etc.). Abel, the editor, wrote a very clear program." [13]

This program announced the scope of *VVV* as poetry, art, anthropology, sociology, and psychology, a range not too dissimilar from that of *Minotaure.* The handsomely produced first issue, with a cover by Max Ernst, contained contributions by, among others, Claude Lévi-Strauss, William Carlos Williams, Masson, Motherwell, Seligmann, Aimé Césaire, Gordon Onslow Ford, and, as a conciliatory gesture, Charles Henri Ford. Since an American was needed to act as editor, at least in name, Matta had proposed Motherwell, but at the outset Breton found him obtuse over the translation of the term "social consciousness" and David Hare was asked to lend his name instead. During his brief tenure as editor, Motherwell wrote to William Carlos Williams asking him to be the American literary editor. His letter includes a statement that makes clear where he stood vis-à-vis Surrealism at that point: "Now I have taken a partisan stand, in the creative sense that Surrealist automatism is the basis of my painting." [14] It is likely that more of the editing was done by Lionel Abel, as Matta suggests, since David Hare's letters of the time indicate a very shaky command of written English. In any event, the real control of "Triple V" was firmly in the hands of Breton and Max Ernst and its key essay was Breton's "Prolegomena to Third Manifesto of Surrealism—or else," which appeared both in French and in an English translation by Abel.

Breton had been promising a new manifesto, but to anyone who had hoped for galvanizing proclamations like those of 1924 and 1929 the "Prolegomena" must have seemed vague and anticlimactic. After a preamble that delivered salvos against Dalí, Aragon, and his old friend Eluard, as well as against those "who follow either the Bible or Lenin," he declared himself against all conformism, even a "too evident Surrealist conformism," and he deplored the number of imitators that the best-known Surrealists had already attracted—"Tomorrow it will be Matta's turn to be imitated." He maintained that the very principle of opposition needed to be fortified—"I give my vote to those who rise . . . I declare myself for the minority which

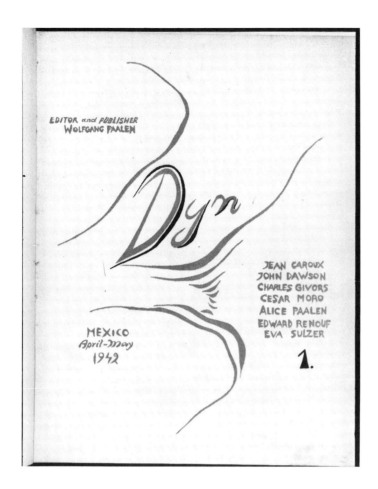

is ever reborn to act as a lever." Then he takes up a theme central to his beliefs, the fallacies of rationalism: "The sudden convulsion of this planet as we witness today is enough to make us question the adequacy, let alone the necessity, of the modes of knowledge and action chosen by man during the last historical period."[15]

Finally he turned to the question "Can society exist without a social myth?" — a question with which "some of the most lucid minds of the time have been grappling"; he mentioned Caillois, Duthuit, Masson, Mabille, Leonora Carrington, and Seligmann, among others. One of Breton's central postulates was that without a social myth a society does not exist. Mythic activity, according to Breton, has a dual purpose, therapeutic and mind-expanding. Far from contributing to oppression, mythic activity can and must participate in the emancipation of the mind.

He had long reflected on the subjective nature of time and space, an interest that must have been rekindled in his conversations with Matta. Out of these conversations grew the following proposal for a new myth, that of the Great Transparents:

Man is perhaps not the center, not the focus of the universe. One may go so far as to believe that there exists above him on the animal level beings whose behavior is as alien to him as his own must be to the day fly or the whale. There is nothing that would necessarily prevent such beings from completely escaping his sensory frame of reference since these beings might avail themselves of a type of camouflage, which no matter how you imagine it becomes plausible when you consider the theory of form and what has been discovered about mimetic animals.[16]

David Hare, *The Retroactive Wish as a Reality*, 1942, altered photograph,
reproduced in *VVV* no. 2-3, 1943.

In support of these hypothetical beings he quotes Novalis and William James and even cites the nineteenth-century scientist Emile Duclaux, who speculated on the existence of "beings whose albumens are straight."

Matta did a drawing entitled *The Great Transparents* to accompany the essay. Kurt Seligmann painted *Melusine and the Great Transparents*. Gerome Kamrowski, although he referred to the Great Transparents in retrospect as "a myth that didn't fly," did several paintings that evoke the invisible beings of Breton's new myth. One, of 1945, is actually entitled *Part I, The Great Invisibles: Script for an Impossible Documentary*. The idea of transparent beings took hold in a variety of ways and had its reverberations on a number of canvases, especially when merged with the renewed interest in Marcel Duchamp's *Large Glass*. As already suggested, the mystique surrounding glass and transparency, like the veiling of subject, intrigued this New York nucleus of European and American artists, Matta even going so far as to coin a word, "vitreurs," for the transparent beings who began to populate his canvases in 1944.

An indication of the way *VVV* was received may be seen in fragments of the July correspondence between Meyer Schapiro and Kurt Seligmann. Schapiro, who had formed a genuine intellectual friendship with Breton, his neighbor in Greenwich Village, received his copy of *VVV* in Vermont and wrote as follows to Seligmann:

The children tore it from my hands and have already read most of it and explored the pictures. Since they know so many of the contributors, they feel it is addressed to them. I had to explain at length the statistical chart of preferences in monsters and myths, a game they want to play as well. I haven't read the whole issue yet, but plucked the berries here and there, yours among the first, in a delicious, uncritical indolence. Here is my signboard of the condensed headlines, like the London newsbills.

  IS DOG MAN'S TRUEST
  FRIEND? SURREALIST
  SATRAP SAYS NO. NEW
  NEW SOCIAL MYTH IMMINENT
  BRILLIANT MINDS CAIRO
  NEW YORK RIO DISCUSS
  PROBLEM. SAVANT CONJE
  CTURES STRAIGHT ALBU
  MEN MEN. SPHINX STILL
  FAVORITE BLOODY NUN
  LAST. . . . .

Do you know the secret of the "straight albumens?" I will give you a hint: this man, who hunts the transparent whales in whose invisible entrails we live, tells time by a clock of which the hands turn leftward: 12, 11, 10 . . . 1, 1, 12, 10 . . . ; however, he is so formed that he can never see us inside the transparent whale (formed like one-way glass), but in physical equations he allows for our existence by adding a X on both sides for the possible unknown (like the pious Jews who say: "There are ten people present, not counting the invisible spirits, known only to God and the angels"). There is in the translation the awful implication that you and I have crooked or curved albumens; this is too ghastly for words. This is the issue on which surrealism may well fall; it is an assault on the construction de l'homme.[17]

Seligmann's response to Schapiro has been censored by nibbling mice, but enough remains to make his attitude clear: "The only qualification I can find for that issue is lousy. Specially lousy because the poverty of its thoughts, the obvious avoidance of having any clear parti-pris, the lack of new ideas is hidden under a dark red velvet mantle of [illegible]. I can only say one thing about Surrealism [missing] definitely dead."[18]

Nor was Matta any more pleased, despite his participation and the inclusion of Motherwell's essay on the perfidy of late De Chirico. He wrote to Onslow Ford: "*VVV* has turned into a democratic organ . . . everybody must have his percentage of the space and the original idea of a laboratory for the word and form in all its suicidal possibilities is gone. So much so that I am thinking of starting a different publication."[19] When he received his copy Onslow Ford wrote Matta:

Congratulations on les Grands Transparents which I like body and soul, really exciting and has filled me full of ideas. But apart from André's magnificent article, I find it rather difficult to get the direction that VVV is taking. Why were you and Bob not front page? Why was there no mention of Esteban? Why should corpses be imitated instead of trampled upon? Or maybe I misunderstood Abel's introduction. Anyway, best of luck with the next number. You can afford to be tough as they cannot do without you.[20]

Breton's "Prolegomena" was the occasion for the appearance in the summer issue of *View* of "Breton—A Dialogue" by the left-wing poet Harold Rosenberg, a scenario in which three intellectuals discuss the need for a new myth. One of the three agrees with Breton, saying that men cannot be set in motion together unless they are "filled with a powerful subjective vision." The second believes that society must be organized by science and that myths are an expression of ignorance. The third treads a middle ground, rejecting the "enslaving fiction of the supernatural I" and proposing that only "through the solidarity of his natural self with all other selves will the individual become entirely unique and real." This third position in the debate, obviously Rosenberg's, sees myths as "images that unify societies only to disintegrate humanity into warring cults," and holds that the production of myths has become the function of "Goebbels, Mussolini, and thousands of editors, advertising men, and information specialists."[21] A groundwork was already being laid here for the particular interpretation Rosenberg was to bring to abstract expressionism in the next decade, as well as for his lack of sympathy with Surrealism.

Despite these reservations, there is no doubt that some Americans were impressed by *VVV.* Jeanne Reynal expressed her praise in glowing terms, saying there was nothing else like it. And indeed there wasn't, for Breton's idea of a publication embodying the marvelous was certainly an anomaly among U.S. reviews. Inconsistencies in typefaces and colors of paper, combinations of drawings, photography, and

Gerome Kamrowski, *Part I, The Great Invisibles: Script for an Impossible Documentary*, 1945, oil on canvas, 72½ x 48 inches; courtesy the Washburn Gallery.

Marcel Duchamp with "found" readymade, Sanary, 1942, photograph by André Gomes.

old engravings, and uneasy juxtapositions of texts that might be anthropology on one page, poetry on the next, made perusing an issue of *VVV* at the very least an adventure in the unexpected. No matter how well the individual inclusions stood up under critical scrutiny, the ensemble was indeed out of the ordinary and made other publications seem pedestrian by comparison.

By the time *VVV* appeared in June a contingent of its contributors had gathered in Wellfleet on Cape Cod, where Matta had been living since May. A disgruntled Breton, who had been forced to accept employment at the Voice of America (where he joined Robert Lebel, Claude Lévi-Strauss, Denis de Rougemont, and Georges Duthuit) when Peggy Guggenheim informed him that she could no longer support him and his family, had to remain in the hot city. Guggenheim rented a summer house from John Phillips (later to be the second husband of Agnes Gorky), who recalls that the Surrealists came there because his wife had met Matta in a gallery in New York. In addition to the Mattas, who were installed in a more remote cottage, there were Max Ernst, Peggy Guggenheim, Leonora Carrington, Motherwell and his Mexican wife María, David Hare, and Jacqueline Lamba and Aube who became friends with the Phillips' daughters. The spy paranoia on the east coast led to suspicions of foreigners, especially Matta whose lonely house on the ocean had blackout shutters that the FBI thought might be signaling enemy U-boats. Phillips was under suspicion because of his tenants, and when the German-born Ernst showed up the local authorities actually took him into custody, questioned him at length, and finally released him after confiscating his flashlight.

"Problems with the electric generator took me over there frequently," landlord Phillips recalled. "They were very theatrical. They made me nervous, but they weren't boring. They wanted to project something by the way they walked, talked, and looked. I had the impression that they weren't thinking much outside the perimeters of their own emotional stuff. All the jokes were in-jokes. I think my wife joined in some of the games they were always playing. Peggy Vail [Guggenheim] was doing transformations of bottles and I remember Max Ernst swinging a can of paint with holes punched in the bottom over a canvas spread on the kitchen floor. David Hare was there cavorting with Jacqueline Lamba on the beach. Matta used to go about with a little walking stick and a kerchief. I thought he was absolutely riveting, full of energy and very friendly. Matta did a lot of painting up there and Motherwell who arrived looking very grey flannel suit seemed very impressed by his work." [22]

Matta had written about Motherwell's arrival to Onslow Ford: "Baziotes, Nelson [the painter Ralph Nelson] and Motherwell, especially Bob, are full sphere interested in our pataphysics. Bob will spend the summer around here so we may unfog." [23] He also urged Gordon to "write, sending charts of what you are doing." The use of the navigational term "charts" suggests the emphasis the two painters put on finding a system for portraying the complex multidimensional spaces they envisioned. Matta's letters more often than not contained quickly drawn little diagrams demonstrating his spatial thinking and giving clues to the symbols he used for different spheres of time as well as "psychological space" and "conventional space."

Meanwhile the Surrealist group was at last made complete by the arrival of its "technician of shock," Marcel Duchamp, who reached New York from Marseilles in June. Why Duchamp had delayed so long his departure from Paris and was slow to join the waiting crowds in the south is not clear. He stayed at Sanary where André Gomes photographed him with a readymade he had discovered in a local backyard, as the departures of ships from Marseilles dwindled to a monthly few. Finally through the efforts of Walter Arensberg and/or Katherine Dreier his visa application was granted. Evidently he had not been on the original list compiled for the Emergency Rescue Committee by Alfred Barr, who indicated elsewhere that among the Europeans Duchamp was of little importance, that he had "only done one or two things." [24]

Duchamp had been an instigator of New York Dada during the First World War. While his role in the 1940s was different, his unobtrusive presence was to serve as an ongoing catalytic force, impacting as much on American art of the 1960s as it did on that of the '40s. After staying a few weeks with Max Ernst and Peggy Guggenheim, he moved to the Kieslers' apartment on Fourteenth Street and later to his own place nearby. He attempted to support himself through fabricating and selling replicas of the green valise containing miniature versions of his earlier works. But his principal solution to the problem of earning a living was, according to Patrick Waldberg, to "suppress his needs." He ate very little, drank almost no alcohol, and bought his clothes off of pushcarts on Orchard Street. He was a de facto member of the Surrealist group but would not have referred to himself as a Surrealist. He was, nonetheless, indispensable to Breton's plans for the next collective undertaking of the émigrés, which was to get under way in the fall.

The French desk at the Voice of America where Breton found himself a reluctant employee has been characterized as a "home of exiles and outcasts." Michel Gorde, Chagall's son-in-law, who headed the desk, described it as very isolated, removed from American culture. Unlike the German intellectual émigrés who were deeply alienated from German politics and culture, the French exiles believed that they would and should go home when the war ended. Since they regarded their situation as temporary, many of them made little or no attempt to learn much about American culture. Some found the place quite uncivilized. At the Voice of America they could work in French, write, think, and speak in French. "We were," said Albert Guerard, "an incredible foreign legion. It was the refuge of all displaced persons." [25] Breton was a broadcaster, which meant he had to be at the office before dawn. Then he had to read in his elegant intonations a prepared script of American propaganda, a role that was distasteful and humiliating for someone who believed neither in nationalism nor in war. Breton, recollected Denis de Rougemont, "would appear at 5 a.m. at the end of the large room, supremely courteous and with the patient air of a lion who has decided to ignore the bars of his cage. He lent us his noble voice but he kept for himself his tinge of irony and solemn carriage. . . . He held success at arm's length, leaving it to Salvador Dalí to make money out of a movement even more prestigious here than in Paris: Surrealism." [26]

Actually the battery of heavyweight intellectuals employed there were probably seldom heard in France, since the station did not have sufficient signal strength to overcome the problems with eastward transmission. The broadcasts were sent by recording or telephone message to England where they were then transmitted by the BBC, often in edited form and not always identified as the Voice of America. Hence it cannot be said that they exerted much influence in Vichy France. Probably the most important consequence of the French desk operation was an improved understanding of the United States on the part of those refugees who returned to influential roles in the postwar years, such as Pierre Lazareff, who became the editor of *Paris Soir*, or Jacques Maritain, noted Catholic philosopher, whose ideas about democracy were broadened by his U.S. stay.[27]

The French refugee colony was rife with disagreement over who should be in command of the Free French forces, and by extension who should govern France at the war's end. Roosevelt steadfastly refused to acknowledge General De Gaulle as the leader in exile, influenced in part by Alexis Léger, an implacable anti-Gaullist, well connected in Washington. Even the relief organizations set up to help alleviate conditions of privation in Europe aligned themselves with one or another of the quarreling factions, France Forever proclaiming a range of Gaullist orientations and the Free French Relief supporting Roosevelt's choice of General Giraud. Antoine de St.-Exupéry who later disappeared with his plane in the North African desert, wrote a letter that was published in the *New York Times* in November and in France in December, in which he pointed out the futility of these quarrels among émigrés and said that the decisions should be left to the British and Americans.[28] This did not earn him much favor with either refugee faction, since the exiles were already apprehensive that they would have neither a voice in the peace process nor a role in the shaping of postwar France.

Breton apparently maintained his characteristic detachment from these political rivalries, while he occupied himself with Surrealism's destiny in the New World. In September he had the consolation of the arrival on the scene of an American recruit, which he took as a sign that Surrealism was taking hold in the Western Hemisphere. Charles Duits, a Harvard student of mixed Dutch and American background, was a rebellious seventeen-year-old when he discovered *VVV* in a bookstore and forthwith determined to make contact with Breton and the Surrealist movement. When he crossed the threshold of the Eleventh Street walk-up, he was already prepared to be the acolyte Breton hoped for, and, as he later wrote, the course of his entire life was altered from that moment on.[29] Within a week he attended his first gathering of the Surrealist group; within several months his work was published in *VVV*; twenty-five years later he was to write the most perspicacious memoir of Breton yet published. As Kurt Seligmann told him with some amusement at the first meeting, "You may not know it, but you are about to break many ties. You will soon see."[30] Robert Lebel knew Duits's parents in a different milieu and was told by them, "Our son has become acquainted with some terrible people."[31]

For two years Duits shadowed the New York Surrealists. "I went almost every day to openings, chatted with one or another of the Surrealists; then we would go downtown to eat in Little Italy and end up at the studio of one painter or another . . . until dawn began to devour the nighttime stars. In New York one could always encounter either the members of the Surrealist group or other well known artists such as Chagall, Mondrian and Léger, or those whose reputations were still to be

Top: Barn at Kurt and Arlette Seligmann's farm in Sugar Loaf, New York; stone
foundation wall with marks of bullets fired by Marcel Duchamp.

Bottom: Marcel Duchamp, front and back covers of "First Papers of Surrealism"
catalogue showing Seligmann barn with bullet holes.

made, Jackson Pollock, Gorki [sic], David Hare, Baziotes, Motherwell."[32] Duits's character sketches of these individuals and his accounts of their interactions, although they are the observations of a college freshman, recalled after several decades had elapsed, leave one with the impression of a very sociable milieu in which the refugees, despite the lack of cafés that some have blamed for the group's disintegration, managed to see a good deal both of each other and of a circle of American friends.

Particularly revealing are his comments on Breton and Duchamp. "Breton was naturally at the center and Duchamp naturally gravitated to the periphery, but when the latter was present, Breton refused to occupy his usual place. Everyone looked at him, listened to him, but he looked at and listened to Duchamp. Strange humility. . . . The cerebral pearls of Duchamp were made of ideas which were sustained by the objects which he made or signed. These existed by virtue of their implications. Breton admired them as he admired the last poem of Rimbaud."[33] It was to Duchamp that Breton turned whenever it was a question of an exhibition or window display, and in this capacity Duchamp played a role in New York as significant, if not more so, as that he had played in Paris. After all, it was in New York that he had first challenged the sanctity of exhibitions when he submitted a urinal to the 1917 exhibition of the Society of Independent Artists, of whose hanging committee he was a member. It was nothing quite so simple that he had in mind for his return performance a quarter-century later.

Breton wrote to Gordon Onslow Ford at the end of the summer: "Duchamp is in New York. That is the most beautiful acquisition we have had. . . . I am preparing a Surrealist exhibition for October 15. . . . I hope at least there will remain from this exhibition a catalogue which I am busy working on and which I am confident will be something new."[34]

It has been arranged that Breton would undertake the staging of a major exhibition of work by the émigrés that would be a benefit for the Coordinating Council of French Relief Societies. The exhibition was to be installed in the Whitlaw Reid mansion on Madison Avenue, and it was Marcel Duchamp who was asked to devise a plan to camouflage the elaborate décor and gilded moldings of the reception rooms, as well as to develop a concept for the catalogue. The title "First Papers of Surrealism" had considerable current relevance at a time when immigration and the naturalization process were subjects very much on the minds of the refugees. It suggests that Surrealism was taking the initial step toward naturalization and U.S. citizenship, making a bid for New World acceptance.

Duchamp's first response to the challenge was to visit the Seligmanns' tranquil farm in Sugar Loaf, where he took up a gun and fired five shots at the stone wall of the nineteenth-century barn. Since it would have been uncharacteristic of Duchamp to have owned a lethal weapon, it is conceivable that he used the gun that Seligmann kept for protection in his isolated farmhouse. If so it was very likely the same gun from which the bullet was fired that killed Kurt Seligmann twenty years later, not 200 feet from that same barn wall. Duchamp photographed the section of the barn wall with the bullet marks and used the photograph on the front cover of the catalogue for "First Papers," punching out the five bullet holes.

Was this related to that ultimate gratuitous act extolled by the Surrealists, to shoot at random in a crowded street? Is it possible that there was anger in the calm Duchamp's gesture, anger at the wasteful senselessness of the war, the earlier war having cut short the life of his older brother Raymond? Typical of Duchamp's love of puns is the pairing of this front cover with a photograph of a slab of holey Swiss cheese on the back cover. War versus peace, death versus nourishment, hard stone and less impenetrable cheese, puncture versus natural process are some of the responses suggested by this incongruous juxtaposition.

The foreword to the catalogue was written not by Breton but by Sidney Janis, who attempted to demonstrate the logic of Surrealism, explaining that "its moral code is that of science, the disinterested attitude of research. . . . Surrealist art transmutes subjective elements into visual images. Pictorially it gives form to the anatomy of intangible reality, the grain of modern sensibilities . . . dreams, totems, myth and fable."[35] The poet Robert Allerton Parker contributed an essay in praise of eccentrics and visionaries, "Explorers of the Pluriverse." There followed fourteen pages devoted to myths, either surviving or in formation, ending with the Great Transparents, illustrated with David Hare's composite photograph of a figure half consumed in flames. The chosen myths were pagan, Christian, medieval, and contemporary, and they were represented by old engravings and photographs and twentieth-century paintings in the Surrealists' favorite process of analogy. Analogical also were the portraits of the artists included alongside the reproductions of their paintings, for example, Walker Evans's photograph of a sharecropper standing in for Leonora Carrington. There were also examples of "outsider" art, such as the American primitive Morris Hirshfield, and, to round it out, thoughts on painting written that year in letters from Henri Matisse to his son Pierre. In other words the catalogue ran true to form as a Surrealist document, intended to disorient the would-be reader through both format and provocative juxtaposition of text and image.

A pun on the title page refers to the installation devised by Duchamp: "hanging by André Breton his twine Marcel Duchamp." "Twine" indeed was the most salient aspect of the show. As he had made the décor of the Galerie des Beaux-Arts disappear in 1938 by hanging 1,000 empty coal sacks from the ceiling, he upstaged the mansion's ornate interiors by stringing five miles of twine between the temporary partitions on which the works of art were hung. Perceived by many as a barrier, although actually there were openings permitting passage from section to section, the crisscrossing network of string might be better understood as lines of connection and emanation, suggesting the multiplicity of interrelationships between the works on display. It has also been proposed that the idea came to him from the cracks in his *Large Glass,* which he had so carefully preserved in his laborious restoration. There the cracks preserve transparency yet testify to the tangibility of the glass as an obstacle, a function somewhat analogous to that of the twine. And of course there was the allusion to the thread of Ariadne that led Theseus out of the Minotaur's labyrinth in the Surrealists' favorite myth. The idea that the web of lines had a serious, perhaps metaphysical import is reinforced by Breton's stern veto of the thousand folded paper birds that Alexander Calder had begun to place in the string meshes. Susanna Coggeshall remembers with a touch of exasperation being one of the several stringers of twine working under Duchamp's direction without benefit of explanation. The bafflement and confusion generated by the web was compounded during the opening by the contortions of the viewers trying to navigate the room and by the presence of children bouncing a ball in and around the webs of string. One of the children was March Avery, who recalls having been asked by Sidney Janis to bring a friend and play in the maze (along with the Janis sons). "We were encouraged to run about and I remember feeling somewhat uncomfortable both because I didn't think it was proper behavior for an opening and also because I sensed that some of the guests were of the same opinion." [36]

"String is boring. So is Surrealism," wrote Robert Coates in a review of "First Papers" in the *New Yorker.* "It has grown tired, tedious and a little repetitive. The earlier work is better." [37] However, he had praise for Matta's "scintillating" *The Earth Is a Man* and the "grandiose" *Meditation on an Oakleaf* by Masson. The latter canvas announced a new content and new way of working on the part of Masson, and it must have made an impact on the artists who saw it. It was painted in bold red, blue, yellow, and white on a black ground that stood for the earth as the source of growth and regeneration. The fact that the horizontal earth coincides with the vertical picture plane indicates a break with his earlier illusionistic approach to painting in favor of the flat surface. Caught in the upward spiral of the composition are suggestions of roots, the paths of things growing, a golden yellow for the force of the sun, blue weaving through the composition as sky meets the earth, shapes that relate to the oak leaf's scalloped silhouette, and, near the lower edge, enclosed as if in a seed or womb, an embryonic white form on which is painted a tilted wine glass, a symbol of the wine-loving artist, according to a member of his family.

During the war Americans were urged to grow their own vegetables in "victory gardens"; accordingly Masson began digging in the dark, rich Connecticut earth and produced tomato plants of spectacular height. This experience prompted him to adopt dark backgrounds to convey the idea of germination and transformation within the earth. At the top of *Meditation on an Oakleaf* there appears a confrontational animal head. Masson explained this last in an interview when he returned to France: "In New England there are oak trees three times larger than here, the leaves also. The weeds are three times larger than here and the insects gigantic, for there is an astonishing fauna and it remains very wild 250 kilometers from New York . . . so I put a wildcat in my painting." [38]

André Masson, *Meditation on an Oakleaf,* 1942, tempera, pastel, and sand on canvas, 40 x 33 inches; The Museum of Modern Art, New York.

Masson's friend and patron Saidie May bought his *There Is No Finished World* from the exhibition. (In order to do this she sold one of her earlier Massons, *Tauromachia,* to her sister, Blance Adler, who in turn donated it to the Baltimore Museum.) No doubt it was at Saidie May's request that Masson made a labeled diagram of the symbolic content of the work. Since he wrote the labels in French, a duplicate diagram was included on which Rose Masson wrote the English translation, and both were sent off with an inscription by both Massons. Thus the artist's own key to his complex symbolic program is available. The figure on the left is Pan, representing the three kingdoms of nature, animal, vegetable, mineral = Man; in the center is the Earth Mother or Demeter, representing fecundity, the sufferings of childbirth, and the source of life; and the right-hand figure is the Minotaur, ruling the labyrinth and in charge of the somber side of existence, the prenatal world, murder, and death. Around them are the symbols of five myths, Icarus, the Sphinx, the Ark, the Gorgons, and the Tower of Babel. The subject of the whole, he explained, is the precariousness of human life, and the fate of its enterprise, always threatened, destroyed, and recommenced.

Another painting of special significance in the "First Papers" exhibition was singled out by the reviewer for *Time* magazine: "A huge Freudian nightmare by Surrealist Ernst was painted especially for the exhibition. *Surrealism and Painting* depicted a nest of multi-colored bosomy birds with a semi-human arm emerging to paint its creator's conception of the disorderly universe."[39] This canvas, sometimes known as *Surrealism Paints a Painting,* more than any other from the previous twenty years provides a direct illustration of what Surrealism purported to be doing. The central image that remotely suggests featherless birds also reminds one in color and form of viscera or layers of the cortex. The rubbery form that it sends forth traces linear paths on the canvas similar to those achieved by a rhythmically swung drip can. The implication is that Surrealist painting comes from an unfathomable source, the whisperings of the magical bird Loplop, the guts, some inaccessible region of the brain. It was a graphic lesson in the process, and the American audience could hardly fail to get the point.

Another Ernst painting being shown for the first time whose meaning could not have been obscure to any audience was *La Planète affolée.* Here the lines produced by paint dripping from the oscillating punctured can move in a tangled skein above a band of decalcomania-derived geological formations suggestive of the southwestern landscape Ernst had admired. It appears that the planet's orbit is gyrating wildly, thrust out of balance no doubt by the aggressions that encircle the Earth. There were no *double entendres,* no chance encounters of disparate objects, no witty transformations in these two new canvases. Rather Ernst was straightforwardly using the language of form. It may be that Ernst was never again quite the poet of disruptive paradox that he had been during the 1920s and 1930s, that he was already entering a new post-Surrealist phase.

Threading one's way through the maze one could also have seen Matta's *The Earth Is a Man,* discussed earlier, and Gordon Onslow Ford's *First Five Horizons,* a painting that has since disappeared. The latter was another of those important paintings, like *Propaganda for Love* and *Transparent Woman,* that Onslow Ford executed

between 1940 and his departure for Mexico in 1941; he believes it was the first
painting he completed after meeting Jacqueline Johnson and he sees it as marking a
transition from a symbolic dreamworld to an inner world that has its own reality.

The Earth is primordial and made mostly of simple curves that originate from behind the
dotted lines that mark the horizons. Reclining in the landscape is a female personage who is
playing with a seed ball spewed from the volcano and seems to be pregnant with a live-line
being. The vertical male is of a different nature than the world, a visitor who is in need of
being integrated into the spirit of the landscape. . . . There are black liberated shadows and on
the right-hand side a highrise chequerboard (influence of NYC) with holes looking through
to dizzying depths. Many sensitive points are touching each other—an early stage of an ecol-
ogy in which everything is in contact with everything else.[40]

In its visual and conceptual complexity *First Five Horizons* makes an interesting contrast with Motherwell's *El Miedo de la Obscuridad,* a rather static rectilinear
abstraction reproduced in the catalogue on the facing page.

"First Papers" was the first exhibition in which American painters had been
invited to show alongside the émigrés. Included among the Americans were William
Baziotes, Alexander Calder, John Goodwin, David Hare, Robert Motherwell, Ralph
Nelson, Barbara Reis, Kay Sage, and Laurence Vail—a list largely compiled on a
social basis. According to Motherwell, he was asked to invite Jackson Pollock to
exhibit, but Pollock declined on the grounds that he was not a group person. Perhaps
the most interesting American inclusion was Baziotes's *The Butterflies of Leonardo
da Vinci,* a painting in which he explored space through multiple linear perspectives
that appear to have been inspired by Matta's drawings. While it is very different from
the soft lyricism of his subsequent work, *Butterflies* at least shows Baziotes as open
to experiment with automatist line and attempting to find a direction of his own
toward evocative, ambiguous imagery.

"The show at the Reid Mansion," according to Peter Busa, "was a focal point
for young artists who were meeting the European Surrealists. This was a great period
for us in the New York art community."[41] At the very least the show demonstrated
that there were other options than those offered in the "Artists for Victory" exhibition mounted by the Metropolitan Museum of Art the following month, a juried
show in which regionalist work predominated and a landscape by John Steuart Curry
won first prize.

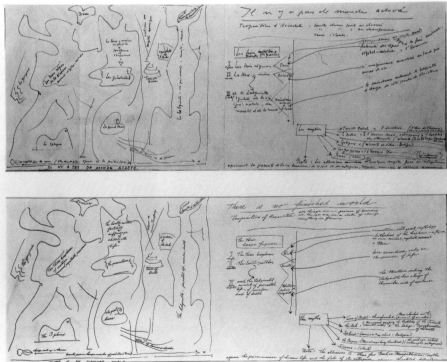

Below: Max Ernst, *Surrealism and Painting,* 1942, oil on canvas, 77 x 92 inches; The Menil Collection, Houston.

Opposite: Gordon Onslow Ford, *First Five Horizons,* 1941, oil on canvas, 46 x 60½ inches; present whereabouts unknown.

The cover of the November 2 issue of *Time* featured the general in command of U.S. forces on Guadalcanal, that island turned into living hell at the low point of the war in the Pacific. On the inside pages appeared an account of the culture those far-flung U.S. forces were fighting to save:

As art lovers emerged from dimmed out Manhattan streets, they encountered a blinding white light. "That's day," said the patroness of Surrealism, Peggy Guggenheim, shielding her eyes from a mass of blue-white electric bulbs. "Isn't it awful?" Day illumined a "painting library"

enclosed in a purple tarpaulin where art lovers were invited to sit on narrow ledges, armless rockers, and, by turning unframed canvases hung from triangular columns, study the exhibits from any angle they desired. . . .

Beyond the painting library, gallery goers enter a kind of artistic Coney Island. Here are shadow boxes, peepholes, in one of which, by raising a handle is revealed a brilliantly lighted canvas by Swiss painter Paul Klee. Another peepshow, manipulated by turning a huge ship's wheel, shows a rotating exhibit of reproductions of all the works, including a miniature toilet for MEN by screwball Surrealist Marcel Duchamp. Beyond these gadgets mankind swarms into what seems to be a decorated subway . . . canvases by England's Leonora Carrington, Spain's Miró, Chile's Matta, all their works unframed, suspended in the air from wooden arms protruding from concave plywood walls. Every two minutes a roar as of an approaching train is heard, lights go out on one side of the gallery, pop on at the other.[42]

Following the opening of "First Papers" by one week, Peggy Guggenheim had opened Art of This Century, a museum and gallery, at 30 West 57th Street, only four blocks from the building where Baroness Hilla Rebay presided over Peggy's uncle Solomon Guggenheim's Museum of Non-Objective Art. Acting on a suggestion from Howard Putzel, Guggenheim had hired Frederick Kiesler to transform the loft space

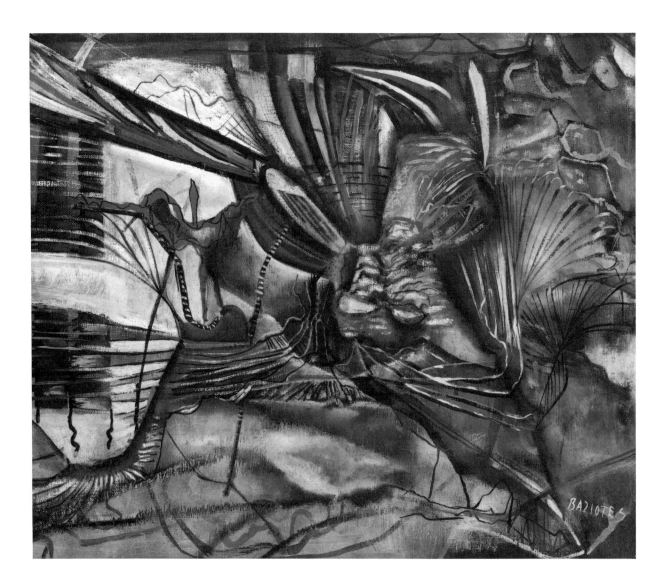

William Baziotes, *The Butterflies of Leonardo da Vinci,* 1942, oil on canvas, 19¼ x 23 inches; estate of William Baziotes, courtesy Blum Helman Gallery.

she had rented into a suitable setting for New York's most up-to-the-minute collection of European modern art. Chiefly a theoretician and visionary, the diminutive Viennese architect had had few opportunities to put his theories into practice. He seized wholeheartedly the occasion Guggenheim offered and set about creating four distinct spaces in which the barriers between viewer and artwork were to be dissolved, in which he felt the work of art could "resume its generic function as an active, organic factor in human life."

This unique showcase, it must be remembered, was on the seventh floor of a building that had a grocery store on the street level, so it was unlikely to be visited except by those already in the know. It was one of those architectural events with a long posterity, however, which would have more impact through the photographs taken of it by Berenice Abbott and others than during the five years of its actual existence. Revolutionary as it was, Kiesler's design cannot be said to have greatly influenced exhibition installation during the subsequent half-century, with the possible exception of Uncle Solomon's museum, where all the frames were removed from the paintings when James Johnson Sweeney became the museum's director in 1951 and whose design with curving exhibition walls from which the paintings would be projected in space was presented by Frank Lloyd Wright in 1948. Although Wright had already tried out the curving walls and spiral ramp in a San Francisco store, he may well have followed Kiesler's precedent when it came to installing paintings as part of a continuous environment by attaching them on arms that projected from the wall surface. In any event Kiesler's design did not lack for publicity at the time; that winter and spring at least three major magazines featured shots of the gallery. *Vogue* used it as a background for fashion models, *Interiors* reproduced Berenice Abbott's photographs of the main tunnel, and *Architectural Forum* used it to accompany Kiesler's statement about presenting "the artist's work as a vital entity in a spatial whole."

Wartime shortages of workers and materials had delayed the gallery's opening by two weeks, but the fact that "First Papers" had opened a week earlier did not diminish either the attendance or the press coverage, although some reporters, such as Emily Genauer writing in the *World Telegram,* covered both newsworthy installations together. By all accounts the gallery was packed at the opening, which was a benefit for the Red Cross. At the opening *Newsweek*'s reporter asked Kiesler why he had arranged for an alternating light at 3½-second intervals. The designer's response, which was reported under the heading "Isms Rampant," was: "It's dynamic, it pulsates like your blood. Ordinary museum lighting makes a painting dead."[43] In the same article the reporter noted that Peggy Guggenheim wore a Calder mobile in one ear and a little painting of a pink desert by Tanguy in the other. Thus did this new impresario of the arts signify her impartiality between the abstract and surreal contingents represented in her collection. Those unmatched earrings, one by an American, the other French, might have also been read as prophetic of the melting pot of European and American art that her gallery was to become, for it was within the eccentric spaces of Art of This Century that the younger Americans began to be shown, first side by side with the Europeans, then in solo exhibitions, and it was at 30 West 57th Street that the nucleus of the future New York School might first have been discerned by an alert viewer.

According to its press release, Art of This Century was to be not only a showcase for Guggenheim's collection but also a "center where artists will be welcome and where they can feel that they are cooperating in establishing a research laboratory for new ideas," the same language Hayter had used about Atelier 17. After the opening exhibition, which consisted entirely of the collection she had formed during the preceding five years, Guggenheim intended to mount theme exhibitions and to seek out new talent through an annual juried salon as well as to show the artists in her own émigré circle. Since her motive in collecting had been to assemble a systematic survey

Frederick Kiesler Seated in the Surrealist Gallery of Art of This Century, 1942,
photograph by Berenice Abbott; courtesy Mrs. Lillian Kiesler.

of twentieth-century art movements from cubism, purism, and suprematism through late Surrealism, any new artists whom she chose to exhibit could, by association, appear to be the successors to this progression. Unfortunately her buying had been done in a hurry, under the guidance of others, and her uneven collection gives the impression of having been formed according to the principle of "one of each significant artist or period of an artist" rather than with an eye for work of exceptional quality. As she began introducing more Americans later in her first season, the question may legitimately be asked whether genuine perspicacity, social reasons, or amorous expectations most strongly guided her selection of artists. The fact remains that, whatever her personal motivations may have been, Peggy Guggenheim's gallery was the first place—long before the Museum of Modern Art—where it was possible to make a connection between the succession of modernist styles abroad and the experiments under way in some of the cold-water flats in downtown New York. Whether by chance or intention, Guggenheim was, in effect, a constructor of history.

One further exhibition to be added to the Surrealist roster for 1942 was the New York debut of Wifredo Lam at the Pierre Matisse gallery on November 17. Letters from Lam in Cuba to Breton that fall thank him for including him in "First Papers" and for the introduction for the Pierre Matisse catalogue; he mentions that the works on paper for the exhibition have been shipped. Evidently Lam had been pursuing in Cuba the direction in which the collaboration with Breton on *Fata Morgana* had impelled him in Marseilles. From Picasso, who had so powerfully influenced him, he kept a freedom of improvisation and the capacity to fuse multiple aspects of a figure on a single plane. From Surrealism came the inspiration to use Caribbean sources such as the jungle peopled with spirits and a world in which there is no firm demarcation between the normal and the supernatural, where birds can be ancestors and plants and animals are interchangeable. Drawing upon the primitive elements of his own heritage, he could also provide an example to Americans intrigued by Amerindian art of ways in which indigenous tradition and modernism could be integrated.

Concurrent with this flurry of Surrealist activity and attendant publicity in New York was the November 8 landing of American troops in North Africa, where they joined the British forces under Montgomery in combat with General Rommel's army. This was interpreted in Germany as a sign that an Allied landing in Europe might come from the Mediterranean. To forestall any such move, German and Italian soldiers moved into the unoccupied zone of France, concentrating their efforts on the

venerable seaport of Marseilles, setting fire to the old city and rounding up thousands for deportation. Thus came the tragic end of Marseilles as the last hope for the dwindling number of refugees who had lingered there. Those who remained of the group that had gathered at Air Bel—Jacques Hérold, Victory Brauner, Henriette and André Gomes—scattered in the countryside, finding refuge where they could and living lives of fear and privation. Among those who sought a rural refuge and anonymity was Lou Straus Ernst. The visa and affidavits Jimmy Ernst had managed to get for her had moved slowly through the bureaucratic process and had been cabled to Marseilles in October, but she still had to wait for a French exit visa and in a few weeks it was too late. The following year she was arrested by the Gestapo and interned in the deportation camp at Drancy. She died in Auschwitz.

Even as they were drawing media coverage with their attention-getting showcases, a number of fissures were at work that would fragment the wedge that the Surrealists had driven into the New York art world. To the gauntlet of *Dyn* flung northward in the spring, Paalen had added two more issues in the summer and fall in which there was every indication that he was building a serious challenge to Surrealism, not only in the articles he wrote or assembled but in the style of painting he was evolving. Seen with the benefit of hindsight, his vertiginous allover abstractions fall naturally into the category of proto–abstract expressionism, although his inspiration derived at least in part from his reading in contemporary physics.

Wifredo Lam, *Deity,* 1942, watercolor and crayon on paper, 41½ x 33¼ inches;
The Baltimore Museum of Art, Bequest of Saidie A. May.

Another split in the ranks threatened when Matta decided to form his own splinter group because he disapproved of the too inclusive nature of *VVV* and wanted to push Surrealism in what he felt was its true direction. He enlisted Motherwell and Baziotes to help round up a few other artists who might be interested in working toward some kind of manifestation and suggested that they meet in his studio to work together and see if they might formulate a new direction. His hope was that something would emerge that would be sufficiently new and exciting to make an impact as an exhibition at Art of This Century. Evidently Peggy Guggenheim had already expressed an interest in showing "the new American automatists." Baziotes suggested a few artists he knew who were committed to exploring new possibilities—Pollock, de Kooning, Busa, and Kamrowski. Motherwell remembered calling on Pollock with Baziotes and spending four or five hours talking to him about Surrealism and automatism. Surprisingly Pollock showed up when they began meeting at Matta's studio. So did Busa and Kamrowski, but de Kooning could not at that point see that automatism held any solutions to the problems he was struggling with. He was evidently averse to a group undertaking of this kind, as well as unenthusiastic about automatism. One account says that Hans Hofmann was also approached, but it is difficult to imagine that this veteran of assorted modern movements who had for decades run his own school could have been seriously considered a candidate for Matta's band of Young Turks. (This is not to say that Hofmann did not experiment with dripped paint, as the misdated canvas *Spring* demonstrates, or that the gestural did not play an increasing role in his work during the 1940s.)[44] Thus it came about that for perhaps half a dozen Saturday afternoons in the late fall and early winter Peter Busa, Gerome Kamrowski, Pollock, Motherwell, and Baziotes met and worked together in Matta's studio. Although Matta includes Gorky in his recent recollections of these sessions, other participants have stated that it wasn't until the following year that the two worked closely together. While Rothko was beginning several years of Surrealist-inspired work, close inspection of his works on paper of 1942–1943 reveals a fairly labored, even deliberate process, rather than the kind of immediate and spontaneous work done at the Matta sessions.

These meetings, according to Kamrowski, "were fairly structured. We would bring our work, discuss it, and analyze the images. Matta was trying to project certain ideas, to get people to visualize time, to develop some sort of symbol, and as you drew automatically to see what would be a common connector."[45] Matta, as we have seen, had developed a system for indicating space and time (Gordon Onslow Ford maintains that it was not consistent, but that the symbols changed each time he interpreted them) and his work was predicated on this, not on the classic Surrealist play of antitheses. Not that he ignored eroticism; his erotic drawings are straightforwardly uninhibited and graphically detailed, with no *double entendres* or veiling of the subject, while the erotic content of the paintings of this period is less overt.

Peter Busa recounted that "Matta would look at our work and make comments as to what dimension we were reflecting. He also had organic attitudes and was interested in whether you were reflecting a rhythm that would be associated with water or with fir or with rock forms. The things that Pollock did were really outstanding because he had a very natural exuberance about this point of view. He

Mark Rothko, *Untitled*, c. 1944, watercolor and ink over graphite on wove paper, 20¹⁵⁄₁₆ x 14⁷⁄₈ inches; National Gallery of Art, Washington, Gift of the Mark Rothko Foundation.

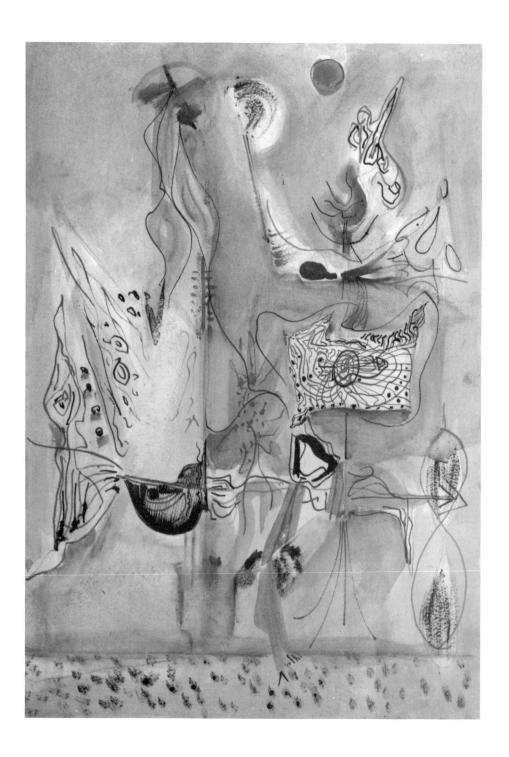

worked in wash and ink—most of us did. . . . One didn't have an image to begin with, but rather a hand and a motor ability. If one trusted the ability just to move one's hand, one could tap many of the sources of the images and come up with not only a discernible Surrealist image, but at the same time a certain amount of freedom." [46] Peter Busa had been a Benton student at the Art Students League and had known Pollock since that time and was a friend of Gorky's as well, since they had both been maverick abstractionists in the Artists Union. Along with Baziotes he had been one of the last artists on the Federal Art Project in 1941, and through him he had already been introduced to automatism. "Bill got us all to practice automatic drawings," Busa said of Baziotes, "and he insisted on the Surrealist use of the automatic image. I had a hard time reconciling that kind of doodling with my formalist background and in the end I didn't achieve anything by trying to combine the two. . . . Baziotes was always going on about aspects of Surrealism which didn't really interest me very much, but then I realized that what interested him deeply was not Surrealism, but the value of the metaphor for an experience." [47]

One can sense from the various recollections the kind of catalytic force Matta exerted and the way in which he helped his American friends break through the barriers to spontaneous expression. However, it is clear that there were differences of interpretation. When Kamrowski mentions Matta's ideas about time and Busa speaks of his interest in "what dimension we were reflecting," they are referring to a visionary aspect of Matta with which neither was completely comfortable. They were preoccupied with their newfound gestural freedom, while, according to Matta, "what interested me was to see if they could apply the system that was to me fascinating at the time, to use morphology about my psychic responses to life." [48] More recently Matta commented on Motherwell's participation, saying he was "more interesting from a theoretical point of view, in his way of expressing images more or less similar to those I was feeling." [49]

Motherwell in later years did not recall participating in these sessions, only recruiting, but in a 1967 interview he gave a detailed account and said that they had always seemed to him to be the "beginnings of what later became known as Abstract Expressionism." [50] And in 1950 he wrote to Tom Hess, editor of *Art News,* saying: "Don't underestimate the influence of the Surrealist state of mind on the young American painters in those days or that through them we had our first understanding of automatism as a technique." [51]

Despite various lapses of memory—Matta's recent recollections tend to telescope and confuse events—it does seem clear that something did happen in Matta's studio during those sessions that left its imprint on the participants, even it if was just his idea that "reality can only be represented in a state of perpetual transformation." He hoped that the Americans would open themselves to what he called simultaneous worlds. He talked to them about interplanetary communication and extrasensory perception and loaned Peter Busa a book about mental telepathy. He spoke about morphology as a way of seeing the different states of matter simultaneously. Kamrowski, with his familiarity with Thompson's *On Growth and Form* and his interest in crystallography, flow patterns of electric energy, and the new microbiological photographs, perhaps best understood what Matta meant by morphology.

Some of his gouaches from 1942–1943, such as *Forest Forms* and *Night Journey,* suggest stages of transformation from seed to larger organisms to breakdown and dispersal, indicated by the use of transparent layers of color that break through dark, opaque surroundings. Dotted lines of direction such as Matta used in his drawings and diagrams appear in *Night Journey* and *Revolve and Devolve.*

The Matta sessions did not last long—recollections vary—as it became evident that the Americans were not interested in following his forays into the occult. Nor did they really take to carrying out his "assignments," such as drawing what they were feeling at each hour of the day in order to see whether there was any concordance at specific times. Perhaps others shared Busa's reservations about automatism. He was troubled by the fact that it was supposed to be unpredictable, yet he felt that the mechanical means of execution produced results that were exactly the opposite. Later Matta was to say that the Americans took the empty forms and ignored the content. However, unlike Matta, each of these painters, with the exception of Motherwell, had behind him years of work and training that had involved a good deal of indoctrination in formalist principles. For them automatism or blind chance remained largely a way of getting into a painting, a gamble that something interesting might emerge, rather than a passport to unseen worlds or a means of conveying the connections and systems underlying visually perceived phenomena that fascinated Matta. As for Pollock, he had already had considerable time to absorb automatism into his working process, first at the Siqueiros workshop, then with Baziotes, as well as in the drawings done for his Jungian analyst Dr. Henderson. The latter drawings had accustomed him to an analytical and psychological approach, although the symbols that surfaced in them differed from the psychic phenomena that interested Matta. However, it may well be that all these experiences played a cumulative role in Pollock's formation. For none of the painters involved was it a definitive commitment, but it opened the possibility that a few young Americans might indeed develop a new style that advanced beyond Europe's last avant-garde and that they might form a group and be known, if not as automatists, then as something else not yet named. When they met again in the 1960s Busa said to Matta: "It was your presence, Matta, that personalized Surrealism for us. . . . Surrealism was a fuse that lit up the American scene." [52]

In Motherwell's version of the story it was Matta who abandoned the project and returned to Breton's fold, leaving the Americans to take the ideas in whatever direction they wanted. One consequence was the bond that formed between these

243

William Baziotes, *Untitled*, c. 1942, gouache with frottage and ink on paper, 9 x
11⅝ inches; estate of William Baziotes, courtesy Blum Helman Gallery.

Gerome Kamrowski, *Transformation*, 1943, enamel on jute, 23 x 32 inches;
courtesy the Washburn Gallery.

Below: Peter Busa, *Untitled,* 1943, gouache on paper, 10½ x 13½ inches; courtesy Christopher Busa.

Opposite: Jackson Pollock, *Stenographic Figure,* 1942, oil on linen, 40 x 56 inches; The Museum of Modern Art, New York, Mr. and Mrs. Walter Bareiss Fund.

painters, a kind of loose association that would resurface at the end of the decade as the New York School. Pollock, Motherwell, Baziotes, and their wives also got together in the evenings to write automatist poetry. So by the start of 1943 there was a handful of American artists who were identified with the Surrealists and who had undergone a kind of indoctrination into Surrealism's ideas and practices.

If Breton was ruffled by the defections, actual or threatened, from the Surrealist ranks, he gave no indication of it in his talk on December 10 to a group of Yale students, under the auspices of the French Department. As unwavering as ever in his antirationalist stance, he said: "We must make a tabula rasa of conventional modes of thought. False rationalism usurps the rights of a true reason." He explained that he was restrained by his situation as a refugee from being too explicit about his political views, but he did get across the idea that Hitler and Mussolini were symptoms rather than sources of evil. "That evil will not be cured simply by eliminating them."

It is an important text in that, first of all, it lucidly sets forth the origins in the First World War of the Surrealist antiwar stance, and secondly in that it offers a view, certainly novel in the United States at the time, of the debasement of language as partly responsible for the present world in chaos. At the outset, Breton addressed the students as young men about to go to war and identified their position with that of his generation in 1917. He did not speak in detail of what he had personally witnessed as an orderly close to the front lines, but he did describe the image that haunted him of Apollinaire as he had seen him on a furlough in Paris, his head still bandaged after the trepanning necessitated by the head wounds from which he eventually died—on the day of the Armistice. Apollinaire, who "of all people saw that it was not enough to put the world back on the old system," wrote in his poem "La Victoire" which Breton quoted: "Man is searching out a new language about which no grammarian of any language will have anything to say. The word is sudden and it is God who trembles."

Breton went on to quote one of his colleagues at the Voice of America, Denis de Rougemont: "The 20th century will appear in the future as a kind of verbal nightmare, a delirious century of prostitution of words. . . . Alas what have we done with the word. Is it possible we are killing for misunderstandings?" This is in part, he explained, due to our overspecialization, the masters of our time being only expert in their specialty and refusing to go beyond their sphere. "We must guard against the

Peter Busa and Matta at the preview of "Matta: Recent Paintings," The Walker Art
Center, Minneapolis, December 1966; courtesy Christopher Busa.

world being divided into groups of individuals who are more and more specialized
. . . we must give back to man the sense of his absolute dependence on the community
of all men." [53]

Breton also reiterated his faith in the instinctiveness and intrinsic virtue of
youth. "Surrealism was born of an affirmation of faith in the genius of youth," he
proclaimed, citing the movement's heroes, Jarry who wrote *Ubu Roi* at the age of
fifteen, Rimbaud who finished his work at eighteen, and Lautréamont dead at
twenty-four. And he reasserted his belief in one word above all others: *liberté*—"it
has been the passionate pursuit of freedom which has motivated Surrealist activity
from the outset." He explained Surrealism's many schisms as the self-disqualifying
process of those who compromised the insistence on total freedom. As an example
he cited Dalí who ceased to oppose fascism when he painted a portrait of the Spanish
ambassador, the representative of Franco, oppressor of his country and murderer of
the closest friend of Dalí's youth, García Lorca.

He may have been regarded in New Haven as just one more guest speaker, but
his lecture was considered sufficiently important abroad to have been published in
the review *Fontaine,* directed by Max Pol Fouchet, printed in Algeria and circulated
in Vichy France. The only public lecture by Breton during his stay in the United
States, an indication perhaps of the relative lack of interest in literary Surrealism,

was regarded as a significant event in the annals of Surrealism. Fouchet, in the same issue of *Fontaine,* wrote on "le Surréalisme aux Etats Unis," describing its continuation in *View* and *VVV* and calling it "since 1918 the only movement directed toward the emancipation of man." [54]

By the close of 1942 Surrealism had done a good deal more than establish a beachhead. With solo exhibitions in established galleries, a major collective manifestation in a mansion on Madison Avenue, the newest and most novel gallery space in New York prepared to serve as its showcase, its own publication, the allegiance of important curators, a responsive press, and the potential adherence of some young American artists, Surrealism seemed on its way to dominating the artistic advance guard of the Western Hemisphere. However, what actually happened in the next several years did not follow this scenario. The interaction between the émigrés and the milieu into which they were displaced produced not a clone but a new precipitate. That milieu also provoked changes in the émigrés, individually and as a group. It may be that 1942 witnessed the last flare-up of the dying flame of the Surrealist movement.

What does seem extraordinary, looking back over the works the refugee artists exhibited in 1942, is not simply that they kept working under enormously difficult and disheartening conditions, but that each of them attained new levels of development in their painting. The works mentioned or discussed in this chapter rank high among the significant works of twentieth-century art in terms of fully realized innovation in form and technique and in terms of affective power. One might posit that the survival mechanism is in play here. Each of these artists whether by chance or conscious decision left a continent engulfed by war or, later, a country defeated and occupied. It seems as if the momentum of the course of action that they took, the momentum of survivors, carried over into their work, producing a surge of energy that pushed it to new heights. Especially when this work is seen in contrast to the art produced in Vichy France—and thousands of artists did go on producing and exhibiting during the occupation—the difference in vitality and individual innovation is striking.

Added to the survivor theory must be the impact of a new milieu. Only one of these artists, Seligmann, had previously been on the North American continent. For the others this was a new encounter, and they each responded to different aspects of the "marvelous" that they discovered in the topography and flora and fauna of the New World. Whether it was Masson, awe-struck by the lavish foliage and autumn colors of the New England woodlands, Tanguy, Seligmann, and Ernst encountering the rock formations of the Southwest, or Matta and Onslow Ford in volcanic Mexico, the vastness and natural spectacles of the continent impelled them to broach new subject matter, to invent new forms, and to deal with space in a multiperspectival way.

Thirdly, as the foregoing makes evident, they had feedback and a support system that encouraged the directions they were pursuing. In crossing the Atlantic, they had gone from being a clique of outsiders to being, if not distinguished visitors, at least sufficiently consequential to be regarded with a certain amount of awe and respect, a situation in which it was difficult to maintain a revolutionary stance.

The sullen greatness of this high plateau where death is ever more present than

life, its peculiar asteroid quality, its emptiness under a fathomless sky whose

clouds are piled up so high that one grasps immediately the thirteen heavens of

Indian mythology . . . the pyramids of the Sun and of the Moon, the jade and

turquoise mosaics on masks with eyes of meteoric iron and, above all, the

primeval spectacle, to witness the birth of a volcano . . .

Wolfgang Paalen in a letter to Gustav Regler

The underlying pre-Columbian culture, often thinly veiled by a European veneer, along with the volcanic landscape and exotic vegetation, made Mexico the Surrealist country par excellence. The tensions between its dual cultures, represented on the one hand by the unabashedly wealthy descendants of the colonists and on the other by the Neolithic lifestyle of the Indian villages, suited the Surrealist sense of paradox. Their anticlericalism appreciated the irony of the ornate Catholic cathedrals built of the stones of the same Aztec pyramids that had formed platforms for human sacrifices to Huitilopochtli. And the relics of earlier Mesoamerican worship embedded in the décor of Catholic churches became Surrealist subversive objects.

In addition Mexico offered a sanctuary without posing embarrassing questions for Europeans from a broad spectrum of national and political backgrounds. Thus those such as Benjamin Péret and Victor Serge whose participation in the Spanish Civil War and the October Revolution made them ineligible for U.S. visas found refuge in Mexico among a remarkable mix of European intellectuals, practitioners of the arts, and feuding political factionalists. Against a background that combined the remnants of an archaic Indian culture, the autocratic imprint of a decadent colonialism, and a modern revolutionary government, the displaced Europeans learned to live with the inequities of a multitiered society and to adapt to a different tempo. Deracinated themselves, in touch with the reminders of bloodthirsty ritual practices and a seemingly timeless Neolithic village life in a land where smoldering violence, like its volcanos, was not far beneath the surface, they found old vendettas erupting in new ways. Where else would one of a country's most eminent artists, David Siqueiros, have been implicated in the attempted assassination of the world's most famous political refugee, Leon Trotsky? "I found in Mexico," said Matta after four months there in 1941, "a class violence. The silence between foreigner, Spaniard, and Indian was a frightening silence of drawn knives. My painting, *Years of Fear,* is about the interior battlefield." [1]

Wolfgang Paalen, with his wife, Alice Rahon, and their friend and benefactress, Eva Sulzer, settled in San Angel on the outskirts of Mexico City in the fall of 1939, following their trip to British Columbia. Even in a place that played host to an amaz-

Matta, *Years of Fear,* 1941, oil on canvas, 44 x 56 inches; Solomon R.
Guggenheim Museum, New York.

ing collection of international refugees, this trio must have stirred some curiosity.
The aristocratic-looking Paalen was the son of a businessman from one of Austria's
prominent Jewish families and a Catholic mother who suffered from melancholia.
His wife, Alice Rahon, was a woman of extraordinary beauty, a beauty only en-
hanced by the fact that she was slightly crippled. She had been Picasso's mistress
during the mid-1930s, but had left him to return to Paalen. She had a sharp French
wit with a caustic edge and Paalen greatly respected her taste and judgment. Eva
Sulzer, who had had an earlier friendship with Paalen, remained steadfastly devoted
to both Wolfgang and Alice and was the financial mainstay of this curious ménage à

trois. Frequenters of their household in San Angel described Eva as silent, practical, and homespun, with a passion for cats who swarmed all over the place. She was the chauffeur, housekeeper, and guardian angel.

The house they shared in the Via Obregón was seen by visitors as "an en-chanted place," filled with Surrealist paintings and objects from Paalen's earlier col-lection of Aegean antiquities as well as his recent pre-Columbian acquisitions. He must have enjoyed the confrontation in his living room of a female Cycladic figure

Above: Wolfgang Paalen in his studio in San Angel, 1942, photograph by Walter Reuter.

Paalen's home and studio, at left, in the Vía Obregón, San Angel.

in marble and a stone Aztec corn goddess. Across the patio Paalen built a high-ceilinged studio in which there was an array of creative fetishes, including a whale penis six feet long laid across the rafters as a reminder of the virility needed for creative work. Against one wall of the studio was the fifteen-foot-high carved façade of a Tlingit hut that he had acquired in British Columbia in the summer of 1939. The small entrance to the hut had been through the carved mouth of a bear.

Although Paalen was something of a Marxist, he was a strong anti-Stalinist and feared Rivera, who lived behind a cactus fence a few blocks away in the studio-home Juan O'Gorman had designed for him. Rivera wore a holster with a gun and a bullet-laden belt and liked to say that the greatest pleasure was to kill, while Paalen was delicate in health and had occasional heart trouble. At the same time he was passionately competitive. He concealed the fact that one of his parents was Jewish, which was not extraordinary under the circumstances, yet undoubtedly a source of some of the anxieties that beset him. He remained deeply disturbed over the fact that one of his brothers had committed suicide and another had disappeared. He told his American neighbor, Edward Renouf: "All my life is seeing if I can find my brother again."[2]

Soon after his arrival Paalen met the Peruvian artist and poet César Moro and helped him to prepare a large international Surrealist exhibition that opened in January 1940 at the Galeria de Arte Mexicano. In the catalogue André Breton was given credit as an organizer of the exhibition along with Moro and Paalen, thus reinforcing its official Surrealist credentials, although Breton, at the time in military service in France, can have had little to do with it.[3] To the usual European representatives of Surrealism were added Kahlo, Rivera, and eight other Mexican painters, along with the photographs of Manuel Alvarez Bravo and a selection of ancient Mexican objects from Rivera's collection. No North Americans were included, an indication that the organizers were ignorant of or did not take seriously the few reverberations of Surre-

International Exhibition of Surrealism, Mexico, 1940, cover of catalogue with photograph by Manuel Alvarez Bravo.

alism that had appeared on canvases north of the border. In his catalogue introduction Moro wrote: "For the first time in centuries we witness a heavenly combustion in Mexico. A thousand tokens mingle and are seen in the conjugation of constellations which renew the brilliant pre-Columbian night."[4] Clearly Mexico awaited Surrealism with a greater sense of affinity than did artists in the United States. Indeed there was a deep vein in Latin American culture, more apparent in literature than in the visual arts, that the Surrealists recognized and claimed as kindred. An artist such as Frida Kahlo might have little desire to be designated Surrealist despite Breton's appropriation of her; she had been furious with the Surrealists at the time of the Paris exhibition Breton had supposedly arranged for her in the winter of 1938–1939 and she did not wish her art, arrived at through her own excruciating suffering, to be claimed by any group. However, whether attributable to parallel affinities or intermingling influences or a combination of both, the fact remains that to this day there is a distinct sense of kinship between Surrealism and Mexican art and literature.

During the spring of 1940 Paalen traveled to New York for a show of his work at the Julien Levy gallery. The exhibition included the fumages he had been doing in Paris in 1939, but there were also paintings that reverberated with memories of his recent visit to the Northwest coast, pictures that, according to Gustav Regler, "conjure up the tracks and shapes of furry animals, the great forest and wide expanses of snow and which are particularly distinguished by a strange quality of white."[5] A work that demonstrates the transitional phase Paalen was in and that can be seen almost as proto-abstract expressionist is *Somewhere in Me*. Here the "personnages" of his earlier canvases (see *Saturnian Princes II*) have dissolved into lines and auras and circular nuclei; the whole canvas has become an energized "field" in which shapes and ground are barely distinguishable one from the other. Since Matta was going through an analogous phase and also had a show that month at Julien Levy, the two exhibitions may have been seen as indicative of a new direction.

Although he later told Gustav Regler that his stay in New York had convinced him that Surrealism had lost its revolutionary impetus, Paalen continued his correspondence with Breton while the latter was still in Vichy France. Evidently he hoped that when Breton reached the Western Hemisphere he would be willing to undertake a revision of the fundamental premises of Surrealism, a revision that would accommodate the philosophical implications of the latest scientific discoveries. When Breton proved unwilling to consider this course of action, Paalen decided to pursue his own avenue of exploration toward an art that would relate to the theories of contemporary physicists.

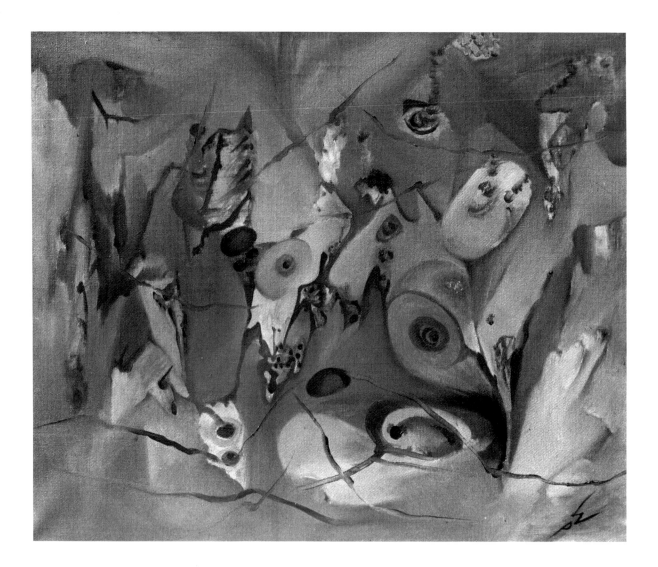

He was troubled by what he perceived as a dualism between "the Surrealist omnipotence of the Irrational and the Marxist omnipotence of Reason." Seeking a synthesis of imagination and reason, he immersed himself in the study of physics and the American pragmatic philosophers, in particular John Dewey. And he began to move his painting in an entirely original direction. As we have seen, his 1940 *Somewhere in Me* with its allover composition, its drifts of color and floating nuclei distributed randomly over the surface, its freely gestural, spontaneous execution, and the total absence of clues to a decipherable subject matter mark a definitive break with the premises of Surrealism. It was shortly after this, in 1941, that he began his large triptych called *The First Spatials,* which was to become, on its completion four years later, a major manifestation of his struggle to give visual form to the concept of matter as energy.

Opposite: Wolfgang Paalen, *Somewhere in Me,* 1940, oil on canvas, 15 x 18
inches; collection Harold and Gertrud Parker.

Below: Wolfgang Paalen, *Discovery of Infra-Space I,* 1940, Conte crayon, 30⅝ x
22⅝ inches; The Museum of Modern Art, New York.

At this point he received a visit from the neophyte American painter Bob Motherwell, bearing an introduction from an artist whom Paalen liked and respected, Kurt Seligmann. Although Motherwell's first reaction to Mexico had been unfavorable, he decided, after meeting Paalen, to stay on during the fall months. He maintained that he was not in the last influenced by Paalen, but that their dialogue was based on a reciprocal exchange of information about Surrealism in return for information about the American pragmatic philosophers. He went almost daily to the house in the Via Obregón and evidently did some painting in Paalen's studio. He was working his way through the styles of various artists—Miró, Picasso, Matisse—in order to learn about composition, and during that fall he made one of his first oil paintings, a seated figure, *Maria,* inspired by the Mexican actress María Ferreira whom he would shortly marry. It is possible that the attentive presence of a responsive young American helped confirm Paalen in his intention of starting a movement of his own, devoted to developing a way beyond Surrealism. Paalen attempted to enlist Motherwell as a collaborator on the publication that was to be the mouthpiece for his movement, hoping for financial as well as technical help. Although this failed, Motherwell was to prove of considerable assistance, translating articles—*Dyn* was to be an English-language publication, directed at a New York audience—contributing an article of his own, and almost certainly advising on the young American artists who were to be included in the last issue.[6]

Instead of Motherwell, Paalen engaged as his assistant Edward Renouf, who had come to Mexico at the suggestion of Julien Levy to learn something about Surrealist painting from him and who was studying with Carlos Mérida. According to Renouf, Paalen was in a deep way infatuated with Breton and had been infected by him with the bug of being the head of an intellectual movement. He desperately wanted Motherwell as a disciple, as well as Renouf himself and a Canadian artist, John Dawson. Renouf's impression was that he lacked the leadership and charisma for such a role and had no genuine empathy. In translating his writing from French to English, Renouf attempted to make it less pompous and pretentious, removing some of the authoritarian flourishes. It was Renouf's name that appeared on the masthead as assistant editor, although he was later replaced by Gustav Regler. In Renouf's estimate Mexico was very uncongenial to Paalen. "He disliked the Spanish language and made no attempt at assimilation. It was to New York that he looked for acceptance and potential influence."[7]

Meanwhile the number of Surrealists in Mexico was augmented by the arrival late in 1941 of Remedios Varo and Benjamin Péret, who had been able to get on a boat to Casablanca and thence to Mexico on the *Serpa Pinto* after Peggy Guggenheim had guaranteed the payment of their passage. By the time Péret left Marseilles only Hérold and Brauner remained at Air Bel; Domínguez had returned to Paris,

Robert Rius had married and gone to Perpignan, and Fry had been expelled in August. "We are finally installed here," Péret wrote to Seligmann in February, "unfortunately suffering from the 2,400 meters altitude, both dead with fatigue and both having heart ailments. And from the financial point of view things are still worse. All the refugees here (Italians, Spanish, German, Israeli) except the French have rescue committees that support them during their first difficult months. I have not succeeded in earning a single centime despite the most persistent and desperate efforts, with the result that I have not even been able to regularize my situation with the Mexican authorities which will cause me problems one of these days." [8]

Shortly thereafter the Surrealists in New York donated works to a sale to raise money to help Péret. Writing to thank Breton for the check, Péret also asked if an exhibition of Brauner's work could be arranged in New York in order to raise the $500 necessary to bring him over, and he proposed asking Peggy Guggenheim and Alfred Barr to intervene with the President of Mexico to get Brauner a visa. Not only was the latter in poor health, but news had come of the arrest of Fry's assistant Jean Gemahling and there was no knowing what other arrests might follow.

By the spring Péret could report to Breton that a very distracted Leonora Carrington had arrived with her Mexican husband Renato Leduc, bringing welcome news of New York, that Esteban Frances had also moved to Mexico City, that Victor Serge was feeling seriously threatened by rumors of an assassination plan and had left the city, and that he had seen Paalen and the first issue of *Dyn* and had not been unduly impressed. Péret proposed gathering the Mexican contingent of Surrealists to discuss a review of their own and suggested that they do a special Mexican issue of *VVV*. Publication of the long poem *Fata Morgana,* which Breton had turned over to Gallimard in Marseilles together with Lam's illustrations, had been forbidden by Vichy, and Péret had brought the proofs with him to Mexico. He sent them off to Roger Caillois in Brazil, where a French-language edition was published not longer after the poem was published in New York in an English translation by Clark Mills. (Unfortunately only the Péret half of the correspondence with Breton during the years of exile is accessible. Some fifteen letters written by Breton from New York will not become available until 2017. Judging from Péret's responses these letters should provide a considerable amount of missing information about Breton's state of mind and his efforts to maintain a New York-based Surrealist group during the war years.)

Onslow Ford and Jacqueline Johnson arrived in Mexico in the summer of 1941. After a few months in Oaxaca and a visit with Matta during his summer sojourn in Taxco, they sought out a location that would be more remote and found an old mill, El Molino, that had been abandoned during the revolution in the Tarascan village of Erongaricuaro. With the help of the villagers, who spoke only in Tarascan, they proceeded to rehabilitate the building to make living and studio quarters. In a letter to Breton Onslow Ford described "studios such as Picasso has often dreamed of, an admirable view of the lake, herbs to cure illnesses and tranquility to heal maladies of the spirit." [9]

There, facing the lake and the rim of mountains on the horizon, Onslow Ford began a long horizontal painting that was to occupy him for many months. Called *The Luminous Land,* it reflected his new immersion in nature and the timeless world of the Indians. Writing to Breton, he described the effect of his new surroundings: "Whether I want it or not, the depths of my imagination are stronger than I am and it's there that I live. More and more I am moving away from people and noise and coming closer to nature." [10]

His first paintings in Mexico had been on the theme of the painter and his muse, very likely reflecting the state of harmony in which he found himself with Jacqueline. Of one of these, *The Circuit of the Light Knight through the Dark Queen,* he said he had "found a language of forms and colors that has its own reality." In this painting the landscape is associated with the female persona while the male is portrayed as a geometrically constructed "pioneer figure poised to discover the landscape of the Muse." The latter appears less integrated with, perhaps even alien to, the landscape surroundings. Onslow Ford worked long and laboriously on this canvas to achieve effects of transparency by layering small dots of yellow and green over a blue ground; changing color was one way of achieving the effect of moving through a transparent plane into another space. This layering process led

Below: Gordon Onslow Ford, *The Circuit of the Light Knight through the Dark Queen*, 1942, oil on canvas, 38½ x 50 inches; private collection.

him to the use of auras made with small touches of color over a contrasting underpainting that might be understood as the spirit emanations of his personnages.

Onslow Ford was still following a practice of keeping notebooks at his bedside and attempting to draw his dreams while still in a semiawake state, so that in its genesis his work was spontaneous and automatist. Yet a large work like *The Luminous Land* was months in the making, its light-dark contrasts carefully worked out with lines giving off light on one side, dark on the other, creating the sense that what is behind is also in front, that planes are continually interpenetrating. The painting is laden with references to earlier images: De Chirico manikins decomposed into planks of wood, linear networks like warped checkerboards inspired by the Poincaré mathematical models ("Divers types de points coniques" was the model that influenced Onslow Ford the most), constructions derived from cubism, and various "planets," flares, and six-pointed stars. At the same time, however, the long horizontal stretch of the landscape with translucent watery intervals and mountainous shapes is deeply permeated by the setting in which it was painted. Originally a painted border, cut off by a careless framer, provided contrasting warm colors that repeated in negative some of the lines of the central composition. It was a painting planned with the utmost deliberation, painstakingly executed, and far removed from automatist spontaneity. Recalling the months of labor it had entailed, Onslow Ford commented: "There we were in a timeless stone age world while the rest of the globe was in turmoil. I was the only painter who had the isolation and leisure to work out something like this."[11]

He wrote frequently to André Breton in New York during that first year in Erongaricuaro, recounting his dreams, describing his paintings, affirming his gratitude to Surrealism. This last he must have thought necessary as Paalen had announced his break with Surrealism and had asked Onslow Ford and Esteban Frances to join him in his new project. "Naturally we refused. It is to you that I give my entire confidence." It was not until Mary 1943 that he drafted a letter saying that he could no longer call himself a Surrealist, but that he still hoped for a visit from Breton and a continuation of their correspondence. It was at this time that he and his wife joined forces with Paalen as contributors to *Dyn*. Esteban Frances, who had managed to get from France to South America, came to join the Onslow Fords in Erongaricuaro

Gordon and Jacqueline Onslow Ford in dugout canoe, Erongaricuaro, c. 1943;
photograph courtesy Gordon Onslow Ford.

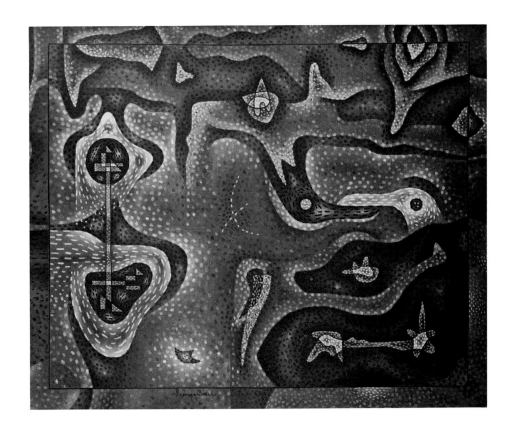

Gordon Onslow Ford, *The Painter and the Muse*, 1943, oil on canvas, 39¾ x 49 inches, private collection.

Gordon Onslow Ford and Esteban Frances at El Molino, c. 1942; photograph courtesy of Gordon Onslow Ford.

Gordon Onslow Ford, drawing for *The Luminous Land,* 1942, chalk on cardboard,
22⅜ x 32½ inches; private collection.

Gordon Onslow Ford, *The Luminous Land,* 1943, oil on masonite, 39½ x 79
inches; private collection.

The Mexican Connection

where his authoritative presence impressed the restive villagers. A roughly drawn floor plan of El Molino has "Esteban's studio" marked on it. It is not clear how long Frances stayed in Erongaricuaro; Péret reported his presence in Mexico City in 1942 and the end of the war found him in New York.

Although it was a long trip from Erongaricuaro to Mexico City, Onslow Ford formed a friendship with Paalen, partly based on their shared interest in pre-Columbian art, an interest that had become a passion for Paalen and subsequently something of a business as well. Onslow Ford had a great respect for Paalen's knowledge of early Mexican art and his sense for where it was to be found. He describes trips made by Paalen into remote sections of the interior in pursuit of fabled treasures and tells of the day Paalen pulled a long green jade bead out of the debris beside their garden wall. Paalen devoted an issue of *Dyn* to the subject of pre-Columbian art, publishing in its objects that he had brought with him from British Columbia as well as Eva Sulzer's photographs of totems *in situ.* He planned a book entitled *Paysage totémique,* with his articles from *Dyn* as preliminary chapters.

Benjamin Péret also began to involve himself in the study of local traditions and wrote to Seligmann in a more cheerful tone in June 1942 saying: "I have begun to occupy myself with an anthology of myths, legends, and folktales from America, from both the present and the pre-Columbian period. Naturally I am writing from the point of view of the marvelous and I am sure there is material for a magnificent collection." He also mentioned that he was doing a radio broadcast, "an artistic chronicle," that he had a tiny garden, and that Remedios had been able to buy brushes and paint and had begun to work.[12]

In the spring of 1942 the first issue of Paalen's new review appeared, pregnant with the promise of a new art. Its title, *Dyn,* was derived from the Greek word for possible (or to be able) and the red letters on its yellow cover were written in such a way as to express something of the kinetic quality of the word. Its text was predominantly in English, with some articles and poems appearing in French and a few entries in both languages. The fact that one of its key articles, Paalen's "Farewell to Surrealism," appeared only in French indicates that it was particularly directed at Breton and the New York Surrealists. And the fact that two additional articles by Paalen appeared in both French and English implies that he wished to propose a new direction to the European refugees as well as to the younger Americans who were part of their circle.

Paalen was thus throwing down a gauntlet to Breton and attempting to establish himself as the spokesman for a new direction in painting. That he did indeed have such ambitions is confirmed by Renouf, who contributed a short article, "Regionalism in Painting," and several drawings to the first issue. The other contributors included Paalen's wife Alice with two written contributions and a gouache, Eva Sulzer with photographs from their British Columbian trip, and César Moro with a selection of poems. Little apparently is known about the two other painters who are included, John Dawson and Jean Caroux, and the suggestion has been made that some of the works appearing under other names were actually painted or written by Paalen himself in order to give the impression that the nucleus of a new movement existed. Judging from Onslow Ford's letter to Breton, Paalen had tried to enlist both him and Esteban Frances in his new endeavor.

In his "Farewell" Paalen acknowledged his debt to Surrealism, especially as it liberated him from "the north pole of art," that is, the years spent in the "rigid formalism" of Abstraction/Creation. He mentioned past disagreements over the emphasis on Hegelian thought and discarded dialectical materialism as well as all other isms. "It is no longer the function of specialists, of psychologists, sociologists, even of philosophers, but of the artist himself to understand and communicate the objective value of his message, especially that artist who has vanquished the dualism between inspiration and reason.... For him there will no longer exist the false alternative of sacrificing the magic of his work to comprehension or of renouncing adult thought for the sake of childlike faith."[13]

With these words Paalen rejected Surrealism's emphasis on raw material from the psyche and on pure automatism (although he acknowledged that the latter was nearly always a means, not an end in itself), and urged joining that "most precious of human faculties, imagination," with the capacity for objective reason. What this new art would be like he spelled out in the same issue in his article "The New Image," which was translated into English by Motherwell. Here Paalen indulged in some begrudging comments on Dalí, Calas, Abstraction/Creation, and art critics in general and traced the development of an art that increasingly moved away from the "prolongation of a perceived entity" in favor of projecting a "new realization which does not have to be referred for its meaning to an object already existing." He saw the true value of an artistic image as deriving from its capacity "to prefigure, to express potentially a new order of things." In concluding, he wrote: "The great lesson of modern art that leaves us filled with hope is that what will be need not be legitimized by what is. The possible does not have to be justified by the known."[14]

In "Art and Science" in the third issue, he elaborates further: "The new directions of physics as much as those of art led me to a potential concept of reality opposed to any concept of deterministic finality. This concept, which I shall call dynastic (from the Greek word *dynaton:* the possible) or the Philosophy of the Possible, excludes any kind of mysticism and metaphysics, because it includes the equal necessity of art and science. . . . The new theme will be a plastic cosmogony, which means no longer a symbolization or interpretation but, through the specific means of art, a direct visualization of forces which move our bodies and minds."[15] In these words, written in 1942, we read both the title of the first journal of the abstract expressionists, *Possibilities,* whose sole issue appeared in 1947, and a precise description of what Jackson Pollock began to do with paint in 1946 as he gave visual form to "the forces that move our bodies and minds." It's not quite as foresighted as Baudelaire's elegant description of impressionist painting twenty years before it came into existence, but Paalen can be credited with intuiting, if not directly influencing, a coming direction in painting. Jackson Pollock had all five numbers of *Dyn* in his library, and among Paalen's papers was a Pollock brush drawing.

In the second and third issues of *Dyn* three particular concerns are emphasized by Paalen and his contributors. The first is a firm opposition to dialectical materialism; the second is an interest, both anthropological and aesthetic, in the Indian art of the Western Hemisphere; and the third is a rapprochement of art and science, which last had the most direct relation to Paalen's own work. In *Dyn* no. 2 under the title "Inquiry on Dialectical Materialism" he published the responses to a questionnaire sent out that spring to Lionel Abel, Breton, Calas, Albert Einstein, James T. Farrell, Clement Greenberg, Sidney Hook, Dwight Macdonald, Philip Rahv, Bertrand Russell, Meyer Schapiro, and others. Most of the above were Trotskyists and half were contributors to *Partisan Review,* which Rahv had moved out of the Stalinist orbit in 1936 and which was one of *Dyn*'s advertisers. Paalen was clearly trying to establish his credentials with intellectuals of the Trotskyist left and to draw into his orbit some of those who were to gain standing as influential critics of literature and the arts by the later 1940s. The question of what could be salvaged from dialectical materialism was one that concerned the Trotskyist left at the time. Meyer Schapiro recalled inviting Breton to his home one evening for a discussion with Jean van Heijenoort, Ernest Nagel, and A. J. Ayers on the question of whether it was possible to have Marxism without dialectical materialism.

As far as his understanding of physics is concerned, Paalen apparently favored Heisenberg and the uncertainty principle over a mechanistic view of the universe. The paintings and drawings reproduced in these issues have in common a concern with a certain kind of kinetic linearity and a tendency to work in a flowing allover motion that was particularly evident in Paalen's *Chromatic Polarities,* reproduced in *Dyn* no. 2, but also echoed in the drawings of Renouf, Alice Paalen's *Moraines,* and the paintings of Jean Carroux.

Opposite: Wolfgang Paalen, *Chromatic Polarities,* 1942; private collection.

Below: Edward Renouf, *Quaternity,* 1942, oil on canvas, 29½ x 22 inches; present whereabouts unknown.

The direction of Paalen's own painting can be judged by the remarkable *Space Unbound* of 1941, a work in which the nuclei of *Somewhere in Me* have expanded outward into whorls of line that spin against each other, conveying a sense of implacable physical forces. The sense of unleashed energy is conveyed through simultaneous contrasts of color as well as by the spinning lines. This work comes as close to illustrating the concept of matter as energy as any work painted up to this time. In the same year he started his triptych *Les Premières spatiales* in which he introduces the parabola, which became a key shape in his monumental cosmogon series. One might say "direction" more than "shape," as a parabola is infinitely expandable, turns on course swiftly, and has no fixed beginning or end. In Paalen's own words: "A picture may say, I am that short stretch where the parabola comes out of the

Opposite top: Alice Paalen (Rahon), *Moraines,* oil on canvas, 25½ x 25½ inches; present whereabouts unknown.

Opposite bottom: Wolfgang Paalen, *Space Unbound,* 1941, oil on canvas, 114 x 145 cm; private collection.

infinite, turns and returns into the infinite." [16] Three parabolas circling toward and away from each other became the motif for canvases such as *Tripolarity* of 1944 as well as the symbol for *Dyn*. "All things become alive at the touch of the parabola," Paalen told Gustav Regler. Some of Paalen's paintings such as *Nuclear Wheel* of 1942 appear to reflect his study of diagrams of molecular structure and other illustrations from the physics books he was accumulating in his library.

Another theme that infiltrates his painting along with that of physics is pre-Columbian art. Forms and symbols connected with his study of the art of the Pacific Northwest and of Mexico are suggested by some of the configurations and colors of his work. In a double issue of *Dyn* (nos. 4 and 5, 1943) devoted to pre-Columbian art, he reproduced the large carved and painted face from the façade of the Tlingit hut that occupied one wall of his studio. Its colors of white, black, and reddish brown, its geometric simplification, and its larger-than-life aura of a spirit form were all elements reflected in one way or another in Paalen's painting. Most particularly his use of a dark negative space to unify the dashes of color yet let them float detached on a field, held together as if by magnetic force, echoes of the mode of composition of the Tlingit façade.

This same double issue of *Dyn* included photographs by Eva Sulzer, writings by the noted anthropologist Miguel Covarrubias, and Paalen's own insightful comments on Amerindian art. He approached it from a Jungian point of view, with the intent of penetrating the archetypal forms to reveal material from the collective unconscious in an ambitious attempt to bind the spirit forms of Indian art to the disembodied energy of theoretical physics. Paalen was a cultivate and cosmopolitan intellectual as well as a painter and was equally articulate in poetic descriptions such as that of his visit to the cave paintings at Altamira (in the pre-Lascaux thirties) and in theoretical discourse such as his discussion of the shortcomings of dialectical materialism in "Suggestion for an Objective Morality." [17] While his counterparts in New York might vaguely talk of their quest for myth in terms once described by Meyer Schapiro as "nightschool metaphysics," he was able to present his point of view in articulate and well-documented form, giving a rationale with a basis in both science and artistic tradition that could justify, if not explain, what was taking shape on canvases in New York and Mexico.

Perhaps those who were to emerge as the most influential critics of the decade did not read his essays, although seven of them were anthologized by Wittenborn in *Form and Sense* in 1945, or were stung by his reference to art critics as those incapable of doing anything else. In any event, scant attention was paid to the role of either his essays or his paintings when it came to describing the genesis of abstract expressionism, yet from a more objective distance both indeed seem to provide a missing link.

This becomes glaringly evident when we turn to the last issue of *Dyn,* which appeared in 1944. Here, published between the same covers, are paintings and drawings by the émigrés (Matta, Onslow Ford, Hayter, Hélion, Alice and Wolfgang Paalen, and Eva Sulzer) and by the Americans (Baziotes, Xenia Cage, Calder, Holtzman, Motherwell, Pollock, and Jeanne Reynal) as well as a sculpture by David Smith. In addition to literary selections by César Moro, Anaïs Nin, Jacqueline Johnson, and Gustav Regler, there is a transcription of a lecture, "The Modern Painter's World," that Robert Motherwell had given at Mt. Holyoke College. In this talk he rejected surrealist automatism as a pseudo-solution of the problem of fathoming the unconscious—"it's really a plastic weapon with which to invent new forms"—and advocated a painting that resulted from the interplay of a sentient being and the external world, or "painting as a medium in which the mind can actualize itself." [18]

Having redefined the function of automatism, Motherwell turned to the question of the artist and society. He declared that the artist should be free from social concerns as long as he worked in a society where the middle class remained dominant. He argued that "the artist has no alternative to formalism as long as modern society is dominated by the love of property. He strengthens his formalism with his other advantages, his increased knowledge of history and modern science, his connections with the eternal, the aesthetic, and his relations with the folk and, finally, his very opposition to middle class society gives him a certain strength." [19]

Thus, with a few sweeping and not always logically founded statements Motherwell set the stage for a depoliticized art that would assume commodity status— what else?—in a property-loving society and, by the formal values it projected, contribute to the quality of life of that society. Since the young, ingenuous author of these words was to be both a financial and articulate verbal contributor to the publication of justifications and explanations of the emerging American art, especially in his 1947 single-issue journal, *Possibilities,* his brief for an apolitical, formalist art can be seen as a major plank in a new artistic platform.

Paalen's contribution to what was to be the last issue of *Dyn* was an essay entitled "The Meaning of Cubism Today." Here he explored the analogies between physics, "which stopped conceiving of space as static," and analytical cubism, which was able to create a "new continuum of space-light in which light and shade are no longer illusionistic means, but are integrated in the plastic matter like the polarity of graphic rhythms and color rhythms." Acknowledging that the "pure cubist constellations will shine always," he goes on to voice his concern with articulating non-

Robert Motherwell, *The Door (Mexico),* 1943, ink and watercolor on paper
mounted on board, 13¼ x 10 inches; collection Thomas Mark Futter.

anthropomorphic elements: "The picture with a subject is finished, and finished too, the picture object, the by-product of architecture. No more painting with a subject, but no picture without a theme. Paintings that are balance beams of scales whose plates are the microcosm and the macrocosm, picture-beings." Concluding, he hailed "those who leave for an expanse, whose maps are still to be sounded: the new space."[20]

Clearly the paintings and drawings reproduced in the 1944 *Dyn* suggest that a new style was in the making. A mode of painterly abstraction that hinted at latent symbols was apparent in the work of Baziotes and Motherwell; an abstract symbolism (described by Onslow Ford as "inner world images beyond dreams") characterized both the cerebral work of Gordon Onslow Ford and Matta's drawing of exploding space; and a swift automatist line appeared to be the basis for graphic work by both Hayter and David Smith. However, the most strikingly innovative work among all those reproduced is Jackson Pollock's *Moon Woman Cuts the Circle*. There is a visceral impact to the paint, a rhythmic organization provided by the repeated crescent forms, and an urgency to the brush drawing that give this work, for all its awkwardness, a forceful presence. The strong primary color offset by calligraphic fragments in black and white, the sense of a recalcitrant image lurking just below the level of recognition, and the exploitation of the entire canvas surface while veering away from the edges combine to confront the viewer with a new kind of

Matta, untitled gouache, 1943, with dedication to Paalen; present whereabouts unknown.

painting, at once authentic in its expressionist force and divorced from previous styles.

Anyone picking up this issue of *Dyn* could hardly fail to recognize the novelty of the art it showed. In fact there are at least two documented instances of members of the U.S. armed forces seeing it in army base libraries and making pilgrimages after the war, Lee Mullican to find Paalen and Harry Jackson to find Pollock. The new art didn't fall under the heading of Surrealism, but it was not yet namable as anything else. No one had published the above-named artists as a group before and no Pollock had been reproduced in color. The story of the two years and six numbers of *Dyn* is in capsule form the story of the decline of one art movement and the genesis of another, starting with Paalen's recognition that Surrealism was no longer valid, his articulation of the importance of new developments in physics (while the Manhattan Project was secretly gathering momentum), his attempts to expand a too inflexible Marxism, his capacity to look beyond Western culture, and his search for an art in his own work and that of others that placed itself at the center of changing awareness in a changing world. How much of a role his paintings and his writings played in inspiring the direction of this new art is not quantitatively measurable, but there is no question that from his quiet corner of San Angel he was sending forth images and ideas that had not previously been formulated, and that these were seen and read and discussed in New York and beyond.

Circumstances, however, prevented Paalen from achieving the kind of fruition that some of the younger artists whose work he published were to attain. The end of his marriage, the failure of a second marriage, attempts to rebuild his life, first in San Francisco, then in Paris, and a scandal involving smuggled antiquities interrupted the momentum of his work and finally obscured the importance of his accomplishment.

While there was little recognition of the foreign artistic presence on the part of Mexican officialdom—the thirties had, after all, been a time of trying to redress the balance in favor of Mexican tradition over European influence—there was one gallery in Mexico City, the Galería de Arte Mexicano, that was generally hospitable to the Surrealists. Its director, Ines Amor, had hosted the International Surrealist exhibition of 1939–1940, and since then had shown a continued interest in the Europeans. On Paalen's recommendation she agreed to mount a Kurt Seligmann exhibition in the summer of 1943 and the Seligmanns finally made their long-postponed trip to Mexico. There they visited the Paalen household and were also reunited with Frida Kahlo, who had been a guest at their home during her trip to Paris in the winter of

Above: Jackson Pollock, *Moon Woman Cuts the Circle*, 1943, oil on canvas;
Centre Georges Pompidou, Musée National d'Art Moderne.

Opposite: Stanley William Hayter, pen drawings reproduced in *Dyn*, 1943; present
whereabouts unknown.

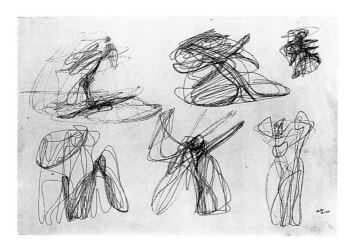

1938–1939. Arlette Seligmann, who was in the truest sense a *femme enfant,* kept in mind only one detail of the Mexican trip, that in Kahlo's "blue house" she was shown a doll that she had given her in Paris four years earlier. After their return to the United States Esteban Frances wrote them saying how much their visit had meant to the small circle of refugees in Mexico and that the exhibition had made a deep impression. In response to Seligmann's request for press notices, however, he regretfully reported that there had been little attention in the press, only one article with a reproduction in *Hoy* of which he was not able to obtain a copy.[21]

Frances also lamented in the same letter that he was "en panne" and had passed three months without being able to work, partly due to the effects of the climate on his health, partly to uncertainty about a New York exhibition that was finally planned for Durlacher in the coming October. Kirk Askew of the Durlacher gallery was also Seligmann's dealer at that time, so very probably Seligmann was instrumental in arranging the show. Frances did not travel to New York for the exhibition, but wrote to Seligmann voicing various concerns: too few paintings—again he had not worked much during that year—and regrets about the titles; he would have preferred to exhibit them without titles, but yielded to pressure from Askew. Frances seems to have been especially grateful for Seligmann's words of friendship and interest, the only ones he had heard from New York during his exhibition. He was by most accounts a person of abrupt mood shifts and did not have close friends in the New York Surrealist group; possibly Breton held against him his relationship with Lamba. It was probably due to Seligmann's good standing with the *View* circle that his New York exhibition received any attention at all and that he was invited to do a *View* cover that year.

Yet the paintings he exhibited were brilliant, a compendium of the various devices that he and Matta and Onslow Ford had developed for representing transparency and non-Euclidean space with the addition of a range of fully saturated color that evokes Mexican *artes populares.* A work such as his untitled mixed media on paper of 1941–1942 seems to bring Chiricoesque space to a volcanic Mexican landscape in which a hybrid idol is ritualistically centered while forms suggesting phantom spirits coalesce out of the earth and sky. The sections of geometric patterning and the dominant black, white, and red palette are unmistakably Mexican in their inspiration. More complex is the larger oil on canvas, also untitled, of 1943, a canvas in which he seems to have packed all his painterly knowledge, to such an extent that the viewer is lost in a profusion of different modes of spatial rendering. The very abundance of intriguing detail and metaphorical allusion in this painting mitigates against its being perceived as a coherent work, but as a repertory of possible modes of abstract symbolism it is unique in its time. Despite his problems of health and money, Frances, like others of the émigré artists, appears to have made bold strides in his painting during the early years of his "exile" and did not in later years equal his achievement of 1941 to 1945.

In Mexico City Frances frequented the modest home of Remedios Varo (a former lover) and Benjamin Péret. Located in the Calle Gabino Barreda near the center of the older section of Mexico City, the tenement building in which they lived was ramshackle at best; one entered through a window and had to be careful to avoid the holes in the floor. Many refugee friends came to stay in that house, including in the summer of 1943 Pierre Mabille and his wife, rather to Péret's annoyance. In 1944 Leonora Carrington also came to share their home after her wartime marriage of convenience came to an end. She soon began a relationship with an old friend of Varo's, the Hungarian-born photographer Chiqui Weisz, whom she married in 1946. The painter Gunther Gerzso and the photographer Kati Horna and her husband, José, were also part of this circle. A painting by Gerzso of 1944, *The Days of Gabino Barreda Street,* commemorates this establishment and the refugees who gathered there. Thinly disguised portraits include Varo in the foreground in a catlike mask, Carrington with her nude torso entwined in vines, Péret as a collection of symbols enclosed in a triangle that rises from trousers seated on a table of twisted roots or vines, a veiled Esteban Frances in the background surrounded by paintings of nudes, and the head of Gerzso himself peering from a box on the ground.[22]

Above: Frida Kahlo, Arlette and Kurt Seligmann, and an unidentified person, Mexico, 1943.

Opposite: Esteban Frances, *Untitled,* 1943, oil on canvas; private collection.

Péret's letters to Breton, devoted to news of mutual friends and matters concerning publications as they are, give no indication of the creative currents that intensified existence in the derelict building in the Calle Gabino Barreda. It was a circle far more informal than that of Paalen, one whose members excised in precarious circumstances and were more concerned with the struggle for survival than with establishing a position and issuing statements. The central force in this group seems to have been Remedios Varo, intuitive, spontaneous, able to nurture the spirit of play despite the hard conditions, inspiring the creativity of others even though she had little time to create herself. It was Remedios who was the principal support of the household, finding work as a decorator of furniture, a costume designer, a builder of small dioramas, and an illustrator of promotional literature for the Bayer pharmaceutical company. This last endeavor, which provided the most sustained income, afforded an opportunity to use her Surrealist's turn of mind, as well as the meticulous technique she had long since mastered, to visualize the insomniac's anxiety or a body racked by the pain of rheumatism. The illustrations for Bayer, which she did under a different name, and the medical and scientific literature to which she was exposed, were instrumental in infusing a component of scientific imagery into her later work.

The addition of Leonora Carrington to the Gabino Barreda group turned out to be of significance for both Varo and herself. There was a great deal that the two women already shared, including their relationships with male Surrealists and their difficult escapes from France after the outbreak of war, during which time Varo was interned and Carrington was put in a mental institution. Both were beautiful, sought-after women determined to establish their own identities through their art. Using what each needed from the male-dominated Surrealist movement, they proceeded to weave fabulous stories using a kind of stream of consciousness prose and to paint in a delicate, translucent style the visionary material that they delved into together. In other circumstances and in a different country neither woman might have found the kind of liberation that they found together in a country that made no claims on them, cast them in no social mold.

Both Péret and Frances mention in letters written in 1944 that the painting of Leonora Carrington is impressive. That two male Surrealists would gratuitously volunteer this information is itself impressive. Indeed unless they needed them to swell the numbers of adherents for a particular exhibition or publication, the male

Above: Esteban Frances, *Composición surrealista,* 1944, pen, ink, and gouache on paper, 18½ x 25 inches; private collection, New York.

writers and poets of the movement seem to have attributed little importance to the creative identities of the women in their lives. Carrington was an exception. The facts that Ernst rescued her paintings from St.-Martin along with his, that her *Self-Portrait* was featured on the front page of *View,* which also published her stories, and that she was the only woman included in the photograph of the émigrés taken in 1942 in Peggy Guggenheim's apartment (with the exception of Peggy herself and the American photographer Berenice Abbott), indicate that she was regarded as an individual artist in her own right, not just appended to the movement as a wife or girlfriend.

Esteban Frances brought to Carrington's studio the eccentric English patron of Surrealism Edward James. Not only did he buy some of her paintings, but he arranged an exhibition for her at Pierre Matisse and wrote the catalogue essay. He described his visit to her studio: "a combined kitchen, nursery, bedroom, kennel and junk store, peeling whitewash on the wall, poorly lit, dog and cat populated—the disorder was apocalyptic." In her he saw "a ruthless English intellectual in revolt

against all the hypocrisies of her homeland, against the bourgeois fears and false moralities of her conventional background and sheltered upbringing."[23]

Meanwhile, from his stone age village Gordon Onslow Ford described for Matta a "life that goes on as in a dream. The rains have gone and the sky is wave after wave of blue, down to a Chirico pale green horizon. The maize has been gathered and the corn planted."[24] From this isolated spot Onslow Ford carried on a correspondence with his old friends from the Surrealist group, whether the displacements of the war, which was never mentioned, had landed them in New York or in Mexico. For a time he wrote as a Surrealist, taking a partisan interest in the conflicts that had arisen in New York between the circle around *View,* which tended to be more artistically conservative, and the younger Surrealists who were part of Breton's entourage. Matta wrote comparing Wellfleet to Trevignon, where they had summered in 1938, but even more lonely. The drawings that were habitually part of his letters here include a horizontal/vertical grid labeled as "time," a warped or wavy grid as "movement, water and transparency," dotted concentric circles as "space," and receding transparent squares as "destiny." "Write," he asked, "sending charts of what you are doing."[25]

"I have been going into spaces until my head swims," Onslow Ford responded. "We are all so occupied making our home in the old mill that I have only been painting in the sky and the mountains on the horizon, slowly gathering energy to explode in my studio when it is ready."[26] Spaces, charts, transparency—this was the vocabulary of psychological morphology with its emphasis on multidimensionality and transcending vision. What Matta achieved by moving his brush across the canvas with a rapidity born of certainty, Onslow Ford worked at with patient deliberation, putting the paint on in small methodical dots. "My first pictures were monochrome," he wrote, "(blue, blue and blue) where I searched for the molten matter of which my world is made. Now I have it, and more easily than before the personages were born."[27]

During the next several years Onslow Ford attuned himself more and more to the rhythms of the natural world around him and to the village life. He learned to paddle a dugout canoe as swiftly and silently as the Indians and he gained their wary trust. Gradually the bright colors of the market place, with its arrays of fruits and vegetables and the woven serapes hanging in the strong sunlight, infiltrated his painting. In *Country Feast* the background is a dazzling pink with strongly contrasting lines and shapes in brilliant colors interspersed over it. He wrote to Paalen: "The countryside, the atmosphere of the Tarascan Indians, their vision of the universe, have me in their spell. It is so different from Paris and from African art and I feel more than ever convinced that something culturally very important, far removed from Surrealism, is going to happen on this continent."[28]

Paalen's mind was on New York, however. He wrote to Onslow Ford that he had heard from Motherwell about the latter's exhibition with Peggy Guggenheim and had decided that it was the place for the him to show. Although Onslow Ford did not feel he ranked high with Peggy Guggenheim, he wrote on Paalen's behalf, saying: "In my opinion it has been modern physics rather than the Mexican landscape that has been Paalen's inspiration, although it is impossible to live here and not be influenced by the dramatic light effects. He has succeeded in contributing a new concept of space that no one can ignore." [29] Whether or not she was swayed by Onslow Ford's recommendation, Guggenheim did agree to give Paalen a show in April 1945, following his February exhibition at the Galeria de Arte Mexicano. The show, comprising mainly paintings from 1944, included two major works, *The Cosmogons* and *First Spatials,* which he had worked on from 1941 to 1944. He thus joined a gallery roster that already included the Americans whose work had been published for the first time in *Dyn*—Baziotes, Motherwell, and Pollock—and who surely already knew the essay "Art and Science" dealing with the crisis of subject that he excerpted in the catalogue.

The best verbal elucidation of what Paalen was attempting in the paintings he showed in 1945 appears in Gustav Regler's 1947 book on Paalen, which friends of the artist believe was written mostly by Paalen himself:

He creates a sort of magnetic field of emotion in which square and round dots and elliptical segments of color are organized into constellations that are limited only by the orbits of their own particles—thus evoking interstellar space. . . . In the Cosmogons series the interactivity of the spectator and the universe is rhythmically expressed. There is no longer any arbitrary encrustation of anthropomorphic fragments or any non-figurative puritanism. The radiant curves coordinate themselves into great "personages" which are the new protagonists of the eternal Promethean play. . . . The planetary sense becomes a true cosmic consciousness. There is no longer the life and the death of a being, any individual landscape, the knotting and untying of any particular situation, but rather the circle of the eternal coming and passing. [30]

If this is indeed Paalen's explanation of his recent paintings he seems to be positing a synthesis of his scientific readings (in the same paragraph he refers to a description of the atom in Brace Lemon's *Cosmic Rays Thus Far*) with the idea of the disembodied spirit form akin to Breton's Great Transparents or Onslow Ford's "live-line beings." The word Paalen uses, *personnages,* is the same one Onslow Ford

uses to describe the form-structures in Tanguy's horizonless spaces as well as the spirit presences in his own paintings. Further light is cast on this notion by a play that Paalen wrote in 1946 called *The Cosmogons,* the typescript of which was among Kurt Seligmann's papers. The play, which apparently was never published or performed, gives a distinctly science fiction impression through its personifications of celestial forces. Paalen's desire to mediate between the scientific and the occult found far more eloquent realization in painting than in this rather wooden interplanetary drama, but the latter does at least amplify the nature of the populated space he envisioned.

Meanwhile, Onslow Ford felt more and more an affinity for what Paalen was attempting. In a 1946 letter to Paalen he wrote: "Your vision of space has been a revelation to me every day. This year I too have made two small space studies which have opened up new vistas."[31] He described this new style a few months later in a letter to Herbert Read: "My latest pictures are in a technique of dots and lines that suggest transparency rather than surface."[32] Like Paalen he was allowing space to intervene between the lines and was using the brush in a more calligraphic way as he prepared for his next major voyage, a departure from Mexico to the west coast of the United States.

Paalen's and Onslow Ford's concepts of space were becoming sufficiently close that when they both found themselves in San Francisco after the war, they formed, together with Lee Mullican, a movement called Dynaton. The words used to describe

Opposite: Gordon Onslow Ford, *Country Feast,* 1944, oil on canvas, 33¼ x 49 inches; private collection.

Below: Wolfgang Paalen, *The Cosmogons,* 1944, oil on canvas, 244 x 236 cm; collection of Robert and Rebecca Anthoine.

it sound like Paalen's: "The Dynaton is a limitless continuum in which all forms of reality are potentially implicit. The unconscious urge for a self-transcending understanding of the world had become conscious in a meta-plastic vision. Meta-plastic painting is a sort of active meditation which leads to a new concept of reality. This concept assumes that the imponderable is as important as the measurable." [33]

While the web of words woven around the artworks may have been different, the direction in which Paalen's work and ideas were moving parallels that of some of the future abstract expressionists in New York and indeed of a number of artists who were not part of that group. While it may not be possible to establish a direct cause and effect relationship, one can't dismiss Paalen, his writings, and his 1945 and 1946

New York exhibitions as a factor in the direction that postwar painting took. In a period when the publication of the writings of artists was a rarity, Wittenborn published a collection of Paalen's essays, *Form and Sense,* in 1945, probably on the advice of Motherwell, who played a significant role in the Problems of Contemporary Art series that the publisher had just initiated. This book of intelligent observations and speculative thoughts on art from the archaic to the most modern circulated not only in the small New York art world but also in Paris where it was sold at the Galerie Maeght. Given the relationship that existed between Paalen and some of the younger New York painters, it can be assumed that Paalen's paintings and his writing were, if not a direct inspiration, at least a corroboration of the responses they were having to the phenomenon of global war, to atomic physics, and to the historical point at which Western art had arrived.

In spite of the remoteness of their village, the Onslow Fords had a number of visitors from New York, including in 1944 Jacqueline Lamba and Aube, who were brought there by Esteban Frances and stayed for an extended visit; Karl Nierendorf, who was to give Onslow Ford a one-man show in 1946; and in 1945 Matta with a new wife. Onslow Ford found the latter greatly changed in four years and voiced a real divergence between them as he described Matta's "ironic preoccupation with the human animal" in his new work. Neophyte painters like William Fett and Richard Bowman sought out Onslow Ford because they had seen or heard about his work. "Young Americans have been coming and going in the house," he wrote to Paalen. "In spite of a great resistance to making the leap from bourgeois to revolutionary, I do like them."[34] In addition the Onslow Fords' home was the long-term refuge of Victor Serge, who lived in fear of Stalin's henchmen, believing he was next after Trotsky on the hit list.

A debate over the impact of Surrealism on Mexican art continues without much prospect of resolution.[35] What was surreal to the offspring of the European bourgeoisie was reality to the Mexicans, as one writer put it, which is perhaps why Mexico became the home of choice for some of the refugees after the war's end. Although Surrealism tried to claim Kahlo and María Izquierdo, their strong individual styles had been long established by 1940. For the decade before the Surrealists arrived Mexican artists had been trying to throw off the yoke of European tradition. Apart from the achievements of the decade's great mural painters, there existed something of a stylistic vacuum that in a sense invited experimentation, invention, and an improvisatory mingling of styles and imagery from different sources. That some of what filled this vacuum might be seen as having affinities with Surrealism is only natural in a country whose rich and highly sophisticated past culture survives everywhere beneath the superimposed European traditions. Gunther Gerzso is the most obvious example of the temporary impact of Surrealism on a Mexican painter, especially in works strongly influenced by Onslow Ford, but he was already Europeanized, both by parentage and a prewar period of study abroad.

It is possible, however, that there was more absorption of Surrealism than is discernible from a later vantage point. When Ines Amor organized an exhibition of younger Mexican artists for New York's Knoedler Gallery in 1945, a reviewer noted that "Surrealism of international flavor has supplanted the vigorous native genre and social protest." Singled out to demonstrate the point was José Chávez Morado, whose grotesque creatures were "as old as Bosch, as new as Seligmann, sifted through his own lively imagination."[36] A similar point was made by Rosamund Frost in *Art News,* which devoted a page to three concurrent Mexican shows. She saw some of the younger artists, such as Juan Soriano, as combining the power of the older social crusaders with a disturbing, often surreal imagery. At Carlos Mérida's one-man show at Nierendorf, she saw work that "fused the Maya tradition with the modern language," including that of Miró. In contrast to a new vitality of the Mexicans, Frost felt that "our own U.S. painting dwindles into something literal, cautious, even a trifle pedestrian."[37]

As far as the reverse impact is concerned, that of Mexico on the refugees, here too there is not a great deal to be collectively applied. Apart from Ines Amor at the Galería de Arte Mexicano, there was no particular art apparatus as in New York, waiting and eager to promote the Europeans, so that opportunities to exhibit, sell, and receive feedback were fairly curtailed. What did affect them, as we have seen, was the day-to-day presence of the pre-Columbian legacy and the volcanic Mexican landscape with its exotic vegetation. Volcanic imagery erupted in paintings and poetry. In *Air méxicain* Péret wrote of the volcano—"the fire, draped in mourning, flares out of all its pores/the spray of sperm and blood veils its face tattooed with lava"—as a symbol of revolutionary Mexico."[38] In the first issue of *Dyn* Alice Rahon apostrophized the volcano visible from Mexico City: "Ixtaccihuatl, named by the gods, the sleeping woman, her face turned toward the rising sun. Always a young giantess, a white lover of snow and millenary dawns . . ."[39] As we have seen, volcanoes had a special significance for Matta, and his 1941 stay in Mexico set off a series of paintings inspired by the idea of an exploding earth, an image with which he identified his physical self. Paalen, Onslow Ford, and others were profoundly stirred by the eruption of a new volcano in 1943 in a cornfield next to the town of Paricutin and made the long trip to witness its birth travails. This event entered into the mythology of the Surrealists in Mexico and became part of the litany of the marvelous in its expanded New World version. The violent eruption of the earth into flame was the perfect exemplification of Breton's dictum on convulsive beauty.

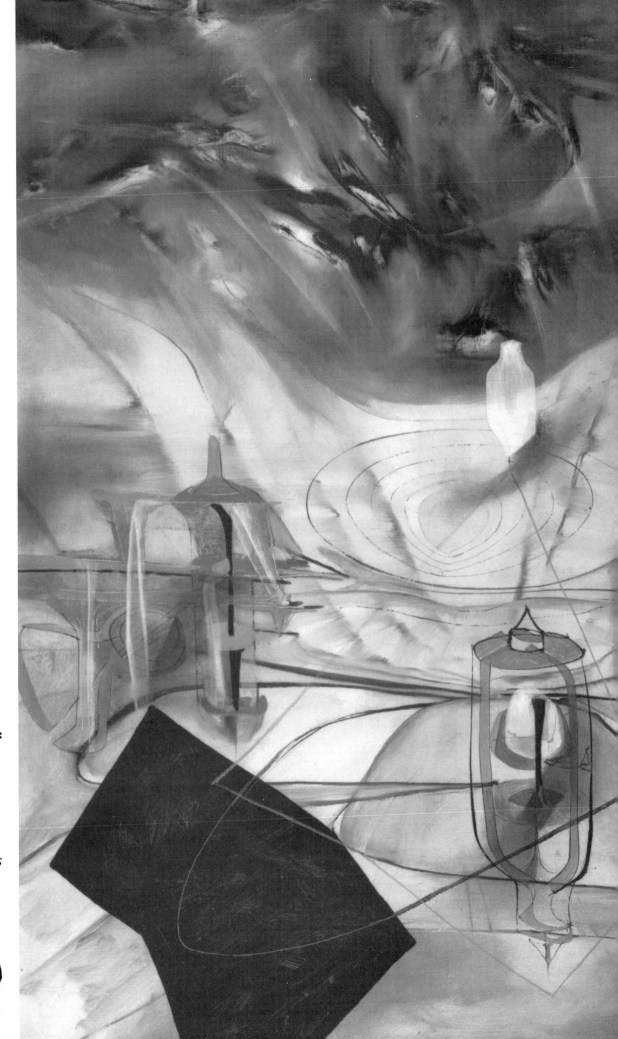

8 New York, 1943:

A New

Momentum Begins

One would expect the triumphs of 1942 to have led to the establishing of Surrealism on a firm footing in the United States and the adherence of some of the younger American artists to have swelled the ranks, just as Breton had originally envisioned when he made his decision to try to regroup in the New World. However, this objective was doomed from within and without. As Seligmann foresaw at the time the Surrealists arrived in New York, they brought their quarrels with them. Duchamp reported to Tzara in Paris that the cohesiveness that bound the band of exiles had quickly changed to a policy of "every man for himself."[1]

Seligmann was one of the first to go, expelled by Breton in 1943 because he disagreed over the interpretation of one of the Tarot cards (correctly, according to Meyer Schapiro). Seligmann's continued involvement with the *View* circle—one of his cyclonic brush drawings appeared on the cover of the first issue of 1943—may also have exacerbated the tensions with Breton. Breton's stance vis-à-vis *View* is reflected in an angry telegram he sent to Péret when the latter sent the manuscript of his introduction to Mexican folktales to *View* at Charles Henri Ford's request. After *VVV* ceased publication in 1944, Breton was again willing to contribute to *View,* as he did for the special Duchamp issue in 1945.

1943 also saw the expulsion of Masson for the most apparently trivial of reasons. Masson had not only done a cover for *View,* but he had agreed to do a curtain for a performance that was to benefit the Free French, with a design that included a French flag. For Breton this amounted to condoning nationalism, and he declared Masson no longer a Surrealist. For the latter, who had been in and out of Surrealism before, this was a nonsensical gesture. He had little use for Breton's dictatorial posturings, including his assumption of authority over who was or was not a Surrealist. "I was born a Surrealist," Masson would say, unfazed by Breton. From Mexico Péret applauded the rupture with Seligmann, regretted Masson's "confusion," and told tales on Motherwell.[2]

1943 was the year of breakups of another kind. Jacqueline Lamba definitively left Breton and moved into an apartment of her own on Bleecker Street. The following year she married David Hare after his divorce from Susanna Wilson. In June Anne Matta gave birth to twin boys, an event that became legendary in the annals of Surrealism. The Surrealists were all sufficiently conversant with ethnology to be aware of the special beliefs that attach to the birth of twins, and even after both sons were tragically dead the Matta twins were spoken of in epochal terms. Their arrival, however, precipitated Matta's move from the tiny apartment in Patchin Place and his taking refuge for a time in the apartment of Isabelle Waldberg, whose husband Patrick was overseas for the Office of War Information. After the Mattas were divorced he married Patricia Kane, who left him after several years for Pierre Matisse, who divorced his American wife Teeny who in 1953 became the wife of Marcel Duchamp. Meanwhile the sculptor Isamu Noguchi provided comfort and much-needed assistance to Anne Matta. And in the spring of 1943 Max Ernst walked out of his year-old marriage to Peggy Guggenheim to live with Dorothea Tanning, the painter whom he had met at Julien Levy's gallery the previous summer. From a distance Péret chimed in again, saying he was glad that Max had escaped and the Gougou must be furious.[3]

Even among the Surrealists, who were noted for changing partners, or at least sharing them, this was a high count for a single year. The significant consequence for artistic developments was that Peggy Guggenheim, having at the end of 1942 launched a gallery essentially filled with European art, was prompted to start looking elsewhere, both for works to exhibit and for a social circle. The natural place for her to turn was to those young American artists who had frequented the Surrealist group or were introduced to her by her assistant Jimmy Ernst and his successor, the insightful Howard Putzel. She began to stage a series of innovative shows: an invitational collage exhibition, an exhibition of women artists, and a "spring salon" for the showing of relatively unknown artists. Matta urged her to see the work of Jackson Pollock, with the result that she commissioned a twenty-foot mural and launched him in a one-man exhibition. Solo exhibitions for Motherwell, Baziotes, and Rothko followed in the 1944–1945 season.

So much for the quarrels among refugees. Another kind of quarrel also began warming up in 1943 and this took the form of American attacks, chauvinist and otherwise, on the Surrealist émigrés. The negative comments did not come at first from the artists, who were still in awe of the Europeans, but from self-styled spokesmen on artistic matters. In the April issue of *American Mercury* Klaus Mann shrilly belabored the "chi-chi Surrealists" and their "Park Avenue friends" as symbolic of the political and social decadence that had produced Hitlerism. Referring to them as "parlor anarchists playing lurid games" and "spoiled *enfants terribles* of a cosmopolitan cafe society," he bitterly denounced their flight: "Millions may die and worlds may crash, but the Breton coterie will be carried to safety and comfort on the wings of benevolent angels."[4] He implied that Peggy Guggenheim had transported a

planeload of Surrealists in lieu of more deserving refugees and that the lot of them were living it up in New York society.

"What I am trying to point out," Mann wrote, "is the subtle and profound affinity between the murderous destruction of the Nazis and the playful destructiveness—of values, forms, sentiments, deep-rooted affections—of certain artistic movements, of which Surrealism is the latest and most spectacular exemplification. . . . I am against Surrealism because I have seen what the world looks like with every esthetic and moral preoccupation being absent. It looks like hell or like a Surrealist painting."

It is a strange attack by a refugee on refugees, especially in the light of the respectful treatment accorded both Klaus Mann and his father in the United States. In fact it was Thomas Mann who, together with Alfred Barr, had provided the Emergency Rescue Committee with a list of important persons who should be brought out of Europe. Klaus Mann's ire may have been roused at this time by the Surrealists'

Above: Kurt Seligmann, study for the cover of *View,* used for no. 1, 1943.

Opposite: Julio de Diego, David Hare, Jacqueline Lamba, Aube Breton, c. 1943.

New York, 1943: A New Momentum Begins

nonparticipatory status as opposed to his own involvement—in 1943 he became an American citizen and enlisted in the U.S. Army. His policy of engagement had led him to start a literary antifascist journal, *Sammlung,* in Europe in 1933, shortly after his own exile from Germany began. He had founded a similar journal, *Decision,* with a notable list of international contributors, at the end of 1940 in New York, but had been forced to discontinue it after a year for lack of funds (see chapter 5). Possibly he felt bitter over what he perceived as the financial and public relations success of the "frivolous" Surrealists. In 1949, unable to reassimilate himself in a postwar Germany that still refused to publish his books, Mann committed suicide.

Peyton Boswell, the editor of *Art Digest,* compounded Mann's attack by reprinting portions of it in the May 15 issue, along with his own gleeful comments. He described the "Dali-Breton-Ernst crowd" as "clever businessmen who know all the local stops of the publicity racket," but he also appended a mitigating question and answer:

Is surrealism contributing anything of lasting value to the sum total of art history? The answer is yes. Perhaps the weakest factor in American art is its poverty of imagination, its unthinking insistence upon painting endless miles of literal landscapes, insipid still lifes, static figures. The surrealists are stimulating Americans to use their eyes less and their minds more, to develop their imagination.[5]

Another salvo was fired by Sam Kootz who in 1945 would open a gallery and become a major promoter of the abstract expressionists. Kootz had already issued a challenge to American artists to be more experimental, to come up with fresh talent and new ideas, in a letter to the *New York Times* in 1941. In the spring of 1943 his *New Frontiers in American Painting* appeared, with a sixty-page introductory survey of twentieth-century art in which he took the opportunity to lambast Surrealism. "The decay evident in Surrealism results from an unhealthy conception of the function of painting," he opined, and went on to criticize the "peep-show pornography" of Max Ernst's 1942 exhibition. He saw it as finding fashionable acceptance with

an audience thrilled by its chi-chi eroticism. This fine leavening of sex-titillation, together with a forceful insistence upon elaborate, meaningless detail, is the pay-off to Surrealism's decay. When painters begin to smirk at sex, to tell squalid little jokes behind their fans, the spectator should begin to recognize the destiny of that form of painting. . . . So ardent has been the attack upon the American public by our flossier refugees (Ernst, Tanguy, Dali, Matta, *et al.*), so well regarded are they in the high places of our museums and galleries, that our American spectators may very well make the mistake that this is an important development in contemporary painting. . . . Surrealism may be the current music hall favorite, but I am convinced that its unwholesome show will have only a short run on the boards.[6]

Toward the end of his introduction Kootz set forth his program for the American artist, urging the affirmation in art of democracy as a way of life. The painter must combat reactionary forces, be "at home with all the advanced ideograms of today," and make his painting "vibrate with the spirit of those forward thrusts." The painter must "lead others in new spiritual adventures and invent a technique to give them the proper expression . . . In short he has a responsibility to go forward."[7]

What we see developing during 1943 and 1944 then is a distinct sense on the part of artists as well as in the more forward-looking sectors of the art apparatus that American art must change and that it must do so by absorbing European modernism in such a way that it comes out ahead of it. In 1943 the absorption process was still going on, but the seeds of a rejection of those who had helped to spawn a new American art were starting to germinate.

1943 also saw the turning point in the war. American and British troops fought Rommel back in the North African desert, for the first time exploding the myth of Nazi invincibility, and then established a foothold on the European continent with landings in southern Italy. Finally retreat across the Pacific was halted and American ships and planes were ready to begin the slow island-to-island advance toward Japan. The Russians held fast in Stalingrad and Leningrad, opting for starvation rather than the certain horrors of surrender to German troops. The invitation Hitler had printed to a New Year's celebration in Leningrad's best hotel proved to be overly optimistic as the city held out under a four-hundred-day siege. The British endured the worst year of the Blitz, but their bomber pilots, alongside American planes and flyers, were beginning to effectively retaliate. Amidst all the news bulletins of hard-fought battles, bloody beachheads, and growing casualty lists, one salient fact emerged: the United States was demonstrating a military power, a leadership capacity, and a heroic anti-fascist stance that marked a changed role in the world. It follows that American artists who had come of age during the Depression years would begin to feel a new kind of empowerment and even a sense that the artist too could be heroic.

What happened to American art as a consequence has less to do with a changing image and style than it does with the way American artists perceived themselves and were perceived by an American public. These changes were gradual and almost imperceptible, but cumulatively they amounted to a major westward shift in the leadership of world art. The groundwork for this may well have been laid in 1943, a year that saw the flowering of what has been called abstract surrealism among some of the younger American artists. It was also a year in which these efforts were acknowledged and encouraged by inclusion in exhibitions at Art of This Century and the new renegade Norlyst Gallery and even by a glimmer of recognition in the press and among art cognoscenti.

The opening on March 15, 1943, of the Norlyst Gallery on West 56th Street offered a preview of a new style of gallery that was to proliferate in the 1950s, galleries dedicated to showing experimental work, operating on a shoestring in unfashionable locations, some of them actually artist-run cooperatives. It was opened by Jimmy Ernst's friend, Elenor Lust, whose aim was to try to do something for struggling artists whose efforts had not yet been brought to public attention. Ernst left the employ of Art of This Century in order to help her realize this ambition. He struggled with the carpentry and lighting and selected most of the fifty artists who were included in the gallery's opening show in March. A heterogeneous group comprised the first exhibition, including enough of the Americans who had been inspired by Surrealism to constitute a unifying direction. Among those contributing to this impression were Baziotes, Busa, Kamrowski, and Motherwell from the Matta studio sessions of the preceding months, as well as Gottlieb, Boris Margo, Rothko, John Ferren, Andre Racz, and Jimmy Ernst. Jackson Pollock would also have been on this roster if Jimmy Ernst's visit to his studio with the suggestion that he put a painting in the first show had not resulted in a misunderstanding; this was shortly before Pollock attracted the interest of Peggy Guggenheim.

Some of the more established galleries looked askance at this haphazard upstart gallery, especially when it showed the carpentered animal sculptures of Louise Nevelson, and at least one artist—Gerome Kamrowski—had to show there under an assumed name so that the Baroness Rebay would not cut off his stipend. The gallery operated informally and artists were welcome to stop by for talk and a glass of wine in the late afternoon. Among those who would drop in at the day's end were Gottlieb and Rothko, both of whom were strongly attracted to Surrealism. The Gottliebs lived in Brooklyn, so, according to Esta Gottlieb, Adolph saw little of the émigré artists. However, she also said that "the Surrealists and Surrealism affected most of the artists at that time, although I think at certain times they would deny that. But the mythical image was certainly something which related to Surrealism."[8]

Above: Jimmy Ernst, *Flying Dutchman,* 1942, oil on canvas, 20 x 18⅛ inches; The Museum of Modern Art, New York, purchase.

New York, 1943: A New Momentum Begins

During 1942 Gottlieb developed the style for which he first became known, usually referred to as pictographic. Although this work has time and again been linked to Native American rock painting, Gottlieb himself asserted that his practice of dividing the canvas into compartments was inspired by early Italian Renaissance altarpieces. "A kind of fragmentation of images was my original motivation. . . . It's a mistake to link my painting with primitive art—it's completely modern." [9] Although much of Gottlieb's output from this period was destroyed in a 1943 studio fire, one can establish his abstract-surreal direction from a few surviving examples such as *Pictograph (Yellow and Violet),* 1942, and *Pictograph #4,* 1943. The earlier work is essentially a rectilinear abstraction with a few shapes suggestive of facial features added. By 1943 the images—eyes, hands, human profiles—had proliferated and filled every available compartment. A sequential view of the two works reveals that he started with essentially an abstract or nonobjective painting and proceeded to work over it in a Surrealist-inspired process, arriving subjectively, through free association, at images and symbols that he maintained he couldn't explain. Recollecting in 1972, he observed:

Adolph Gottlieb, *Pictograph #4*, 1943, oil on canvas, 35¼ x 22⅛ inches; Adolph and Esta Gottlieb Foundation, Inc., New York.

My interest in Freud and Jung started with my interest in Surrealism—because the Surrealists were interested in Freudian theories of dreams. In the early 1940s I was very much influenced by Surrealism and was using a type of free-association which was one of the Surrealist techniques. I was putting images into the compartments of my painting as if I were doing automatic writing. . . . I admired Miró, early Dalí, Max Ernst; the automatism of Masson certainly was an influence. At the same time Rothko was also doing some mythological subjects, partly semi-abstract, partly Surrealist in style.[10]

Rothko had been for several years diligently working his way out of the representational style of his 1930s painting. In 1942 he painted a series of Procrustean figure compositions with parts of bodies wedged into restrictive spaces (it is said that Rothko retained an angry memory of being swaddled long beyond infancy in Russia) and profile and frontal heads congealed into a single mass. During 1943 he opened up the spaces and turned his figures into linear abstractions. These transparent linear presences suggest performers in a dramatic narrative in which only a few clues to the literal content remain. The many works on paper of this period show Rothko grappling over and over with the problems of image and abstraction. Although these ink and wash drawings have the appearance of improvisations, produced in an automatist fashion, a number actually have pencil drawing under the inked lines and tinted washes. Many of these works are organized by vertical and horizontal divisions of the paper, like a cross; washes are applied, sometimes rubbed into the paper, and then ink-drawn looping and squiggly lines introduce personages. The lines are often rough, as if they had been drawn with a matchstick, and in places they have been allowed to blur into the wet paint. It appears that here and there a razor has been used to scrape away paint so that the textured white paper shows through. Despite the technical experimentation, the overall impression is of deliberation rather than spontaneity, of cerebration and studied decision-making in a prolonged struggle to "veil" the content which he had maintained was essential to art.

The process that Rothko was laboriously enacting in the 1940s is analogous to the one by which Kandinsky between 1908 and 1912 gradually "veiled" his imagery. Both artists were too cerebral to make sudden leaps into the unknown. Sloughing off the "material" world entailed a series of carefully plotted steps, although Rothko had the advantage of the Surrealist precedent to draw upon while Kandinsky, sustained only by his anthroposophical beliefs, was on his own. The notion of veiling was one that cropped up in discussions of Surrealism such as James Johnson

Sweeney's 1942 article "What Tanguy Veils and Reveals,"[11] and it also offered a viable means of bridging the gap between subject matter and the "empty house of abstraction" that was Rothko's major preoccupation. Oddly, although the rationalization was totally different, the means used by Kandinsky and the abstract surrealists were similar in that both separated line and color; for Kandinsky the color was the aura and line the spiritual essence, while for Matta, Gorky, and Rothko from 1942 to 1944 color was a means of dematerializing and giving emotional tone to the latent imagery. Line stood for movement in time and space for Matta; for Rothko it was usually a skeletal residue of form; and for Gorky, who was passionate about drawing, it was both a caressing delineation of form and a trajectory from one shape to the next.

What Surrealism evidently provided for Rothko is a kind of "open sesame," a means of proceeding that enabled him to leave behind the drab visual data of his

Mark Rothko, *Untitled (Rothko number 3079.40)*, c. 1942, oil on canvas, 23⅞ x 31⅞ inches; National Gallery of Art, Washington, gift of the Mark Rothko Foundation.

earlier work and move toward what he felt were more universal essences. He credited the Surrealists with discovering "the vital resource of the atavistic memory or prophetic dream" [12] and for "uncovering the glossary of myth and establishing a congruity between the phantasmagoria of the unconscious and the objects of everyday life." [13] According to the photographer Aaron Siskind, who was a good friend of Rothko during the 1940s, "He liked Matta a great deal. He told me he thought Matta was really one of the great painters—and if you look at his biomorphic forms you can see how much Matta influenced him because Matta was a very brilliant and skillful painter, while Mark really had to work at it." [14]

Among the artists in the opening exhibition at the Norlyst Gallery was the Russian-born Boris Margo, who had been identified as an American Surrealist by Onslow Ford in his 1941 New School lectures. Margo had been working in a spontaneous visionary manner using decalcomania since the 1930s. "I dream onto canvas," wrote Margo in 1941. [15] Although fiercely independent in his art world dealings—or lack thereof—Margo seems to have taken a great interest in the émigrés and there are developments in his work at this time that may be attributed to the inspiration of Matta. This can be seen specifically in the crisp linear brush drawing over diaphanous color areas. Like Matta, Margo used lines to accent the edges of certain forms, but he also made them operate separately to suggest multiple perspectives akin to Matta's so-called non-Euclidean spaces. Rothko and Margo shared a studio in 1943–1944. It is interesting to note that Margo at this time had moved away from his densely worked decalcomania paintings and was painting linear personages not altogether different from what Rothko seems to have been trying to do.

Charles Seliger was not yet twenty when he stopped in at Art of This Century one afternoon and struck up an acquaintance with Jimmy Ernst. Totally without art school training, Seliger had left high school in the tenth grade to go to work and at the same time started painting at night. He had come across Ozenfant's *Foundations of Modern Painting* and in 1941 was doing "little Kandinsky-ish abstractions." He had also read Herbert Read's *Surrealism* and he knew who Jimmy Ernst was when he saw him behind the desk. After they had talked for a while, Ernst said, "I'm starting a new gallery. Would you like to help us paint the walls?" [16] Thus it came about that Seliger's small abstractions were included in the first exhibitions at Norlyst and that he met Breton, Matta, Pollock, and Rothko and the whole Surrealist crowd.

"I loved the Surrealists," Seliger recently reminisced. "I found it so fascinating what paint could produce. I think absolutely that the Surrealists had the most im-

New York, 1943: A New Momentum Begins

Charles Seliger, *Confrontation*, 1944, oil on canvas, 27¾ x 27 inches; courtesy
Michael Rosenfeld Gallery.

portant impact. Matta and Gordon Onslow Ford were very interesting for me. I don't
know where my work came from. The license that they gave opened up everything.
The question was, what forms do you use as a starting point? I used insects for quite
a while." [17]

Starting as he had, without preconceptions, Seliger allowed the process to lead
him. The earliest works he exhibited are evocations of plant and insect forms and
share the biomorphic characteristics of works by some of his contemporaries. Increasingly, however, he seems to have been drawn toward expressing a sense of natural processes. The specific references to plant and insect forms become less
discernible; instead there is a kind of labyrinthian journey for the eye as it traces out
the convolutions of the biomorphic forms that suggest more than anything else an
ongoing metamorphosis on a microcosmic level.

Biomorphism also characterizes the painting that Gerome Kamrowski was doing in 1943–1944. As he recalled, "The Museum of Science and Industry had X-
rays of plants and photographs of microorganisms. It spread everywhere—Matta,
Tchelitchew—it was a cultural commodity of the time." [18] Kamrowski's biomorphism
is well exemplified in *Emotional Season #1* with its delicate and varied suggestions
of morphology, in the sense that Matta applied the term to the process of growth
and transformation. Kamrowski establishes an undulating upward flow that engulfs
shapes of leaves pressed into the paint, nuclei surrounded by concentric circles suggesting seeds expanding outward and bursting, fine-lined tendrils, tufts of thistle-
down, airborne seeds, all adrift in a mysterious blue-black space. There is a certain
kinship with Masson's telluric paintings, not only in subject but in the willingness to
suspend gravity and use the entire surface of the painting as a field of action.

All the while he had been working in the Museum of Modern Art mailroom
and then as Peggy Guggenheim's assistant, developing his own circle of friends and
becoming fluent in English, Jimmy Ernst had also been painting into the small hours
of the morning. Innately skillful, with a fine precise touch, he began with a kind of
illusionistic surreal painting and then moved toward biomorphic and abstract surrealism, influenced first by Onslow Ford and then by Baziotes in whose studio he
painted on weekends. What he produced in 1943–1944 was a mélange of linear abstraction and a delicately shaded biomorphism. In the press release for his debut
show at the Norlyst Gallery in April 1943 Jimmy Ernst separated himself from Surrealism: "He believes that a painter can rely on certain principles of Surrealism without
identifying himself with the movement. . . . He attempts to translate into art forms

the scientific inquiries of this generation. This is the presentation of the effect of this new scientific age upon a young artist." [19]

In June Gottlieb and Rothko achieved a certain notoriety by engaging in an exchange with *New York Times* art critic Edwin Alden Jewell. These two long-time friends were active in the Federation of Modern Painters and Sculptors; in fact, Gottlieb served as its president in the mid-1940s. (The Federation, it will be remembered, was founded in 1939 by artists who pulled out of the Communist-dominated Artists Congress after it had passed a resolution supporting the Nazi-Soviet pact.) The Federation's third annual exhibition opened in March 1943 at the Wildenstein Galleries. In reviewing it Jewell commented on his mystification in front of Rothko's *Syrian Bull* and Gottlieb's *Rape of Persephone,* stating that he could not see how their works fit in with the program of globalization called for in the show's catalogue. Gottlieb phoned the *Times* and asked if Jewell would like an explanation. The resulting, now famous, statement was published on June 13 along with reproductions of their paintings that filled most of the Sunday art page under the heading "The New Globalism." The statement began: "To us art is an unknown world which can be explored only by those willing to take risks," and ended with the assertion that "subject matter is crucial and only that subject matter is valid which is tragic and timeless." They also stressed the need for "large, unequivocal shapes" and flat forms that "destroy illusion and reveal the truth." [20]

Opposite below: Gerome Kamrowski, *Emotional Season #1,* 1943, gouache and collage, 22 x 30 inches; courtesy the Washburn Gallery.

Below: Mark Rothko, *Birth of the Cephalopods (Rothko number 3058.44),* 1943, oil on canvas, 39⅝ x 53¹¹⁄₁₆ inches; National Gallery of Art, Washington, gift of the Mark Rothko Foundation.

In preparing their statement Rothko and Gottlieb had help and advice from their friend Barnett Newman. Earlier in the year Newman had written the catalogue text for the American Modern Artists show held at the Riverside Museum in protest against the isolationism of the Artists for Victory Show at the Metropolitan Museum the previous fall. In it he advocated a modern art that would reflect a new America, one that might "become the cultural center of the world." Newman, according to Esta Gottlieb, was "not painting, but [was] an art intellectual" who wanted a role as "an American André Breton."[21] For the next few years he was mainly visible through short catalogue texts that he wrote for exhibitions at the gallery of his employer, Betty Parsons, although in 1945 he painted some works on paper that appear to be

the result of automatist experiments. For more than one firsthand observer of this period these three artists were a triumvirate who discussed and carried out strategic moves that would place them in the vanguard of American art.

Matta, having given up his plan to make a palace revolution, made peace with Breton and worked with him and Duchamp on a new double issue of *VVV* that appeared in March 1943. He contributed a sequence of drawings to accompany a long poem, "Le jour est un attentat," by the young George Duits, both poem and drawings inspired by the experience of New York City, and his fiery, prophetically ominous painting *The Year 1944* was reproduced. New artists in this issue were Kamrowski, Lam, Gypsy Rose Lee, Kay Sage, the Swiss painter Sonia Sekula, David Hare with several altered photographs and collages done in collaboration with Jacqueline Lamba, Barbara Reis, Susanna Hare, and Dorothea Tanning, with two of her most important works, *Birthday* and *Children's Game*. With all these additions, some of them rank amateurs, Breton seemed determined to create the impression that Surrealist momentum was building in the Western Hemisphere. It is interesting to note the increasing amount of space devoted to women artists in *VVV* whereas they had been virtually absent from *Minotaure*. Some credit for this is due to Peggy Guggenheim and her January exhibition of thirty-one women artists, since most of *VVV*'s choices were also in the Art of This Century show.

Jacqueline Lamba was currently painting some strong visionary works, somewhat along the lines of Matta and Esteban Frances but with a diaphanous quality and a fluidity that marked them as distinctly her own. Despite the fact that Breton signaled approbation by reproducing her work in each number of *VVV*, when he returned to his Montmartre atelier after the war he discarded or destroyed all the paintings Lamba had left there, so little evidence remains of her artistic evolution. Apparently Lamba reached new strength as a painter at the time she was breaking up with Breton, only to flounder and lose her way after her marriage to David Hare. Looking back over her work in her Paris studio when she was in her seventies she seemed to realize this as she summed up her dilemma: "If I had been less beautiful I would have been a better painter."[22]

On the same page with Lamba's *Non, il ne fait qu'en chercher* appeared Carrington's *La Dame ovale* with an idol-like figure in a landscape that looks like the background in a quattrocento painting, animals whose tails become trees and four stags' heads on a punctured heart-shaped structure. At the age of twenty-six, Carrington had marked out a highly original direction involving emblematic imagery drawn from magic, alchemy, and folklore filtered through an imagination that had been heightened by the terrifying experience of the sanatorium in Santander. In New York Breton found her a wonderfully spontaneous and uninhibited spirit of revolt, sharing his black humor, putting mustard on her feet in a restaurant, or preparing

Opposite top: Jacqueline Lamba in her studio on Bleecker Street with two of her paintings, photograph from *VVV* no. 2-3, 1943.

Opposite bottom: Leonora Carrington, *La Dame ovale*, c. 1942–1943, reproduced in *VVV* no. 2-3, 1943.

New York, 1943: A New Momentum Begins

for her friends a repast of hare stuffed with oysters following a sixteenth-century English recipe. In no way beholden to the claims of the modern tradition or to Surrealism other than for the license it gave her own originality, she was to continue to fruitfully mine this lode during the coming years in Mexico.

In 1986 Motherwell characterized Gerome Kamrowski as "the most Surrealist of us all,"[23] possibly because Kamrowski did not develop the reservations about Surrealism that Motherwell himself came to have after a few years. It is true that Kamrowski enjoyed the stimulus of various Surrealist ideas, and that he stayed with it longer than the others, having a show in Paris with a catalogue introduction by Breton as late as 1950, but the paintings he created during the mid-1940s were in no sense Surrealist look-alikes. His contribution to the 1943 *VVV* included a "panoramagraph," featuring scattered images and quotations linked by free-flowing lines of connectedness, and a page labeled the "story of man" laid out in a format resembling the shadow boxes he had been making by cutting out amoeboid openings in the cover of a black box to reveal small vignettes clipped from engraved textbook illustrations.

Despite his imminent ouster from the group, Seligmann was featured with four separate entries in the second issue of *VVV*, including drawings of the four seasons, a "Prognostication by Paracelsus," and one engraving from the Oedipus suite that he had done to accompany a text translated by Meyer Schapiro. Seligmann was something of an anomaly in the Breton circle, part of it and yet apart, as one might have gathered from his disapproving comments on the first *VVV*. He made conscientious attempts to establish and maintain cordial relations with all factions and with a growing network of American acquaintances, and he helped financially in small ways within the refugee circle. On his own press he pulled the prints for the portfolio that had been intended to finance *VVV*, and he seems never to have been too busy to write a letter of introduction to a dealer or a job recommendation for one of his colleagues or for the younger artists he came to know. Most of the émigrés visited him in Sugar Loaf at one time or another and kept in touch with him via postcards as they journeyed around the country. Only Max Ernst, who had been the witness at his wedding in Paris in 1935, seems never to have written. Yet one has the sense that Seligmann was tolerated more than respected as an artist, partly because he was in a position to be helpful, for example with his connection to Georges Wildenstein in 1938 or through the network his command of English made it possible for him to establish in the United States.

While Seligmann's archaizing paintings and graphic work sold, especially to the Chicago collector Earl Lugdin, and entered museum collections, they cannot be said to have made much impact on young painters. He nevertheless remains very much a part of the collective image of Surrealism in exile, not only because of the old-masterish craft of his cryptic paintings, but also because of his scholarly interest in

Gerome Kamrowski, *Panoramagraph*, from *VVV* no. 2-3, 1943.

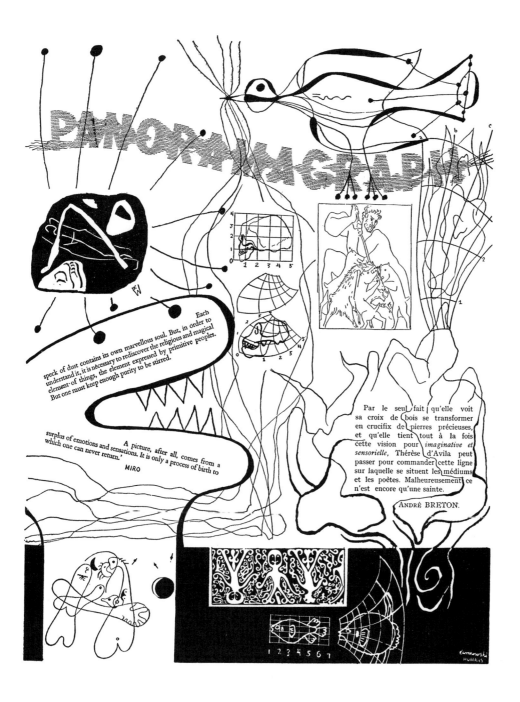

arcane works on magic and alchemy. This was manifest in his writing for *View* and *VVV*, in the evenings of magic held in his New York studio, and ultimately in his *History of Magic*, a unique compendium of esoteric information published by Pantheon in 1948 and reprinted in many subsequent editions in three languages. To maintain contact with a European past that he missed sorely in the New World he went to considerable lengths during the war years to find rare books on magic and the occult, many of which dated from the seventeenth and eighteenth centuries, and when he wrote for *View* or *VVV* it was usually on a subject gleaned from his arcane readings.

In 1943 Seligmann moved from Nierendorf to the Durlacher Gallery, whose director was Kirk Askew, and thus into the Askews' lively social circle. His new dealer asked Seligmann to provide him with explanations of the imagery in the paint-

Kurt Seligmann, *Rendez-vous of the Elements*, 1942, oil on canvas; present whereabouts unknown.

New York, 1943: A New Momentum Begins

ings included in his March exhibition at the gallery. The artist, punctilious as usual, wrote out explanations such as the following for *Rendezvous of the Elements:*

A dream I had as a child: my mother and another woman attempting to sail across the sea on a small raft which could not carry us three. Frightened, my mother's companion held onto a strange being emerging from the water, and a warning voice calling me louder and louder flies through the air, hits my ear finally like thunder, and awakens me. This dream of earth, water and air was apparently a marking stone in my psychological development. Plastically, I wished to express these forms or groups of forms, which are hostile and hold together only through imaginary lines, curves and angles, forming the scheme of the composition.[24]

He associated this image with Watteau's *Embarkation from Cythera,* only he imagines that when the couple "steps into the fragile little boat and starts a voyage that was thought to be a Sunday trip, the boat disappears on the horizon. An endless journey is ahead, full of the strangest adventures, most of them lacking the assurance and elegance Watteau used to love."[25] Since he painted two nearly identical versions of this theme—an unusual practice for him—it must have had special significance in his psychological formation. At any rate his explanation provides us with a much-needed clue to the convoluted process that gave rise to his hermetic-seeming paintings, a process far removed from gestural automatism.

Another explanation written out for Askew casts light on Seligmann's cyclonic paintings and drawings of 1942–1943. He described one of these canvases as follows: "This is an interpretation of the southwestern American landscape. They are psychological landscapes with anthropomorphic elements; living beings seem to detach themselves from tortuous geological formations. A world in formation—not the heroic landscapes of prehistory, but rather a lyrical one."[26] His encounter with the awesome scale and visible geological history of the Grand Canyon and the fantastic rocks thrusting out of the desert landscape of Arizona and New Mexico prompted Seligmann to consider the potent forces that shaped these wonders. Exhilarated by the contrast between America's "unsettled land and virgin nature" and the European landscape "where civilizations lie buried under every acre," he attempted to express the vast and indifferent nature of the New World.

The cyclonic shapes were used for other purposes as well. In *Melusine and the Great Transparents,* swirling forms suggest the gigantic hovering invisible beings that Breton had posited in his attempt to create a new myth. This painting was reproduced in the April 15 issue of *Art News,* whose reviewer found a change toward "non-representational forms of much greater interest" and considered his "vocabulary as original as that of any surrealist now in America." The outlines of the cyclonic form, it will be remembered, were derived from the quasi-automatist practice of projecting broken glass through a polarizing lens and tracing the resulting lines directly on the paper or canvas, a process Seligmann had used for the décor of Hanya Holm's ballet *The Golden Fleece* in 1941 as well as for a *View* cover in 1943. This abstract "spirit form" partakes in the "occultization" that was in vogue in Surrealism at the time, but it also has a bizarre historical footnote: in 1949 a cyclone, virtually unheard of in that part of New York State, swept through Sugar Loaf, leveling Seligmann's studio barn. It is tempting to imagine that the author of the *History of Magic* may have been something of a conjuror himself. At the very least the American artists seeing his work were exposed to the ways a contemporary artist could reuse the past, to the notion of a hermetic iconography, and to another, somewhat circuitous way of releasing the imagination.

Seligmann was strangely silent about the war in his correspondence as well as in these written descriptions of his imagery. However, since it was characteristic of him to hide his intentions or leave them deliberately ambiguous and to encode his meanings in cryptic images, there may be another layer of anxious symbolism in the

Kurt Seligmann, *Aurora,* 1942, graphite on paper; present whereabouts unknown.

New York, 1943: A New Momentum Begins

Kurt Seligmann, *Melusine and the Great Transparents,* 1943, oil on canvas, 74.3
x 61 cm; The Art Institute of Chicago, Mary and Earl Ludgin Collection.

paintings of the war years that he did not articulate. Despite the complacency of his letters to Switzerland, his involvement in the various exiles' projects, and his attentiveness to his own professional status, he was not ignorant of the fate of millions of Jews left within reach of Hitler, as newspaper clippings found among his papers testify. "My mind is as black as the backgrounds in my paintings" was scrawled on a piece of paper found among his miscellaneous letters.

The spring of 1943 saw a number of exhibitions featuring the émigrés, including a show of works from the past year by Masson (sharing the billing with Klee) at Buchholz, Hayter at Willard (the Museum of Modern Art purchased his print *Laocoon* and it was reproduced in *Art News*), a show of Max Ernst's collages and drawings at Julien Levy (marking the publication of *Misfortunes of the Immortals* by Ernst and Eluard), watercolors by a new recruit to Surrealism, Enrico Donati, at the New School, and in June an exhibition of works by Calder and Tanguy at Pierre Matisse. A reviewer pigeonholed Calder as a Surrealist "because of his bone and peanut shapes" and felt that Tanguy's "animation of his world has really gotten underway"; Calder's constellations were seen as "exploding from walls or ceiling."[27] All this activity took place against a background of American art that was still preponderantly conservative and realistic, so that the curving metal supports and cut-out shapes of Calder's stabiles and mobiles, along with the lunar tonality and

Stanley William Hayter, *Laocoon*, 1943, engraving and soft ground etching, plate 12¼ x 21¾ inches; The Museum of Modern Art, New York.

New York, 1943: A New Momentum Begins

Enrico Donati, *Troublefête*, 1944, oil on canvas, 40 x 30 inches; private collection.

intricate marmoreal constructions in Tanguy's paintings and the curved walls and biomorphic furniture of Kiesler, achieved instant recognition as indicators of the progressive European influence in art.

When Enrico Donati exhibited at the New School, the art historian Lionello Venturi immediately saw affinities with Surrealism and arranged for an introduction to Breton. Although he had not known the Surrealists in Europe, where he had grown up, Donati had been using automatism for some time and he also shared their ethnographic interest, having made his own youthful pilgrimage to American Indian reservations in the Southwest and in Canada in 1934. Like Duchamp he had a deep interest in alchemy, so much so that for several years he worked on a series of seemingly abstract paintings that are actually allegories of alchemical processes. For Donati's next exhibition, at the Passedoit Gallery in 1944, Breton provided a glowing catalogue essay that drew him into the Surrealist ranks. As was his practice while in New York, Breton also wrote out titles for the paintings on small slips of paper, overriding Donati's hesitations about their seeming unrelatedness.

Two sculptors also helped to fill the gap left by defections and expulsions. One was Isamu Noguchi, who at forty-five had a considerable career behind him but who was just entering on the most surreal phase of his work. Of Japanese/American parentage, Noguchi in 1942 had become a voluntary intern in an internment camp in Poston, Arizona, in the hope of improving conditions for the Japanese Americans who had been forcibly placed there. On his return to New York in 1943 he moved into a studio in MacDougal Alley and became part of the Greenwich Village circle of American and émigré artists. He was a good friend of Arshile Gorky; in the summer of 1941 they had driven to California together, along with Gorky's future wife, Agnes Magruder. Noguchi began to carve large slabs of marble which he stood upright at angles to each other so that they intersected through various perforations. The softened edges and ovoid openings gave these sculptures the look of having been lifted from a Tanguy painting. Indeed Alfred Barr told Noguchi that his marble *Kouros* had been turned down for purchase by the Modern because Sweeney felt that it looked too much like a Tanguy.

The other sculptor, David Hare, was part of the Surrealist family by virtue of being Kay Sage's cousin and the future husband of Jacqueline Lamba. Accepted first as the creator of altered photographs that were distinctly surreal, he had by 1943 turned to sculpture and was experimenting with various techniques for achieving open-form sculpture, including some precariously fragile plaster pieces.

On April 1 a show of Matta drawings opened at Julien Levy's gallery. The artist was characterized in *Art News* as an "apostle of light, lightheartedness and legerdemain," and the drawings were described as "story-telling abstractions with a touch of alchemy; each sheet contains nine separate but related sketches developing the

Isamu Noguchi, *Kouros*, 1944, pink Georgia marble, height about 9 feet 9 inches;
Metropolitan Museum of Art, Fletcher Fund.

New York, 1943: A New Momentum Begins

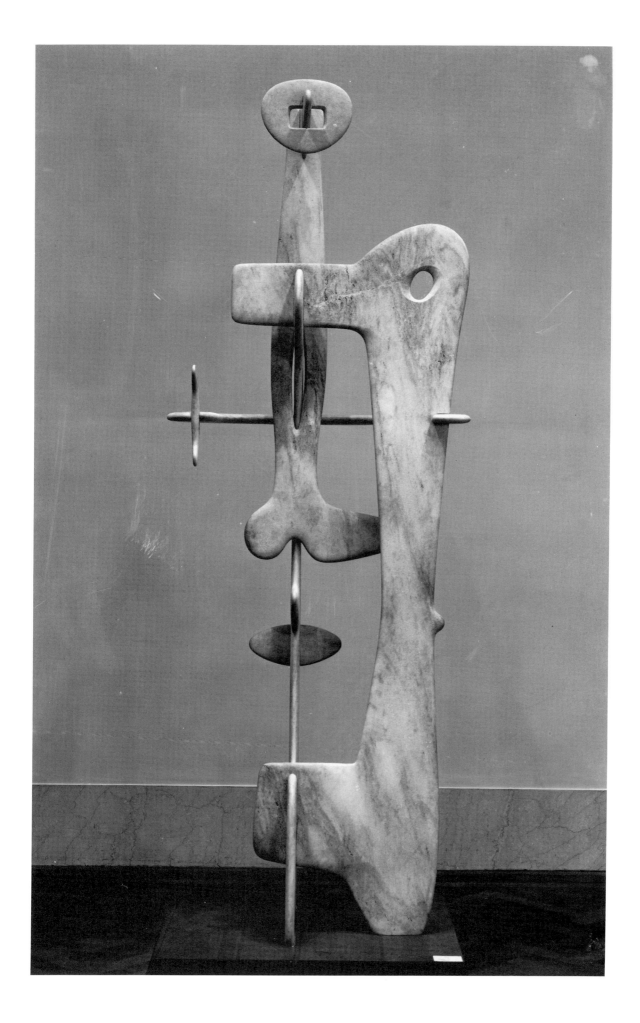

narrative with a comic strip sequence."[28] Of all the émigrés it was Matta whose name really became a household word in the small New York art world. A prodigious worker, he managed to put forth a new vision on one after another of what were in those days large-scale canvases, offering a dazzling way beyond both Surrealism and geometric abstraction. The erudition and capacity to make multilingual plays on words evident in his titles made a mockery of the self-important mythological titles of Rothko and Gottlieb. Where others plodded he leapt nimbly. He even teased the somewhat humorless Breton, who nonetheless continued to regard him as Surrealism's young star, playing much the same role as Dalí had in 1929. Breton wrote glowing tributes to him and asked him to do the cover for the final *VVV* and to illustrate the major work of his American years, *Arcane 17*. John Meyers, who had come to New York from Buffalo as an eager young poet and was working in the *View* office, noted in his journal: "If you ask me who is the most talked about painter in town I would say it was Matta."[29] According to Kamrowski, "Matta had a lot of energy and it was really Matta who swung the thing."[30] And Robert Lebel recalled: "The real influence was Matta. After he left all that pertained to that movement was forgotten."[31]

However, there was one mind that held Matta in thrall, one artist who had already probed the mental territory that Matta had set out to explore. Years earlier Matta had been turned away from architecture and toward painting when he read an article on Marcel Duchamp in *Cahiers d'Art*. Now Duchamp was living a few blocks away at 231 West Fourteenth Street, easily accessible to the young Chilean; in fact they lunched together frequently. Matta's absolute irreverence, witty iconoclasm, and predilection for plays on words, as well as his interest in alchemy and the occult, must have provided the basis for a stimulating exchange between the two. Writing in 1947, Soby described them as having been close and devoted friends and quoted Duchamp as remarking that for him Matta was the only young painter of talent visible anywhere.[32] When Duchamp wrote the entry for Matta in Katherine Dreier's *Société Anonyme* catalogue he did so in terms of high regard. And as a testimony to the multiple ways in which their minds met he made a present to Matta of his altered readymade, *L.H.O.O.Q.*

Breton had written: "The thing that constitutes the strength of Marcel Duchamp is his disdain for the thesis."[33] In a milieu given to pronouncements, perhaps it was the unassertive nature of Duchamp that made him a catalytic force. Quietly a Duchamp mystique developed—"He knew everything and never read anything," Patrick Waldberg said of him. "In his apartment there were piles of books with the pages uncut, but he knew what was in them"[34]—and young American artists began knocking on his door. Since he did not have a gallery and little about him had appeared in print, the booklet *Duchamp's Glass, an Analytical Reflection*, which Matta

Marcel Duchamp, *The Bride Stripped Bare by Her Bachelors, Even, as Installed in Katherine Dreier's House in Milford, Connecticut, 1948*, photograph by John Schiff; The Philadelphia Museum of Art.

New York, 1943: A New Momentum Begins

and Katherine Dreier published in 1944, must have contributed to this underground reputation.

Not only was Duchamp available in person, but in 1943 his masterpiece, *The Bride Stripped Bare by Her Bachelors, Even*—or *The Large Glass*—was loaned by Katherine Dreier to the Museum of Modern Art, where it went on public display for the first time since its debut in Brooklyn in 1926, with the added feature of the repaired shattered glass. Its presence had an impact on a number of artists, none more so than Matta. *The Large Glass* coincided perfectly with Matta's occult, erotic, and morphological interests: it incorporates perspective for the watermill and illusionistic rendering for the chocolate grinder, yet is flat, it is solid and physically divides the room, yet keeps it open visually, even incorporating it within the frame of the artwork, and it offers a multilayered imagery ranging from a mechanistic view of human sexual functioning to alchemy. In response Matta embarked on a series of paintings that has sometimes been considered as a "Duchampian suite."[35]

Already in *Locus Solus*, which was painted before Duchamp arrived in New York, Matta had interrupted his diaphanous areas of sponged and wiped color with delicate linear networks that set up multiple systems of perspective. In a letter to Onslow Ford he had explained his code for levels of space and time with small diagrams in which an outer circle was labeled "conventional space, akin to the watch in time" and an inner circle was "psychological space, in which everything becomes concrete."[36] Lines tangent to the circles indicate time, while degrees of transparency stand for receding time; smaller, more precise forms indicate conventional movement in the present. He took the title, *Locus Solus*, from the 1914 proto–science fiction novel by Raymond Roussel, and the seven delicate constructions in the painting may represent the seven "bachelor machines" in the park of the villa Roussel describes. In this painting Matta began to intercept his fluid spaces with opaque planes that disrupted any semblance of spatial continuity. These developed into the black rhomboids that are suspended like antimatter in his paintings of 1943–1944, including the large triptychs of 1943, *Prince of Blood* and *La Vertue noire*. One can't help noting the resemblance of these opaque tetrahedrons to the cut-out metal shapes suspended on the slender wire armatures of Calder's mobiles featured in his MoMA show of 1943. (The term mobile was coined by Duchamp.) They have also been seen as magical tetragrams and as deriving from the Poincaré models illustrating the warping of planes at the confluence of space and time.

In 1943 Matta introduced negative lines, that is lines made not with the brush but with a razor that cut slender troughs through the dark painted grounds, as in *Membranes of Space* or *Composition in Magenta*. Several Duchampian links have been proposed for these lines or spatial membranes: for example the cracks running through the *Large Glass* and the web of string from the "First Papers" installation.

It is likely that Duchamp's oblique, cerebral approaches to content were as significant to Matta as the transparency, spatial punning, and motion of his actual works. This is strongly suggested in *Le Pendu* with its cataclysmic violence and suspended, tightly enclosed embryonic shape, which has been seen as relating to the Tarot card of that name, to Duchamp's *Pendu Femelle,* and to the pregnancy of Anne Matta.[37]

Perhaps the culminating work in his dialogue with Duchamp is *Vertige d'Eros* of 1944, which alludes to erotic experience just as Duchamp does in the *Large Glass.* The broken concentric circles tilting in space suggest the rotations of the chocolate grinder, the malic molds, and the water wheel; the vaginal shape at the upper left parallels the bride; the five pearl-like suspended shapes—astral eggs?—may connote fertilization as well as having alchemical references. The iridescent glow in the dark ground gives an underwater effect, like the fluids of prenatal existence. Even the Eros of the title may allude to Duchamp's alias, Rrose Sélavy.

The most avowedly Duchampian of Matta's paintings is *The Bachelors, Twenty Years After* of 1943 which was done specifically as an homage and was included in the booklet that he wrote with Katherine Dreier. In this painting Duchamp's carefully contrived stationary mechanisms have been set in motion: levers and pistons appear to move up and down while circular forms rotate and what look like philosophers' stones circle in space by themselves. The objects pictured are tinged with glowing color, opalescent like substances transformed by heat; a small crimson "flame" appears at the base of each beaker—"the alchemical alembics" that take the place of Duchamp's malic molds; and there appear to be colored gasses at the upper left. The effect of mechanical motion brings it closer to Tinguely than to the restrained and enigmatic *Bride Stripped Bare by Her Bachelors, Even.*

The observations in the booklet's brief text focus on the idea of the image as an act that must be completed by the spectator. "This dynamic reality, at once reflecting, enveloping and penetrating the observer, when grasped by the intentional act of consciousness, is the essence of a spiritual experience."[38] The text was very likely the work of Katherine Dreier as it gives no inkling of what Matta must have known about the underlying meanings of the work, nor are there any of his witty *double entendres.*

Among the various progeny spawned by the public appearance of the *Large Glass* or by Matta's interpretation of it, shown in his 1944 exhibition at Pierre Matisse, are two 1944 paintings by Rothko, *Gyrations on Four Planes* and *Slow Swirl at the Edge of the Sea.* The first is particularly a departure for Rothko in its apparently mechanical imagery and the experiment with multidimensional space. The second has been regarded as marking his own betrothal, since he had recently married for the second time. Rothko evidently told William Rubin that the second of these works was definitely inspired by the Duchamp and Matta works on the theme of betrothal.[39] Gerome Kamrowski's *Revolve and Devolve* is also Duchampian in lineage.

Although Matta has been credited with being the intermediary through which other artists were inspired by the *Large Glass*, the fact that it was newly on view at the Museum of Modern Art may have in itself been sufficient introduction. Gorky, whose 1947 *Betrothal I* and *Betrothal II* have been connected with Duchamp,[40] had, as mentioned earlier, a reproduction of Duchamp's *Bride* (the original belonged to Julien Levy) tacked on his studio wall when Kamrowski visited him in 1936. Since the period when Gorky was closest to Matta coincided with the latter's Duchampian

Matta, *The Vertigo of Eros*, 1944, oil on canvas, 77 x 99 inches; The Museum of Modern Art, New York, given anonymously.

New York, 1943: A New Momentum Begins

Below: Matta, *The Bachelors, Twenty Years After,* 1943, oil on canvas, 127 x
96.4 cm; Philadelphia Museum of Art, purchased: Edith H. Bell Fund, Edward and
Althea Budd Fund, and Museum funds.

phase, it is certainly conceivable that his interest in Duchamp was rekindled and the
project of doing an adaptation with his own encoded symbols began to take shape
at that time.

According to Peter Busa it was he who introduced Gorky to Matta, probably
at a party at Matta's apartment. In New York since 1933, Busa had been in Benton's
class at the League with Pollock, then at Hofmann's school in its early days on 57th
Street, and had worked in the mural division of the Federal Art Project. He met Matta
in 1940 at a party at Francis Lee's and, as we have seen, he was a skeptical participant
in the sessions at Matta's studio. (Later he had a show of drip paintings at Art of
This Century, participated in the Iconograph group, was in on the founding of the
Artists Club, and showed in the Ninth Street show.) He lived on Fifteenth Street

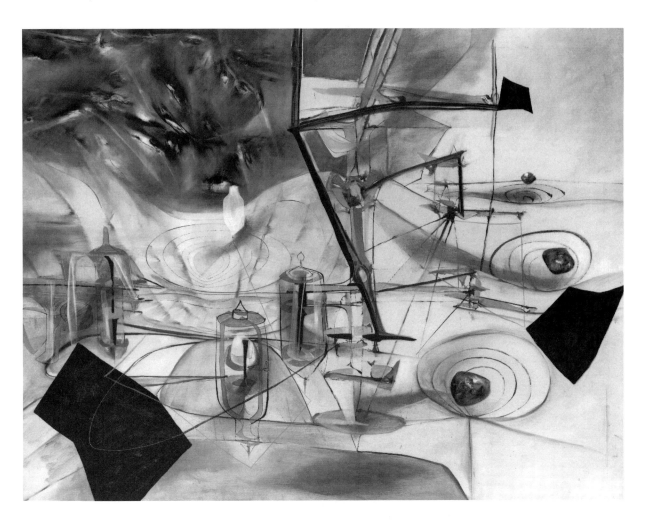

New York, 1943: A New Momentum Begins

Opposite top: Mark Rothko, *Gyrations on Four Planes*, 1944, oil on canvas, 24¼ x 48¼ inches; The Philadelphia Museum of Art, gift of the Mark Rothko Foundation.

Opposite bottom: Gerome Kamrowski, *Revolve and Devolve*, 1943, gouache on paper, 20 x 29 inches; courtesy the Washburn Gallery.

directly across Union Square from Gorky and saw him frequently. He was good friends with Baziotes, Pollock, and Kamrowski, and he knew most of the downtown artists of the 1930s and 1940s. Since he had a wife and five children to support he began taking teaching jobs away from New York, so that he was not around when the solidarity of the artists' community began to splinter. For all the above reasons plus the fact that there seems to have been little that was careerist about him, his recollections and recorded interviews seem relatively devoid of self-serving agendas. His words imply that there is a moral value attached to art and convey a sense of the open-ended, risk-taking approach of the younger American artists during the war years. When he quotes Motherwell as saying, "Just pretend you're not afraid," the words take on real meaning in the context of the unknown frontiers that the artists were moving toward.[41]

According to Busa, Gorky's interest in Matta at first was negligible:

He told him he thought he painted too thin. In those days Gorky was painting rather heavy. You could hardly lift his paintings and his palettes were so loaded with paint that they were like shields. Matta said he didn't think he painted so thin. An infantile conversation went on. Finally Gorky raised himself to his full height and said "OK, let me put it this way. You don't paint so thin, I don't paint so thick," and there was a lot of laughter.[42]

Busa also said that the period when Gorky worked closely with Matta was later than the fall 1942 studio sessions. Gorky was in Virginia during the summer of 1943 and went there again for nine months starting in the spring of 1944. His period of closest work with Matta was very likely in the spring of 1943, before that summer in Virginia when he "first learned to look into the grass." During that summer he executed his first crayon and pencil drawings in a calligraphic style and in a medium long used by Matta; in some of the drawings he even uses the dotted circle that was Matta's way of indicating a certain movement in space. After mid-1944 a close collaboration is unlikely because at that point Matta's work had veered in a literal figurative direction that can have held little interest for Gorky.

It is plausible that Matta inspired him to "look into the grass." "It was the botanical that got me started," Matta had said of his beginnings as an artist.[43] For him it had not been a case of looking directly into the grass, but of looking at micro-photographs of parts of plants and drawing freely from them to produce his fantastic drawings of the late 1930s. Some of these fantastic drawings had been included in

his 1940 exhibition at the Julien Levy Gallery, where it would be uncharacteristic for Gorky not to have seen them. If we look at Gorky's drawings from 1943, for example his study for *The Liver Is the Cockscomb,* it is a simple matter to see how plants, blossoms, and grasses provided a starting point for an almost hallucinatory elaboration and transmutation.

Of this collaboration Meyer Schapiro, who was well acquainted with both artists, wrote:

The artist he admired now was a brother rather than a father, and a younger brother. In Matta he found for the first time a painter whose language, once mastered, he could use as freely himself. From Matta came the idea of the canvas as a field of prodigious excitement, unloosed energies, bright reds and yellows opposed to cold greys, a new Futurism of the organic as well as of mechanical forces. Gorky could draw his own conclusions from Matta's art without waiting for the inventor; he was able to build on it independently as Braque did upon the forms created jointly by Picasso and himself. The encounter with Matta was, it seems to me, a decisive point in Gorky's liberation from enslavement to other artists.[44]

"It was Matta," Schapiro also said, "who showed Gorky how to flow on thinned paint and to draw with his brush."[45] Sidney Janis, who had known Gorky

Above: Arshile Gorky, *Virginia Landscape,* 1943, pencil and colored crayons on paper, 17 x 22 inches; Metropolitan Museum of Art, promised gift of Muriel Kallis Newman. The Muriel Kallis Steinberg Newman Collection.

New York, 1943: A New Momentum Begins

Below: Arshile Gorky, *Garden in Sochi,* c. 1943, oil on canvas, 31 x 39 inches; The Museum of Modern Art, New York, acquired through the Lillie P. Bliss Bequest.

since the 1930s, was of the same opinion. If one compares the earlier and later versions of *Garden in Sochi* it is easy to see what Schapiro was referring to. While the composition resembles Miró's *Still Life with Old Shoe,* which had been in the 1941 Museum of Modern Art exhibition, the paint in the first version is still thickly applied and heavily textured; edges are still sharply defined; and the Miró-like playfulness of the forms is nullified by the leaden quality of the paint. In the version dated 1943 white paint is loosely brushed on to form a translucent ground while a spontaneous, looping line provides contours for floating shapes whose bright colors, also freely brushed, avoid coinciding with the contour lines. This was the point at which Gorky began to break new ground and to develop a way of working that differed markedly from that of either the Surrealists or his American contemporaries, one that suited the need of his poetic nature for a lyrical, expressive mode.

The working relationship between the two artists is not a simple one to decipher. Gorky, it must be remembered, was nearly ten years older than Matta and he had won his artistic liberty by working through a sequence of styles that he felt

passionately about. He had taught at the Grand Central Art School and had painted at least three major mural series, while Matta when they met have been working in oil for less than four years and had bravura as one of his principal assets. Gorky had a profound regard for painting, from Pompeian wall painting to the masters of modernism, and he haunted museums, while Matta was more interested in the nontraditional—in the primitive, the occult, and considerations of time and space. On the other hand, there is the record of Gorky's habits of appropriation, artistic and literary, and the example of the poetic letters he wrote that were lifted verbatim from other sources. According to Busa, "Gorky used to say to a group of friends: 'Let's admit we are all bankrupt.' He would question the others and no one would admit it, but for him this attitude about being bankrupt was a way of getting to a magical situation where he could face this area of nothingness." [46]

The flowering of Gorky's art between 1942 and his death in 1948 remains a phenomenon without parallel in American art, both for the breathtaking beauty of the actual paintings and the posthumous significance they have taken on. It is such a multilayered body of work and so complex in its sources that no one of the historians, critics, friends, and disciples who have written on it has succeeded in fully uncovering its genesis, either in terms of Gorky's personal and artistic history or in the context of Surrealism. Despite his ultimate rejection of the Surrealism that had enchanted him, the fact remains that Gorky was during his last six years the artist who most eloquently bridged the space between waning Surrealism and nascent abstract expressionism. A generation of young artists seeing his memorial exhibition in the old Whitney Museum on Eighth Street in 1951 took Gorky as their point of departure. His achievement, like that of Cézanne, was one that could be built on, one that opened up more possibilities than it closed out, in contrast to the major members of the New York School who by the early fifties each had their signature style marked out. Because the point at which Gorky arrived between 1942 and 1944 was so crucial, a close look at this development and the literature on it is critical for the story that unfolds in this book.

Valuable insight through firsthand observation is offered by Ethel Schwabacher, Julien Levy, and Harold Rosenberg in books that are personal tributes to the artist, but each is naturally colored by the nature of the relationship the writer had with Gorky and flawed by selective and not always accurate memory. Of the more objective scholarly examinations of the meanings layered in his work by far the most illuminating is that of Harry Rand, who through careful scrutiny of the numerous preliminary drawings deciphers the concealed content of the later paintings, a content of which not even those closest to the artist seem to have been aware. Thanks to Rand's detective work we are able to trace Gorky's gradual, deliberate process of "veiling," the term used by Breton in describing Tanguy's painting in his 1942 article in *View,* "What Tanguy Veils and Reveals." What Gorky was doing is wholly analogous to the steps in concealment that Rothko was working through at precisely the same time, although usually with more mythology than autobiography in his subject matter. Matta and Onslow Ford had also been following the practice of encoding an at least partially concealed content in their paintings, a content that in the case of Matta was often made more cryptic by his punning titles. Even Kurt Seligmann's archaizing figures had a very specific, if hermetic, iconography, a symbolism that was often personal and contemporary in its relevance. And by most accounts a specific recollected image or experience underlay even the most abstract of Pollock's drip paintings, and the steps by which he arrived at what Kamrowski called his "greater freedoms" clearly passed through an image-concealing or image-destroying phase. So there is nothing unique in Gorky's use of this device except the failure of most contemporary commentators to remark on it, as they noted instead the breakdown of distinction between positive and negative space, the separation of line and color, and the emphasis on the canvas surface as a field of action.

However, Rand's analysis does not take fully into account the Surrealist context in which Gorky's evolution occurred, or the qualities in the work of Masson, Tanguy, and Matta that validated his goals and pointed out some of the ways to move toward them. Masson considered Gorky his only friend among American artists, and Julien Levy quoted Gorky's recollection of Masson saying: "I do not paint in front of nature but within nature."[47] Two things were transpiring in Masson's work during the summer of 1942, the time of Gorky's first stay in Connecticut. One was an immersion in nature, as he had described it to Saidie May, resulting from the combined impact of New England vegetation and climatic extremes and his fascination with the telluric. Another was a different approach to the canvas surface, a way of conceiving not of pictorial space but of a flat surface on which the artist makes marks that activate and utilize the entire field, as described by Masson in "Painting Is a Wager." This developed partly in response to Masson's desire to deal with what was happening simultaneously within the earth and above ground. Also, as we have seen, a painting such as *Meditation on an Oakleaf* was laden with symbols alluding to personal experience.

At this time Masson kept a considerable amount of brush drawing visible in his final work, as well as continuing to do the fine pen drawing in conventional techniques that paralleled the masterful drawing that had long been a crucial aspect of Gorky's oeuvre. From an aesthetic standpoint it seems likely that Gorky would have

found more to admire in the work of Masson than in that of Tanguy, who was also a Connecticut neighbor, but the idea of hermetic meanings sealed into the latter's fanciful yet precise constructions may well have helped to open other horizons to Gorky. Julien Levy felt that Tanguy was the last artist to whom Gorky "apprenticed" himself.[48]

Gorky also admired Kandinsky, whose work was accessible to him at the Museum of Non-Objective Art. From Kandinsky's paintings of 1910–1914 he would also have observed the way a brush-drawn black line can be used quite separately from color, as well as how to make color appear to lift and hang suspended in space. However, unless he intuited it on his own, there was no one at that time to point out the sign language that underlay Kandinsky's ostensibly subjectless works, including Will Grohmann whose book on Kandinsky he owned. Given Gorky's capacity for absorbing from other artists and the multiple sources available to him, it is impossible to quantify the relative influence from Masson, Kandinsky, and Matta that

Above: Arshile Gorky, *The Liver Is the Cockscomb*, 1944, oil on canvas, 73¼ x 98 inches; Albright Knox Art Gallery, gift of Seymour H. Knox.

New York, 1943: A New Momentum Begins

made possible his breakthrough in 1943. Schapiro's certainty on the matter of Matta's influence and the mention of it by Busa, Calas, Greenberg, and Levy, among others, coupled with visual evidence, indicates that some specific interchange took place, but its exact nature and the extent to which it was reciprocal remain difficult to assess.

A useful exercise is to place Gorky's large (72-by-98-inch) *The Liver Is the Cockscomb* of 1944 alongside a Matta of comparable importance such as *The Earth Is a Man* (illustrated in chapter 6), which had been shown in 1942. The most palpable distinction is in the vastly differing uses of space; space—exploding, infinite, and multiperspectival—is virtually Matta's central subject, and everything is caught up in conflicting gravitational pulls. For Gorky here and always, space is finite and conventional, a self-contained interior or a stage on which his various personages perform. The facture is also different, Gorky using small painterly touches of the brush, sometimes as part of a shimmering, translucent overpainting, while Matta's paint is flowed on and wiped off with no visible trace of a brush. In Gorky's painting a firm, fluent brush-drawn line establishes contours and connections, while the linear structure at the center of *The Earth Is a Man* is so fragile as to be barely noticeable. (Another émigré artist who had known the Surrealists in Paris, Gabor Peterdi, may actually be responsible for the changing role of line in Gorky's painting; Peterdi, who worked as a graphic artist, suggested to Gorky that he use a lettering brush because its long bristles could hold enough ink or paint to make a continuous unbroken line of considerable length.)[49] Color is a different matter. In his early paintings Matta used paint right from the tube, unmixed and fully saturated so that the red, blue, and yellow primaries tend to dominate these paintings as they do in *The Earth Is a Man*. Gorky seems not only to have adopted the palette, but to have floated one color inside another as Matta does on the right side of his painting. The effect is one of lifting and suspending the forms, thus putting them into a dreamlike or visionary mode. And ultimately it is this dream space that is the closest link between the paintings by the two artists.

Following his summer in Virginia in 1943, Gorky returned to his Union Square studio in New York, and it was probably during that winter of 1943–1944 that he accompanied Noguchi to the dinner at the home of Jeanne Reynal where he was introduced to Breton. His meeting with Breton can have been no later than the winter of 1943–1944, since Breton describes a gesture made by the daughter of "my friend Arshile Gorky" in *Arcane 17* which was written in the summer of 1944. A photo shows the two together in the Connecticut countryside with Gorky's daughter Maro, who was born in 1943. When he wrote an essay on Gorky's painting in early 1945 Breton referred to the "wild and tender personality which Gorky hides."

That the Gorkys were well acquainted with Breton is also evident in the letters Jeanne Reynal wrote to Agnes Gorky from Soda Springs, California, where she was living from 1943 to 1945. Not only does she mention Breton's favorable response to Gorky's work, but she frequently comes to Breton's defense, discusses his books, and praises "the quality of poetry he injects into ordinary experience." "The night I dined with you and HE was there, HE said, rather sadly, 'La femme change, mais c'est toujours le même amour.' And in December 1944: "Oh have no fear of M. Breton. He might be dangerous for the shallow ambitions, but for you and Arshile there is nothing of this sort."[50]

Breton was quick to claim Gorky for Surrealism. He is said to have provided titles for some of Gorky's paintings from 1944–1945—Robert Lebel recollected having translated these titles for the artist—and he wrote the catalogue essay for Gorky's first New York exhibition in 1945 and included a section on Gorky in the edition of

André Breton in Connecticut with Gorky and his daughter Maro, c. 1944.

New York, 1943: A New Momentum Begins

Surrealism and Painting that he was preparing for Brentano's. The only reason one can imagine for Gorky not being included in the fourth and last *VVV* is that it was already prepared for publication by the time their relationship developed.

Gorky seemed heartened by this supportive interest on the part of the distinguished European poet, leader of a movement that had intrigued him since the early 1930s. Breton had a way of making each artist feel uniquely important, and apparently for Gorky his interest and approval brought a sense of validation and of artistic belonging. At this time, then, Gorky had no objection to being regarded as a Surrealist. His friend Sidney Janis included him in the Surrealist section of his book *Abstract and Surrealist Art in America*. Apparently he used some of the titles that Breton jotted down for his paintings, and he participated in the International Surrealist Exhibition in Paris in 1947. According to Motherwell he was at the time of his death thought of as a Surrealist. However, despite the annexation by Breton, the loose designation "abstract surrealist" that floated around in the mid-1940s, and the fulfillment of belonging to something that came out of the European tradition, Gorky's motivation and practice were almost the inverse of Surrealist motivation and practice, something that he himself could state unequivocally by 1947. A perusal of the many drawings that preceded each of both the large and moderate-size paintings makes it clear that even his most spontaneously painted works were carefully planned and deliberately plotted. All during the thirties he had stood fast in support of artistic quality and an exalted artistic tradition, and he had covered reams of paper with drawings intended to improve his art rather than to reveal his psyche. It was enough for him to pursue art as a high calling and he does not seem to have thought of it as a means to bring about a revolution, either in consciousness or in society.

The experimentation among younger American artists was being carried on largely without benefit of a support system or the possibility of feedback except from other artists. That this situation gradually changed was due in large part to Peggy Guggenheim, whose gallery had opened with such éclat at the end of 1942. Not only was she the principal connecting point for the European and American artists, but she had access both to influential curators and critics and to potential buyers among her wealthy friends and relatives. In 1943 she set about staging a series of innovative group exhibitions that offered opportunities for unknown Americans to be showcased alongside noted Europeans. The first, an exhibition of thirty-one women, was reportedly proposed by Duchamp and offered a heterogeneous mix put together at least partly on a social basis. Novices from the inner circle such as Guggenheim's daughter, Pegeen Vail, and the Reises' daughter Barbara, Gypsy Rose Lee, amateur painter and professional strip tease artist, and Surrealist regulars Fini, Carrington, Sage, Lamba, and Oppenheim were shown along with diverse Americans, including Louise Nevelson, I. Rice Pereira, and Buffie Johnson. A newcomer who fit perfectly into the general Surrealist tenor of the show was Dorothea Tanning, who placed an accomplished academic style in the service of a distinctive, slightly chilling personal vision in *Birthday* and *Children's Games*.

To replace Jimmy Ernst as her gallery assistant, Peggy Guggenheim hired Howard Putzel, who seems to have given her confidence to move beyond the European circles and to show unknown Americans. The Americans to whom she turned were those who had already exhibited with the Surrealists in "First Papers" or whom she had met through them. According to Matta it was he who first drew Guggenheim's attention to Pollock and brought her to his studio. Sidney Janis had already visited Pollock's studio and had mentioned his work to Putzel, and the latter also urged Guggenheim to see his work. When she was planning an international collage exhibition in the spring, the first exhibition of its kind to be held in the United States, she suggested to Motherwell, Baziotes, and Pollock that they try making some collages and, depending on how they turned out, she said she would put them in the exhibition. Kamrowski, Hare, Ad Reinhardt, and Jimmy Ernst were also included, alongside such international figures as Arp, Miró, Max Ernst, Picasso, and Schwitters.

Exhilarated yet somewhat intimidated at the idea of exhibiting with internationally known artists, Motherwell and Pollock got together in the latter's studio to try their hand at this unfamiliar medium. Motherwell described Pollock's approach as violent—"he burnt it with matches and spit on it," while for him it was a discovery of a wholly sympathetic process—"like making beautiful love for the first time." [51] His affinity for collage began at that point and soon he had a stack of collages that he showed to Matta who said, "These are really you. Why don't you do more and make them bigger?" [52] The result was the large collage *Pancho Villa Dead and Alive*, which was purchased almost immediately by the Museum of Modern Art.

Whereas the Surrealists had primarily used collage to yield provocative juxtapositions of antithetical images, Motherwell and Pollock adopted a painterly approach to the task, trying to work with an automatist spontaneity that emphasized process but also took composition into consideration. In his early collage, *The Joy of Living*, Motherwell used torn and pasted papers, a cut-out from a map, black polyhedrons and linear constructions similar to those in Matta's most recent works, spatters, blurred edges, and passages of gestural brush drawing on a softly brushed diaphanous ground. A largely irresolute work whose main virtue was in its declaration of freedom to mix media and be bound by no existing style, it was nonetheless purchased from Peggy Guggenheim by Masson's benefactor Saidie May, who also

Robert Motherwell, *The Joy of Living*, 1943, mixed media, collaged on cardboard,
110.5 x 85.4 cm; The Baltimore Museum of Art, Bequest of Saidie A. May.

had the perspicacity to buy Baziotes's collage *The Drugged Balloonist*. While collage never became an important medium for Baziotes, he certainly went all-out in this effort for Peggy Guggenheim. Insect wings, leaves, cut-outs from glossy magazines, papers of extraordinary texture, a propeller seen in perspective, and quick-drying poured paint are delicately juxtaposed to create passages of poetic suggestion and a mood akin to the dreamy, metaphorical tone of his paintings.

Most of the Americans in the collage show were included in Guggenheim's Spring Salon, which followed in May. Among those added to their number were Virginia Admiral, Peter Busa, Xenia Cage, Morris Graves, Ibram Lassaw, I. Rice Pereira, and André Racz. Only artists under thirty-five were allowed to submit works to a jury consisting of Guggenheim, Duchamp, Mondrian, Putzel, Sweeney, and Soby. This was the famous instance in which Mondrian spoke in a strongly positive vein in support of Pollock after Guggenheim had presented his entry *Stenographic Figure* in a disparaging fashion. Mondrian's comment, "I think this is the most interesting work I've seen so far in America," not only convinced Guggenheim, who was soon repeating it as her own opinion, but provided Pollock with much-needed approval from an artist-hero. (It should be noted for the record that Mondrian had an agenda of his own, the inclusion in the exhibition of his friend and benefactor, Harry Holzman, and he hoped by demonstrating broad-mindedness to promote a similar tolerance in Guggenheim.)[53]

Above: William Baziotes, *The Drugged Balloonist*, 1943, collage, 18¼ x 24 inches; The Baltimore Museum of Art, Bequest of Saidie A. May.

New York, 1943: A New Momentum Begins

Putzel had met Pollock during the previous year and had written about him in glowing terms to Onslow Ford in November 1942: "I have discovered an American genius. . . . Matta speaks very enthusiastically about Pollock's work and so, surprisingly, does Soby." [54] His strong support, coupled with Matta's enthusiasm, finally brought about Peggy Guggenheim's June visit to the fifth-floor walk-up on Eighth Street that housed Pollock and Lee Krasner and their work. The outcome of the meeting was a contract with Guggenheim that would provide Pollock with $150 a month against sales of his paintings, which meant that he could leave his job at the Museum of Non-Objective Art. A one-man exhibition at Art of This Century was scheduled for late that same year, and Guggenheim commissioned him to do a nineteen-foot mural for the entryway of the house she was about to move into. In one sweep a significant change had been effected, not only for Pollock but for the direction of American Art. Now an unknown American artist had a contract and a stipend from a dealer just as Tanguy and Matta had from Pierre Matisse. A thirty-one-year-old American was to be given a one-man exhibition by a patroness of the arts noted for her championship of European moderns. Further, he had a commission for a painting on a scale that neither he nor most of his contemporaries had contemplated outside of the Federal Art Project. During the ensuing months he was caught up in a frenzy of work as he prepared for his Art of This Century show in November.

In the summer of 1943 Max Ernst took Dorothea Tanning to see the land of the red cliffs that had impressed him so strongly on the return trip from California two years earlier. They stayed on into the autumn at a working ranch near Sedona, Arizona. The spell it exerted on them was sufficiently strong that they returned in 1945, built a house with their own hands, and made it their home for six years. The fantastic rock formations seemed to come out of an Ernst painting of the 1930s, as he had observed on his earlier trip, and the exotic color of the rocks, alternately violet, red, and orange, lent the entire prospect a visionary aura. In his "Biographical Notes" Ernst gave a detailed description of the flora and fauna of the "oasis of Sedona," and mentions the rock formations that "resembled a great variety of things" as well as the abundance of color, "the red ochre of the soil . . . the pink bark of the ponderosa pines." [55] In describing the "unobtrusive kindness and wholly natural hospitality of the bipeds," he extended his comment to the several Indian tribes, including the Hopis.

Ernst's large *Vox Angelica,* painted during that summer, marks a departure in his work that parallels the point of departure he had reached in his life. A four-part oil on canvas, divided into smaller segments by *trompe-l'oeil* inner frames, it offers a reprise of Ernstian themes, interspersed by sections painted in imitation wood grain and others of a flat opaque blue. Its retrospective elements include the anthropomorphic mechanical instruments, recalling his transformations of 1918–1920, the wood grain frottages that became petrified forests in the late 1920s, the lush, tangled vegetation of 1936–1938, the decalcomania landscapes of recent vintage, the crisscrossing lines obtained with the punctured paint can on a pendulum, stenciled leaves, phantom silhouettes of the Eiffel Tower and the Chrysler Building, abstract color studies, birds, constellations, and much more. This painting and other similarly compartmented works such as *Painting for Children* were shown at Julien Levy's gallery in 1944. There were no sales and the show was the occasion for an extremely negative review by Greenberg.

The event that most clearly signaled the incipient decline of the Surrealist era in New York and the birth of the unique hybrid it had provoked was the Pollock exhibition in November at Art of This Century, even though few perceived its significance at the time. In 1942 Pollock had produced very little, ostensibly because the Project kept those artists who were still on its rolls busy with defense-related work. However, three fairly large paintings appear to have been near completion by the end of that year, *Moon Woman, Male and Female,* and *Stenographic Figure.* All three signify a momentous change in his work, a change in scale, scope, and assurance but also a change in paint application and treatment of the image. The rough, raw, turbulent handling of paint is still forcibly present, but it is mitigated by what is at times an almost felicitous calligraphy. Over the solid areas of color run large sweeping movements of the brush and over these in thinner line are quick, electrifying gestural lines, a kind of abstract writing with occasional recognizable letters and numbers that activates much of the canvas surface.

Although veiling is perhaps too delicate a way of describing Pollock's treatment of his underlying subject matter, it does suggest the affinity between his painting process and that of some of the Surrealists and their American colleagues, especially Rothko and Gorky. A number of writers on Pollock, most notably Naifeh and Smith in their exhaustive biography, have pointed out that Pollock's paintings of the mid-1940s began with a repertoire of recurring subjects: his family, Lee Krasner, recollected scenes from his youth, and totemic animals. The process of transformation seems to have alternated between a kind of violence-tinged interaction with the subject and the impulse to establish a unifying rhythm. As these contradictory impulses vie with each other the edges of shapes disappear, paint strokes cross over into the surrounding space, and the positive/negative distinction begins to break down. The act of giving form and the act of obliterating it merge, as they were to do so often in the abstract expressionist years to come.

It is impossible to quantify the relative input from the different sources acting on Pollock as he moved ahead in these three paintings and then swung into a succession of new canvases in the months before his Art of This Century show. Despite his ambivalence about the sessions in Matta's studio, which took place at the time his painting was beginning to come together, it is hard to believe that Matta's rapid brush drawing and cryptic symbols did not have some bearing on Pollock's introduction of calligraphic notation and independent line into his paintings. Among the places where pages of cryptic symbols could have crossed his horizon were *View* (Seligmann's articles), *VVV* (Claude Lévi-Strauss on Indian tattoos), and *Dyn* (the Amerindian number with drawings of Maya hieroglyphs). He may not have shared Matta's interest in telepathy or non-Euclidean space, but he must have observed the pyrotechnics of his brush drawing. (Gordon Onslow Ford maintained that he and Matta tried to draw faster than the speed of thought in order to work from a truly unconscious state.) From what we know about Pollock in his studio, especially the twenty-four-hour marathon in which he painted Peggy Guggenheim's mural, he worked at a speed that precluded conscious decision-making.

The sessions with Matta also reinforced the experience of several years earlier when he had made spontaneous drawings for his Jungian analyst, Dr. Henderson. However, the fact that Matta announced specific subjects to which the artists were supposed to respond without conscious deliberation irritated Pollock, and he eventually left the Matta project in annoyance. Yet it may well have served as a catalyst that helped him bring together the Siqueiros experience, the lacquer dripping with Baziotes and Kamrowski, and the psychoanalytic practice of accessing the unconscious through drawing. Pollock's 1943 painting *Burning Landscape* evokes Matta's volcanic works of 1941–1942, both in the amorphous flow of paint and the cataclysmic imagery. In addition Pollock was exposed to at least two other validating sources from Surrealism in transformation: the current painting of Masson and the art and ideas of Wolfgang Paalen, whose journal *Dyn* was among Pollock's books. Pollock was not a reader, his friends maintain, but he looked, and in the three issues of *Dyn* that appeared in 1942 he could have seen paintings such as Paalen's *Chromatic Polarities,* which are characterized by an allover energizing of the canvas surface through strong rhythmic brush drawing. If he did glance at *Dyn*'s written content he could have read in "Art and Science" Paalen's prescription for a new kind of painting that would be "a direct visualization of the forces that move our bodies and minds." [56]

As for Masson, there have been several probably apocryphal stories about Pollock's responses to Masson including his saying "I'm going to paint me a *Pasiphaë*" when he saw Masson's painting of that title at the Buchholz Gallery in 1944, reportedly at the suggestion of Greenberg. In fact, during 1942–1943 it would have been hard for Pollock to avoid seeing Masson's work, given the number of exhibitions and reproductions in which it appeared. As we have seen there was both an overt and a symbolic content in Masson's painting, such as *There Is No Perfect World* or *Meditation on an Oakleaf*. In the latter, shapes flow into one another across the canvas plane, positive and negative spaces fuse, and differing systems of representation are combined.

A further Surrealist source has been suggested for the work in Pollock's first exhibition: the arcane pictographic signs in *Guardians of the Secret* appear to have been influenced by a short essay Kurt Seligmann wrote for *View*, "Magic Circles," in which he reproduced two pages from Cornelius Agrippa's *Fourth Book of Occult Philosophy*, identifying the astrological and alchemical characters symbolic of good and evil spirits. A number of roughly equivalent signs are used by Pollock.[57]

There is another way in which Masson, Matta, and Paalen served Pollock: they prepared an audience for his work. Conditioned to see with Surrealism's inner eye and to appreciate the gestural qualities of automatism, influential figures such as Soby and Sweeney were ready to approach Pollock with an open mind and prepared to give him the benefit of the doubt, if not to offer immediate acclaim. As we have seen, the more experimental American artists and progressive critics during the war years were facing a void that they could not fill with any of the existing styles. The canvases covered with thick turbulently applied paint that bordered on chaos by the tormented but compelling thirty-one-year-old from Cody, Wyoming, just might offer an idea of what could fill that void.

Even before Pollock's show was hung, Soby let Peggy Guggenheim know that the Museum of Modern Art was interested in buying *The She Wolf*, a clumsy-looking painting of an animal that had started as a bull but had metamorphosed into an ungainly hybrid along the way. (Coincidentally Masson, inspired by his "savage" surroundings, did two works on the theme of the wolf in 1943, *Le Loup garou*, Museum of Modern Art, and *Le Loup couleur d'automne*, Grenoble Museum.) Sweeney apparently had gone to see Pollock's work in 1942 at the urging of Herbert Matter and may even have mentioned him to Guggenheim; he was willing to write a short catalogue introduction for the show and produced a cautious, somewhat ambivalent piece. He referred to Pollock's talent as "volcanic" and "undisciplined, lavish, explosive and untidy." Despite the ire that this aroused in Pollock, Sweeney's intentions were not necessarily negative. "What we need," he continued, "is more young men who paint from inner impulse without an ear to what the critic or spectator may feel—painters who will risk spoiling a canvas to say something in their own way. Pollock is one."

Jackson Pollock, *Burning Landscape,* 1943, oil on gesso on canvas, 36 x 28⁷⁄₁₆
inches; Yale University Art Gallery, gift of Peggy Guggenheim.

Although, with the exception of a single drawing, there were no sales during the exhibition, the show did prove to be provocative. Artists who came in considerable numbers reacted with comments that ranged from anger and dismay to the kind of approval that Pollock's friend Ruben Kadish voiced when he said that Jackson had "cracked the whole thing open." Motherwell wrote on the show for *Partisan Review,* claiming that "Pollock represents one of the younger generation's chances. There are not three other painters of whom this could be said." [58]

Reviews appeared in eight publications with most of the critics taking an equivocal stand. However, the general consensus was that they had encountered something that could not be lightly dismissed. Several critics sounded a new note of chauvinism, emphasizing that this was an American artist. [59] Clement Greenberg, who had recently started writing art reviews for the *Nation,* dwelt on the "mud" of the paint, finding it the "equivalent of that American chiaroscuro which dominated Melville, Hawthorne, and Poe and has best been translated into painting by Blakelock and Ryder." He was congratulatory that the artist had "come out on the other side" of a series of influences—Miró, Picasso, Mexican painting—but, adopting a pedagogical tone that was to become a hallmark of his criticism, he warned that "in his search for a style he is liable to relapse into an influence." [60]

The nineteen-foot canvas for Peggy Guggenheim's mural had remained stretched and leaning against the wall of Pollock's studio since July. It was still blank a day before the deadline for its delivery. He began to paint just after nightfall, so the story goes, and fifteen hours later the huge painting had been completed. Pollock recounted the story to several friends over the years: "I had a vision. It was a stampede." He evidently started painting his memory of the Grand Canyon and wild mustangs on the run and the figures of those who had been there with him. No sooner was the subject brushed in with big black lines than the process of "veiling" or, more accurately, obliterating began as he added "every animal in the American West." "Cows and horses, antelopes and buffaloes. Everything is charging across that goddamn surface." [61] In the end they had vanished with scarcely a trace, and what remained was the energy registered by the process itself and the sense of a precarious stasis reached in the course of the simultaneous painting in and painting out, precisely what Harold Rosenberg would later dub "Action Painting."

So at the end of 1943, as American and British troops fought their way up the Italian peninsula and American forces began the costly battles over Pacific islands whose names are written in blood—Guadalcanal, Iwo Jima, and Okinawa—Surrealism was no longer the newest thing in town and the first step had been taken toward the building of an American momentum. While some art experts such as Sidney Janis thought that this momentum could be seamlessly grafted onto European modernism, there were others who held that the new American art could attain its manhood, so to speak, only by rejection of the European art and artists closest at hand: the Surrealist émigrés. In 1944 both these tactics were to be in play.

Jackson Pollock, *The She Wolf*, 1943, oil, gouache, and plaster on canvas, 41⅞ x
67 inches; The Museum of Modern Art, New York.

9 New York, 1944-1945: *Young Cherry Trees Secured against Hares*

A facetious title for a volume of his selected poems was spotted by André Breton during a random stroll through a bookstore. In the midst of a display of books on agriculture, the phrase "Young cherry trees secured against hares" caught his attention. He may not have understood its meaning, but the word "hare" was all too familiar since that was the name of the young American who had served as editor for *VVV* and who was the cause of Jacqueline Lamba's leaving him. The irritant power of the dislocated phrase and the word with a double sense were combined with a double image on the book's exterior devised by Duchamp, the ever-ready accomplice. Over a Benday dot ground on the dust jacket he imprinted in green a photographic image of the Statue of Liberty with a hole cut out of the head; through this hole appears the face of Breton, printed directly beneath on the book's cover. Thus the poet becomes the personification of liberty, the true liberty offered by Surrealism which was, like the statue, French in origin. The image also suggests a monument in honor of a force that has taken possession of the city, a notion in which there was a touch of Duchampian irony since it represented the opposite of what was actually happening.

Not only had Breton been losing his old guard, but even new recruits like Georges Duits and Motherwell began distancing themselves, and others of the American painters took a separatist stance emboldened by Peggy Guggenheim's support and interest. "I moved away from Surrealism around 1944 almost as quickly as I had moved into it," Motherwell recollected.[1] The years 1944 and 1945 saw both the continued atomization of the émigré group and the growing visibility of the Americans who had, however briefly, been linked with that circle.

The last issue of *VVV*, which Breton brought out in February 1944, reflects Surrealism's changing cast of characters and growing diversification. Among the newly included were Jimmy Ernst, Gunther Gerzso, Dorothea Tanning, Donati, Julio de Diego, Esteban Frances, Isabelle Waldberg, and seventeen-year-old Philip Lamantia, who had sent Breton his poems while still in high school. A *vagina dentata* contributed by Matta animated the cover. More of the text of this issue was in French, suggesting a retreat from the goal of reaching an American audience or forging a new Franco-American Surrealism.

The last issue of *Dyn*, which appeared soon after, was more cohesive and prophetic of a new direction in art, including as it did paintings by a core group of "abstract surrealists" (see chapter 7). Compared to Paalen's clearly stated position—

"no painting with a subject and no painting without a theme"[2]—and the visual evidence he published to support it, *VVV* appears lacking in direction. If the unifying center of a group for Breton was a publication, the center was not holding very well in 1944.

The press in general, however, was beginning to take note of the "American Surrealists." In April *Harpers Bazaar* ran an article in which James Johnson Sweeney introduced five artists: Milton Avery, Gorky, Morris Graves, Matta, and Pollock, each of whom he saw as holding "the promise of a new and encouraging phase of American art." He pointed out that young American painters, "having seen some of their idols here as refugees working to find fresh ways of expressing themselves," have now realized that modern art is "something which is constantly developing and must continue to develop—always in a new direction."[3] He praised the new vocabulary of forms that were born of Gorky's having "looked into the grass" and saw Matta's new emphasis on structural lines as the basis of his most successful work to date. Pollock's *She Wolf*, which was reproduced in color, was purchased by the Museum of Modern Art shortly after the article appeared, despite Alfred Barr's aversion to Pollock.

In February *Arts and Architecture* published what purported to be an interview with Pollock, conducted by Motherwell, which included the following statement:

I accept the fact that the important painting of the last one hundred years was done in France. American painters have generally missed the point of modern painting from beginning to end. Thus the fact that good European moderns are now here is very important, for they bring with them an understanding of the problems of modern painting. I am particularly impressed with the concept of the source of art being the unconscious. The idea of an isolated American painting, so popular in this country during the '30s seems absurd to me . . . the basic problems of contemporary painting are independent of any country.[4]

It was Motherwell, by his own account, who actually wrote this statement.[5] There is no question that it reflects his desire to graft American art onto a European modern tradition with which he felt more of an affinity than some of the other "American Surrealists." This nostalgia for the European, that is, French, is a leitmotif that pervaded his art and public pronouncements well into the 1950s. Thus the Mexican influence began to be replaced by Gallicisms: wrappers from Gauloise cigarettes, envelopes with foreign stamps and postmarks, scrawled phrases in French, and above

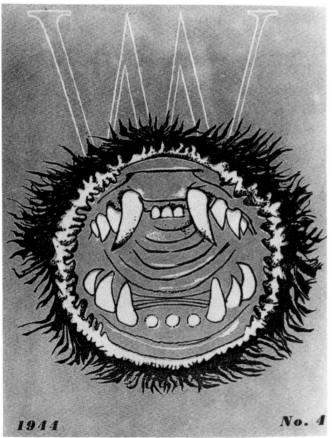

all the exercise of a kind of taste that was the antithesis of Pollock's raw paint handling. In 1944 he asked the French architect Pierre Chareau to transform a Quonset hut into a home and studio for himself and María in Amagansett on eastern Long Island. The result was a series of horizontal planes intersecting the half-circle of the metal Quonset, characteristic of Chareau's predilection for architectural collage and industrial materials.

Sidney Janis was even more eager than Motherwell to merge American art into an international mainstream. As a collector, Janis had concentrated on European art, convinced that American art wasn't up to the same standard. His chief interest in America had been naive artists, a subject on which he and his wife wrote a book. Both Breton and Ernst had expressed interest in his work on American autodidacts. However, in 1942 Janis began systematically collecting names and visiting artists' studios in order to gather material for a different kind of book, *Abstract and Surrealist Art in America.* His motivation arose from his conviction that American artists had been influenced by the exiles, and he wanted to show the work of both together. At first no publisher would take the book, but Janis persisted, encouraged by the artists who gathered in Gorky's studio to pledge their support. Finally in 1944 Jeanne Reynal's brother brought it out under the imprint of Reynal and Hitchcock, and for years it remained the only book to acknowledge that there was enough nonrealist art in America to constitute a genuine modernist movement. Twenty-nine artists were included under the abstract designation, twenty-eight under the Surrealist heading, and fifteen in a section devoted to "American Works by Artists in Exile."

Two themes were emphasized in Janis's introduction, the scientific background of modern art and the continuity of culture. "Surrealism," he wrote, "has consistently made an ordered scientific attempt to release the creative impulse, mainly through its adaptation of psychoanalytic techniques and especially through a system of tapping the resources of the unconscious."[6] Because he felt that he and his wife had been considered "kooks" in their early days of acquiring modern art, it was important for him to anchor the work in a rational structure akin to that of science. Thus he referred to "man manipulating the lever of contemporary culture upon the fulcrum of science." To graft the new American art onto an older European tradition he wrote: "By their authority the artists in exile . . . have produced that heightened activity which comes from personal contact besides nurturing in Americans—painters and public alike—a reasuring sense of the permanence of our common culture."[7]

Although Janis took the view, convenient for organizational purposes, that contemporary art was made up of "two antithetical directions, abstraction and surre-

alism, which were allied to the undercurrents of opposing directions which have persisted for centuries," some of the artists he included were not nearly so certain about these divisions and questioned whether they belonged in the abstract or the Surrealist section. Arguably the fit was an uncomfortable one in instances such as Abraham Rattner (abstract section) or social realist Howard Taft Lorenz (Surrealist section). However, Janis also included a paragraph reconciling Surrealism and abstraction,

Robert Motherwell in the house designed for him by Pierre Chareau in 1944 in
Amagansett, Long Island. Photograph by Hans Namuth, courtesy the Dedalus Foundation.

saying that in certain painters "there was a fusion of elements from each." As examples he mentioned David Hare, Gottlieb, Rothko, and Gorky; he described Motherwell as a former member of the Surrealist circle who still retained Surrealist ideas while approaching pure abstraction. Deciding who was an émigré was also something of a problem. Albers and Hans Hofmann were assimilated into the abstract section (Hofmann, according to Janis, did not at the time consider himself an abstract painter, but painted an abstraction so he could be included in the book),[8] Hayter into the Surrealist section, while Mondrian, Léger, Chagall, and the European Surrealists were assigned to the special section "American Painting by Artists in Exile." Each artist had a work reproduced, together with a personal statement.

The main thrust of Janis's book was to create a seamless continuity between European and American modernism, legitimizing the latter by its lineage and preparing the way for its succession to a place at the forefront of art history. The book appeared in 1944, but even before its publication the Mortimer Brandt gallery mounted an exhibition based on it at 15 East 57th Street, the very space in which Janis himself was to open a gallery in 1948. Another supporter of American modernism, Grace McCann Morley, perhaps prompted by Jeanne Reynal, asked for the exhibition at the San Francisco Museum and en route it was shown in four other cities. Thus a basis was laid for an overview of the new trends in American art years before the Museum of Modern Art seriously addressed the question.

Among the artists represented in the Surrealist section were Gottlieb, Rothko, Baziotes, Hare, Kamrowski, Margo, Andre Racz, Jimmy Ernst, Joseph Cornell, and Dorothea Tanning, all acknowledged as part of the expanded Surrealist group, socially or artistically. In addition there were two paintings that broke new ground in a bold and assured manner, Pollock's *She Wolf* and Gorky's *The Liver Is the Coxcomb*. Anyone leafing through Janis's book could get a sense that a new direction had opened in American art and might also observe that a half-dozen of the works reproduced were stylistically reminiscent of Matta's *The Disasters of Mysticism,* which was reproduced in the section on "Artists in Exile."

Upheavals at the Museum of Modern Art may have been responsible for the Museum's failure to acknowledge the new American experimental art during the 1940s. In 1944 Alfred Barr was removed from his position as director of painting and sculpture and given a space off the library in which to write his books. The post was partially filled by Soby and a curator, Dorothy Miller, whose husband, Holger Cahill, had directed the Federal Art Project. In 1947 Sweeney accepted the job, but he left in less than two years. Like Janis, who was a long-time member of the Museum's Advisory Council, Soby and others in charge at MoMA felt that there was nothing in American art that could hold up alongside the best European modern work, an attitude that provoked picket lines of artists outside the entrance. However, there were exceptions that permitted a glimpse of what was going on in the United States, such as the 1944 "Art in Progress" exhibition that marked the fifteenth anniversary of the Museum's founding.

Intended as an assessment of current directions, "Art in Progress" included recent work by Surrealists Dalí, Ernst, Hayter, Tanguy, Masson, Miró, and Matta, who was represented by his stunning *Vertige d'Eros*. It also included several Americans with Surrealist leanings, Peter Blume, Walter Quirt, and Gorky; the latter was represented by the 1941 *Garden in Sochi,* which had been donated to the Museum. Quirt's *The Tranquillity of Previous Existence* was also from 1941, when he and Matta had both been showing with Julien Levy, and his work had definite affinities with that of Matta. Other Americans in the show represented a spectrum of figurative styles that included the social realism of Jack Levine and Philip Evergood, modified modernists such as Milton Avery and Paul Burlin, and American realists such as Edward Hopper. Despite the heavy emphasis on Surrealism, there was scarcely a nod in the direction of those who were beginning to be called American Surrealists, whose work could be seen at the Norlyst Gallery or at Art of This Century a few blocks from the Museum. (Two years later, when Miller put together her first "14 Americans" show, four of the artists—Noguchi, Hare, Motherwell, and Gorky—were from this group.) Reviewing "Art in Progress" in the *Nation,* Clement Greenberg complained: "The extreme eclecticism now prevailing in art is unhealthy and it should be counteracted. The selection indicates no positive policy in respect to art being produced at the moment—an 'uneven catholicity.'"[9] He dismissed Blume, Dalí, and Tchelitchew as irrelevant, an indication of his mounting aversion to what he considered illustrative art. Greenberg would soon set a course designed to counteract what he perceived as "unhealthy eclecticism."

In April, following a one-man show for Hans Hofmann, Peggy Guggenheim assembled an exhibition called "Twenty Paintings, First Showing in America." To a roster of well-known Europeans she added Rothko's *Entombment,* David Hare's *The Frog is a Heart,* Pollock's *Pasiphaë,* and works by Motherwell, Isabelle Waldberg, Laurence Vail, and others. Although the Pollock work has often been mentioned as having been inspired by Masson's *Pasiphaë,* the title was "a later graft," supplied by Sweeney, who also provided Pollock with the story of the Minoan queen's infatuation with the bull—his notes on this story remained among Pollock's papers.[10] Whatever the source of the title, the Pollock painting with its swelling central form and allover activity of grafitti-like signs had an explosive force that commanded attention. If there was a Masson connection, it lay more in the mode of painting; the deployment of calligraphic brushstrokes over a darker ground, the swirling movement, the adherence to the picture plane, and the use of cryptic symbols are all characteristic of the new style Masson had evolved by 1942 in works such as *Meditation on an Oakleaf*.

"Twenty Paintings" was followed by a sequel to the 1943 Spring Salon, with Alfred Barr added to the jury. *Art Digest* announced the show saying: "Young Surrealists under thirty-five are invited to submit." Clement Greenberg did not find much virtue in the latter. "These young artists lack force and erudition, lack profound obsessions and aim at felicity more often than complete expression." He made passing mention of "Jackson Pollock's inflated pastel and gouache," but ended on a more positive note: "William Baziotes has painted an experiment rather than a picture, but it makes one more curious about his particular future than about that of any other painter present." [11]

By the summer Greenberg had taken a new tack. With increasing confidence in voicing his own opinion, he launched a double-barreled attack on Surrealism in two successive numbers of the *Nation* (August 12 and 19). He started with a negatively charged comparison of the Surrealists to the pre-Raphaelites on the basis that both sought to change the structure of industrialized society and that both attempted to reinvigorate academicism. How the pre-Raphaelites' nostalgia for a sentimentalized version of the past resembled Surrealism's attempts to subvert the hegemony of rationalism through the liberation of the unconscious is not spelled out. Greenberg then sought to separate the Surrealists of whom he approved—Miró, Arp, and Masson who used automatism as a "primary factor"—from those of whom he disapproved—Ernst, Dalí, Tanguy, and Magritte who illustrated the fantastic in literal detail; "Ernst's volcanic landscapes," he wrote, "look like exceptionally well manufactured scenic postcards." The principal crime of the second group was that they were outside the "tradition of painting which runs from Manet through Impressionism, Fauvism, and Cubism [which] created the first original style since the French Revolution, and the only original one our bourgeois society has been capable of." [12] In other words these artists challenged the inviolability of the modernist tradition which Greenberg held sacred by "taking refuge in the ancient arsenal provided by the traditions of oil painting."

Thus Greenberg, in conformity with his Marxist background, laid the groundwork for the dialectical process he was to continue to follow, a dialectic that opposed the reactionary, that is, the illustrative, to a narrowly construed modernism that above all else eschewed volumetric rendering in favor of flatness and respect for the sacrosanct picture plane. By setting up the Surrealists as a target he could discredit

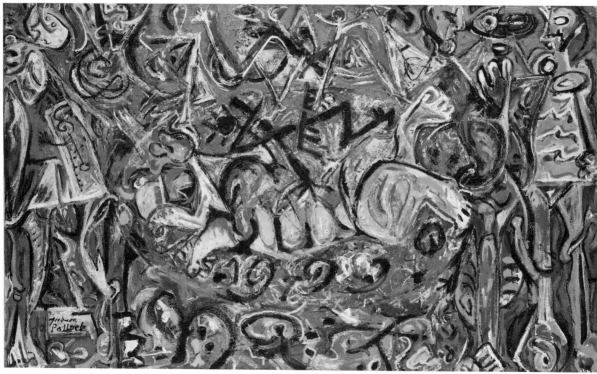

the last existing avant-garde and install a legitimate heir to the modern tradition. Who that heir was to be would become evident in the reviews he wrote in the fall.

Greenberg had deliberately sought to be provocative. On August 23 he wrote to Baziotes regarding the two articles: "I want to know what you frankly think of it. Don't pull any punches . . . I'm now waiting for lightning to descend, or hoping rather that it will descend, for it may not at all. The Surrealists have probably got too tired." [13] If they were tired it would have to have been from vacationing, as that summer they were mostly gathered in or near Amagansett where Motherwell had settled and where the Pollocks would soon acquire a house. Among those who were summering on eastern Long Island were the Hayters, Max Ernst, Lionel Abel, Noguchi, Becky Reis who arrived carrying one of the Matta twins while Anne carried the other, Laurence Vail and children, Jean Hélion, May and Harold Rosenberg, Luchita (soon to be Paalen), and Anaïs Nin. Most of this gathering is described by Motherwell in a letter to Baziotes, a letter in which he speaks with enthusiasm of Masson, Chareau, Hayter, and Hélion, but advises Baziotes to break with the young Surrealists "who are ignorant and sterile." [14] As for Max Ernst, he was too occupied with making sculpture in the garage of his rented house, expanding from plaster chessmen to the large *King Playing with the Queen,* to be troubled by Greenberg's vitriol.

If Greenberg has been hoping for a counterattack from Breton he was doomed to disappointment—Surrealism's principal spokesman was a thousand miles away in an isolated cabin on Canada's Gaspé Peninsula, where he would remain into October. He was accompanied by the new woman in his life, Elisa Varo, the wife of a Chilean diplomat. He had met her the previous January when, in the midst of a snowstorm, he had stopped for lunch at a favorite refugee hangout, Chez Larré, and had noticed a woman with an overwhelming sadness on her face. He subsequently learned that her eleven-year-old daughter had drowned the previous summer while at a camp in Cape Cod and that she herself had attempted suicide. Breton, who had written in *Plein marge*: "I have looked only at women at odds with their time," was instantly drawn to her. The following year Elisa became his third wife and remained with him the rest of his life.

In August the newsreels showed truckloads of American G.I.s driving down the Champs-Elysées and Charles de Gaulle, head and shoulders above the cheering crowds, returning to Paris as the Germans retreated eastward. Realizing that his days in the Western Hemisphere were numbered, Breton had gone off with Elisa to spend the late summer and fall on the Gaspé where he wrote his last major analogical

Max Ernst, *The King Playing with the Queen,* 1944, cast 1954, bronze, 27¾ x 33
x 21¼ inches; The Menil Collection, Houston.

work, *Arcane 17*. It is a diffuse meditation on love, on utopian social theory, and on esotericism as the key to universal symbolism; throughout its pages one motif continually recurrs, awe of that vast conjunction of land, sea, and sky spreading away from the looming, often fog-shrouded Rocher Percé. Its pages are given over to descriptions of the mystical revelations that came to him as he experienced the crashing surf against the fantastic rock formations—the Rocher Percé had split, and from a certain angle one side looked like an organ, the other like a profile of Bach—and lived in daily contact with the evidence of a planet in permanent flux. For the first time he seemed to come to terms with the forces of nature and to find in them a reconciling vision. He took special pleasure in visits to Bonaventure Island, one of the largest seabird sanctuaries in the world. He was particularly intrigued by the myriad birds' nests wedged into the crevices, so that the face of the rock was alive with fluttering wings.

Our attention was riveted to the sight offered by the sheer face of the island fringed from step to step with a living snow foam ceaselessly recreated by the bold and capricious strokes of a blue trowel . . . during a beautiful quarter of an hour my thoughts had been willing to turn into white oats in that thresher . . . poetic thought . . . to remain what it is—a conductor of mental electricity—must above all charge itself in isolated surroundings.[15]

Like Masson in rural Connecticut and Ernst in the Southwest, Breton, far from the Deux Magots, found his poetry regenerated by the spectacular natural surroundings he discovered in the New World. *Arcane 17* was published in December by Brentano's in an edition of 325, with illustrations by Matta relating to the Tarot cards and in some copies an original drawing by Gorky.

The fall season for the Surrealist circle in New York got under way in October with one-person shows of Kay Sage at Julien Levy, Esteban Frances at Durlacher, and the debut of Baziotes, followed by that of Motherwell, at Art of This Century. Guggenheim, encouraged by Putzel, was strongly supportive of Baziotes and had bought $450 worth of paintings in order to allow him a span of worry-free painting time to prepare for his autumn show. Suddenly the difficulties that had blocked his painting evaporated and he was able to complete twenty-eight works before the October opening. Motherwell, who helped him hang the show, recalled Baziotes's feeling of apprehension at seeing his work detached and thrust into public view. Baziotes himself described the experience as "strange; the most astonishing people would come and buy. [These included collector Sam Lewison and a young Air Force officer,

Thomas Hess.] It was a very exciting period. Fantastic, leading a lonely life, no connection with the world, thrown, thrust into it suddenly."[16] For Baziotes who a few years earlier had been eking out an existence on WPA allotments, having to beg a few dollars from his brother when a check was late, this turn of events partook of that aura of the marvelous that he identified with Surrealism. Baziotes acknowledged as crucial his meeting Onslow Ford and Matta at Francis Lee's loft, which led him to develop "a Surrealist attitude toward things—an image coming in from the unconscious, making irrational elements work together . . . I love the mysterious in painting."[17]

Baziotes also mentioned Kurt Seligmann as being very supportive in wanting to help him exhibit his work. He would occasionally bring his work to show Seligmann on Saturday mornings. In his article "The Evil Eye" Seligmann wrote that "one of the most feared magico-diabolic forces is fascination through the evil eye," and he connected this with the Cyclops, thus possibly inspiring Baziotes's painting of that name.[18] Baziotes described some of the imagery that came to him after a crisis— "prostitutes with syphilis on their legs, perverts, all kinds of insane . . . an odalisque with a big cobra looming out of a vase, all completely unexpected."[19] In a letter to Alfred Barr on the genesis of the painting *Dwarf* he mentioned a World War I amputee, an eye like that of a lizard, the teeth of a crocodile, a feminine sexual symbol.[20]

William Baziotes, *The Parachutists,* 1944, duco enamel on canvas, 30 x 40 inches; estate of William Baziotes, Blum Helman Gallery.

For Janis's book he made the statement: "There is always a subject in my mind that is more important than anything else . . . I may not recognize it until a long time afterward." [21] Whereas his earlier works, notably *The Butterflies of Leonardo da Vinci*, which had hung in "First Papers" in 1942, were inspired by plant and insect life, the paintings in the 1944 show such as *The Wine Glass, The Balcony,* or *The Parachutist* were more abstract and based on a gridlike structure interrupted by curvilinear forms. A similar synthesis between abstraction and Surrealist fantasy would be apparent in Motherwell's show a few weeks later. The two painters had been close between 1942 and 1944, and, as mentioned above, had even gotten together on occasion, along with their wives and Jackson Pollock and Lee Krasner, to try their hand at automatist poetry. Baziotes worked in a more nuanced, painterly manner, trying for greater translucency of surface, but at this point, before he developed his own idiom, it appears that he and Motherwell sought similar paths of reconciliation between cubism and Surrealism.

Greenberg's new tactic, to simultaneously attack Surrealism and promote Guggenheim's young Americans, became more obvious when he wrote on Baziotes's first one-man show, which opened on October 4. He described him as "unadulterated talent, natural painter and all painter," issued his customary advice—"Baziotes will become an emphatically good painter when he forces himself to let his pictures 'cook' untouched for months before finishing them"—and concluded: "He already confronts us with big, substantial art, filled with real emotion and the true sense of our time." [22] Greenberg also had words of praise for Peggy Guggenheim "for her enterprise in presenting young and unrecognized artists. Two of the abstract painters she has recently introduced, Jackson Pollock and William Baziotes . . . have already placed themselves among the six or seven best young painters we possess."

Motherwell's first one-man show followed at the end of October. It was heavily Mexican and/or Spanish in theme, including such works as *Zapata Imprisoned* and *The Little Spanish Prison*; María Motherwell's father had been a general in the time of Pancho Villa, so the artist had heard direct accounts of the revolution. His collage, *Pancho Villa Dead and Alive*, done in 1943 after Matta had advised him to work larger, was inspired by a photograph of Pancho Villa after he had been shot from Anita Brenner's book *The Wind That Swept Mexico;* it was purchased in the year it was made by the Museum of Modern Art. In addition, the tragic outcome of the Spanish Civil War already loomed large as a subject that would recur in his work for decades.

By 1944 Motherwell had detached himself from Surrealism, although he would continue to use what he called "plastic [rather than psychic] automatism" throughout his career. He acknowledged his debt to Matta when he advised Baziotes that he needed someone to "make a map" for him. "Matta used to do it for me when I was filled with instinct, but now I begin to see the whole terrain." [23] Motherwell's essay in the final issue of *Dyn* made clear his desire to stand apart from Surrealism. However, his subsequent comments on the subject are characteristically ambivalent, ranging from "We were catalyzed by something we detested" to "It was one of the most illuminating experiences of my life; they talked about moral concerns while the American artists talked about money." [24]

Motherwell had little desire to follow Breton's path of perpetual revolution. For him it was sufficient to stop with aesthetics, precisely that which Breton had sought to eliminate when he proposed a psychic automatism free of aesthetic and moral considerations. That Motherwell was also concerned with a possible reconciliation between abstraction and Surrealism is evident in the combination of the geometric and the gestural that characterizes many of the paintings in his first exhibition. In the statement accompanying the reproduction of his painting in Janis's book, Motherwell wrote:

Robert Motherwell, *Pancho Villa Dead and Alive*, 1943, gouache and oil with cut
and pasted paper on cardboard, 28 x 35⅞ inches; The Museum of Modern Art,
New York, purchase.

The Spanish Prison, like all of my works, consists of a dialectic between the conscious (straight lines, designed shapes, weighed color, abstract language) and the unconscious (soft lines, obscured shapes . . .) resolved into a synthesis which differs as a whole from either. The hidden Spanish prisoner must represent the anxieties of modern life, the intense Spanish-Indian color, splendor of any life.[25]

Greenberg wrote more reservedly on this show—"It is through his very awkwardness that Motherwell makes his specific contribution"—and offered the following advice: "*Joy of Living* points Motherwell's only direction, the direction he must go to realize his talent, of which he has plenty . . . let him stop thinking instead of painting himself through."[26]

Already in 1944 some of the fundamental tenets of abstract expressionism were being formulated: the idea of the hidden, even unconscious, subject latent in every work and the tension between automatism and an underlying structure ultimately derived from cubism and geometric abstraction. Greenberg, perhaps bolstered by his discussions with Hans Hofmann and Lee Krasner, grasped the formalist aspects of this new direction while ignoring the content. Reversing his position of the previous spring, he announced his candidates for the avant-garde position from which he had dislodged the Surrealists. "The future of American painting depends on what Motherwell, Baziotes, Pollock and only a comparatively few others do from now on."[27]

If Greenberg had written the review two months later, he might have added two more names, those of David Hare and Rothko, both of whom had been introduced by Guggenheim in an earlier group exhibition and who were now given solo shows, Hare in November and Rothko in January. Hare had progressed from surreal photographs produced by heating and thus deforming the negatives to sculpture in the fragile medium of plaster-covered wire. His home in Roxbury was near Calder's studio and he had become interested in the kinetic possibilities of sculpture, which he applied to his sculptural translations of mythological images.

Rothko's January debut offered a sampling of his experimental approaches of the previous two years, including the Duchampian *Gyrations on Four Planes* and the *Syrian Bull,* which had baffled the *Times* critic Jewell in 1943. There were works whose images were drawn from Greek tragedy, such as *The Sacrifice of Iphigenia* and *Tiresias,* and the biomorphic *Birth of the Cephalopods,* in addition to the autobiographical *Slow Swirl by the Edge of the Sea.* He also showed his *Entombment I* and *Entombment II,* turning to another source for inspiration, Christian mythology and

Above: David Hare, *House of the Sun,* 1945, cement; formerly collection Edgar
Kaufman, Jr., photograph courtesy estate of David Hare.

Opposite top: Mark Rothko, *Entombment I,* 1946, gouache, pen, and ink on
paper, 20⅛ x 25¼ inches; Whitney Museum of American Art.

Opposite bottom: Wolfgang Paalen, *Gyra,* 14⅜ x 14 inches, Solomon R.
Guggenheim Museum.

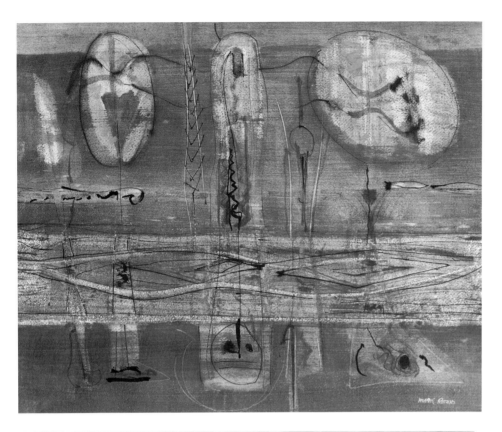

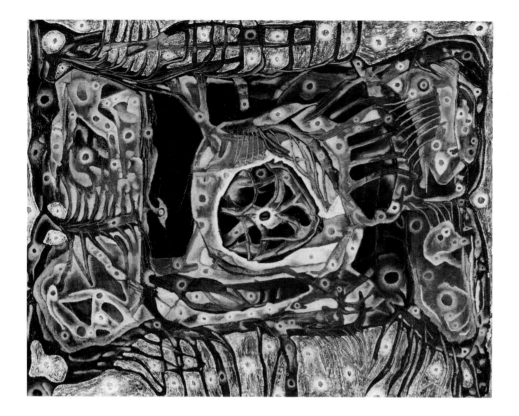

the Renaissance Pietà.[28] Thus this first Rothko show made clear the transitional process the artist was undergoing, as he carefully worked out his subject matter and then proceded to "veil" it in such a way that the viewer could sense the underlying allusions while responding also to the color, line, and hovering shapes. While not a Surrealist in the sense of partaking in its revolutionary stance, Rothko was using what he understood as its methods, particularly those of Matta and possibly Onslow Ford, to move toward abstraction.

The 1944–1945 season at Art of This Century was richly promising. The debuts of Baziotes, Hare, Motherwell, and Rothko were followed by Pollock's second exhibition and the first New York showing of Paalen's post-Surrealist work. (Continuing her policy of featuring women artists, Guggenheim also gave one-person exhibitions to Isabelle Waldberg and Alice Rahon Paalen and in June staged a show of thirty women artists, both abstract and surreal.) This sequence of six exhibitions, together with Gorky's first exhibition at Julien Levy, Jimmy Ernst's debut at Norlyst, and shows for Gottlieb and Charles Seliger at Gallery 67, all featuring work that in one way or another went beyond Surrealism yet sprang from Surrealist sources, confirmed that there was a new direction taking shape, referred to as abstract surrealism.

As American divisions rolled eastward too fast and were caught in the last desperate ground battle of the war, the Battle of the Bulge, the way was being prepared

Opposite: Charles Seliger, *Cave,* 1945, oil on canvas, 22 x 28 inches; courtesy
Michael Rosenfeld Gallery.

Below: Richard Pousette Dart, *Pegeen,* 1943, oil on linen, 127 x 132 cm; Detroit
Institute of Art, Founders Society Purchase, W. Hawkins Ferry Fund.

for a new art that would suit the U.S. postwar stance as the banner-carrier for individual liberty and a triumphant world power, an art that would be both personal and heroic. It was to be another four years before the form that this art would take became evident to the world at large, and in 1944–1945 it is safe to say that none of the artists realized what lay ahead, although a few dealers and critics were playing their hunches.

Washington art dealer David Porter followed his hunches out on a limb with a February exhibition he called "Personal Statement: Painting Prophecy, 1950." Porter, who was a friend of Peggy Guggenheim and Howard Putzel, built the show around the American artists they had introduced: Baziotes, Motherwell, Pollock, and Rothko, along with Jimmy Ernst, Gottlieb, de Kooning, Pousette Dart, and Bradley Walker Tomlin, in other words the core of the future New York School. Porter saw them as "forming a new set of painting ideologies and a new school of art, for which the war has been a catalytic agent," and he regarded the exhibition as a "prophecy of a widespread understanding of this new kind of painting five years hence."[29] He printed statements by the artists in the catalogue and characterized their works as flowing "from the artist's brush in response to a deep and spiritual need arising from the conditions of our time."

Howard Putzel, nominally Guggenheim's assistant but later acknowledged by her to have served in many ways as a mentor, seems to have grasped better than anyone the import of what was happening as he brought his discerning eye to bear on the new painting. In the summer of 1944 he announced his departure from Art of This Century in order to found his own Gallery 67. His untimely death a year later meant that he missed seeing his hunches pay off, but he had been one of the very first to appreciate Pollock and from the start was a firm supporter of Baziotes. The second exhibition at his gallery, "Forty American Moderns," brought together many of the artists who would by the end of the decade be referred to as the New York School. Putzel was no ordinary merchandiser of art. He was possessed of an intellect that sought to explore the sources of the work he exhibited; to this end he instituted informal Saturday morning discussion sessions for artists and critics at the gallery.

In the late spring Putzel perspicaciously addressed the changing situation in art with a show he called "A Problem for Critics." The problem was how to characterize or name the new art that he referred to as a "new metamorphism."[30] He thus predated by five years the more official taking up of this question in 1950 during a three-day discussion at Studio 35 among a group of the New York School artists together with Alfred Barr. That Putzel saw a blending of later Surrealism into what would eventually be called abstract expressionism is evident from his inclusion of Matta and Masson along with Gorky, Gottlieb, Hofmann, Lee Krasner, Pollock, Pousette

Richard Pousette Dart, *Figure*, 1946, oil on canvas, 80 x 50 inches; estate of the artist.

Dart, Rothko, and Seliger. (Arp, Miró, and Picasso were hung separately as forerunners.) "I believe we see real American painting beginning now," he wrote in the statement accompanying the exhibition.[31]

The critics who responded to the exhibition failed to come up with an answer to the question, but they were in accord in recognizing the problem. Robert Coates wrote: "A new school of painting is developing in this country. It is small as yet, no bigger than a baby's fist, but it is noticeable if you get around to the galleries much."[32] The *Art Digest*'s Maude Riley was more cautious: "I won't say that a new ism is not about to be born."[33] And Greenberg, although he had some reservations and caveats, endorsed the concept: "There is no question that Mr. Putzel has hold of something here."[34]

Julien Levy, discharged from the army, reopened his gallery and was somewhat disgruntled to find that the work that he had pioneered in showing during the thirties had been enjoying star billing and that others were given the credit for it. He could console himself, however, with the return of Max Ernst, liberated from Art of This Century, and take pride in the fact that it was he who introduced Arshile Gorky's recent paintings in the spring of 1945 with a catalogue essay by André Breton. This brief essay, "The Eyespring," became the penultimate chapter of the new edition of *Surrealism and Painting*, which Brentano's published that year. Breton emphasized that Gorky was, "of all the Surrealist artists, the only one who maintains direct contact with nature—sits down to paint before her," but he added that Gorky treated nature as a cryptogram, that he could "decode nature to reveal the very rhythm of life." Stating that "the key to the mental prison . . . lies in the free and unlimited play of analogies," Breton continued: "we have recently admired a canvas, signed by Gorky, entitled *The Liver Is the Comb of the Cock*, which can serve as the great door opening to the analogical world."[35]

The identification with the Surrealists, while it provided temporary support, cost Gorky painfully when it came to Greenberg, who wrote in the *Nation*, "Gorky has at last taken the easy way out, corrupted by the example of the worldly imported Surrealists."[36] By Gorky's second show a year later Greenberg had changed his mind and wrote that these were "some of the best modern paintings turned out by an American." And by early 1948 he was to declare Gorky's *Betrothal* the best work in the Whitney Annual and to write of his March 1948 show at Julien Levy: "he is the equal of any painter of his own generation, anywhere." He subsequently settled for the following line: "again he submitted his art to an influence, Matta . . . who is inveterately flashy and superficial. It took Gorky's more solid craft, profounder culture as a painter, and more selfless devotion to art to make many of Matta's ideas look substantial."[37]

The works in Gorky's first show that drew Greenberg's negative comments were indeed from what appeared to be his most automatist, that is, most free-flowing

Below: Arshile Gorky, *Water of the Flowery Mill,* 1944, oil on canvas, 42½ x 38¾ inches; Metropolitan Museum of Art, New York, George A. Hearn Fund.

phase: *Water of the Flowery Mill, How My Mother's Apron Unfolds in My Life, The Leaf of the Artichoke Is an Owl,* and *One Year the Milkweed* are characterized by an allover use of the painting surface, loosely brushed, runny paint, and separation of line from color. They lend themselves to being categorized as proto–abstract expressionist works, but here appearances are deceptive—underlying each were preliminary studies and careful deliberation quite in opposition to either automatist or abstract expressionist processes.

The Gorky exhibition took place in March, concurrently with Gottlieb's first exhibition and Pollock's second show, all staged by dealers who had previously featured Surrealism. Pollock had been in a slump until a few weeks before his show, and most of the paintings were done in a burst of energy at the last moment. One of

his few activities that winter had been to accompany his close friend Ruben Kadish to Atelier 17, now located on Eighth Street across from Pollock's apartment. Kadish, who had been an assistant to Hayter, had a key to the loft, so they would work there during hours when the place was empty, etching plates and pulling proofs. Later the story circulated that Hayter had been a teacher of Pollock, but Kadish emphasized that "Pollock did not like working in the shop nor was he carried away by etching. The plates were never editioned during his lifetime and they began to exist only after his death." [38] Despite Kadish's testimony, the prints later pulled from these plates are of genuine significance because they provide evidence for an interim stage in Pollock's transition to a more linear way of working; in addition, numbers 4, 6, 7, and 10 are the first of his works in which the entire surface is used in an allover manner. Since they were unfinished, they also provide, if one looks closely, a clue to the way the initial image is absorbed into and obliterated by the linear flow.

There are several ways in which working at Atelier 17 might have contributed to the direction in which Pollock was moving. One is the emphasis that Hayter himself put on line and the way in which his teaching stressed the allover use of the plate, especially the creation of an allover texture either through line or by means of loose woven cloth or crumpled paper pressed into a soft ground. In his essay "Line and Space of the Image," which appeared in the December 1944 issue of *View*, Hayter described his concept of "space-line" as a means of registering "imaginary space," unlimited in direction and not confined to "one order of time." He discussed "the trace" as an elementary human process, involving motion and the exercise of force,

Above: Jackson Pollock, *Untitled (7)*, 1945, printed 1967, engraving and
drypoint, printed in brown black, plate 15¾ x 23¾ inches; The Museum of
Modern Art, New York, gift of Lee Krasner Pollock.

André Masson, *Abduction (Rapt)*, 1942, printed 1958, drypoint, 12⅛ x 15¹⁵⁄₁₆ inches; anonymous extended loan to The Museum of Modern Art, New York.

but not "primarily associated with the exact reproduction of the immediate visual experience because the trace resembles astonishingly few phenomena in external nature." He then listed nine different functions of the trace or line in representation, depending on the relationship of the trace to the plane of the plate. Whether Pollock heard these ideas from Hayter himself or read them in *View*, the notion of the trace must have reinforced the direction in which he was moving.

Another possible inspiration at Atelier 17 would have been that can of bitumen (described in chapter 5) suspended on a compound pendulum, moving and dripping slowly onto the paper spread out below. Further, according to Hayter, a proof of Masson's print *Abduction (Rapt),* with its image reduced to lines running wildly over the entire surface, hung in the studio and would have been seen by Pollock.[39] The print offers a striking contrast with the artist's rape paintings and drawings of the early 1930s in the use of line not to define contour but to indicate direction and unleashed energy.

Some of the paintings hurriedly done for Pollock's March show reflect the all-over nature of his etchings as well as their linearity. *Night Mist*, for example, is a filagree of light-toned brush drawing over a dark ground in which there are virtually no solidly painted shapes. Distinctions between positive and negative space break down, leaving a surface covered with gestural markings. This is the manner in which all nine of the plates he etched were carried out. Whether he cared for printmaking or not, the nature of the process dictated the use of line, and for Pollock also line was becoming a trajectory rather than a means of defining a contour.

Nearly half of the thirteen paintings in the March exhibition were in light tones on dark grounds. In this Pollock followed Masson who, in order to suggest processes going on within the earth, had begun in 1942 to use a flattened synthetic space with a flow of bright colored shapes and lines over black grounds. Other Pollock canvases from that show, such as the *Portrait of H.M.,* however, consisted of a struggle between the lights and darks, with each continually overlapping the other and staccato strokes of black and white imposing a diagonal organization. Also shown was the 9-foot *There Were Seven in Eight* which he had started after the Guggenheim mural and allowed to lie fallow for nearly a year. When he finally renewed his attack on the canvas, he was unable to give it the rhythmic unity of *Mural* and the result is little more than eclectic chaos. His final addition to this painting was a thin, looping, back-circling black line overrunning the canvas as if he thought that this would tie the disparate elements into a whole. It is similar to the line used by Masson in *Abduction (Rapt)* or his own line in the etchings he had just done.

Matta did an even larger canvas, *X Space and the Ego,* for his show the same month at Pierre Matisse, and the race for size was on. In general, limitations of space and funds had obliged artists to work on modest-size canvases; when Richard Pousette Dart painted his ten-foot *Symphony No. 1, the Transcendental* in 1942, other painters shook their heads over the futility of working on such a scale unless it was a commissioned work. However, there is little doubt that Pollock's Guggenheim *Mural* posed a challenge, goading painters to work on a heroic scale and to consider the new relationship with the canvas that this imposed on both artist and viewer. Matta rose to the challenge with two fourteen-foot paintings, *Science, conscience et patience du vitreur* and *X Space.*

Size was only one of the attention-getting components of Matta's new canvases: his previously uninhabited paintings appeared to have been taken over by invaders

Jackson Pollock, *Night Mist,* 1945, oil on canvas, 36 x 74 inches; Norton Gallery of Art, West Palm Beach, Florida.

Top: Richard Pousette Dart, *Symphony No. 1, the Transcendental,* 1942, oil on canvas, 90 x 120 inches; estate of the artist.

Bottom: Matta, *X Space and the Ego,* 1945, oil on canvas, 202.2 x 457.2 cm; Centre Georges Pompidou, Musée National d'Art Moderne.

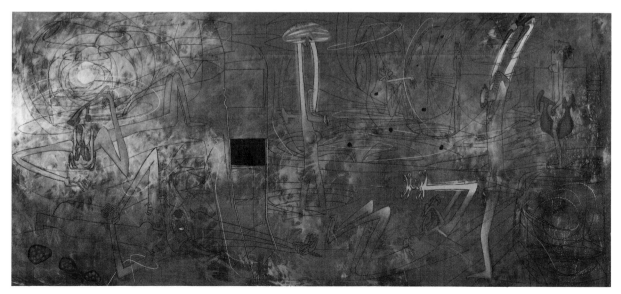

from another planet. Faceless quasi-human tubular figures were twisted into contorted poses or galvanized by a current from the wiry lines that spun in loops and circles across the surface of these new works. Were these the "Great Transparents" that Matta had illustrated for Breton when he announced his new myth in the first issue of *VVV*? Was their shape inspired by Giacometti's *Invisible Object,* the plaster for which Matta had just acquired? or by Hopi kachinas? or by Wifredo Lam's elongated jungle figures? All have been suggested as sources. Matta has said that he introduced these totem-personages because he wanted to deal with the full scope of history, in particular the revelations that were beginning to reach the West about the extent of the deportations and the fate of millions of deportees. He leaves it ambiguous as to whether his humanoids are perpetrators or victims. They are all caught up in something sadistic and terrifying, but the activity takes place on a dehumanized plane where the viewer cannot find a point of entry.

Without the seductive color and vertiginous but alluring spaces, Matta's new paintings verged on the cartoonish, leading Greenberg to actually refer to him as "that little comic stripper." Even Breton was initially upset by this change in direction, so much so that Matta painted out his first large populated canvas. The American painters who had been influenced by Matta could not follow him into this new literal style. Kamrowski accused him of "doing science fiction." They had been able to ignore the occult element that had entered later Surrealism as long as it was veiled in abstraction, leaving interpretation as an intuitive and personal matter. When it surfaced in illustrational form they parted ways with their former mentor.

Paalen, whose show followed that of Pollock at Art of This Century, was also involved with a new kind of supernatural figuration in his *Cosmogons*. For all his attention to physics and his extensive scientific library, Paalen apparently needed some form of suprahuman being to personify physical forces. About this time he wrote the script for a play, *The Cosmonauts,* that features just such humanoids in a science fiction setting. In explaining his Cosmogon series to Gustav Regler he spoke of the *constellation man,* which reappears among the orbiting particles of interstellar space "to represent the human presence reintegrated into this universe. . . . The radiant curves coordinate themselves into great 'personnages' which are the new protagonists of the eternal Promethean play." [40]

However, what was visible in the paintings that projected from the curved walls at Art of This Century was a system of disconnected rectangular marks of the brush that lent itself to interpretation as a kind of atomic vision appropriate to a period when the formula $E = mc^2$ was entering into public knowledge. In other words Paalen's new paintings could be seen as a portrayal of matter as energy, sometimes cohering, sometimes dispersed over a field, and as such they contributed to the form-dissolving process that was changing the look of painting.

Opposite: Enrico Donati, *Feet after Magritte,* for Brentano's window on the occasion of the publication of Breton's *Le Surréalisme et la peinture,* 1945; photograph courtesy of the artist.

Dedicated as it was to the showcasing of American art, the Whitney Museum had taken little cognizance of the émigré presence until it was about to come to an end. From March 13 to April 11 the Whitney's smallish quarters on Eighth Street played host to "European Artists in America," in recognition of "the international spirit which has played so important a part in the American art of our day." However, the museum's approach was, as *View*'s reviewer put it, "encyclopedic" rather than selective, so that the impact of specific artists like Masson, Tanguy, and Ernst was watered down by the inclusion of all the refugee artists who could be identified. The exhibition marked the end of a period during which American art had been inseminated, so to speak, by a European presence. Less than a month after the show closed came the unconditional surrender of Germany on May 8, and the refugees now could contemplate a return to Europe. But return was not a simple matter. For many a partial assimilation into American life and into a culture transformed by their presence made the choice to return difficult. Most postponed the decision until the situation in Europe stabilized and many eventually chose to remain in the United States.

Of the Surrealists only Masson made immediate plans to go back to France. Breton, who had been so uncomfortable during his exile, now got some inkling of what would lie ahead on his return to Paris from the reception given Sartre when he arrived in New York in January 1945 as a correspondant for *Combat,* a single-sheet newspaper of opposition that had been founded in Algeria by Albert Camus in 1943. Eight French journalists were invited by the State Department for a two-month stay. In New York they were put up at the Plaza Hotel and dressed by a Fifth Avenue department store courtesy of the Office of War Information. They were feted and regarded as heroes and invited to the White House, where they met Roosevelt just weeks before the President's death; they also had the opportunity to meet with the European exiles, notably Mann, Brecht, and Marcuse. Although Sartre arrived with a journalist's credentials, he soon became the subject of interviews himself. A new word, existentialism, began to be bandied about in intellectual circles and was even explained in *Time* magazine, while photographs of Sartre appeared widely in the press. John Meyers recorded in his journal the following exchange in the *View* office:

"I think," said Charles one afternoon, "that Surrealism is on its way out."

"And what is on its way in?" I asked.

"Existentialism, Honey. Existentialism." [41]

Meyers reported that the lecture by Sartre sponsored by *View* filled the Carnegie Recital Hall "to the rafters" and that half the audience was "people from the 57th Street art world." Sartre's *No Exit* was produced by Oliver Smith in a translation by Paul Bowles, and a Greenwich Village chanteuse, Stella Brooks, added to her repertoire a song called "Existentialism Blues."

The attraction of the French philosopher (Sartre himself refused that designation) lay primarily in the aura that accompanied him of one who had not capitulated during the Occupation but had nurtured the spirit of resistance, if not its actual practice. His philosophy, as explained by *Time*—"One is free to act, but one must act to be free"—was well suited to the needs of the moment, as it replaced sectarian ideology with a open-ended program of engagement. Furthermore he represented the non-Communist opposition, which made him acceptable to the Trotskyist intellectuals and useful in terms of the American postwar policy of containing communism then being formulated. His belief that "we can only make ourselves absolute by fighting passionately in our time, by loving it passionately and by consenting to perish entirely with it"[42] could be as applicable to the Cold War as it had been to the Occupation.

One would not know from Sartre's dispatches to *Combat* that a substantial wartime French colony even existed in New York; there was not a word of significant reunions or the activities of the Free French. He wrote disappointingly superficial reports on the United States—the New Yorker eats two pounds of meat a week, mostly chopped beef; there is full employment with wages up to sixty cents an hour; there is a fixation on mechanical equipment, refrigerators, telephones; the crowds seem to be without gaiety—but probably gave the French, still suffering severe deprivations, the kind of information they wanted to hear. This de Toquevillian impulse to scrutinize Americans stemmed from a growing awareness of the part they were to play in the postwar world and a dawning recognition that the role of France was diminished as decisions continued to be made in tripartite meetings of the Americans, British, and Soviets.

Breton learned during the course of a long meeting with Sartre that the press in liberated Paris was dominated by the Stalinists and that consequently his antagonists Eluard and Aragon were in positions of power. Sartre's reports on the strength of the Communists in France influenced Breton's decision to postpone his return and, casting about for a source of income, he asked Pierre Mabille, now a cultural attaché, to arrange for him to lecture in Haiti. In the meantime for Breton the regular round of group activities subsided in importance, although he continued to write introductions for artists' catalogues and even contemplated a new issue of *VVV* consecrated to the theme of liberty. He added his American adherents to the new edition of *Surrealism and Painting* that Brentano's published in 1945. To mark the occasion Donati worked with Duchamp and Matta on the display for the store's Fifth Avenue window. Reproduced on the jacket of the book was the famous Magritte painting of feet metamorphosing into shoes. For the window Donati fabricated a three-dimensional version of the feet/shoes. Perhaps it was the nearly naked headless mannequin that disturbed Bretano's; at any rate the whole thing had to be moved around the corner to the Gotham Book Mart on 47th Street.

An earlier Surrealist-originated Brentano's window marking the publication of de Rougemont's *La Part du Diable* had been allowed to stay in place. For that window Seligmann had painted a background of diabolic emblems borrowed from sixteenth-century occultists; from the ceiling Duchamp had finally been able to suspend open umbrellas that looked like bat wings; an antiques dealer loaned his collection of figurines of the devil from fifteen countries; and in the center a few fistfuls of Mexican jumping beans trembled on a black-covered table. From time to time crowds gathered as a passing exorcist was moved to try his powers in front of the window.

Jubilation over the end of the war in Europe was not without its sobering counterpart in the accumulated reports and actual news photos that had been coming out of German territory occupied by Allied troops. On April 13 *Combat* printed a detailed description of the heaps of bodies stacked liked dried kindling in the just-liberated Buchenwald camp, where the living were barely distinguishable from the dead. That same day de Gaulle met with the repatriated women from Ravensbruck to hear the accounts of the surviving one-third of the 150,000 women who had been imprisoned there. It would still be months before the full extent of the death camp toll would be known, and years before the release of the film footage made by the British army recording the naked walking male and female skeletons that provided forced labor in Hitler's underground munitions factories. In January Lincoln Kirstein writing from France for the *Magazine of Art* described the retrospective honoring Max Jacob, the poet friend of Apollinaire and Picasso who had died or committed suicide at the deportation camp of Drancy. Not until the fall of 1945 did his former colleagues receive definitive word of the death of the Surrealist poet Robert Desnos, whose hypnotic trances had been so important for 1920s Surrealism. Desnos had been arrested and deported for activities in the underground press during the occupation. After being shifted from Buchenwald to a camp in Czechoslovakia he was one of 800 wasted prisoners who took to the road when their camp was abandoned by the retreating Germans. Only thirty had the strength to survive; Desnos was one of the hundreds to die of typhus, recognized at the last from the one poem he carried with him by the young intern who cared for him in his final hours. Desnos's earlier essay on Duchamp had appeared that spring in the special Duchamp issue of *View*.

They were also to learn the tragic fate of Sylvain Itkine, the radical theater director who had participated in the Surrealists' activities at Air Bel. Arrested by the

French police for Resistance activities, he had been turned over to the Gestapo, tortured, and killed. In December 1944 Péret wrote a newsy letter from Mexico to the Surrealist poet Robert Rius, not knowing that he had been shot six months earlier. Rius had been captured when he attempted to join the Maquis in the Forest of Fontainebleau in June. Months after the liberation the *charnier* of Fontainebleau was discovered and Jean François Chabrun, who went to identify the body, could only recognize Rius by the ski boots that he had loaned him.

As these and countless other grim facts emerged it must have dawned on the émigrés that the reintegration in postwar France of those who had spent the war years in New York was going to have its problematic aspects. The outlook for the Surrealist contingent, known for being antiwar and anti-Stalinist, was particularly bleak, as they might have gathered if they read René Huyghe's "Letter from Paris" in the *Magazine of Art* in November. Huyghe, chief curator of paintings at the Louvre, wrote: "Applied to the surface of yesterday's world, surrealism, that corrosive, digs out of it unthought of and curious designs, but when that world has been resurrected, one no longer dreams of discrediting what remains to it. Thus surrealism is dead." [43]

In the summer of 1945 Breton and Elisa went to Reno for a divorce and remarriage, which took place on July 31. He carried with him on the long train trip the complete works of the nineteenth-century utopian socialist Charles Fourier and spent the required six-week waiting period in Nevada in the study of Fourier's views on social harmony. He began writing his "Ode to Fourier" in the garden of their Reno lodgings and subsequently incorporated some of his impressions of the Zuñi and Hopi villages they visited with Jeanne Reynal. Reynal came from California to meet them in Reno and drove them to Tahoe and Virginia City. She described Breton, ever on the lookout for the marvelous, as having been fascinated by the minerals as he climbed over the dumps at Silver City, combing them for crystals. After their marriage she drove the Bretons to Santa Fe via the Grand Canyon. Along the way they explored the mesas looking for petroglyphs and stopped at pueblos where they saw "the extraordinary Indian dances—the antelope dance and the snake dances which are very beautiful with the men and snakes as brothers showing no fear." Reynal described this trip to Agnes Gorky: "We saw so much that was beautiful and we owe all this to André you know who put it on a plane of exaltation where one hopes really to remain forever, but of course one will slip back too fast, very much too fast, into the rut predestined." She also reported that "André thinks Gorky's work is more important than anything else. He thinks he should go to Paris." [44]

Breton rounded out his stay in the Western Hemisphere with several months in Haiti, where Pierre Mabille had arranged a series of lectures. Since an uprising took place on the day following one of his lectures, he took credit for having inspired it; this has often been repeated as historical fact, but eyewitnesses maintain that it had been in the making long before Breton came on the scene. He did have the opportunity to attend voodoo ceremonies and was fascinated with "the Haitian will to transform the world of everyday appearances and capacity for surrendering reality to higher powers." While in Haiti Breton was shown a copy of the just-published *L'Histoire du surréalisme* by Maurice Nadeau. That this first French attempt to write an objective historical account should end so definitively in 1940, giving the impression that there was no place for Surrealism in liberated France, upset Breton no end. Had no one in France read the articles he had contributed during the war to *Fontaine* or more recently to *Labyrinthe*? (Fontaine had been published monthly during the war in small print on cheap paper in Algiers by Max Pol Fouchet and distributed in the unoccupied zone. Not only had it printed Breton's Yale lecture and selections from his "Prolegomena to a Third Manifesto" but it had reproduced the artists-in-exile photo and described *View* and *VVV*, the latter as a successor to *Minotaure*.) He began to wonder just what kind of reception lay ahead in Europe, and his doubts were not calmed by his meeting in March with *Combat*'s editor, Albert Camus, who reiterated that Communist organizations controlled the press and publishing in postwar France. What role would be left to him and his colleagues in the face of the all-powerful National Committee of Intellectuals that had emerged out of the Resistance?

In the fall of 1945 Peggy Guggenheim staged an Autumn Salon. Nine of the twenty-nine artists included were to be part of the core New York School, as it was to be immortalized in a famous *Life* magazine photograph in 1951 under the heading "the Irascibles." New to the gallery were de Kooning, Pousette Dart, Gottlieb, and Clyfford Still. De Kooning exhibited *The Wave*, the closest he came to a kind of biomorphic Surrealism. Only two of the one-time Surrealists, Hayter and Paalen, were included. Although Tanguy, Ernst, Seligmann, and Matta remained in the United States in the immediate postwar years and continued to exhibit, visibility as a group had virtually come to an end as far as New York was concerned. New York's new importance was noted by art dealer Daniel Henry Kahnweiler, who had been in hiding in France during the war. Writing on the state of painting in Paris he commented: "It has been suggested that the center of painting has shifted and that New York has become a modern Alexandria, an international metropolis of the arts."[45]

In the avant-garde slot created by and for the émigrés, appropriating some of their ideas as well as the support system that had formed around them, a new loosely structured American group was taking shape. It had no platform; it had no poet-

spokesman; and no one knew what to call it, let alone how to describe it. Its tentative nature is exemplified by both the title and contents of the single-issue journal *Possibilities* that Motherwell and Rosenberg brought out in 1947. If there was anything these artists held in common in 1945 it was their open-ended approach to art, the value they placed on the act of painting directly from "the self," and their stance of truculent individualism. The existence of this ad hoc group, combined with the vacuum left by the retreating Europeans, made it evident even before V.E. Day that an expanded and transformed abstract surrealism was the likely heir apparent to European modernism and would provide the art movement required by the United States postwar role as the world's strongest economic and military power. Both the artists and the critical, curatorial, and marketing apparatus were falling into place by the end of 1945. When Pollock's old friend James Brooks got out of the army he found that "the New York School was all set up."[46] Brooks, whose last painting before the war was the 240-foot *History of Flight,* found that he had a lot of catching up to do if he was going to play in the same league as his old friends. Because many others also missed or overlooked or deliberately forgot the beginning of abstract expressionism and the catalytic role of the Surrealist émigrés, the story tended to disappear as American painting moved toward its triumph in the postwar years.

Opposite: Willem de Kooning, *The Wave,* ca. 1942–1944, oil on fiberboard, 48 x 48 inches; National Museum of American Art, Smithsonian Institution.

Below: Arshile Gorky, *The Unattainable,* 1945, oil on canvas, 104.8 x 74.3 cm; The Baltimore Museum of Art.

Paris, 1945–1947:

In the Time

of Lean Cows

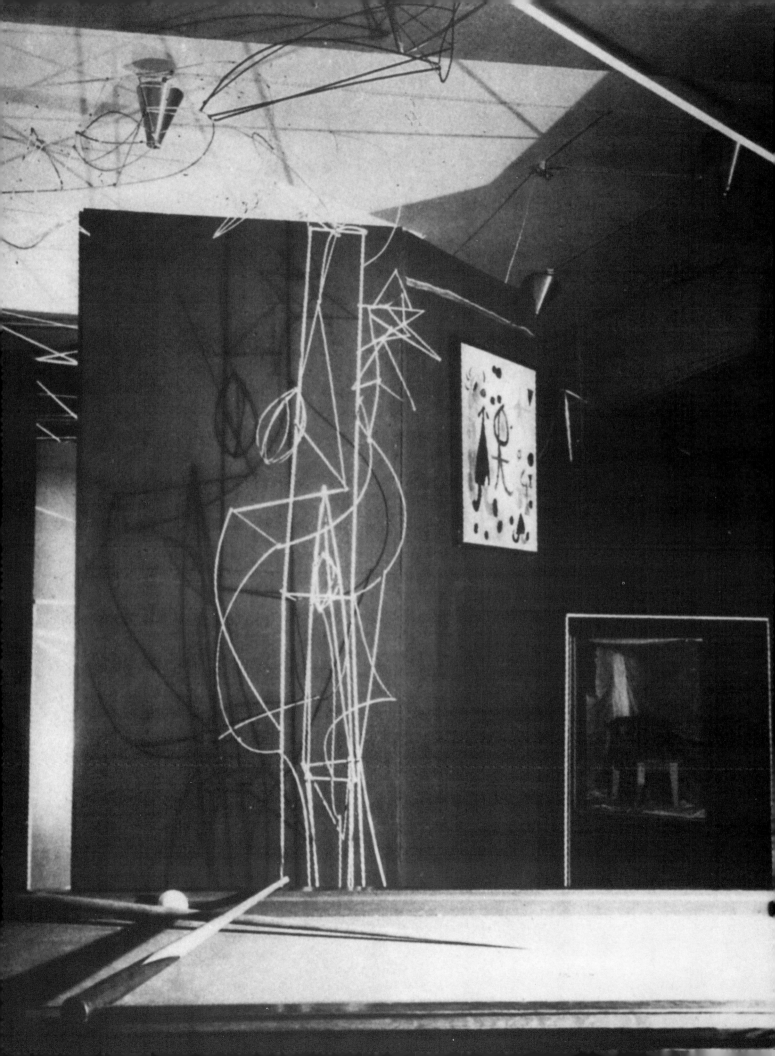

The liberation of Paris in the summer of 1944 and the final surrender of Germany in May of 1945 were followed by a period of recriminations and political feuding that has left a mark on half a century of French intellectual life. Even as Franco-German cooperation grows, a bitter dialogue continues between old adversaries within a factionalized France. In the immediate postwar years the situation was envenomed by many intellectuals who chose to flaunt their antagonisms rather than to resolve old differences. People were quick to join the game of "resistancialism" and to hide the many forms of collaboration in which they had participated. The leadership of the left inflamed the working classes against the "collaborationist bourgeoisie" and claimed sole proprietorship of the Resistance, which took on increasingly heroic and mythic proportions.

There was little talk of the role of the French police in sending more than 200,000 French Jews to Drancy and other deportation camps and turning over to the Gestapo the German aliens who had taken refuge in France. There was little mention of the art galleries that had catered unabashedly to the Nazis or of the artists who, in order to exhibit, had signed the register asserting that they were French and were not Jewish, while the middle-of-the-road painting that had met with Vichy and Nazi approval continued to flourish in the postwar art world.[1] To be sure, there were scapegoats and showy trials and a few suicides, notably that of the editor of the *Nouvelle Revue Française,* Drieu La Rochelle (Laval also attempted it). Joining in the witch hunt for the major offenders seemed to be a way of exonerating oneself for the minor acts of collaboration that many had found necessary for survival. As for those who had spent the war years in the United States, few returned to positions of influence in postwar France, although there are exceptions such as Pierre Lazareff who became editor of the conservative newspaper *France Soir.* Decades later the questions "Was it necessary to leave France? Was it necessary to stay despite the risks? are still being debated."[2]

Since the major figures of the Surrealist movement had been absent from France and since their earlier antiwar, antinationalist position had been loudly proclaimed, there can have been little expectation that Surrealism could reclaim its prewar avant-garde leadership. Such was, nonetheless, the hope of the group of young writers and artists, led by Noël Arnaud, who had endeavored to keep Surrealism alive in France during the war years with a series of clandestine publications appearing under the imprint of La Main à Plume. The group responsible for this literary production had put it out at great risk, moving constantly from one location to another, falsifying a censor's number, and participating in various Resistance activities. Their first pamphlet, dated May 1941, called for a rallying of Surrealists—"it is the duty of all the Surrealists to raise their hand." They managed to put out some thirty collective and individual pamphlet-style publications during the war years, among them the first French publication of Breton's *Pleine marge*, contributions from Picasso, Arp, and Eluard, and work by the young writers of the group. Their efforts were reinforced by Brauner and Hérold, who had gradually made their way back to Paris. As peace approached, however, and their political differences became stronger than the common enemy that had held them together, they broke up in factionalism, and their publications ceased in May 1944. Since Arnaud, like the preponderance of those who had carried on clandestine anti-Nazi activities, was allied with the Communists, there was little likelihood of forming a united Surrealist front with the returning émigrés.

And where were those older figures around whom the wartime Surrealists might have rallied when peace came? Breton, as we have seen, had sought to delay his return because of the unpropitious political climate in postwar France. Marcel Duchamp was in New York, choosing not to return to "that basket of crabs" as he referred to Paris.[3] Max Ernst had married the American painter Dorothea Tanning (at a double ceremony in Los Angeles with Man Ray and Juliet Browner) and they were homesteading in Sedona, Arizona. Tanguy was pining for France and consoling himself with martinis in rural Connecticut. Miró, having spent the war years in Spain, was in the United States working on a mural for a Cincinnati hotel. The Masson family returned to France in October 1945, but they were living with one of Rose's sisters near Poitiers. There Masson was celebrating peace and the survival of Rose's family by painting the French landscape, quite putting aside the flattened way of working and the telluric themes he had taken up in Connecticut. The dark grounds of so many of his U.S. works had given way to an obsession with light. A few months after his return an exhibition of the work Masson had done in exile was held at the Leiris Gallery (formerly the Galerie Simon which had been the gallery of Kahnweiler, forced to change its name and ownership during the war). Evidently there was considerable anticipation over the prospect of seeing the work of the first artist returned from New York. At least one reviewer found Masson's show reassuring. Calling it one of the most important shows in Paris, he wrote:

One might have feared that far from the Parisian ambience, the works painted by artists during their *séjour américain* might have suffered from the unfavorable surroundings and become sterilized. The evolution of Masson shows on the contrary a detente of the surrealist cerebration toward a stronger pictorial tendency. The figures are almost absorbed into abstraction, guided by plastic necessity, and more importance is given to color.[4]

Among the paintings Masson exhibited was one of the last works he had painted in the United States, *Elk Attacked by Dogs,* from his series on the theme of Actaeon, the youth who was turned to a stag and devoured by his own hounds. This painting could easily give rise to the reviewer's observation that the "figures are almost absorbed into abstraction." Although a similar observation might have been made about some of Masson's rape paintings of the early 1930s, the new work was far more painterly and gestural, so that the image was dissolved in the energized surface created by the activity of the brushstrokes and the texture of the pigment. In many ways the painting seems closer to canvases Pollock was to paint in 1946 or to the late 1940s work of de Kooning than to Masson's own paintings of a few years earlier. However, it was to be a while before Masson himself built on the work of his American period. Instead he spent months drawing the landscape with particular attention to its shimmering qualities of light, as if, as he himself said, in celebration

Above: André Masson, *Elk Attacked by Dogs,* 1945, oil on canvas, 20⅛ x 25⅛ inches; Hirshhorn Museum and Sculpture Garden, Smithsonian Institution, Gift of Joseph Hirshhorn.

of peace and the French countryside. Curt Valentin continued to show his work in New York and to fulfill the requests of the Masson family for some of the items they missed in that postwar time of austerity in France. Not until the mid-1950s did Masson begin to recapitulate aspects of his American work, even to the extent of experimenting with quick-drying paint and the gestural effects used by Pollock whose work he went to Geneva to see.

It was late May of 1946 when Breton finally crossed the courtyard at 42 rue Fontaine and climbed the four curving flights of stairs to the studio apartment that he had occupied from 1921 to 1940. A friend had stayed in the apartment during part of his absence and his father had continued to pay the rent; he found the paintings, African carvings, and flea market objects as he had left them. However, during the skirmishes that had preceded the liberation of Paris bullets had broken the skylight, and Breton attached great significance to the fact that one had lodged in the temple of a plaster mask of Paul Eluard. They had no money; rain poured through the broken skylight; and he, Elisa, and Aube had to live in the studio and one small adjoining room. Not only was the Paris to which he had returned austere in the immediate postwar years, but it was also by no means disposed to issue a hero's welcome to those who had fled to the Western Hemisphere. The press, as he had been forewarned, was dominated by the Communists; Sartre occupied the intellectual position of the greatest visibility; the old Surrealist group could not be reconstituted since most were still in the West or were, for Breton, politically unacceptable, having aligned themselves with the Communist Party.

There was a moment of hope when Breton received a visit from Noël Arnaud, the young poet who had kept the flame of Surrealism alive during the occupation, but it soon became apparent that their Trotskyist/Stalinist differences would prevent a united front. Arnaud and his youthful colleagues, Jacques Bureau, Jean-François Chabrun, and Marc Patin, addressed a critical letter to Breton, maintaining that they had kept faith with Surrealism under the most difficult circumstances while he had, in effect, deserted.[5] How deep the resentments ran against those who had spent the Occupation years abroad may be judged from the words written by Chabrun thirty years later:

We also have played "exquisite corpses." With folded scraps of paper. And also in quite another way. Killed, shot, exterminated in concentration camps, fallen with weapons in hand, eight dead, that's a lot, a lot for a group which had scarcely fifteen regular members, sometimes twenty or twenty-five at most. The heavy silence of the dead paralyzes us who were—who are forever—amputated of them.[6]

Georges Bataille commented on the return of his one-time colleagues, emphasizing the contrasting programs of engagement and nonengagement of Surrealism and existentialism:

The surrealist decision is thus a decision not to make decisions (the free play of the spirit would be betrayed if I subordinated it to some predetermined result). The profound difference between surrealism and the existentialism of Jean Paul Sartre lies in the nature of the existence of freedom. If I don't enslave it, freedom will exist. Poetry, words, no longer having to serve a useful function, break loose and this letting loose is the image of the free existence, which can only exist in the instant.[7]

Word of Breton's activities in New York had preceded his return. As we have seen, his Yale lecture on "Surrealism between the Wars" had been printed in *Fontaine* and circulated in Vichy France. In February and March of 1945 the text he had written for the book on Peggy Guggenheim's collection, "Genesis and Artistic Perspectives of Surrealism," was published in *Labyrinthe*, Albert Skira's new Geneva-based review of the arts. *Labyrinthe* had made its debut shortly after the liberation of Paris and, although published in Switzerland, it was essentially occupied with the French cultural scene at a time when France, still at war and in economic disarray, could not manage such a publication. Although it was printed in black and white on cheap paper in a newspaper format in contrast with its lavish predecessor *Minotaure*, its texts by a variety of well-known authors, accompanied by copious, well-printed illustrations, offered a good preview of what the artistic priorities and issues of post-war Paris might be. In short, it provides a perspective of the intellectual climate that greeted the returning Breton.

While *Minotaure* had been preempted in midstream by the Surrealists, *Labyrinthe* appeared determinedly pluralistic, featuring Eluard, Breton, and Sartre in turn. Its contents included reproductions of past and contemporary art and articles dealing with photography, film, and literature, including recent American novels, as well as summaries of reviews in the Paris press when they began to appear. Despite the statement by Charly Guyot in the January 1945 issue that "today's heros are Sartre, Beauvoir, Camus, Malraux, and Aragon,"[8] the next issue contained selections from the Buenos Aires edition of Breton's *Fata Morgana* and an announcement of his imminent return to Europe. Max Pol Fouchet, interviewed for the June issue, gave front place in contemporary literature to Camus and Sartre and referred to Malraux as "the most important and most intelligent writer in France today. . . . These three have a tremendous influence on the young intellectuals." Asked if he is forgetting Surrealism, he replied, "Surrealism remains the most important accomplishment in French literature since 1918. Nothing is more important. Far from being dead, it is giving us wonderful works: *Un beau ténébreux* by Julien Gracq, for example. Many of us wait with impatience the return of André Breton from New York."[9]

In August André Rousseau contributed a letter from Paris headed "Du Surréalisme à Jean Paul Sartre," in which he envisaged a need to prolong and renew Surrealism as a revolt against "pretended realities" and was critical of Sartre's nihilism and his view of a humanity closed to love.[10] Yet a few months later *Labyrinthe* printed an introduction by Jean Cassou, Resistance activist and curator at the Louvre, to a new book by Tristan Tzara. "Surrealism," wrote Cassou, "enclosed itself in the obligation to pursue at all costs, frenetically, arrogantly the issue of a transcendence which it was only willing to find in itself. It thus attributed to itself a power which in the final analysis consisted of imitating or pretending to have the powers of that which primitives and occultists called magic."[11]

There followed an excerpt from a forthcoming preface by Sartre, "La Liberté cartésienne," and a description of the first issue of a new review directed by Sartre, *Les Temps Modernes,* whose slogan was "for a literature of engagement" and whose contents included a short story by Richard Wright, political commentary by Raymond Aron, and Merleau-Ponty's "La Guerre a eu lieu." Deciding that it owed its readers a clarification of existentialism, *Labyrinthe* then published an article by Jean Wahl that began: "There is a lot of talk about Existentialism in Paris and Greenwich Village; here is a brief history of the theories." He traced the contributions of Kierkegaard, Jaspers, and Heidegger and discussed Sartre's transformation of Heidegger. In conclusion, he wrote, "To be or not to be has once more become the question; we are seeing a new mode of philosophy, not of essence, but of existence."[12] That spring, under the sponsorship of *Labyrinthe,* Sartre and Beauvoir made a lecture tour in Switzerland.

Thus the postwar intellectual battleground of the left—it should be remembered that the Communists held a third of the seats in the reconstituted Assembly and together with the Socialists formed a majority—was laid out as a three-way contest between the non-Communist left led by Sartre and Camus, Breton and the Trotskyist Surrealists, and dedicated adherents of the Communist Party like Aragon, Eluard, and Tzara. One thing was certain: Sartre, referred to by some as a café messiah, had moved up to star billing. Breton had for three decades been able to annex to Surrealism some of the most iconoclastic talents of his day. In the decimated intellectual world of Paris in the mid-forties, as the crimes perpetrated by the Nazis and their French collaborators unfolded daily, the revolution in consciousness seemed less crucial than recovery from the wounds of war and the immediate political struggle going on that would determine the future of France. Sartre's open-ended philosophy of engagement had more practical application both retrospectively to the war years and to the postwar situation than Breton's policy of detachment.

Nonetheless Breton still had some clout, and soon after his return a photograph of him with his collection of kachinas was published in *Le Littéraire* together with an interview.[13] He was called on to participate in a gathering at the Théâtre Sara-Bernhardt in support of Antonin Artaud, who had been released from the Rodez

asylum. When Breton met with his cohort of the 1920s at the Deux Magots, he found that Artaud was convinced that he, Breton, had died ten years earlier and that in his present incarnation he was the tool of his enemies. Despite his dislike of speaking in public Breton appeared at the theater where the *tout Paris* was gathered, some say as much to see the returned Breton as to pay homage to the outcast Artaud. Hailing Artaud, Breton said that in another society, less imbued with rationalism, "he would have been a shaman because he had passed to the other side of the mirror and had seen what it is not given to the rest of use to know."[14] Taking up the question of existentialism, he insisted that he had nothing but derision for all forms of engagement that were not directed toward his own triple objective: to transform the world, change life, and restructure human consciousness.[15]

Encouraged by the number of young people who made contact with him, Breton set about reconstituting a Surrealist group. He gathered together old members such as Victor Brauner, Jacques Hérold, and Marcel Jean, along with new young recruits, and the daily meetings at the Deux Magots or the café in the Place Blanche recommenced. One of these youthful recruits, Alain Jouffroy, has described the pro-

Above: André Breton in his apartment in the rue Fontaine with a Hopi kachina, *Le Littéraire* 29, October 1946.

cess by which Breton drew him into the group following their meeting at an inn at Huelgoat in the Finistère in the summer of 1946. Arriving at a gathering at the café in the Place Blanche in response to a telegram from Breton, Jouffroy, who was eighteen at the time, found himself being proposed for inclusion and passed on by the assembled group, who all voted in the affirmative so as not to displease Breton.[16]

By the end of 1946 Breton began to feel that it was time to give a sign that Surrealism had survived and was alive and well in postwar Paris and he began consulting with Duchamp, who was in Paris in the early winter, about a possible manifestation. In February the following announcement appeared in *Combat:*

Since his return André Breton has been content to observe. Now he is preparing, in close secrecy, his reentry and that of the Surrealist group, a sensational exhibit to be held in the month of May. The director of one of the most luxurious Paris galleries has agreed and it is said that he is even underwriting the cost. It will be a "grand plat surréaliste" with Duchamp as the great producer—one counts on him not simply to repeat the exhibition of 1938. . . . But Surrealism is not true to itself without dissidence and excommunications. It is considered today that Picasso has no claim to Surrealism; others who are excluded are thinking of grouping around him for a different exhibition.[17]

The gallery in question was the prestigious Maeght Gallery in the rue de Teheran. Its director, Aimé Maeght, was attempting to enliven a dull Paris art scene still bereft of many of the major prewar dealers who had taken refuge in New York. He lived, of course, from the art of the past, according to Jacques Kober who managed the gallery, but he wanted to present exhibitions that were exciting and forward-looking. When approached by Breton, Maeght decided that it would be good publicity to host a major Surrealist manifestation and that the gallery was large enough to accommodate the proposed exhibition. He did not foresee the complicated and expensive installation and the problems he would have with the landlord over the curtain of rain that was part of the Duchamp/Kiesler plan. And he may not have been aware of the potential consequences of the political feuds that surrounded Surrealism.

Breton sent out a letter of invitation in which he voiced his hope of surpassing all their earlier manifestations in the expression of the search for a new myth. He proposed a layout that would retrace the successive phases of an initiation. On the ground floor would appear the pre-Surrealists and "those who have ceased to gravitate in its orbit: Chirico, Picasso, Masson, Dalí, Paalen, Magritte, Domínguez." The twenty-one steps leading to the gallery's upper level were to represent the spines of books with titles corresponding to the twenty-one major arcana of the Tarot, le Mat or Fou excepted. A Hall of Superstitions to be realized by Kiesler, Duchamp, and

Matta was to open onto a labyrinth composed of twelve octagonal recesses, each containing an altar like those used in voodoo with propitiatory offerings dedicated to a being linked to one of the twelve signs of the zodiac. In the remaining spaces works submitted by all those who regarded themselves as Surrealists were to be installed. Breton included a plan of the gallery and described the specifications for altars, calling upon each recipient of his letter to submit proposals for their participation in the exhibition.[18] Among the acquiescent responses to Breton's letter, the negative reaction of Artaud stands out. Rejecting the concept of ritual initiation, he called for "active, energetic, irredeemable, and perpetual insurrection against everything that pretends to exist."[19]

Already in February Maeght was protesting over the expense into which the Surrealists were leading him, but when Breton suggested he might cancel the show, Maeght decided he didn't want to lose the publicity the exhibition would bring, despite the cost.[20] However, Maeght didn't wait for the Surrealist International Exhibition to begin his attempts to enliven the dormant Paris art scene. In the spring he imported an exhibition of the work of experimental American artists from the newly opened Kootz Gallery in New York. Included were the very artists who had been most influenced by the European émigrés and who had been introduced by Peggy Guggenheim and Howard Putzel—Baziotes, Gottlieb, and Motherwell—as well as Romare Bearden, Carl Holty, and Byron Browne.

In his brief text for the catalogue Harold Rosenberg asserted that these six American painters "had applied to the needs of their special passions the international idiom of twentieth century painting—an idiom that . . . achieves much of its energy, inventiveness and glory . . . through assimilating all national vestiges into a transcendental world style." Rosenberg also tilted the motivation of these artists toward existentialism, writing of their "unique loneliness of a depth that is reached perhaps nowhere else in the world" [!] and of their belief in "their ability to dissociate some personal essence of their experience and rescue it as the beginning of a new world."[21]

The show was a financial and critical disaster. Jean José Marchand, reviewing the show for *Combat,* characterized the Americans as derivative pasticheurs who couldn't paint and he found in the show ample cause for what he called "American art's inferiority complex vis-à-vis Europe."[22] The show was indeed premature both from the standpoint of the work included and from that of a French culture struggling to maintain its identity in the face of an American onslaught, most acutely felt in the area of film, with literature a close second.

In the months before the Surrealist exhibition opened Breton and his reconstituted group were embroiled in a number of controversies that bear out Duchamp's characterization of Paris as a "basket of crabs." The founder of Dada, Tristan Tzara, was now a Stalinist, and he called on the Surrealists to unite with the Communists for an engaged art. When Tzara was scheduled to lecture in the great amphitheater of the Sorbonne on "Postwar Surrealism" Breton refused an invitation to be a respondent, preferring as in days of old to heckle and disrupt from the audience. As Tzara intoned that Surrealism had been "absent from this war, from our hearts, and from our actions," Breton made loud dissenting comments, drank from the lecturer's glass of water, and stirred the audience into vociferous confusion.[23]

The young writers from the Main à Plume days decided that it was time to challenge Breton's exclusive right to speak for Surrealism. Led by Christian Dotremont, they founded a group called Revolutionary Surrealism that was clearly aligned with the Communist Party. It included an international component made up of Belgians, Danes, Czechs, Dutch, and even Germans. They put out a broadside, "Les Grands Transparents," that was essentially a satirical attack on Breton's leaning toward the occult and a denunciation of his abandonment of dialectical materialism.

At the same time Breton was attacked from another quarter. In Sartre's essay series in *Les Temps Moderns,* "Qu'est-ce que la littérature?," the fourth and fifth installments took up the question of Surrealism. Sartre's case against it lay primarily in its lack of engagement and in its pretensions of being revolutionary while essentially ignoring the proletariat. "The Surrealists don't destroy reality," he maintained, "they put it in parentheses. . . . They are really only a radicalized version of the *Grand Meaulnes.* Just as the preceding generation destroyed bourgeois life while preserving it in all its nuances, they want to cleanse themselves of original sin without renouncing the advantages of their position. . . . The Trotskyists are using Surrealism as an instrument of disruption." In essence Sartre accused the Surrealists of remaining part of the bourgeoisie and of having as their only audience the cultivated bourgeoisie. "They are parasites of the class that they insult. . . . They were all victims," he continued, "of the disaster of 1940. That is, when the moment of action came none of them was prepared for it. Some took their own lives, others went into exile; those who have come back are in exile among us . . . in the time of lean cows they have nothing to say to us."[24]

Sartre's dismissal of Surrealism did not prevent the opening of a "Secrétariat général du Surréalisme," with a small office in the fifteenth arrondisement, directed by Georges Henein, Henri Pastoureau, and Sarane Alexandrian. Nor did it impede the publication or reissuing of a number of Breton's books—a new edition of the manifestos, a French edition of *Arcane 17,* and his "Ode to Charles Fourier." Reviewing these publications, Maurice Nadeau took issue with Sartre for limiting the significance of Surrealism to a time gone by, for considering it only as the product of the "other after war" with no present validity. "The presence of Breton is always felt as undesirable, provocative, and out of place," he wrote, but maintained that his voice was always necessary to counter the foggy ideas of "conformists, cowards, and compromisers," saying that the manifestos were still timely and should be reread every year.[25]

On May 31 the front page of *Combat* carried an interview with Breton and a drawing of his profile by Maurice Henry. Questioned by Dominique Arban about the present significance of automatic writing, Breton maintained that it had "acted by continuous infiltration and had mined the field of expression," and he warned away those who "want to immolate it on the altar of reason." He went on to say that he held Sartre in "high intellectual esteem in spite of his Baudelaire which was certainly not mine; we are of very different mental formations." Questioned about the ethical program of Surrealism, he reminded his interviewer that "psychic automatism was described in the First Manifesto as being 'outside all aesthetic or moral considerations.'" It was never intended as a code of ethical behavior or a moral philosophy, he maintained, implying that it did not function on the same plane as existentialism.

Shortly thereafter some fifty artists and writers signed a statement that was published as "Rupture Inaugurale." Written by Henri Pastoureau, it was based on the responses to a questionnaire that took up matters such as: in what manner is Surrealist activity to be exercised? and in what areas? in politics does the end justify the means? can religion offer anything helpful to mankind? Essentially they called for a post-Christian morality, voicing the possibility of a new religion, to which Péret, still in Mexico, objected on the grounds that a new mysticism had its dangers and that poetry itself obviated the need for religion.

While he occupied himself with the details of the upcoming exhibition Breton also took the time to arrange Paris shows and write catalogue introductions for his recruits from the Western Hemisphere, Hare, Donati, Kamrowski, and Maria Martins, as well as for Matta, Hérold, and Toyen. Meanwhile in New York Duchamp, assisted by Donati, worked on the cover for the exhibition catalogue that Maeght was to publish. It was far more startling than the 1938 *Dictionnaire abrégé* or the bullet-riddled cover for "First Papers." Jacques Kober, the gallery's director wrote to Donati: "The cover you have put together is completely revolting, it's marvelous in a world that eats away at itself."[26] He was referring to *Prière de toucher,* the words inscribed under a sponge rubber breast on a black velvet ground. According to Donati, "Duchamp created a plaster, then came to see me and said 'I would like to put this on the cover.' I made them all and painted every nipple. I put in the black velvet because I thought it looked naked. I said to Marcel, 'Please touch,' and he said, 'Prière de toucher,' and that was it."[27]

Breton's letter of invitation/explanation was printed in the catalogue, along with a letter from Péret proposing noises and *nourritures.*[28] The 150-page catalogue contained written contributions from thirty authors, including Georges Bataille who wrote on "The Absence of Myth," Henry Miller on his journeys in France, Arp with a tribute to his late wife, Sophie Taeuber, and Brauner who saw the whole event in a satirical light. There were also reproductions of the work of most of the exhibiting artists. In short the 1947 catalogue was an elaborate compendium of offerings by those who regarded themselves as having any affinity with the postwar Surrealist movement. (Some of the exhibitors were added after the catalogue had gone to press so that their names do not appear among the eighty-five contributors listed.) However, for those who responded to Duchamp's invitation to touch and opened the cover of this opus it must have presented a confusing potpourri, disorienting indeed as was the Surrealists' wont, but conveying a sense that the movement had lost its subversive edge as it mired itself in the occult. The ethnological interests of earlier Surrealism had given way to a form of emulation of the primitive that could hardly come across as authentic when practiced by sophisticated Parisians.

The exhibition that finally opened on July 8 was, as Breton had promised, devoted to alchemy, esotericism, and myth. As planned, the gallery was set up as a place of initiation through which the visitors would traverse the stages necessary to acquire knowledge. One climbed the twenty-one book steps, crossed the Hall of Superstitions, a grotto created by stretching fabric over an irregular framework, and entered a room in which a curtain of rain fell continuously in front of a billiard table at which visitors were invited to play. Then came the labyrinth, inspired by Breton's recent experience with voodoo rituals, with twelve recesses containing altars dedicated to "a being, a category of beings, or an object, real or imaginary, capable of being endowed with a mythical life, such as the Great Invisibles." Among the artists who submitted designs for altars or who actually were on the spot to fabricate them were Lam, Matta, Hérold, and Brauner, and among the most potent of the "mythical" objects created were Brauner's *Wolf-Table,* an elegant little table furnished with a wolf's head and tail, Duchamp's *Gravity Manager,* Lam's altar for "La Chevalure du Falmer" (from Song IV of *Les Chants de Maldoror*), and Hérold's large plaster *Grand Transparent* with a concave mirror set in his belly, in which viewers beheld their distorted features. Breton had tried in vain to persuade Giacometti to allow his *Invisible Object* to be included among the cultic objects, while he himself contributed an altar veiled by a fly-studded green net in homage to Rimbaud's poem "Devotion."[29] Donati's assigned theme was the evil eye, and on his altar he placed a green fist in which an eye was embedded, a "symbol of myself looking at the evil eye."

The artworks by roughly one hundred artists that had been streaming in from twenty-four countries were installed in every available remaining space, including Aimé Maeght's private office. There was a respectable enough showing from the Western Hemisphere—Donati, Gorky, Hare, Kamrowski, Kiesler, Noguchi, Reynal, Sage, Man Ray, and Tanning, as well as Riopelle from Canada—to make it appear

Top: Installation view of the 1947 Surrealist exhibition, designed by Marcel Duchamp and Frederick Kiesler, Galerie Maeght, Paris; photograph courtesy Mrs. Lillian Kiesler.

Right: Installation view of the 1947 Surrealist exhibition, Hall of Superstitions.

Paris, 1945–1947: In the Time of Lean Cows

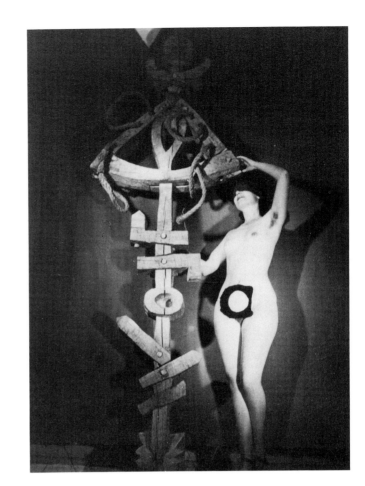

Right: Installation view of the 1947 Surrealist exhibition, Frederick Kiesler's altar.

Bottom: Jacques Hérold, *Le Grand Transparent,* 1946–1947, bronze cast from original plaster made for 1947 Surrealist exhibition; photograph courtesy Galerie Patrice Trigano.

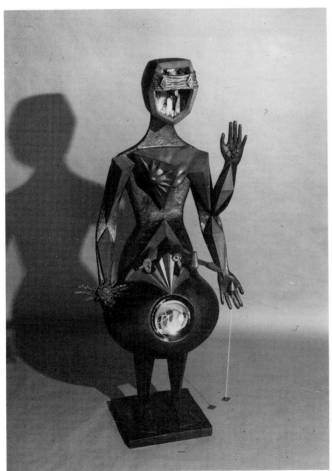

that Surrealism had indeed taken root in the New World during the war. The showing of Hans Richter's U.S.-made film, *Dreams Money Can Buy,* strengthened the impression of a ferment stirred up across the Atlantic by Surrealism. Kiesler, who had come from New York to carry out Duchamp's plans and add some touches of his own, was described as "beating his brains out" and "getting some of the success he had missed these last fourteen years in N.Y." [30]

Because of the delays caused by such a complicated installation, much of Paris was already on vacation by the time the show opened on July 4. This poor timing cut down on the attendance and possibly also on the press coverage, although blame for the latter was placed on Aragon, Breton's one-time comrade in arms and fellow medical student. In postwar Paris Aragon controlled directly or indirectly three-quarters of the media, both radio and the press. In any case the reviews were generally either ironic or diffident. *Figaro*'s reporter Albert Palle summed it up: "We are no longer moved by it . . . the enormous destruction of the world which we lived through during the dark years has emptied surrealism of its explosive force." [31] *Time*'s Paris correspondent was of the same opinion: "After the gas chambers, those heaps of bones and teeth and shoes and eyeglasses, what is there left for the poor Surrealists to shock us with?" [32]

David Hare and Jacqueline Lamba were in Paris in the summer of 1947, and his report on the show to Donati echoed the prevalent French response, that Surrealism definitely belonged to the past:

The show finely opened after all the various disagreements that you can so well emagin since you remember VVV. However the public didn't know all that so they are labering under the imprestion the surealists are one big happy family. Surrealism is accepted as past history. The gallery is crowded with humanity with nothing better to do on an afternoon. There are no discussions, no fights, no real interest and yet it is a suces as a publicety stunt for the gallery. .one would say it was a popular success, but an intellectual failure . . . a small group of people amusing themselves with ideas which they invented in 1929. [33]

Breton soon left the city for the Massif Centrale. He wrote to Kober asking him about the show and saying that he had heard it was controversial, which was all he asked at his age. He referred to the Aragon-controlled press as "infamous." [34] More controversy was still to come. Two weeks before the show was to close members of the Jeunes Surréalistes Révolutionnaires, Arnaud, Dotremont, Jaguer, and others demonstrated outside the Maeght Gallery and distributed a broadside that accused the exhibition of representing the Surrealism of 947, not 1947. Even the gallery's manager Kober signed the statement of protest. [35] It is difficult to say whether it was Breton's occultism or his anti-Stalinism that was more responsible for this outburst. Certainly the exhibition's mystical orientation alienated both press and

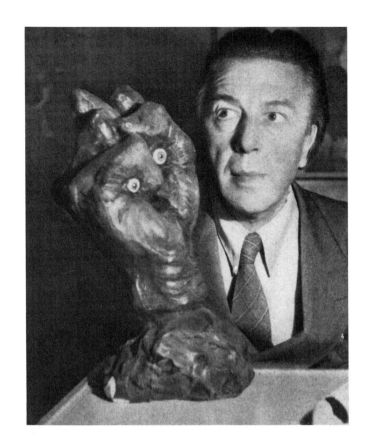

Top: News photo of André Breton with Enrico Donati's *Fist,* summer 1947; courtesy Enrico Donati.

Bottom: Enrico Donati, *Carnavale da Venise,* 1946, oil on canvas, 40 x 50 inches; private collection.

public and Breton was reproached for his interests in utopianism, esotericism, and mysticism. He defended these concerns on the grounds that for him they were a "black light, illuminating an active understanding of man in the universe." [36]

The second International Exhibition of Surrealism closed on October 5, 1947. Writing to Donati in New York, Breton admitted that the exhibition had not been a *succès d'estime* and certainly not a financial success, but allowed that it was important because it had rallied the Surrealists and shown that the movement was still alive. [37] He asked Donati to join with the others in participating in the upcoming Surindépendants exhibition and informed him of plans for Surrealist shows in Prague, Basel, and Lausanne, as well as one in Berlin scheduled for January. He felt that this last was of special importance since nothing was known there of art that had been made outside German borders for the past fourteen years, and he asked him to spread word of it to Marcel, Max Ernst, Yves, Maria, Noguchi, Gorky, Kamrowski, de Diego, and Jeanne Reynal, the New York-based remnant of his group. The Berlin exhibition, although it was to be sponsored by the American embassy and the French cultural services, was vetoed from the Quai d'Orsay, perhaps again due to the power of Breton's enemies.

Despite the tepid reception, the exhibition did garner new recruits for Surrealism among the young, in whom Breton had always put his faith. Jean Schuster was

Above: Gerome Kamrowski, *Strange Sky,* 1945, gouache on Whatman, 22 x 30 inches; collection Kirby Kamrowski.

sixteen when he discovered a book by Breton at the home of a friend. His curiosity roused, he went to see the exhibition at Maeght, passed through the curtain of rain to play billiards, and obtained Breton's address from the gallery. When Schuster arrived at 42 rue Fontaine he found a note beside Breton's name in the entry saying that he gave no interviews and no autographs and to write for an appointment. The young man wrote and was duly given a rendezvous at the café in the Place Blanche at 5:45—fifteen minutes before the regular meeting, which was held at six, seven days of the week, and lasted precisely one and a half hours. If there was serious work to do—an exhibition or a publication—a few of the senior members such as Péret and Legrand would meet in the rue Fontaine after dinner. As an ingénue, Schuster was invited to attend twice a week, and later he became a regular. For the first four years he said nothing at the meetings, but took his poems privately to Breton who would "gently criticize" them. Breton, he recollected, was somewhat ambivalent about his years in the United States. He was full of affection toward those who had been supportive, Schapiro, among others, but felt disgust for the country.[38]

If the 1938 exhibition had marked the end of Surrealism's avant-garde phase, the 1947 show may be seen as putting a close to Surrealism's coda as it was played out during the war years. In 1938 the Surrealists still had the power to disorient; Duchamp's limp coal sacks and the various irreverent mannequins were written into history, as was the very notion of the potent installation, and Dalí's *Rainy Taxi* took on the status of an icon. Much of the work shown was symptomatic of the political restiveness that plagued France, dismay over the triumph of fascism in Spain, and apprehensiveness over the inevitable war. None of this held true nine years later. In a world that had experienced a real-life version of *Ubu Roi* what could a plaster statue say? In the face of the scientific hegemony established by the splitting of the atom and its awesome implications, who was ready to join Breton's flight into the occult? What power was there to Duchamp's curtain of rain for a public that knew of the millions herded to their death in the "showers"?

The period of exile saw a transformation as well as a dispersal of Surrealism. Those who had been its leading iconoclasts in the visual realm—Ernst, Tanguy, and Masson—found their own work deeply affected by their years of exile. Not only did each carry on his work quite detached from the group idea, but each responded to aspects of the physical nature of the North American continent in ways that gave their work greater harmony while diminishing its disorienting effects.

Max Ernst recognized the finale of Surrealism in the United States in the statement he wrote for the *Museum of Modern Art Bulletin* in 1946: "Art is not produced by one artist, but by several. It is to a great degree a product of their exchange of ideas one with another . . . such a communal life as that of the Paris cafés is difficult, if not impossible here. . . . For Breton it was necessary to have a center and in New York he found it impossible to maintain one."[39] What followed the dispersal of the Surrealists was a period of void, as Leo Castelli, a young émigré himself, characterized it.

By the time the International Surrealist Exhibition opened at Maeght, Art of This Century had closed its doors for good and Peggy Guggenheim had returned to Europe. The gallery that had functioned for four and a half seasons as a meeting ground and showcase for European and American artists and that had wet-nursed the infant hybrid that this encounter had helped to produce was gone—even its curving Kiesler-designed walls had been removed, having been sold, thanks to Charles Seliger, to the Franklin Simon clothing store. Gone also was Gallery 67, whose auspicious start had ended abruptly with Howard Putzel's death in 1945. Even Julien Levy, the pioneering promoter of Surrealism, was contemplating ending his career as a dealer. New galleries were opening and taking over some of the artists who had been discovered by these dealers. Betty Parsons, who had been running the contemporary section of the Mortimer Brandt gallery, opened her own gallery in the same space in the fall of 1946, across the hall from Sam Kootz who made good his threat to start promoting American art by opening a gallery and taking on Motherwell, Baziotes, Gottlieb, and a partially Americanized Hans Hofmann. With the exception of the Hugo Gallery which remained Surrealist in orientation, these new galleries felt no need to stress an artistic continuity between the European Surrealists and the new American painting. This does not mean that the notion of an American Surrealism had been completely lost; it was still a force for some of Breton's New York adherents and it continued to impact on unaffiliated painters and on sculptors such as Theodore Roszak and David Smith.

Before leaving for Paris to work on the Maeght installation Kiesler designed the setting for a New York exhibition, entitled "Bloodflames," that opened at the Hugo Gallery in March. Organized by Nicolas Calas, this was one of the few attempts to perpetuate the concept of an American Surrealism in the postwar years. Included were works by Hare, Gorky, Kamrowski, Lam, Matta, Noguchi, Helen Phillips, and Jeanne Reynal, installed in the environment created by Kiesler. In his introduction Calas wrote of the artist's "ex-centric" position and the consequent need to create an "ex-static, out of place commodity." This was to be done by emphasizing "open forms, polycentric constructions, unexpected attractions, and disengagements." He wrote of the artist "who will risk everything," who "will be heroic," who "will aim toward freedom and achieve magic," producing "that alchemy of form and colors which transform an artificial object into an eye emanating light."

In the meantime the other artists who had been perceived as American Surrealists or who had once referred to themselves as such were visible in a spate of one-man exhibitions: in 1946 Motherwell, Hare, Clyfford Still, Baziotes, Peter Busa, Jimmy Ernst, Gorky, Pollock, Rothko, Seliger, and Margo; in 1947 Gorky, Pollock, Stamos, Rothko, Pousette Dart, Still, Margo, Sage, and Gottlieb. Some—Gorky, Noguchi, and Hare—were included in the Museum of Modern Art's "14 Americans"

Farewell party for Max Ernst and Dorothea Tanning, New York, 1946. Above, left to right: Dorothea Tanning, Jimmy Ernst, Frederick Kiesler (photograph courtesy Dorothea Tanning). Below, left to right: Matta, Arlette Seligmann, Frederick Kiesler, Max Ernst, and Nina Lebel (Seligmann archives).

show in 1946. In late 1946 Pollock, who had moved out to eastern Long Island the previous fall, began to lay his canvases down on the floor and to drip quick-drying lacquer paint from sticks and brushes as he walked and stooped and reached out over the surface. The paint landed in thin threads that looped back and forth around the canvas or in heavier globs that dried with a wrinkled skin. The touch of the hand was giving way to the motion of the body as automatism metamorphosed into action and the gesture gained autonomy.

The final installment of the Surrealist incursion was the arrival in New York in February 1947 of Joan Miró. He had come to paint a 7-by-32-foot mural that had been commissioned for the Terrace Hilton Hotel in Cincinnati. A number of New York artists saw him at work on it in the studio that Carl Holty had loaned him for the job, as did Soby who arranged for the completed mural to be shown at the Mu-

seum of Modern Art in October before being installed in the hotel's Sert-designed dining room. Gorky gave a dinner party for Miró in his Union Square studio, and some of the artists found themselves working alongside him as he made prints at Atlelier 17. Since Miró's impact had long since been felt through his many exhibitions at Pierre Matisse and Rosenberg and his 1941 retrospective at the Museum of Modern Art, it is difficult to assess what the impact of this actual visit was. There are some New York artists who remember his quiet presence working among them as a sign of New York's new artistic status, while others were impressed by the 32-foot expanse of canvas he was working on. The voice that had been raised against Surrealism, that of Clement Greenberg, now praised Miró in a handsomely produced monograph.

Above: Dorothea Tanning, *Max in a Blue Boat,* 1947, oil on canvas, 61 x 50 cm;
private collection.

Breton's favorite among American artists, the painter who Masson said was his only friend among American painters, Arshile Gorky, was suffering the double blow of the loss of twenty-seven paintings in the January 1946 fire that destroyed his studio barn and a colostomy the following month. The fire claimed a crucial body of mid-1940s work, for this was the time when Gorky was working his way through Surrealism and forging a new synthesis between Surrealism and abstraction that was of profound significance for the art of the subsequent decade. Despite these major setbacks Gorky had enough work ready for shows with Julien Levy in both 1946 and 1947, while his *The Calendars* in the 1947 Whitney Annual was singled out by Greenberg as the best painting in the show. He described it as reminiscent of Miró's design and Matta's calligraphy and wrote that Gorky was "the only American artist to have completely assimilated French art."[40] It was in 1947 that Gorky wrote bitterly to his sister Vartoosh about Surrealism,[41] although this new attitude was probably as

Above: Matta, *Accidentalité,* 1947, oil on canvas, 192 x 248 cm, private collection, Geneva.

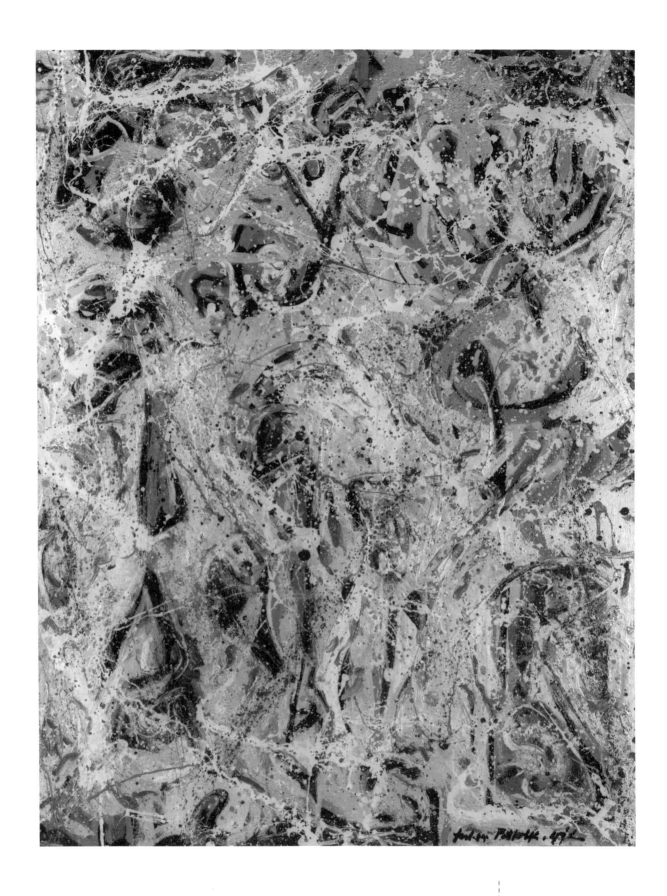

much due to personal reasons—his heavy drinking, his disintegrating marriage, the impotence resulting from his operation—as to artistic, since he showed that year in the Surrealist exhibition at Maeght as well as in "Bloodflames."

Gorky's new work continued to move away from what had appeared as all over abstraction in paintings such as *The Leaf of the Artichoke Is an Owl* and toward a greater emphasis on narrative and drama. At this point, if one accepts Julien Levy's firsthand account, he was inspired by his Connecticut neighbor, Tanguy.[42] Gorky's late work was significant for emerging abstract expressionism in its separation of line and color, the one wire-thin and gracefully precise, the other loose, brushy, and flowing. He was indeed the fulcrum on which the transition from abstract surrealism to abstract expressionism swung. He set a standard for American painters of a dedication to art of the highest quality while exemplifying free experimentation. He "veiled" his subjects, subjects that were acutely real for him, while retaining their poignant and poetic qualities, and he demonstrated the emotive effectiveness of a language of form, reaching from his own subjectivity into that of the viewer. Without the intense liberating experience of Surrealism, the firsthand acquaintance with Masson, Matta, and Tanguy, and the validating approbation of Breton, it is unlikely that Gorky's art would have blossomed as it did in the last years of his too short life.

Occultism was not entirely gone from the New York scene in 1947. It certainly tinged the work that Matta showed at Pierre Matisse both in 1945 and again in 1947, although now manifest in automatons rather than automatism. That year also saw the publication of Seligmann's *History of Magic,* selected by Helen and Kurt Wolf for Pantheon, the première of Balanchine's *The Four Temperaments* with sets and costumes by Seligmann, and his fifth solo New York exhibition. *Art News* featured him in its monthly "spotlight on" page, with Aline Louchheim (later Saarinen) seeing his work as finally free of the "overtones of Nazi-ridden turmoil" and writing of his interest in magic as deriving from "its insistence on the oneness of all things and on their transmutability."[43]

Not only did Surrealism's strongest support among the New York galleries disappear, but so did the periodicals devoted to it. Robert Motherwell and Harold Rosenberg attempted to fill the gap by starting a new journal, *Possibilities,* devoted to artists, writers, and composers (John Cage was the music editor) who "practice in their work their own experience without seeking to transcend it in academic, group or political formulas. Such practice implies the belief that through the conversion of energy something valid may come out, whatever situation one is forced to begin with."[44] The emphasis on open-endedness echos Paalen's notion of "the possible" expressed in the very name of his periodical, *Dyn.* Open-ended is just how the contents of *Possibilities* must have appeared, as one leafed through statements by Baziotes, Rothko, David Smith, and Pollock, an essay by Hayter, a poem by Arp, and an

Jackson Pollock, *Galaxy,* 1947, oil and aluminum on canvas, 43½ x 34 inches;
Joslyn Art Museum, gift of Peggy Guggenheim.

interview with Miró. Even the literary contributions from Lionel Abel, Paul Good-man, and Andrea Caffi refrain from pointing in any specific direction, as if to reverse the tendency of previous avant-garde movements, Surrealism in particular, to set forth dogmatic platforms. Especially significant was the title used by Baziotes, "I Cannot Evolve Any Concrete Theory," and it was he who selected the lines from Valéry on "the silence of painters." The ancestry of *Possibilities* is to be found in the declaration of artistic freedom that Trotsky had insisted on when he and Breton composed their joint statement of 1939. Perhaps it was inherent in the nonprogram-matic nature of this journal that its first promising issue should also have been its last.

Two other short-lived publications also moved into the void left by *View: In-stead,* a broadside that came out in eight numbers put together by Matta and Lionel Abel in 1947–1948, and the well-financed, luxurious *Tiger's Eye,* published by heir-ess Ruth Stephan and her painter husband John, starting in October 1947. *Tiger's Eye* continued the Surrealist tradition with its mixture of painting, poetry, and an-thropology. In its pages are to be found Peruvian weaving, Kwakiutl shaman songs, and artworks by Gottlieb, Stamos, Sage, Baziotes, Max Ernst, Motherwell, Hayter, Kamrowski, Pollock, Still, Newman, Tanguy, Gorky, Matta, Stephan, and Rothko. In short, it perpetuated and augmented what remained of the automatist approach to art and of the Art of This Century/American Surrealist circle for another two years, but without a label. In fact that whole question of a designation—whether one was wanted at all, as well as what it might be—was to be a matter of serious debate in the years to come, and in the opinion of some was never satisfactorily resolved.

By the end of 1947, then, Surrealism had staged its dramatic but unsuccessful attempt at a Paris comeback, while the seeds it had sown in New York were sprouting into a nameless new hybrid, a plant that was already beginning to bear strange fruit. At the point at which this story ends the artists who had embarked on the pathway opened by Surrealism were indeed moving into unknown territory, to a still uncertain reception. The course on which they had embarked, although perceived in hindsight as a road to glory, exacted a price, even while it made millionaires of a few artists, dealers, and a critic or two. Breton had sought to fabricate a myth when he conjured up the Great Transparents. Rothko, Gottlieb, and Newman had tried to revivify old myths. Neither venture was particularly successful in terms of the resonance a myth must evoke. However, they all participated in the generating of a new myth, that of the American artist-hero, seizing and transforming a remnant of Old World culture and turning it into an instrument of power in order to perpetuate and propagandize the New World myth of limitless frontiers and boundless individual freedom. Surre-alism in exile provided the validating lineage for a new aesthetic of risk, even as Surrealism as a movement became history.

Arshile Gorky, *Betrothal,* 1947, oil on canvas, 50⅝ x 39¾ inches; Yale University Art Gallery.

Epilogue   In Paris toward the end of 1948 a notice was sent out to the members in good standing of the Surrealist group under the heading "Decisions." The first decision it announced was that of October 25, 1948, excluding Matta Echaurren from the group for reasons of "moral ignominy and intellectual disqualification." The second, dated November 8, excluded Victor Brauner for breaking Surrealist discipline (*travail fractionnel*) and five others (Alexandrian, Bouvet, Jouffroy, Rodanski, and Tarnaud) for taking the part of Brauner. The first decision had been prompted by the news of the death of Arshile Gorky, who in July had been found hanging from a beam of an outbuilding near his house in Sherman, Connecticut. A letter Breton had received from New York attempted to fix the blame for Gorky's suicide on Matta because of an affair with Gorky's estranged wife. To the Surrealists, summoned by telegram, he announced that Matta was responsible for the death of Gorky. No matter that none of those present knew Gorky and few knew Matta; they all seconded Breton's call for Matta's prompt exclusion—all, that is, except for Victor Brauner, who was not about to condemn a fellow Surrealist for amorality, especially on the strength of an apparently malicious report. Brauner's independent stand led to his own exclusion, voted soon after, along with that of the five others who had agreed with his stand.[1] Thus Surrealism lost two of its strongest remaining artists, Matta and Brauner, leaving the visual side of the movement irreparably weakened. Although there were periodic reconciliations—with Ernst and Paalen, for example, and even with Matta—essentially Surrealism in the strict sense of an influential organized movement in the visual arts was at an end.

There were some in the American art community who had been close to Gorky who did indeed blame his suicide on the amorality of Surrealism. His association with it was seen as the beginning of his path to self-destruction.[2] The great final flowering of his art that the contact with Surrealism had helped to nurture was overlooked as Gorky was turned into a martyr and Surrealism into a scapegoat. Gorky's death was used to justify the collective amnesia regarding the Surrealist émigrés that for decades militated against a historical understanding of the genesis of abstract expressionism. When Robert Motherwell said in 1982, "There is no account of those five years that corresponds in any way with what actually happened,"[3] he was, in effect, acknowledging the conspiracy of silence on the subject. He added that once they had been shown the way by the Surrealists, it was "like King Arthur finding that he could pull the sword from the stone . . . I still shake when I think how that opened the door."[4]

As for the motivations that drove Gorky to take his life just when his years of struggle were beginning to be crowned with success, one can cite the studio fire and the colostomy of 1946, followed in the spring of 1948 by a broken neck, the result of an accident when he was driving with Julien Levy, and the disintegration of his marriage, which had begun with a separation the previous summer.[5] However, there is a strong likelihood that both Gorky's suicide and his paintings were inextricably connected to the tragedies of his early life. On April 25, 1914, several hundred Armenian intellectual, political, and religious leaders in Constantinople were imprisoned and later killed. In the next several years Armenians by the tens of thousands were forcibly removed from their ancestral homelands in Turkey and deported to the Syrian deserts; men and boys were separated from the caravans and shot or butchered; women and children continued on foot for months and were robbed, raped, and massacred; many of the young and the elderly were abandoned. Donald Miller, director of the School of Religion at the University of Southern California, interviewed one hundred survivors who had been children at the time of these events. He found that "their pain is not just the memories of the brutal acts they witnessed, but the suffering of aloneness and abandonment as children. The genocide also ruptured their sense of a morally ordered universe."[6]

The later disasters that befell Gorky may well have opened up old wounds from the atrocities he had witnessed as a child in Turkish Armenia, the grim conditions of the forced one-hundred-mile march to the Caucasian frontier when he was eleven,

Above: Arshile Gorky, The Black Monk ("Last Painting"), 1948, oil on canvas,
30¾ x 39¾ inches; Thyssen Bornemisza collection, Madrid.

and the pain and helplessness he must have felt as he watched his mother die of malnutrition during the famine winter of 1918–1919. Very likely it was these early traumas that overwhelmed Gorky in the end, despite the long struggle to bolster his identity by borrowing the painting style or the words of an artists or poet he admired. His preoccupation with death during his last months is attested to by the stark work simply known as *Last Painting*. Julien Levy identified the source of this work as *The Black Monk,* a short story by Anton Chekov, which "for several weeks he had been reading and rereading, or having read and reread aloud to him."[7] In the story a dying man, Kovrin, who considers himself a failure (and who is separated from his wife), conjures in his delirium the image of a Black Monk who "whispered to him that he was a genius and died only because his feeble mortal body had lost its balance and could no longer serve as the covering of genius."[8] *Last Painting* has been perceptively analyzed by Harry Rand who reveals its fidelity to the Chekov story; in it Gorky seems to have painted his own death wish.

Thought of as a Surrealist by Motherwell at the time of his death, described as such by Gottlieb in a 1950 catalogue introduction, Gorky's late accomplishment can neither be wholly dissociated from Surrealism nor wholly identified with it. Four of the movement's artists were intentionally or unintentionally mentors to him. Like Masson he turned to myth for a portion of his subject matter, in his case drawing more on Armenian than Greek sources. Also, as Masson was doing in Connecticut, Gorky used close-up drawings of botanical forms as the starting point for large compositions, which he transformed with free-flowing paint. Like Tanguy he veiled his subjects but imparted a strong sense of latent content and left clues for the deciphering of this content for those with the persistence to look beyond the felicities of technique. Like Matta he separated brush-drawn line from free-flowing color, but the apparent freedom of his loose runny paint came only after careful plotting in preliminary drawings complete with the traditional grid used for transfer to a larger scale. (Such plotting, we now know, thanks to the availability of his notebooks, also underlay the apparent spontaneity of Miró's painting.) Gorky shared Surrealism's fixation on the erotic, but not its aim of dislocating the senses. The quality of his line and the sensuousness of his color belong to the realm of the lyric poet, not the iconoclast, yet his lyric voice might have remained mute were it not for the models provided by Miró, Masson, Matta, and Tanguy and the approving feedback from Breton.

In January 1951 a memorial show for Gorky opened at the old Whitney Museum on Eighth Street. On the walls of its cramped galleries hung a succession of astonishing paintings, most of which had never been publicly shown. (Pollock wrote: "More than ninety percent of the work I'd never seen before.")[9] When his work could finally be seen as a body Gorky became the artist-hero of the next generation. The new mode of veiled or abstract narration that he had pioneered became one of the linchpins of the New York School. His way of separating his fluent brush drawing from his loosely applied drifts of color provided a starting point for many artists in the 1950s. One didn't need to ferret out the hidden subject in order to respond to the supple line and lyrical color or to intuit that there was an underlying drama. The acknowledged leader of the New York School, de Kooning, described his own artistic formation with the words "I come from 36 Union Square." By the early 1950s scores of younger artists traced their roots to the same place.

On a spring evening in 1951 the light shone brightly from the doorway of a vacant storefront on Ninth Street and a crowd of artists milled about inside and spilled over onto the pavement. The walls were hung with large gestural paintings by the founding members of the artists' club and with works in a variety of styles by their friends and associates, a total of sixty-one in all. No elaborate installation showcased this exhibition, no catalogue perpetuated its memory, and it is known to history simply as the Ninth Street show, in effect the first salon of the New York School. Leo Castelli, not yet the proprietor of a gallery, helped to hang the show in the raw, harshly lit space. The audience was made up mainly of artists with few uptowners or art establishment figures, and there was little press notice of it. What the Ninth Street show signified most of all was the existence of a community of artists, like-minded chiefly in their dedication to an open-ended approach to painting, who had made common cause to deal with what they perceived as their disenfranchisement and to provide a support system that would validate the activity in which they were engaged.

Impromptu and impoverished as this exhibition was, the collective energy that emanated from those walls sent out a signal that was impossible to ignore—the New York School had identified itself. The combination of this event and the Gorky memorial exhibition made it clear that a watershed had been reached in American art in terms of its relation to Old World culture. To be sure, European modernism had been absorbed, but now confident artists shed any last perception of themselves as provincial and moved with conviction into the void left by the departed European refugees. In the interim the periodicals *Possibilities* and *Tiger's Eye,* the Subjects of the Artists School founded by Motherwell, Baziotes, and Rothko, the Friday night lectures there and later at Studio 35, and the start of the artists' club helped to sustain the momentum that had grown out of the American-European points of contact and what had for a brief period been known as abstract surrealism.

A new directorial team was in place at the Museum of Modern Art by 1950, the charismatic and energetic Austrian-born René d'Harnoncourt as director and the Scotsman Andrew Ritchie as director of the department of painting and sculpture, with Alfred Barr restored to a position of influence. In 1951 under Ritchie's direction MoMA presented "Abstract Painting and Sculpture in America." Starting with pioneers such as Joseph Stella, Patrick Henry Bruce, and John Covert, the exhibition culminated with the latest developments in American art: the work of Gorky, de

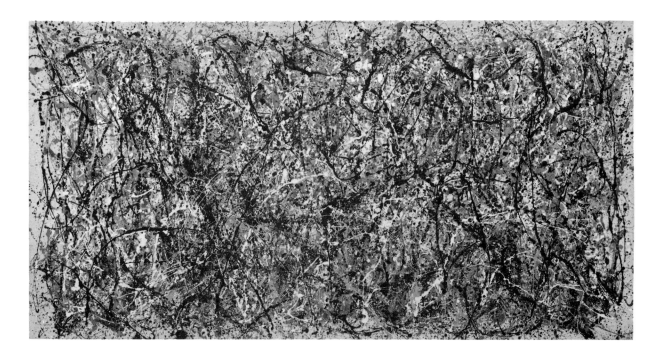

Kooning, Pollock, Motherwell, Baziotes, and Rothko, as well as others who had been known as abstract surrealists, Jimmy Ernst, Kamrowksi, and Seliger. Thus those who were beginning to be called abstract expressionists were given their first major museum exposure in the context of a survey of American art that, with the exception of a brief introductory section of the catalogue, made no reference to European modernism. Instead the works were categorized under such neutral headings as "pure geometric," "naturalist geometric," and "expressionist biomorphic." The new movement in American art, despite its hybrid nature, was made to appear to be the lineal descendant of a hermetic sequence of American abstract artists, the outgrowth of a provincialism finally come of age. MoMA's previously reluctant attitude toward American art is made plain by the fact that out of one hundred and eight works in the show only twelve came from the collection of the museum, although it had been in existence for twenty-two of the forty years covered.

By 1951 the abstract expressionists had official validation as representing the vanguard of American and possibly world art from the institution once dedicated to showcasing European modernism. To replace Peggy Guggenheim they had ambitious and entrepreneurial dealers from the business world such as Sam Kootz and Sidney Janis. To write on their work they had sympathetic, articulate critics, Clement Greenberg, Harold Rosenberg, and the managing editor of *Art News,* Thomas Hess, who that year published the first book on the New York School, *Abstract Painting, Background and American Phase.* Nor were they ignored by the popular press. Without *Life* magazine's famous 1949 article on Pollock and its 1951 publication of a landmark photograph titled "The Irascibles" that has become the standard document for defining the abstract expressionist group, what was happening in Manhat-

Above: Jackson Pollock, *One (Number 31, 1950),* oil and enamel on unprimed canvas, 106 x 209⅝ inches; The Museum of Modern Art, New York, Sidney and Harriet Janis Collection Fund (by exchange).

tan's downtown lofts might have remained the province of a few initiates.[10] With such media coverage the notion of the artist-star taking a place alongside the stars of film and sports gained greater popular currency. Dalí had long since shown how to use the media for personal promotion; now publicity-seeking tactics could become part of an artist's gambit.

The postwar fate of the Surrealist émigrés did not follow a similar trajectory. Their story is one of fragmentation and, for some, personal tragedy. As we have seen, Breton managed to keep the Surrealist movement going in postwar Paris, but with a different cast of characters and a diminished level of response. Masson pursued an independent course, painting the light on the French landscape, collaborating on a project with Sartre. Others of the group—Tanguy, Seligmann, Paalen, Duchamp, Ernst for a time—lingered in the New World, unable to decide between return to the uncertainties of postwar Europe and the fairly comfortable positions and artistic reputations they had established for themselves in the West.

In early March of 1946 the Seligmanns received a postcard from Pegeen Guggenheim inscribed as follows: "Il y a un party chez ma mère (155 E 61) samedi à neuf heures pour nous deux—un farewell party—J'espère vous voir à mon vernissage aussi le même jour. Love, Pegeen." Those departing for France were Pegeen and her recently acquired husband Jean Hélion, soon to be followed by Peggy Guggenheim who was wearying of managing the gallery and wanted to look at postwar European art. While there she took a trip to Venice with Mary McCarthy and her husband and decided to make it her home. She returned to New York for the gallery's last season, closed it in the spring of 1947, and settled into a luxurious life in the city of the Doges, a goodly distance from the art centers to whose turbulent life she had feverishly contributed. Behind her in New York she left a nascent American art movement, launched largely through her activities, as well as memories of an international meltdown at her wild parties.

That same year Max Ernst and Dorothea Tanning returned to Sedona, Arizona, that land of the red rocks that had so much moved him in 1941 and where they had spent five months in 1943. There, facing a sweeping expanse of dramatic rock formations and cactus-studded desert, they built a homestead where they lived, at first without water or electricity, until 1952 when they were able to afford to return to France. Many of Ernst's paintings from the Sedona period are related to these surroundings; in *Landscape with Red Rocks* one can see the profile of recognizable Sedona cliffs. The satirical irreverence and subversive impulse of the earlier years seems to have been calmed during the prolonged confrontation with the natural grandeur that met his eye in all directions.

Tanguy, who visited the Ernsts there in 1951 and made a trip with them to the Grand Canyon, also felt the impact of that boundless chiseled landscape. His late paintings, as densely filled as a city graveyard, have a distinct resemblance to the dozens of square miles of striated rocks cut deeply and with near-geometric precision by the Colorado River that he visited with the Ernsts. Brought up in the Breton tradition that the standing rocks or menhirs have distinct identities, Tanguy may have been particularly sensible to the power of the southwestern rock formations. He seems to have drawn on their vastness and density to express a mood very different from that of his impoverished but free-floating Paris years. There is a claustrophobic quality suggesting impasse to the somber 1954 paintings such as *Multiplication of the Arcs* or *Imaginary Numbers;* there is no open space for the free play of fantasy that his earlier canvases had invited. In 1953 he and Kay Sage made a triumphal circuit through France and Italy where they both had exhibitions, but returned to Connecticut where Tanguy cooked pasta, mixed martinis, and entertained visiting members of his old coterie such as Duchamp and Donati. From time to time the Tanguys exchanged visits with Kurt and Arlette Seligmann. In the last year of his life he took part in Hans Richter's film *8 x 8,* in which Calas and others enacted a surreal drama loosely based on chess. His health impaired by years of alcoholism, Yves Tanguy died of a cerebral hemorrhage in his fifty-fifth year.

In 1947 Gordon Onslow Ford and his wife loaded the fruits of six years' work, his paintings, her manuscripts, and objects of pre-Columbian art, into their car, crossed the Mexican border, and started up the California coast. After a visit with Henry Miller in Big Sur, they continued on to San Francisco. Finding it a sympathetic atmosphere, they rented a house on Telegraph Hill. Later they were joined by Paalen and his second wife Luchita and by the young American painter Lee Mullican, who had discovered *Dyn* at an army base in Hawaii and has sought them out. The three painters proceeded to form a new group based on the ideas that Paalen had been evolving in Mexico, to which they gave the name Dynaton. It was described by Paalen as "a limitless continuum in which all forms of reality are potentially implicit. Possibilities are a part of nature. Nature is what we can know of realized possibilities."[11] The work of the Dynaton group, as shown at the San Francisco Museum in 1951, brought a new concept in art to the Bay area. It was as radical, albeit more philosophically grounded, as the art shown at the Ninth Street show in New York the same year. If the Dynaton artists had not broken apart for personal reasons, their work might have had a much greater impact as a major visual response to a world in which the atom had been split.

Following the Dynaton show Paalen moved to Paris where he rented Kurt Seligmann's house in the Villa Seurat and attended Breton's meetings at the café in the Place Blanche. The innovative force of his 1940s paintings diminished as he developed a more formularized mode of painting in small regular strokes that seemed to represent the fields of force of apparitional beings, similar to those he had introduced in his script for a play, *The Cosmogons,* in 1946. By the middle of the decade Paalen

The "red rocks" of Sedona, Arizona.

Max Ernst, *Landscape with Red Rocks,* 1950, oil on canvas, 28¾ x 36¼ inches;
The Menil Collection, Houston.

Yves Tanguy, *The Mirage of Time*, 1954, oil on canvas, 25½ x 19¾ inches; The
Metropolitan Museum of Art, George A. Hearn Fund.

was back in Mexico where he married an old friend, Isabel Marin, sister of Diego Rivera's first wife, Lupe. There was no sequel to the ground-breaking ideas he had articulated in his essays for *Dyn,* and he was never quite able in his painting to follow through on the implications of his brilliant and prophetic works of the early 1940s. He continued to deal in Mexican antiquities and became implicated in a scandal involving stolen objects. In 1959 he took his life, having arranged by letter in advance for a friend to come to Taxco to collect his body and even having paid beforehand for that friend's expenses at the hotel. To Gordon Onslow Ford he wrote that he was obliged to save what little honor he had. The usual reason given for Paalen's suicide is trouble with the police or with rival antiquities dealers, but there was ample other cause for his suicidal despair, including suicidal tendencies in his family background, anguish over what had befallen family members under the Nazis, and personal relationships beset with problems.

On January 2, 1962, Kurt Seligmann, so the story goes, made a fire in his kitchen stove, set two places at the breakfast table, and went outside to try to shoot the rats who had been eating the feed he had put out for the birds. He slipped and fell on the ice, discharging a bullet into his skull. Secretive and ironic by disposition, given to encoding concealed meanings in his work, Seligmann died in a manner consistent with his character. He had been about to leave for Europe in 1958 when he suffered a heart attack—the receipt for the steamship ticket was still among his belongings when he died—and he carried nitroglycerine pills with him thereafter. His fear of a recurrence forced him to resign from his teaching job at Brooklyn College and give up his New York studio. Isolated in the country, eclipsed by the new American art after his successes of the 1940s, he painted canvases that are characterized by a ribbony disintegration. An example of this late style is *Rubezahl,* named for a Swiss mountain spirit, which evokes a ghostly presence that looms out of the darkness as if coming to claim a mountain traveler. Arlette prevailed on the local authorities to allow her to bury her husband at the farm in Sugar Loaf. His polished granite tombstone still looks out of place among the worn sandstone grave markers

Yves Tanguy, Kay Sage, and Arlette Seligmann in Connecticut, c. 1950.

Wolfgang Paalen, *Nuit Tropicale*, 1948, oil on canvas, 58½ x 55 inches;
collection of Robert and Rebecca Anthoine.

of the Wood family who farmed that land in the nineteenth century, a symbol of his ultimate nonassimilation in his place of refuge.

Kay Sage stayed on in the house she and Tanguy had shared, increasingly lonely, depressed, and alcoholic. She continued to paint and write poetry and devoted a good deal of time to assembling a fully illustrated catalogue raisonné of all Tanguy's known works. In the later 1950s, as her eyesight failed, her creative efforts were increasingly turned toward poetry. An unsuccessful operation for double cataracts led her to attempt to take her life in 1959. Successful exhibitions and the publication of three books of poetry did not alleviate her depression. Just a year after writing Arlette Seligmann a letter of condolence about the death of Kurt Seligmann, the artist who had introduced her to Surrealism, she put a bullet through her heart.

The self-inflicted deaths among the one-time Surrealists were added to by that of Oscar Domínguez, the Surrealist painter from Tenerife who had developed the decalcomania technique. Domínguez had been among the refugees at Air Bel in 1941; unable to leave for the West, he had at least managed not to be returned to

Franco by the Germans and had spent the war years in France. He committed suicide in Paris in 1957. The causes of the high number of suicides among the Surrealists remain unexplored. The movement could be said to have begun with the bullet hole that Jacques Vaché put through his own photograph, a prelude to his death by an overdose of opium in 1919. In the 1920s it was proposed that the truest Surrealist act would be to take a gun out into a crowded street and shoot at random. To examine why so many of those associated with Surrealism turned the gun against themselves might cast some light on the temperaments drawn to the movement as well as on the times during which they lived and died.

Masson spoke of Surrealism as having ended in 1945 when they came back from exile. The Americans he saw as unhampered by tradition and thus completely receptive to automatism. "Pollock," he said, "pushed it to extremes that I myself couldn't have envisioned." [12] He did try his hand at it, however, in the mid-1950s. Later his son Diego rescued from the garbage pail a gestural drip painting that testifies to Masson's interest in the possibilities of the new direction automatism had taken in American hands.

Despite the brilliant work he had shown at Durlacher in 1944, Esteban Frances did not continue a career as a painter. He moved to New York from Mexico and became a successful designer for the stage. Although he had been a strong anti-Falangist, he returned to Spain while Franco was still in power and spent the last years of his life in Mallorca.

Leonora Carrington, Matta, and Gordon Onslow Ford are still alive at this writing. Carrington made Mexico her home, raised two sons there, and developed a close and productive working relationship with Remedios Varo. The personal symbology she has evolved reflects an underlying feminism and a synthesizing knowledge of Celtic and other mythologies, alchemy, and various twentieth-century visionary writers. She is also conversant with recent scientific theory, avoids retrospection, and appears to live in the present moment. Retrospective exhibitions of her work were held in London and Los Angeles in 1992.

Since 1948 Matta has lived mostly in Europe, dividing his time between homes in London, Paris, and Tarquinia; the latter home is in a former monastery constructed above an ancient Etruscan necropolis. In Europe he is thought of by many as the most important living painter, while old prejudice has prevented full acknowledgment in the United States of his brilliant achievement. On his enormous canvases he has conjured spaces that others cannot even envision, using his phenomenal facility and even more phenomenal energy to express the interconnectedness of diverse events happening on different planes at different points in time. The Matta twins are both dead: Sebastian was an early suicide; Gordon Matta Clark, a highly regarded artist, died of cancer at age thirty-five.

Onslow Ford, for whom Gordon Matta Clark was named, has lived nearly forty years on a wooded hillside above a canyon near the Pacific coast, coming out

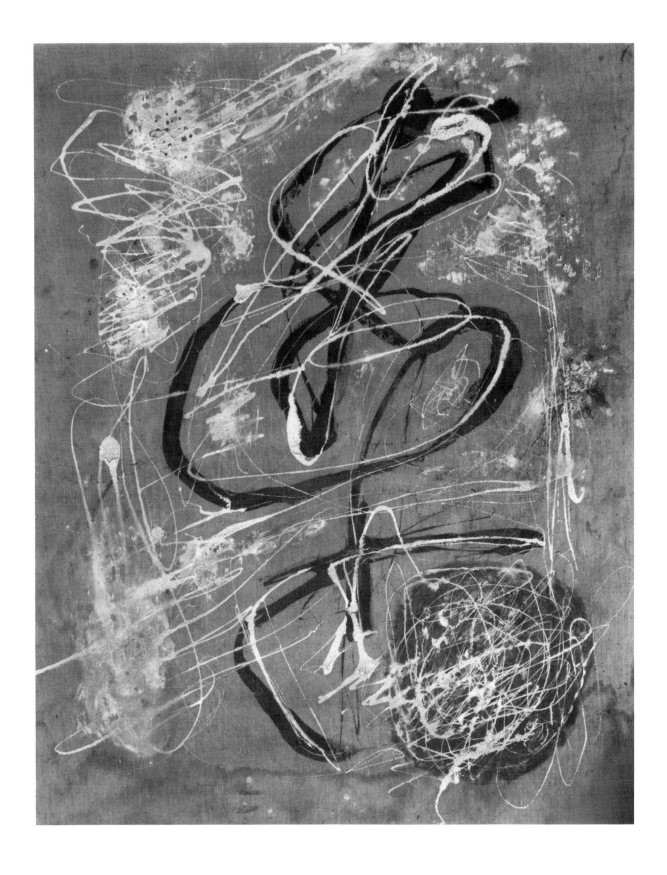

André Masson, *Dance*, 1955, oil on canvas, 100 x 81 cm; collection Diego and
Guite Masson.

of his seclusion for an occasional exhibition or lecture. He has continued his search for a means to express his "inner worlds,—the place where one goes in deep sleep, the dwelling place of spirits." Years of study of oriental calligraphy with a Zen master and years of looking at the sky through the needles of ancient Bishop pines and the star shapes formed by the canopy of bay leaves that shelters the pathways of his nature preserve have given him the means to situate his spirit forms ("live-line beings" he calls them) in what appear to be infinitely expanding spaces. The cohorts of his Surrealist years, especially Tanguy, are still presences for him, but one cannot say he lives in the past, for he has merged past, present, and future into a seamless continuum. For Onslow Ford Surrealism was truly a window opening onto the marvelous; he passed through that opening and discovered the transparent worlds that he has pursued in painting for nearly a half-century.

Maybe that's what it all boils down to—this whole tale of migrations, exhibitions, friends, enemies, old worlds and new—a window into a marvelous, a door to hidden chambers of the mind. However, located at its particular juncture in history, this displacement would seem to have a larger significance. Possibly the Surrealist presence was not needed for the liberation of the American artist's mind and hand that automatism helped to effect. It may be that among the New York artists there would have emerged a willingness to take a chance on possibilities rather than to reiterate certainties, even without the Surrealist émigrés to point out the way. Probably the atmosphere of urgency generated by world-wide war and the daily fact of so much death—in the rubble of London buildings, on Pacific atolls, or behind barbed wire in Germany—had far more impact on New York artists than the presence of a few émigrés in Greenwich Village and western Connecticut. However, this very urgency made it more compelling for the artists to reach out for what was daring

Above: Gordon Onslow Ford, *Sky Play,* 1988.

and precedent-breaking, and in doing this it is clear that they were at times stimulated and prompted by the refugees in their midst who in the wake of the earlier war had embarked on a similar gambit.

Breton had come to North America with the intention of expanding Surrealism. That is what happened, but Surrealism itself was transformed by displacement just as it changed the milieu into which it was displaced. Surrealism as an organized attack on rationalism lost its momentum as its adherents came in contact with the natural wonders of the New World, as they enjoyed minor celebrity status, and as their works became commodities. Set free from group discipline, the artists produced some of their most brilliant works. The fact that Miró, remaining in Europe, had, during the early months of the war, painted his dazzling constellation series leads one to hypothesize a general survival momentum at work in defiance of totalitarianism, a kind of artistic adrenalin responding to danger. Masson's *Meditation on an Oakleaf*, Ernst's *Europe after the Rain*, Paalen's *Cosmogons*, Tanguy's *Through Birds, through Fire, but not through Glass*, Onslow Ford's *Propaganda for Love*, Matta's *The Earth Is a Man*, Seligmann's *Melusine and the Great Transparents*—weren't these extraordinary works of the early 1940s manifestations of the survival power of art in the face of the totalitarian threat?

To put oneself on the edge of the unknown has its risks—witness the number of self-inflicted deaths among the survivors of this displacement, as well as the number of untimely deaths and suicidal behaviors among the former "American Surrealists" in the two decades following the end of the war. The artistic watershed ballyhooed as the "triumph of American painting" was paid for dearly both by its participants and by those who helped to unleash its force. What remains are some of the most significant artworks of the century, produced despite or because of the desperate circumstances during Surrealism's period of exile and the American aftermath. They are works that bear witness to an era of upheaval, an era that revealed the human capacity for total evil and unleashed a capacity for total destruction.

Gordon Onslow Ford with the author, Inverness, California, 1984.

Notes

Much of the source material for this book came from the Kurt Seligmann papers that at this writing are still in my possession; this is indicated by (MS) in the endnotes. They will eventually join the remaining Seligmann papers in the Beinecke Library at Yale University.

Translations from French not otherwise indicated are mine.

Introduction

Epigraph: André Masson, "Life and Liberty," *Art in Australia* 4–5 (March, April, May 1942), p. 11.

[1] Conversation with the author, ca. 1983.

[2] André Masson, *Entretiens avec Georges Charbonnier* (Paris: René Julliard, 1958), p. 67.

[3] Conversation with the author, April 1985.

[4] Museum of Modern Art *Bulletin* 13, no. 4–5 (September 1946), p. 25.

1 France, 1938: The Railroad Station of the Imagination and the Dream

[1] Press comments on the 1938 Surrealist exhibition come from a clipping file in the Seligmann papers (MS). Seligmann employed a clipping service both in Paris and later in the United States. Descriptions of the exhibition and its preparation were compiled from a variety of sources, but principally from Georges Hugnet, "L'exposition surréaliste internationale de 1938," *Preuves* no. 91 (September 1958).

[2] Clippings in Seligmann papers (MS).

[3] Hugnet, "L'exposition surréaliste internationale," p. 40.

[4] Ibid.

[5] *Dictionnaire abrégé du surréalisme* (rpt. Paris: José Corti, 1980), p. 10.

[6] Ibid.

[7] Telford Taylor, *Munich: The Price of Peace* (Garden City: Doubleday, 1979), pp. 561–576.

[8] Ibid.

[9] "On the Time When the Surrealists Were Right," *Manifestoes of Surrealism* (Ann Arbor: University of Michigan Press, 1972), p. 250.

[10] Pierre Mabille, *Égrégores* (Paris: J. Flory, 1938), p. 230.

[11] "Souvenir du Mexique," *Minotaure* no. 12 (May 1939), p. 31.

[12] Mabille, *Égrégores*, p. 232.

[13] Breton, "Visite à Léon Trotsky," in *La Clé des champs* (Paris: Sagittaire, 1953), p. 43.

[14] Arturo Schwartz, *André Breton, Trotsky et l'anarchie* (Paris: UGE, 1977), p. 61.

[15] Jean van Heijenoort, *With Trotsky in Exile* (Cambridge: Harvard University Press, 1978), p. 78.

[16] "Toward a Free Revolutionary Art," translated by Dwight Macdonald, *Partisan Review* 6, no. 1 (Fall 1938).

[17] Ibid.; *London Bulletin* (Fall 1938); *Minotaure* no. 10 (November 1938).

[18] Schwartz, *André Breton, Trotsky et l'anarchie*, p. 60.

[19] Kurt Seligmann, "Entretien avec un Tsimshian," *Minotaure* no. 12–13 (Spring 1939), p. 37. See also Seligmann, "Le Mat Totem de Gédem Skanísh," *Journal de la Société des Américanistes* 31 (1939), pp. 121–128.

[20] Jimmy Ernst, *A Not So Still Life* (New York: St. Martins, 1984), p. 144.

[21] Ibid., p. 146.

[22] Gordon Onslow Ford, *Yves Tanguy and Automatism* (privately published, Inverness, California, 1984).

[23] P. D. Ouspensky, *Tertium Organum* (New York: Random House, 1982), p. 43.

[24] Conversation with the author, March 1985.

[25] This definition of psychological morphology is excerpted from a typescript of Matta's original French statement provided to the author by Gordon Onslow Ford together with his translation.

[26] Keith Eubank, *Munich* (Norman: University of Oklahoma Press, 1963), p. 228.

[27] Jean-Paul Clébert, *Mythologie d'André Masson* (Geneva: Pierre Cailler, 1971), p. 54.

[28] Ibid., p. 57.

[29] For a comparison of a student portrait Seligmann painted of Giacometti and the 1928 *Portrait,* see Sawin, "The Archaizing Surrealism of Kurt Seligmann," *Arts* (February 1986).

[30] Archives of the Art Institute of Chicago.

[31] André Breton, "Prestige d'André Masson," *Minotaure* no. 12–13 (May 1939), p. 13.

2 France, 1939: "The Curtain Has Risen on a Forest Fire"

[1] Janet Flanner, *Paris Was Yesterday* (New York: Viking, 1972), p. 297.

[2] Georges Duthuit, "Enquête," *Cahiers d'Art* 1–4 (1939), pp. 72–73.

[3] For a detailed discussion of the stories in *Le Mur* in relation to Surrealism see William Planck, *Sartre and Surrealism* (Ann Arbor: University of Michigan Press, 1981).

[4] Planck, *Sartre and Surrealism,* p. 39.

[5] This was printed for the first time, courtesy of Stephen Miller, in *Matta* (Paris: Centre Georges Pompidou, Musée National de l'Art Moderne, 1985), p. 269.

[6] Letter from Breton to Seligmann, July 18, 1939, Seligmann papers (MS).

[7] Paalen papers, uncatalogued, made available by Gordon Onslow Ford.

[8] Gordon Onslow Ford, *London Bulletin* 18–20 (1940), p. 29.

[9] André Masson, *Entretiens avec Georges Charbonnier* (Paris: René Julliard, 1958), p. 43.

[10] Postcard to Kurt Seligmann, July 1939, Seligmann papers (MS).

[11] Paalen papers, made available by Gordon Onslow Ford.

[12] Letter of September 16, 1939, probably enclosing the letter to Van Heijenoort. Made available by Gordon Onslow Ford.

[13] Stephen Robeson Miller, "In the Interim: The Constructivist Surrealism of Kay Sage," in *Surrealism and Women,* ed. Mary Ann Caws, Rudolf E. Kuenzli, and Gwen Raaberg (Cambridge: MIT Press, 1991).

[14] J. L., "Specters of 1939," *Art News* 38 (October 7, 1939), p. 9.

[15] James W. Lane, "Tanguy at Pierre Matisse," *Art News* 38 (December 6, 1939).

[16] James W. Lane, "Matter of Matta and of Tchelitchew," *Art News* 38 (May 1, 1940), p. 25.

[17] Seligmann papers (MS).

[18] Seligmann papers (MS).

[19] Seligmann papers (MS).

[20] Robert Motherwell, conversation with the author, April 1982.

[21] Letter from Robert Motherwell to Kurt and Arlette Seligmann, July 1941. Seligmann papers (MS).

[22] Arthur Conte, *Le 1 janvier, 1940* (Paris: Plon, 1977), p. 376.

3 New York, 1939: The Prepared Ground

[1] Julien Levy, *Surrealism* (New York: Black Sun Press, 1936), p. 10.

[2] Interview with the author, November 1987.

[3] Baziotes papers, Archives of American Art, Smithsonian Institution.

[4] Typescript of interview with Jack Taylor, Peter Busa papers, Provincetown.

[5] Jeffrey Wechsler, *Surrealism and American Art* (New Brunswick: Rutgers University Art Gallery, 1977), p. 60.

[6] A note on a scrap of paper from Jimmy Ernst's files reads: "Why does Max doubt the dating of Margo's work?" Could Max Ernst have imagined that no one but Domínguez, from whom he learned the technique of decalcomania, would have thought of using it for artistic purposes?

[7] Typescript of Taylor interview, Peter Busa papers, Provincetown.

[8] Samuel Putnam, "Marxism and Surrealism," *Art Front* 21 (March 1937), p. 10.

[9] *Art Front* 5, no. 3 (February 1935), p. 7.

[10] "The Surrealists," *Art Front* 19 (January 1937), p. 12.

[11] James Thrall Soby papers, Museum of Modern Art Archives.

4 France, 1940–1941: The Marseilles Game

Epigraph: André Breton, "Plein Marge," trans. Edouard Roditi, in *Young Cherry Trees Secured against Hares* (New York: View Editions, 1945).

[1] Paalen papers, made available by Gordon Onslow Ford.

[2] Seligmann papers (MS).

[3] Seligmann papers (MS).

[4] Julien Levy, *Memoir of an Art Gallery* (New York: Putnam, 1977), p. 247.

[5] Susanna Coggeshall, interview with the author, August 1985.

[6] Germana Ferrari, *Matta: Entretiens Morphologiques, Notebook no. 1, 1936–1944* (London: Sistan, 1987), p. 100.

[7] Seligmann papers (MS).

[8] Seligmann papers (MS).

[9] Seligmann papers (MS).

[10] Alma Mahler Werfel, *And the Bridge Is Love* (New York: Harcourt Brace, 1958).

[11] Varian Fry papers, Butler Library, Columbia University.

[12] *Pleine marge* was published as an eight-page leaflet during the occupation in 1942 by the clandestine Main à Plume group. In New York it appeared in French and in an English translation by Edouard Roditi in Breton's *Young Cherry Trees Secured against Hares*.

[13] Varian Fry, *Surrender on Demand* (New York: Random House, 1945), p. 115.

[14] Victor Serge, *Memoirs of a Revolutionary* (London: Oxford, 1963), p. 362.

[15] Françoise Levaillant, *André Masson: les années surréalistes, correspondance 1916–1942* (Paris: La Manufacture, 1990), p. 206.

[16] Fry, *Surrender on Demand*, p. 119.

[17] Helena Benitez, interview with the author, March 1992.

[18] Conversation with the author, March 16, 1992.

[19] Varian Fry papers, Butler Library, Columbia University.

[20] Levaillant, *André Masson: les années surréalistes, correspondance 1916–1942*, p. 454.

[21] Claude Lévi-Strauss, *Tristes Tropiques* (New York: Atheneum, 1964), p. 26.

[22] *Tropiques*, February 1943.

[23] Seligmann papers (MS).

[24] Fry archives, Butler Library, Columbia University.

[25] Conversation with the author, July 1986.

[26] Levaillant, *André Masson: les années surréalistes, correspondance 1916–1942*, p. 487.

[27] Ibid., p. 462.

[28] This was the version of the story told in the 1960s when Max Ernst was criticized for not doing more to save his first wife. It does not appear in the 1945 *Surrender on Demand*.

[29] Seligmann papers (MS).

[30] Fry, *Surrender on Demand*, p. 224.

[31] Fry archives, Butler Library, Columbia University.

5 New York, 1941: In a Land without Myth

[1] *The Diary of Anaïs Nin,* vol. 3 (New York: Harcourt, Brace & World, 1971), p. 77.

[2] *View* 1, no. 3 (October 1940).

[3] Interview with the author, October 1985.

[4] Jacob Kainen, interview with Avis Berman, August 10, 1982, Archives of American Art, Smithsonian Institution.

[5] Nin, *Diary*, vol. 3, p. 126.

[6] Interview with the author, October 2, 1985.

[7] Ibid.

[8] Archives, Fogelman Library, New School for Social Research.

[9] The quotations that follow are from the handwritten lecture notes, which Gordon Onslow Ford graciously permitted me to read.

[10] Jimmy Ernst, *A Not So Still Life* (New York: St. Martin's, 1984), p. 243.

[11] Karlen Mooradian, *Arshile Gorky Adoian* (Chicago: Gilgamesh Press, 1978), p. 282.

[12] A version of this story was told to the author around 1960. It is recounted in two interviews in the Archives of American Art: Jimmy Ernst interviewed by Francine Grey, December 1968, p. 6, and by Paul Cummings, September 20, 1974, p. 58. It is possible that the whole story is apocryphal or that Ernst has placed this exchange earlier than it actually took place. There were many gatherings at the Jumble Shop during the early forties at which there could have been such a conversation.

[13] Christopher Lazare, "Exhibition Review," *Decision* 1, no. 4 (April 1941), p. 6.

[14] Letter dated January 27, 1941, Seligmann papers (MS).

[15] James Johnson Sweeney, *Joan Miró* (New York: Museum of Modern Art, 1941), p. 78.

[16] George L. K. Morris, "Sweeney, Soby, and Surrealism," *Partisan Review* 10, no. 2 (March–April 1942), p. 122.

[17] Clement Greenberg, "Three Current Art Books," *Partisan Review* 10, no. 4 (March–April 1942), p. 127.

[18] André Masson, *Le Plaisir de peindre* (Nice: la Diane, 1950) p. 138.

[19] André Breton, *La Clé des champs* (Paris: UGE, 1973), p. 75.

[20] For a full description of the laborious automatist process Seligmann used for his cyclonic drawings and paintings, see Stefan E. Hauser, "Kurt Seligmann as Draftsman," *Drawing* 16, no. 6 (March–April 1995), 121–126.

[21] Magazine of Art (December 1941).

[22] *Art News* 40 (October 15, 1941), p. 29; *Art News* 41 (April 15–30, 1942), p. 27.

[23] Conversation with the author, April 1983.

[24] André Breton, *L'Amour fou* (Paris: Gallimard, 1936), p. 25.

[25] Nin, *Diary,* vol. 3, p. 144.

[26] Thomas Hess, *Abstract Painting, Background and American Phase* (New York: Viking, 1951), p. 60.

[27] Conversation with the author, November 1987.

[28] Letter to Kurt and Arlette Seligmann, Seligmann papers (MS).

[29] Germana Ferrari, *Matta: Entretiens Morphologiques, Notebook No. 1, 1936–1944* (London: Sistan, 1987), p. 108.

[30] *View* 1 (October 1941), p. 1.

[31] Ibid.

[32] "Life and Liberty," *Art in Australia* 4–5 (March, April, May 1942), p. 11.

6 New York, 1942: Veils and Transparents

Epigraph: Rosamund Frost, "First Fruits of Exile," *Art News* 41 (March 15, 1942).

[14] Statement by Aaron Siskind, October 2, 1982, Rothko project, p. 14, Archives of American Art, Smithsonian Institution.

[15] Quoted in interview with Dorothy Gees Seckler, 1967, Archives of American Art, Smithsonian Institution.

[16] Interview with the author, April 1987.

[17] Ibid.

[18] Interview with the author, November 1987.

[19] Press release written by Jimmy Ernst, March 1943, Eleanor Lust papers, Archives of American Art, Smithsonian Institution, Washington, D.C.

[20] *New York Times,* June 13, 1943, section II, p. 9.

[21] Esta Gottlieb, interview, Archives of American Art, Smithsonian Institution.

[22] Interview with the author, April, 1985.

[23] Telephone interview with the author, November 1986.

[24] Seligmann papers (MS), carbon copy of explanation sent to Askew.

[25] Ibid.

[26] Kirk Askew papers, Archives of American Art, Smithsonian Institution.

[27] *Art News* 42, no. 6 (June/July 1943).

[28] *Art News* 42, no. 4 (April 1, 1943), p. 27.

[29] John Meyers, *Tracking the Marvelous* (New York: Random House, 1983), p. 67.

[30] Interview with the author, November 1986.

[31] Interview with the author, April 1985.

[32] "Matta Echaurren," *Magazine of Art* 40 (March 1947), p. 104.

[33] André Breton, "Marcel Duchamp," *Littérature,* n.s. 5 (October 1922), translated in Marcel Jean, *The Autobiography of Surrealism* (New York: Viking, 1980), p. 86.

[34] Interview with the author, April 1985.

[35] Romy Golan, "Matta, Duchamp et le mythe: un nouveau paradigme pour la dernière phase du surréalisme," in *Matta* (Paris: Centre Georges Pompidou, Musée national d'art moderne, 1985).

[36] Onslow Ford papers.

[37] Golan, "Matta, Duchamp et le mythe," p. 41.

[38] Katherine Dreier and Roberto Matta Echaurren, *Duchamp's Glass* (New York: Société Anonyme, 1944), p. 3.

[39] William Rubin, "Matta aux Etats Unis: une note personelle," in *Matta* (Centre Georges Pompidou), p. 24.

[40] Golan, "Matta, Duchamp et le mythe," p. 43.

[41] Busa, studio notes, courtesy of Cristopher Busa.

[42] Busa, interview with Jack Taylor, c. 1970. A similar story was told to the author by Ethel Baziotes.

[43] Germana Ferrari, *Matta: Entretiens Morphologiques, Notebook no. 1, 1936–1944* (London: Sistan, 1987), p. 31.

[44] Meyer Schapiro, "Gorky: The Creative Influence," *Art News* 56 (September 1957), p. 29.

[45] Conversation with the author, c. 1957.

[46] Typescript of interview with Jack Taylor, c. 1970, p. 3, Peter Busa papers, Provincetown.

[47] Julien Levy, *Arshile Gorky* (New York: Harry N. Abrams, 1966), p. 31.

[48] Julien Levy, *Memoir of an Art Gallery* (New York: Putnam, 1977), p. 285.

[49] Conversation with the author, April 1994.

[50] Letters of Jeanne Reynal to Agnes Gorky, Archives of American Art, Smithsonian Institution.

[51] Videotape shown during Motherwell's Guggenheim Museum show in 1985.

[52] American Masters television program: "Robert Motherwell and Abstract Expressionism."

[53] Steven Naifeh and Gregory White Smith, *Jackson Pollock, An American Saga* (New York: Clarkson Potter, 1989), p. 445.

[54] Letter dated November 2, 1942, Onslow Ford papers.

[55] Max Ernst, "Biographical Notes," reprinted in Werner Spies, *Max Ernst, a Retrospective* (Munich: Prestel, 1991), p. 323.

[56] Paalen, "Art and Science," *Dyn* no. 3 (1942), p. 18.

[57] Ellen G. Landau, *Jackson Pollock* (New York: Abrams, 1989), p. 131; also see footnote.

[58] Robert Motherwell, "Painter's Objects," *Partisan Review* 10, no. 1 (Winter 1944), p. 97.

[59] Naifeh and Smith, *Jackson Pollock*, p. 466.

[60] Clement Greenberg, "Art," *The Nation* 157 (November 27, 1943), p. 621.

[61] Naifeh and Smith, *Jackson Pollock,* p. 468.

9 New York, 1944–1945: Young Cherry Trees Secured against Hares

Epigraph: Mark Rothko, "Personal Statement" written for David Porter Gallery, Washington, D.C., 1945.

[1] Robert Motherwell, interview with the author, March 1982.

[2] Paalen, "The New Image," *Dyn* 1 (Spring 1942), p. 15.

[3] James Johnson Sweeney, *Harpers Bazaar* (April 1944).

[4] Robert Motherwell, "Interview with Jackson Pollock," *Art and Architecture* (February 1945).

[5] Robert Motherwell, telephone interview with the author, November 1985.

[6] Sidney Janis, *Abstract and Surrealist Painting in America* (New York: Reynal and Hitchcock, 1944), p. 6.

[7] Ibid.

[8] Sidney Janis interviewed by Helen Franck, 1967, transcript in Museum of Modern Art Library.

[9] Clement Greenberg, "Art," *The Nation*, 1944, p.

[10] Steven Naifeh and Gregory White Smith, *Jackson Pollock, An American Saga* (New York: Clarkson Potter, 1989), pp. 457–458. Masson's *Pasiphaë* was in the Buchholz Gallery inventory by January 1944, was shown by Paul Rosenberg in April, and was commented on by Clement Greenberg in the *Nation* in May. Pollock had started work on his 6½-by-8-foot canvas before the end of 1943, then put it aside and completed it after he finished Guggenheim's *Mural.* Greenberg reportedly advised him to see the Masson painting and Pollock is even said to have muttered on seeing it "I'm going to paint me a Pasiphaë." The title could have been appropriated as an afterthought at the time of the Guggenheim exhibition, and possibly Sweeney provided his explanation at that time.

[11] Greenberg, "Art," *The Nation* 158 (May 27, 1944), p. 634.

[12] Greenberg, "Art," *The Nation* 159 (August 19, 1944), p. 220. The two essays from *The Nation* of August 12 and 19 were reprinted in England in *Horizon* in January 1945.

[13] Greenberg, letter to Baziotes, August 21, 1944, William Baziotes Papers, Archives of American Art, Smithsonian Institution.

[14] Motherwell, letter of September 6, 1944, to William Baziotes, Baziotes papers, Archives of American Art, Smithsonian Institution.

[15] André Breton, *Arcane 17* (New York: Brentano's, 1945), p. 1.

[16] Donald Paneth, "William Baziotes: a Literary Portrait," unpublished typescript in Baziotes Papers, Archives of American Art, Smithsonian Institution, p. 30.

[17] Ibid.

[18] Seligmann, "The Evil Eye," *VVV* 1 (1942), p. 46. The influence of the Seligmann article on Baziotes's *Cyclops* is suggested by Mona Hadler, "The Art of William Baziotes," Ph.D. dissertation, Columbia University, 1977, p. 169.

[19] Paneth, "William Baziotes: A Literary Portrait," p. 21.

[20] Baziotes, letter to Alfred Barr, copy in Baziotes file, Museum of Modern Art Library.

[21] Sidney Janis, *Abstract and Surrealist Art in America* (New York: Reynal & Hitchcock, 1944), p. 107.

[22] Greenberg, "Art," *The Nation* 159 (November 11, 1944), p. 498.

[23] Motherwell, letter to Baziotes, September 6, 1944, Baziotes papers, Archives of American Art, Smithsonian Institution.

[24] Motherwell, excerpts from videotaped talk, Malone Gill Projects, 1979, on occasion of Case Western Reserve festival, and from a telephone interview with the author.

[25] Janis, *Abstract and Surrealist Art in America,* p. 65.

[26] Greenberg, "Art," *The Nation* 159 (November 11, 1944), p. 568.

[27] Ibid.

[28] According to David Anfam, neither of the works identified as *Entombment I* and *Entombment II* on Guggenheim's list of works exhibited in Rothko's January 1945 show are identical with the two somewhat later paintings of the same titles. There is some confusion about which paintings actually were shown under these titles. I have reproduced the Whitney Museum *Entombment I,* dated 1946, because, despite the later date, it offers a good example of the "veiling" process that Rothko was using. I appreciate David Anfam's knowledgeable assistance in the matter of these multiple *Entombments.*

29 David Porter, "Personal Statement: Painting Prophecy, 1950," exhibition announcement, David Porter Gallery, Washington, D.C., February 1945.

30 Melvin P. Lader, "Peggy Guggenheim's Art of This Century: The Surrealist Milieu and the American Avant-Garde, 1942–1947," Ph.D. dissertation, University of Delaware, 1981, pp. 172ff.

31 Ibid.

32 Robert M. Coates, "The Art Galleries," *The New Yorker* 21 (May 26, 1945), p. 68.

33 Maude Riley, "Insufficient Evidence," *Art Digest* 19 (June 1945), p. 12.

34 Greenberg, "Art," *The Nation* 160 (June 9, 1945), p. 657.

35 André Breton, catalogue text for Gorky's 1945 exhibition at Julien Levy; also published in *Surrealism and Painting* (New York: Brentano's, 1945).

36 Greenberg, "Art," *The Nation* 160 (March 24, 1945).

37 Clement Greenberg, "American Type Painting," *Partisan Review,* Spring 1955.

38 Ruben Kadish, letter to the author, February 15, 1986.

39 That a proof of *Abduction (Rapt)* hung at Atelier 17 was mentioned by Hayter in an interview with the author, as well as in several published articles. However, no edition was made of this print until after Masson's return to France, and there is a theory that since it was a drypoint he may have made it at his home in Connecticut. Since he did eighteen prints at Atelier 17 in New York there is room for some confusion about what proofs may have been hanging there. In an interview with the author Masson asserted that his and Pollock's paths had never crossed, but that he had been told that the latter spent time at his exhibitions.

40 Gustav Regler, *Wolfgang Paalen* (New York: Nierendorf Editions, 1946), p. 53.

41 John Meyers, *Tracking the Marvelous* (New York: Random House, 1983), p. 60.

42 *Horizon* 11, no. 61 (May 1945), p. 312.

43 René Huyghe, "Letter from Paris," *Magazine of Art*, November 1945, p. 272.

44 Jeanne Reynal, letter to Agnes Gorky, Archives of American Art, Smithsonian Institution.

45 *Horizon* 12, no. 67 (July 1945), p. 68.

46 James Brooks, interview with the author, fall 1986.

10 Paris, 1945–1947: In the Time of Lean Cows

Epigraph: Jean Paul Sartre, "Qu'est-ce que la littérature?" 4–5, *Les Temps Modernes* no. 20 (May 1947), p. 1426.

1 Michèle Cone in *Artists under Vichy* (Princeton: Princeton University Press, 1992) details these varying degrees of accommodation and collaboration in the French art world during the Occupation. She reproduces a page from the register for the Salon d'Automne showing the signatures of the exhibiting artists testifying to their Frenchness and non-Jewishness.

2 Gilles Ragache and Jean Robert Ragache, *La Vie quotidienne des écrivans et des artistes sous l'occupation* (Paris: Hachette, 1988), p. 92.

[3] Marcel Duchamp, letter to Tristan Tzara, 1946.

[4] *Labyrinthe* no. 16 (January 15, 1946), p. 6.

[5] Reprinted in Jean Schuster and José Pierre, eds., *Tracts surréalistes et déclarations collectives, 1922–69* (Paris: Le Terrain Vague, 1982), vol. 2, pp. 11–17.

[6] Quoted in Michel Faure, *Histoire du surréalisme sous l'occupation* (Paris: Table Rond, 1982), p. 428. The eight dead referred to are Jean-Claude Diamant Berger, Marc Patin, Hans Schoenhoff, Tita, Jean-Pierre Mulotte, Marco Menegoz, Robert Rius, and Jean Simonpoli.

[7] Georges Bataille, "Le surréalisme et sa différence avec existentialisme," *Critique* no. 2 (July 1946), p. 101.

"La Décision surréaliste est ainsi décision de ne plus décider, l'activité libre de l'esprit serait trahie si je la subordonnais à quelque résultat décidé d'avance. La différence profonde du surréalisme avec l'extentialisme de Jean Paul Sartre tient à ce caractère d'existence de la liberté. Si je ne l'asservis pas, la liberté existera; c'est la poésie, les mots, n'ayant plus à servir à quelque désignation utile, se déchaînent et ce déchaînement est l'image de l'existence libre, qui n'est jamais donnée que dans l'instant."

[8] Charly Guyot, "Jean Paul Sartre et l'experience de l'angoisse," *Labyrinthe* 4 (January 1945), p. 6.

[9] *Labyrinthe* 9 (June 15, 1945), p. 8.

[10] André Rousseau, "Du surréalisme à Jean Paul Sartre," *Labyrinthe* 10 (July 15, 1945), p. 9.

[11] Jean Cassou, "Tristan Tzara et l'humanisme poétique," *Labyrinthe* 14 (November 15, 1945), pp. 1–2.

[12] Jean Wahl, "La vogue de l'existentialisme," *Labyrinthe* 17 (February 15, 1946), p. 6.

[13] "André Breton nous parle," *Le Littéraire* 29 (October 1946), p. 1.

[14] Henri Béhar, *André Breton, le grand indésirable* (Paris: Calmann-Lévy, 1990), p. 378.

[15] This is very likely the same event, although the locale differs from that given in Béhar, reported in *Combat*, June 17, 1947. It is described as having taken place at the Théâtre de Vieux Colombier with an SRO audience of 900 and talks by Gide, Camus, Breton, and Artaud himself. The latter described the effects of electroshock treatment, saying that "when one wakes one is incapable of recovering one's identity [retrouver son moi]."

[16] Alain Jouffroy, *Le Roman vecu* (Paris: Editions Robert Laffont, 1978), p. 152.

[17] *Combat* (February 1947).

[18] A copy of the letter Breton sent to each member of the group was provided to the author by Enrico Donati.

[19] Béhar, *André Breton*, p. 282.

[20] Breton, letter to Donati, February 1947, Donati archives.

[21] Reprinted in *Possibilities* no. 1 (1947).

[22] *Combat*, May 1947.

[23] Béhar, *André Breton*, p. 384.

[24] *Les Temps Modernes* no. 20 (May 1947), p. 1426.

[25] Maurice Nadeau, "Breton, mage du possible," *Combat*, June 20, 1947.

[26] Jacques Kober, letter to Donati, May 8, 1947, Donati archives.

[27] Donati, interview with the author, February 1994.

[28] *Le Surréalisme en 1947* (Paris: Editions Maeght, 1947).

[29] For a detailed eyewitness description see Marcel Jean, *The History of Surrealist Painting* (New York: Grove Press, 1960), pp. 341–344.

[30] David Hare, letter to Donati, August 14, 1947, Donati archives.

[31] Albert Palle, "L'Exposition internationale surréaliste," *Figaro,* July 9, 1947.

[32] *Time,* July 21, 1947.

[33] David Hare, letter to Donati, August 8, 1947, Donati archives (orthography uncorrected).

[34] Breton, letter to Jacques Kober, August 1947.

[35] Information on the response to the exhibition was provided by Jacques Kober in a letter to the author dated March 29, 1992, and a phone conversation on March 3, 1992. Kober had been associated with the Main à Plume group and had been one of the editors of *Pierre à Feu,* published in Nice, the first number of which in August 1944 was dedicated to the Main à Plume.

[36] Béhar, *André Breton,* p. 393.

[37] Breton, letter to Donati, September 14, 1947, Donati archives. Breton also expressed annoyance with Maeght for not disciplining Kober for signing the protest, as well as for careless handling that resulted in damage and loss during the taking down of the exhibition.

[38] Jean Schuster, interview with the author, March 1992. Schuster also emphasized that Breton did not feel a great hostility to Sartre; rather he hoped to work with him to build an anti-Communist left. Both participated in the large rally organized for this purpose by Camus in 1948.

[39] *Museum of Modern Art Bulletin* 13, nos. 4–5 (1946), p. 19.

[40] Greenberg, "Art," *The Nation* 166 (January 10, 1948).

[41] Gorky, letter to Vartoosh, February 17, 1947. Published in *Ararat* no. 4 (Fall 1971). Gorky wrote: "Surrealism is academic art under disguise and anti-esthetic and suspicious of excellence and largely in opposition to modern art. Its claim of liberation is really restrictive because of its narrow rigidity. To its adherents the tradition of art and its quality mean little. They are drunk with psychiatric spontaneity and inexplicable dreams. . . . Their ideas are somewhat strange and flippant, almost playful. Really they are not as earnest about painting as I should like artists to be. Art must always remain earnest."

[42] Julien Levy, *Memoir of an Art Gallery* (New York: Putnam, 1977), p. 285.

[43] Aline Loucheim, "Spotlight on Kurt Seligmann," *Art News* 41 (December 1946).

[44] Title page, *Possibilities* I, winter 1947/8.

Epilogue

[1] A description of this proceeding is given by Alain Jouffroy in *Le Roman vecu* (Paris: Editions Robert Laffont, 1978), pp. 159–163. It was also described to the author by Patrick Waldberg during an interview in April 1985.

[2] See Margaret Osborne, unpublished memoir of Arshile Gorky, on file in the Museum of Modern Art Library. A portion of this appeared in *Art News* 61, no. 10 (February 1963), pp. 42–43.

[3] Conversation with the author, April 1982.

[4] Malone/Gill Projects Inc., taped interview with Robert Motherwell on the occasion of a Surrealist festival at Case Western University, fall 1979, organized by Peter Newington, Jack Roth, and George Holly.

[5] Several letters from Jeanne Reynal, living near Gorky in Twin Lakes, Connecticut, to Agnes Gorky who was in Virginia, written in July and August 1947, shed light on Gorky's state of mind and the state of the marriage. She also comments on "two lovely canvases . . . out of his anguish he always emerges with something that makes no mention of the same." Archives of American Art, N69/66, 665–794.

[6] Donald E. Miller and Lorna Touryan Miller, *Survivors: An Oral History of the Armenian Genocide* (Berkeley: University of California Press, 1993), p. 10.

[7] Julien Levy, *Arshile Gorky* (New York: Harry N. Abrams, 1962), p. 9.

[8] Robert N. Linscott, ed., *The Stories of Anton Chekov* (New York: The Modern Library, 1933), p. 150. This is quoted in Harry Rand, *Arshile Gorky, the Implication of Symbols* (Berkeley: University of California Press, 1991), p. 229. Rand carries his analysis of *Last Painting* further than Levy, providing a detailed correlation between the forms in the painting and the descriptions in the Chekov story and identifying Gorky more specifically with the character of Kovrin.

[9] B. H. Friedman, *Jackson Pollock* (New York: McGraw-Hill, 1972), p. 169.

[10] For a complete account of the circumstances surrounding the publication of "the irascibles" see Bradford Collins, "*Life* Magazine and the Abstract Expressionists, 1948–1959: A Historiographic Study of a Late Bohemian Enterprise," *Art Bulletin,* June 1991, 283–308.

[11] Wolfgang Paalen, "Metaplastic," essay for the Dynaton catalogue, San Francisco Museum of Art, 1951, p. 22.

[12] Interview with Guy Habasque, 1959, quoted in Jean-Paul Clébert, *Mythologie d'André Masson* (Geneva: Pierre Cailler, 1972), p. 75.

Selected Bibliography

Books, Catalogues, and Articles

Abel, Lionel. *The Intellectual Follies: A Memoir of the Literary Venture in New York and Paris.* New York: W. W. Norton, 1984.

Ades, Dawn. *Dada and Surrealism Reviewed.* Catalogue, Hayward Gallery. London: Arts Council of Great Britain, 1978.

Ades, Dawn. *Dalí and Surrealism.* New York: Harper & Row, 1982.

Alexandrian, Sarane. *Surrealist Art.* New York: Praeger, 1970.

Alloway, Lawrence. *William Baziotes: A Memorial Exhibition.* New York: Solomon R. Guggenheim Museum, 1965.

Alquie, Ferdinand. *Entretiens sur le surréalisme.* Paris: Flammarion, 1968.

Andersson, Christiane. *Dirnen—Krieger—Narren, ausgewählte Zeichnungen von Urs Graf.* Basel: GS-Verlag, 1978.

André Masson, Works from 1923–1944. Catalogue. New York: Kouros Gallery, 1986.

Aranda, Francisco. *Luis Buñuel, a Critical Biography.* New York: Da Capo Press, 1976.

Arnaud, Noël. *Avenir du surréalisme.* 2nd series of Feuillets du Quatre Vingt et Un, Le Quesnoy Nord, 1944.

Aron, Raymond. *The Century of Total War.* New York: Doubleday, 1954.

Artforum 5, no. 1 (September 1966). Special issue on Surrealism.

Art Institute of Chicago. *Surrealism and Its Affinities: The Mary Reynolds Collection.* Catalogue. Chicago: Art Institute ofChicago, 1956.

Ashton, Dore. *The New York School: A Cultural Reckoning.* New York: Viking Press, 1972.

Balakian, Anna. *André Breton, Magus of Surrealism.* New York: Oxford University Press, 1971.

Barr, Alfred H., Jr., ed. *Fantastic Art, Dada, Surrealism.* New York: Museum of Modern Art, 1936.

Bataille, Georges. "Le Surréalisme et sa différence avec existentialisme." *Critique,* no. 2 (July 1946).

Bauer, George H. *Sartre and the Artist.* Chicago: University of Chicago Press, 1969.

Baziotes, William. "Notes on Painting." *It Is* (Autumn 1959).

Behar, Henri. *André Breton: le grand indésirable.* Paris: Calmann-Lévy, 1990.

Bénédite, Daniel. *La Filière marseillaise.* Paris: Editions Clancier-Guenaud, 1984.

Benitez, Helena. *Wifredo Lam, Interlude Marseille.* Copenhagen: Edition Blondal, 1993.

Bettelheim, Bruno. *Surviving and Other Essays*. New York: Knopf, 1979.

Birmingham, Ellen. "André Masson in America: The Artist's Achievement in Exile 1941–1945." Ph.D. dissertation, University of Michigan, 1979.

Bloch, Marc. *Strange Defeat: A Statement of Evidence Written in 1940*. London, 1949.

Bonnet, Marguerite. *André Breton, naissance de l'aventure surréaliste*. Paris: José Corti, 1975.

Breton, André. *L'Amour fou* (1936). Paris: Gallimard, 1976.

Breton, André. *Arcane 17*. With illustrations by Matta. New York: Brentano's, 1945.

Breton, André. *La Clé des champs* (1953). Paris: UGE, 1973.

Breton, André. *Entretiens avec André Parinaud, 1913–1952*. Paris: Nouvelle Revue Française, 1954.

Breton, André. "Genesis and Perspectives of Surrealism." *Art of This Century*, catalogue of the Peggy Guggenheim collection. New York: Art of This Century, 1942.

Breton, André. *Manifestoes of Surrealism*. Translated by Richard Seaver and Helen R. Lane. Ann Arbor: University of Michigan Press, 1972.

Breton, André. "Originality and Liberty." *Art in Australia* 4 (December, January, February 1941–1942).

Breton, André. *Pleine marge: eau-forte de Kurt Seligmann*. New York: Nierendorf Gallery, 1943.

Breton, André. *Le Surréalisme et la peinture*. New York: Brentano's, 1945.

Breton, André. *Young Cherry Trees Secured against Hares*. In French, with English translations by Edouard Roditi. New York: View Editions, 1945. Ann Arbor: University of Michigan Press, 1969.

Breton, André. *Yves Tanguy*. New York: Pierre Matisse Editions, 1946.

Breton, André, and Marcel Duchamp. *First Papers of Surrealism*. Catalogue. New York: Coordinating Council of French Relief Societies, 1942.

Breton, André, with André Masson. *Martinique, charmeuse de serpents*. Paris: Pauvert, 1972.

Browder, Clifford. *André Breton—Arbiter of Surrealism*. Geneva: Librairie Droz, 1967.

Brownstone, Gilbert. *André Masson, vagabond du surréalisme*. Paris: Editions Saint-Germain des Pres, 1975.

Chadwick, Whitney. *Myth in Surrealist Painting, 1929–1939*. Ann Arbor: UMI Research Press, 1979.

Chadwick, Whitney. *Women Artists and the Surrealist Movement*. Boston: Little, Brown, 1985.

Champa, Kermit. *Flying Tigers: Painting and Sculpture in New York 1939–1946*. Catalogue. Providence: Bell Gallery, Brown University, 1985.

Chave, Anna. *Mark Rothko: Subjects in Abstraction*. New Haven: Yale University Press, 1989.

Clébert, Jean-Paul. *Mythologie d'André Masson*. Geneva: Pierre Cailler, 1972.

Clifford, James. *The Predicament of Culture: Twentieth-Century Ethnography, Literature, and Art*. Cambridge, Mass.: Harvard University Press, 1988.

Cohen-Solal, Annie. *Sartre 1905–1980*. Paris: Gallimard, 1985.

Cone, Michèle. *Artists under Vichy*. Princeton: Princeton University Press, 1992.

Conte, Arthur. *Le Premier janvier 1940*. Paris: Plon, 1977.

Coply, William. "Portrait of an Artist as a Young Art Dealer." In *Coply: Reflections on a Past Life*. Houston: Institute for the Arts, Rice University, 1979.

Dalí, Salvador. *Diary of a Genius*. Translated by Richard Howard. New York: Doubleday, 1965.

Dalí, Salvador. *The Secret Life of Salvador Dalí*. London: Vision Press, 1948.

Delperrie de Bayac, Jacques. *Histoire du Front populaire*. Paris: Fayard, 1972.

de Rougemont, Denis. *Journal de deux mondes*. Paris: Gallimard, 1946

Dictionnaire abrégé du surréalisme (1938). Paris: José Corti, 1969.

Dorothea Tanning. Paris: Vingtième Siecle, 1977.

Dreier, Katherine S., and Matta Echaurrén. *Duchamp's Glass, an Analytical Reflection*. New York: Société Anonyme, 1944.

Duits, Charles. *André Breton a-t-il dit passe*. Paris: Denoël, 1969.

Ernst, Jimmy. *A Not So Still Life*. New York: St. Martin's, 1984.

Ernst, Max. *Beyond Painting and Other Writings*. New York: Wittenborn, 1948.

Faure, Michel. *Histoire du surréalisme sous l'Occupation*. Paris: La Table Ronde, 1982.

Ferrari, Germana. *Matta: Entretiens Morphologiques, Notebook No. 1, 1936–1944*. London: Sistan, 1987.

Fichner-Rathus, Lois. "Pollock at Atelier 17." *Print Collectors Newsletter* 13, no. 5 (November–December 1982), 162–165.

Flanner, Janet. *Paris Was Yesterday, 1925–1939*. Edited by Irving Drutman. New York: Viking, 1972.

Fontaine, André. *Le Camp d'étrangers des Milles: 1939–1943*. Aix-en-Provence: Edisud, 1989.

Fouchet, Max-Pol. "Le Surréalisme en Amérique." *Fontaine* 32 (1944).

Freeman, Judi. *The Dada and Surrealist Word-Image*. Catalogue, Los Angeles County Museum of Art. Cambridge, Mass.: MIT Press, 1989.

Fry, Varian. *Surrender on Demand*. New York: Random House, 1945.

Galerie Maeght. *Exposition internationale du surréalisme*. Catalogue. Paris: Editions Pierre à Feu, 1947.

Gendel, Milton. "Immagine indelebile." In *Hayter e l'Atelier 17*. Rome: Calcografia, Accademia di San Luca, 1990.

Gerassi, John. *Jean Paul Sartre, Hated Conscience of His Century*. Chicago: University of Chicago Press, 1989.

Gerome Kamrowski: A Retrospective Exhibition. Catalogue. Ann Arbor: University of Michigan Museum of Art, 1983.

Gold, Mary Jayne. *Crossroads Marseilles 1940*. Garden City: Doubleday, 1980.

Goutier, Jean Michel. *Benjamin Péret*. Paris: Editions Henri Veyrier, 1982.

Greenberg, Clement. *The Collected Essays and Criticism*. Edited by John O'Brian. Vol. 1, *Perceptions and Judgments, 1939–1944*; vol. 2, *Arrogant Purpose, 1945–1949*. Chicago: University of Chicago Press, 1986.

Guggenheim, Peggy, ed. *Art of This Century*. New York: Art of This Century, 1942.

Guggenheim, Peggy. *Confessions of an Art Addict*. New York, Macmillan, 1960.

Guggenheim, Peggy. *Out of This Century*. New York: Dial Press, 1946.

Guilbaut, Serge. *How New York Stole the Idea of Modern Art: Abstract Expressionism, Freedom, and the Cold War*. Translated by Arthur Goldhammer. Chicago: University of Chicago Press, 1983.

Hadler, Mona. "The Art of William Baziotes." Ph.D. dissertation, Columbia University, 1977.

Hahn, Otto. *Masson*. New York: Harry N. Abrams, 1965.

Halami, André. *Chantons sous l'Occupation* (film). Paris: Olivier Orban, 1976.

Hare, David. "Art History, Art History on the Wall. Did I, Did I Do It All?" Published under "Communication," *Art News* (June 1967).

Hare, David. "Spaces of the Mind." *Magazine of Art* (February 1950).

Heilbut, Anthony. *Exiled in Paradise*. New York: Viking, 1983.

Hess, Thomas. *Abstract Painting, Background and American Phase*. New York: Viking, 1951.

Hirshfeld, Gerhard, and Patrick Marsh, eds. *Collaboration in France: Politics and Culture during the Nazi Occupation, 1940–44*. New York: St. Martin's, 1989.

Hobbs, Robert, and Gail Levin. *Abstract Expressionism, the Formative Years*. Catalogue. New York: Whitney Museum, 1978.

Hommage to Wolfgang Paalen. Catalogue. Mexico City: Museo de Arte Moderno, 1967.

Hughnet, Georges. "L'Exposition internationale du surréalisme en 1938." *Preuves* (September 1958).

Jackman, Jarrell, and Carla Borden, eds. *The Muses Flee Hitler.* Washington, D.C.: Smithsonian Institution Press, 1983.

Janis, Sidney. *Abstract and Surrealist Art in America.* New York: Reynal & Hitchcock, 1944.

Janis, Sidney. "European Artists Come to New York." *Decision* 2, no. 5–6 (November–December 1941).

Jean, Marcel. *The Autobiography of Surrealism.* New York: Viking, 1980.

Jean, Marcel. *The History of Surrealism.* New York: Grove Press, 1960.

Josephson, Matthew. *Life among the Surrealists: A Memoir.* New York: Holt, Rinehart and Winston, 1962.

Jouffroy, Alain. *Le Roman vécu.* Paris: Editions Robert Laffont, 1978.

Kaplan, Janet. *Unexpected Journeys: The Art and Life of Remedios Varo.* New York: Abbeville, 1988.

Kootz, Samuel. *New Frontiers in American Painting.* New York: Hastings House, 1943.

Kozloff, Max. "An Interview with Matta; an Interview with Robert Motherwell." *Artforum* 4, no. 1 (September 1965).

Kuh, Katherine. "The Present." In catalogue for "Abstract and Surrealist American Art." Chicago: Art Institute of Chicago, 1947.

Lader, Melvin. "Peggy Guggenheim's Art of This Century: The Surrealist Milieu and the American Avant-Garde, 1942–1947." Ph.D. dissertation, University of Delaware, 1981.

Lader, Melvin. *Peggy Guggenheim's Other Legacy.* Catalogue. New York: Solomon R. Guggenheim Museum, 1987.

Lamba, Jacqueline. "La Rencontre Trotsky-Breton." *Les Lettres Nouvelles,* no. 4 (September–October 1975).

Laroche-Sanchez, Evelyne. "L'Aventure mexicaine du surréalisme (1936–1948)." Thesis, 3rd cycle, University of Paris III, 1987.

Laughlin, James, ed. *New Directions in Prose and Poetry, 1940.* Norfolk, Conn.: New Directions, 1940.

Legrand, Gérard. *André Breton en son temps.* Paris: Le Soleil Noir, 1976.

Leiris, Michel, and Georges Limbour. *André Masson et son univers.* Geneva: Trois Collines, 1947.

Levaillant, Françoise. *André Masson: les années surréalistes, correspondance 1916–1942.* Paris: La Manufacture, 1990.

Lévi-Strauss, Claude. *Tristes tropiques.* Translated by John Russell. New York: Atheneum, 1964.

Levy, Julien. *Arshile Gorky.* New York: Harry N. Abrams, 1966.

Levy, Julien. *Memoir of an Art Gallery.* New York: Putnam, 1977.

Levy, Julien. *Surrealism.* New York: Black Sun Press, 1936.

Lottman, Herbert. *The Left Bank: Writers, Artists and Politics from the Popular Front to the Cold War.* New York: Houghton Mifflin, 1982.

Lynes, Russell. *Good Old Modern.* New York: Atheneum, 1973.

Mabille, Pierre. *Égrégores.* Paris: J. Flory, 1938.

Mabille, Pierre. *Le Mirroir du merveilleux.* Paris: Sagittaire, 1940.

Mann, Klaus. "Surrealist Circus." *American Mercury* 56 (February 1943). Excerpted in *Art Digest* 17 (15 May 1943).

Mann, Klaus. *The Turning Point: Thirty-five Years in This Century.* New York: L. B. Fischer, 1942.

Manrique, Jorge Alberto, and Teresa del Conde. *Una mujer en el arte Mexicano—memorias de Ines Amor.* Mexico City: Universidad Nacional Autónoma de México, 1987.

Masson, André. *Anatomie de mon univers.* New York: Curt Valentin, 1943.

Masson, André. *Entretiens avec Georges Charbonnier.* Paris: Julliard, 1958.

Masson, André. "Life and Liberty." *Art in Australia* 4–5 (March, April, May 1942).

Masson, André. *La Mémoire du monde.* Geneva: Skira, 1954.

Masson, André. *Mythology of Being.* New York: Wittenborn, 1942.

Masson, André. "Peindre est un gageure." *Cahiers du Sud,* no. 233 (March 1941). First English translation, *Horizon* 7, no. 39 (March 1943).

Masson, André. *Le Plaisir de peindre.* Nice: La Diane Française, 1950.

Matta. Catalogue. Paris: Centre Georges Pompidou, Musée National d'Art Moderne, 1985.

Mattison, Robert. *Robert Motherwell: The Formative Years.* Ann Arbor: UMI Research Press, 1987.

Mauriac, Claude. "Sartre contre Breton." *Carrefour* 4 (September 1947).

Meyers, John. *Tracking the Marvelous: A Life in the New York Art World.* New York: Random House, 1983.

Michael Rosenfeld Gallery. *Charles Seliger, Nature's Journal.* Catalogue. New York: Michael Rosenfeld Gallery, 1994.

Miller, Donald E., and Lorna Touryan Miller. *Survivors: An Oral History of the Armenian Genocide.* Berkeley: University of California Press, 1993.

Miller, Nancy. *Matta: The First Decade*. Waltham: Rose Art Museum, Brandeis University, 1982.

Miller, Stephen R. "The Surrealist Imagery of Kay Sage." *Art International* 26, no. 4 (September–October 1983).

Mooradian, Karlen. *Arshile Gorky Adoian*. Chicago: Gilgamesh Press, 1978.

Motherwell, Robert. "Beyond the Aesthetic." *Design* (April 1946).

Motherwell, Robert. "Painters' Objects." *Partisan Review* 10, no. 1 (Winter 1944).

Museum of Modern Art Bulletin 13, no. 4–5 (September 1946).

Nadeau, Maurice. *Histoire du surréalisme: documents surréalistes*. 2 vols. Paris: Editions du Seuil, 1945–1948.

Naifeh, Steven, and Gregory White Smith. *Jackson Pollock: An American Saga*. New York: Clarkson N. Potter, 1989.

Neff, Terry Ann R., ed. *In the Mind's Eye: Dada and Surrealism*. Catalogue, Museum of Contemporary Art, Chicago. New York: Abbeville Press, 1985.

Nessen, Susan. "Surrealism in Exile: The Early Years, 1940–42." Ann Arbor: UMI Dissertation Information Service, 1986.

Nin, Anaïs. *The Diary of Anaïs Nin*. 7 vols. New York: Harcourt Brace Jovanovich, 1969–1980.

Noël, Bernard. *Marseille-New York: une liaison surréaliste*. Marseille: André Dimanche, 1985.

O'Connor, Francis V., and Eugene Victor Thaw. *Jackson Pollock: A Catalogue Raisonné of the Paintings, Drawings, and Other Works*. New Haven: Yale University Press, 1978.

O'Hara, Frank. *Jackson Pollock*. New York: George Braziller, 1959.

Onslow Ford, Gordon. *Creation*. Basel: Galerie Schreiner, 1978.

Onslow Ford, Gordon. *Painting in the Instant*. London: Thames & Hudson; New York: Abrams, 1964.

Onslow Ford, Gordon. Retrospective exhibition catalogue. Oakland: Oakland Museum, 1977.

Onslow Ford, Gordon. *Toward a New Subject in Painting*. San Francisco: San Francisco Museum of Art, 1948.

Onslow Ford, Gordon. *Yves Tanguy and Automatism*. Inverness, California: Bishop Pine Press, 1982.

Orwell, George. *Homage to Catalonia* (1938). New York: Penguin, 1962.

Ouspensky, P. D. *Tertium Organum.* New York: Random House, 1982.

Paalen, Wolfgang. *Form and Sense.* Problems in Contemporary Art, no. 1. New York: Wittenborn, 1945.

Penrose, Roland. *Scrapbook: 1900–1981.* London: Thames and Hudson, 1981.

Picon, Gaetan. *Surrealists and Surrealism.* Geneva: Albert Skira; New York: Rizzoli, 1977.

Pierre, José. *L'Aventure surréaliste autour d'André Breton.* Paris: Filipacchi/Artcurial, 1986.

Pierre, José. *Position politique de la peinture surréaliste.* Paris: Musée de Poche, 1975.

Pierre Matisse Gallery. *Yves Tanguy, a Summary of His Works.* With contributions by Kay Sage Tanguy, André Breton, and Paul Eluard. New York: Pierre Matisse Gallery, 1963.

Planck, William. *Sartre and Surrealism.* Ann Arbor: UMI Research Press, 1981.

La Planète affolée. Catalogue, Musées de Marseille. Paris: Flammarion, 1986.

Polcari, Stephen. *Abstract Expressionism and the Modern Experience.* New York: Cambridge University Press, 1991.

Pollock, Jackson. "Jackson Pollock." *Arts and Architecture* 61, no. 2 (February 1944).

Porter, David. "Personal Statement, a Painting Prophecy 1950." Exhibition catalogue. Washington, D.C.: David Porter Gallery, February 1945.

Preble, Michael. *William Baziotes: A Retrospective Exhibition.* With essays by Mona Hadler and Barbara Cavaliere. Newport Beach, California: Newport Harbor Art Museum, 1978.

Provincetown Art Association and Museum. *Life Colors Art: Fifty Years of Painting by Peter Busa.* Provincetown: Provincetown Art Association and Museum, 1992.

Queens Museum. *Remembering the Future: The New York World's Fair from 1939 to 1964.* Catalogue. New York: Rizzoli, 1989.

Ragache, Gilles, and Jean Robert Ragache. *La Vie quotidienne des écrivains et des artistes sous l'Occupation: 1940–1944.* Paris: Hachette, 1988.

Rand, Harry. *Arshile Gorky: The Implication of Symbols* (1980). Berkeley: University of California Press, 1991.

Regler, Gustav. "Four European Painters in Mexico." *Horizon* 16, no. 91 (1947), 95–101.

Regler, Gustav. *Wolfgang Paalen.* New York: Nierendorf Editions, 1946.

Rodríguez Prampolini, Ida. *El surrealismo y el arte fantastico de México.* Mexico City: Universidad Nacional Autónoma de México, 1983.

Rosenberg, Harold. "Breton—a Dialogue." *View* 2, no. 3 (Summer 1942).

Rosenblum, Robert. "Notes on Rothko's Surrealist Years." New York: Pace Gallery, 1981.

Rosenthal, Deborah. "Interview with André Masson." *Arts* (November 1980).

Rubin, William. "Arshile Gorky, Surrealism and the New American Painting." *Art International* 7 (February 1963).

Rubin, William. *Dada and Surrealist Art*. New York: Harry N. Abrams, 1974.

Rubin, William. *Dada, Surrealism and Their Heritage*. New York: Museum of Modern Art, 1968.

Rubin, William. "Matta." *Museum of Modern Art Bulletin* (1957).

Rubin, William. "Notes on Masson and Pollock." *Arts* 34, no. 2 (November 1959).

Rubin, William S., and Carolyn Lanchner. *André Masson*. New York: Museum of Modern Art, 1976.

Rudenstein, Angelica Zander. *Peggy Guggenheim's Collection, Venice*. New York: Harry N. Abrams, 1985.

Sandler, Irving. "Dada, Surrealism and Their Heritage: The Surrealist Émigrés in New York." *Artforum* 6, no. 9 (May 1968).

Sandler, Irving. *The Triumph of American Painting: A History of Abstract Expressionism*. New York: Praeger, 1970.

San Francisco Museum of Art. *Dynaton*. Catalogue. San Francisco: San Francisco Museum of Art, 1951.

Sartre, Jean Paul. *Le Mur*. Paris: Gallimard, 1939.

Sartre, Jean Paul. "Qu'est-ce que la littérature?" *Les Temps Modernes* 20–21 (May, June 1947).

Sartre, Jean Paul. *Situations II*. Paris: Gallimard, 1947.

Sawin, Martica. "The Archaizing Surrealism of Kurt Seligmann." *Arts* (February 1986).

Sawin, Martica. "The Cycloptic Eye, Pataphysics and the Possible." *The Interpretive Link: Abstract Surrealism into Abstract Expressionism*. Newport Beach, California: Newport Harbor Museum, 1986.

Sawin, Martica. "Gerome Kamrowski, the Most Surrealist of Us All." *Arts* (November 1986).

Sawin, Martica. "Prolegomena to a Study of Matta." *Arts* (December 1985).

Sawin, Martica. "Stanley William Hayter, Painter and Printmaker." *Arts* (January 1986).

Sawin, Martica. "El surrealismo etnográfico y la America indígena." In *El surrealismo entre Viejo y Nuevo Mundo*. Catalogue. Las Palmas: Centro Atlantico de Arte Moderno, 1990.

Sawin, Martica. "Les Surréalistes aux États Unis." In *La Planète affolée*. Paris: Flammarion, 1986.

Sawin, Martica. "The Third Man or Automatism American Style." *Art Journal* (Winter 1988).

Schimmel, Paul. *The Interpretive Link: Abstract Surrealism into Abstract Expressionism*. Catalogue. Newport Beach, California: Newport Harbor Art Museum, 1986.

Schuster, Jean, and José Pierre, eds. *Tracts surréalistes et déclarations collectives 1922–69.* 2 vols. Paris: Le Terrain Vague, 1982.

Schwartz, Arturo. "André Breton, Trotsky, et l'Anarchie." Paris: UGE, 1977.

Seghers, Anna. *Transit.* Translated by James A. Galston. Boston: Little, Brown, 1944.

Seligmann, Kurt. *History of Magic.* New York: Pantheon, 1948.

Serge, Victor. "Letter from Mexico." *Horizon* 15, no. 85 (January 1947).

Serge, Victor. *Memoirs of a Revolutionary.* Translated by Peter Sedgwick. London: Oxford University Press, 1963.

Serge, Victor. *S'il est minuit dans le siècle.* Paris: Grasset, 1939.

Shattuck, Roger. *The Innocent Eye: On Modern Literature and the Arts.* New York: Farrar, Straus, Giroux, 1984.

Shirer, Willliam L. *The Collapse of the Third Republic: An Inquiry into the Fall of France in 1940.* New York: Simon and Schuster, 1969.

Simon, Sidney. "Concerning the Beginnings of the New York School 1939–1943: An Interview with Peter Busa and Matta; An interview with Robert Motherwell." *Art International* 11 (Summer 1967).

Soby, James Thrall. "Matta Echaurren." *Magazine of Art* 40 (March 1947), 102–106.

Soby, James Thrall. *Salvador Dalí.* New York: Museum of Modern Art, 1946.

Spies, Werner, ed. *Max Ernst: A Retrospective.* Munich: Prestel, in association with the Tate Gallery, London, 1991.

Stich, Sidra. *Anxious Visions: Surrealist Art.* New York: Abbeville, 1990.

El surrealismo entre Viejo y Nuevo Mundo. Las Palmas: Centro Atlantico de Arte Moderno, 1990.

Sweeney, James Johnson. "Eleven Europeans in America." *The Museum of Modern Art Bulletin* 11, nos. 4–5 (1946), 2–40.

Sweeney, James Johnson. *Miró.* New York: Museum of Modern Art, 1941.

Tanning, Dorothea. *Birthday.* San Francisco: Lapis Press, 1986.

Taylor, Telford. *Munich: The Price of Peace.* Garden City: Doubleday, 1979.

Van Heijenoort, Jean. *With Trotsky in Exile.* Cambridge: Harvard University Press, 1978.

Waldberg, Patrick. *Surrealism.* New York: McGraw-Hill, 1956.

Waldman, Diane. *Arshile Gorky, 1904–1948: A Retrospective.* Catalogue, Solomon R. Guggenheim Museum. New York: Harry N. Abrams, 1981.

Walter Quirt, a Retrospective. Minneapolis: University of Minnesota Gallery, 1980.

Watt, Daniel Cameron. *How War Came: The Immediate Origins of the Second World War, 1938–1939.* New York: Pantheon, 1989.

Wechsler, Jeffrey. *Surrealism and American Art.* Catalogue. New Brunswick: Rutgers University Art Gallery, 1977.

Wechsler, Jeffrey. "Surrealism's Automatic Painting Lesson." *Art News* 76, no. 4 (1977), 44–47.

Weld, Jacqueline. *Peggy, the Wayward Guggenheim.* New York: Dutton, 1986.

Werfel, Alma Mahler, in collaboration with E. B. Ashton. *And the Bridge Is Love.* New York: Harcourt Brace, 1958.

Wolfgang Paalen, between Surrealism and Abstraction. Catalogue. Vienna: Museum moderner Kunst Stiftung Ludwig, 1993.

Wyman, David S. *Paper Walls: America and the Refugee Crisis, 1938–41.* Amherst, Mass., 1968.

Zabriskie Gallery. *Enrico Donati, Surrealist Paintings and Objects from the Forties.* Catalogue. New York: Zabriskie Gallery, 1987.

Periodicals
The dates given beside the periodicals listed indicate the relevant years, not necessarily the entire run of the periodical.

Art Digest, 1938–1950.
Art Front, 1934–1937.
Art News, 1938–1950.
Combat, 1944–1947.
Decision, 1941–1942.
Dyn, 1942–1944.
Fontaine, 1942–1944.
Instead, 1947–1948.
Labyrinthe, 1944–1946.
London Bulletin, 1938–1940.
Magazine of Art, 1944–1948.
La Main à Plume, 1942–1944.
Minotaure, 1–12, 1934–1939.
The Nation, 1942–1947.
Partisan Review, 1938–1950.
Possibilities, single issue, Fall 1947.
View, 1940–1944.
VVV, 1–4, June 1942–February 1944.

Interviews at Archives of American Art, Smithsonian Institution

Rosalind Browne, interviewed by Irving Sandler.

Fritz Bultman, interviewed by Irving Sandler, January 6, 1968.

Peter Busa, interviewed by Dorothy Seckler, May 9, 1965.

Nicolas Calas, interviewed by Paul Cummings.

Leo Castelli, interviewed by Paul Cummings, May 14, 1969.

Jimmy Ernst, interviewed by Paul Cummings, September 20, 1974.

Jimmy Ernst, interviewed by Francine Gray, December 1968.

Adolph Gottlieb, interviewed by Dorothy Seckler.

Esther Gottlieb, interviewed by Phyllis Tuchman, October 22, 1981.

David Hare, interviewed by Dorothy Seckler, January 17, 1968.

Gerome Kamrowski, interviewed by Dennis Barrie, January 22, 1976.

Boris Margo, interviewed by Dorothy Seckler.

Robert Motherwell, interviewed by Paul Cummings, November 24, 1971.

Mark Rothko in his times: includes interviews on the subject of Rothko with Jacob Kainen, Aaron Siskind, Jack Tworkov, Hedda Sterne, Betty Parsons, Dorothy Miller, Herbert Ferber, William Coply, Sally Avery.

Charles Seliger, interviewed by Paul Cummings, May 8, 1968.

James Thrall Soby, interviewed by Paul Cummings, July 7, 1970.

Archives

Archives of American Art, Smithsonian Institution.

Bibliothèque Litteraire Jacques Doucet, the Bibliothèque Sainte-Geneviève, Paris. Breton, Duchamp, and Péret archives.

Peter Busa papers, Provincetown, Massachusetts.

Jimmy Ernst papers, East Hampton, New York.

Varian Fry papers, Butler Library, Columbia University.

Museum of Modern Art: Alfred Barr papers; James Thrall Soby papers; Curt Valentin papers; artists' exhibition files.

Gordon Onslow Ford papers, Inverness, California.

Kurt Seligmann papers, in possession of the author and at the Beinecke Library, Yale University.

Index

Page numbers in italic indicate illustrations.